CAMBRIDGE LIB

Books of enduring scholarly value

Literary Studies

This series provides a high-quality selection of early printings of literary works, textual editions, anthologies and literary criticism which are of lasting scholarly interest. Ranging from Old English to Shakespeare to early twentieth-century work from around the world, these books offer a valuable resource for scholars in reception history, textual editing, and literary studies.

The Orkneyinga Saga

Joseph Anderson (1832–1916), curator of the National Museum of Antiquities of Scotland, edited this version of the saga of the earls of Orkney, translated by Jon Hjaltalin and Gilbert Goudie, and published in 1873. Anderson (whose works on the archaeology of Scotland from the Stone Age to the early Christian era are also reissued in this series) provides a lengthy introduction to the saga, discussing the geography of the islands, and using literary and archaeological material to put the work, which is written in Icelandic and dates from between 1170 and 1220, in context. The first Viking incursions into the islands began in the late eighth century, and the Norwegian king Harald Fairhair gave Orkney to the first earl, Rognvald Eysteinsson, in compensation for the death of his son, in about 870. Anderson also provides notes to the translation, and an appendix with further material from the Icelandic Flateyjarbók.

Cambridge University Press has long been a pioneer in the reissuing of out-of-print titles from its own backlist, producing digital reprints of books that are still sought after by scholars and students but could not be reprinted economically using traditional technology. The Cambridge Library Collection extends this activity to a wider range of books which are still of importance to researchers and professionals, either for the source material they contain, or as landmarks in the history of their academic discipline.

Drawing from the world-renowned collections in the Cambridge University Library and other partner libraries, and guided by the advice of experts in each subject area, Cambridge University Press is using state-of-the-art scanning machines in its own Printing House to capture the content of each book selected for inclusion. The files are processed to give a consistently clear, crisp image, and the books finished to the high quality standard for which the Press is recognised around the world. The latest print-on-demand technology ensures that the books will remain available indefinitely, and that orders for single or multiple copies can quickly be supplied.

The Cambridge Library Collection brings back to life books of enduring scholarly value (including out-of-copyright works originally issued by other publishers) across a wide range of disciplines in the humanities and social sciences and in science and technology.

The Orkneyinga Saga

JOSEPH ANDERSON
JON A. HJALTALIN
GILBERT GOUDIE

CAMBRIDGE
UNIVERSITY PRESS

CAMBRIDGE
UNIVERSITY PRESS

University Printing House, Cambridge, CB2 8BS, United Kingdom

Cambridge University Press is part of the University of Cambridge.

It furthers the University's mission by disseminating knowledge in the pursuit of
education, learning and research at the highest international levels of excellence.

www.cambridge.org
Information on this title: www.cambridge.org/9781108082242

© in this compilation Cambridge University Press 2019

This edition first published 1873
This digitally printed version 2019

ISBN 978-1-108-08224-2 Paperback

THE ORKNEYINGA SAGA

Printed by R. & R. Clark

FOR

EDMONSTON & DOUGLAS, EDINBURGH.

LONDON .   .   . HAMILTON, ADAMS, AND CO.
CAMBRIDGE . . MACMILLAN AND CO.
GLASGOW .   .   . JAMES MACLEHOSE.

Sir H Dryden, delt

Waterston & Son Edin Lith.

ST MAGNUS CATHEDRAL

(South Transept and part of Choir)

THE

ORKNEYINGA SAGA

TRANSLATED FROM THE ICELANDIC
BY JON A. HJALTALIN AND GILBERT GOUDIE

EDITED, WITH NOTES AND INTRODUCTION

By JOSEPH ANDERSON

KEEPER OF THE NATIONAL MUSEUM OF THE ANTIQUARIES OF SCOTLAND

EDINBURGH

EDMONSTON AND DOUGLAS

1873

PREFACE.

The Orkneyinga Saga is the history of the Orkneymen, Earls and Odallers of Norwegian extraction, who established an Earldom of Norway in the Northern Scottish Isles a thousand years ago, and whose descendants for several centuries held sway over the Hebrides and Northern Mainland of Scotland. Commencing with the conquest of the Isles by Harald Har-fagri, the Saga relates the subsequent history of the Earldom of Orkney under the long line of its Norse Jarls, and is, for a period of three centuries and a half, the principal authority for the history of Northern Scotland. The narrative is mainly personal, and therefore picturesque, pourtraying the men in person and character, impartially recording their deeds, and mentioning what was thought of them and their actions at the time. Occasionally the Saga-writer is enabled to do this in the words of a contemporary Skald. The skaldic songs, so often quoted, were the materials from which the Sagas were subsequently elaborated. In estimating their value as historical materials, it must be borne in mind that all history has begun in song. When great events and mighty deeds were preserved for posterity by oral recitation alone, it was necessary that the memory should be enabled to retain its hold of the elements of the story by some extraneous artistic aid, and therefore they were welded by the word-smith's rhymes into a compact and homogeneous " lay." Thus, worked into a poetical setting (as the jeweller mounts

his gems to enhance their value and ensure their preservation),
they passed as heirlooms from generation to generation,
floating on the oral tradition of the people. Snorri Sturluson
tells us that the songs of the skalds who were with Harald
Harfagri in his wars were known and recited in his day, after
an interval of nearly four centuries. " These songs," he says,
" which were sung in the presence of kings and chiefs, or of
their sons, are the materials of our history ; what they tell of
their deeds and battles we take for truth ; for though the
skalds did no doubt praise those in whose presence they stood,
yet no one would dare to relate to a chief what he and those
who heard it knew to be wholly imaginary or false, as that
would not be praise but mockery." Our earliest Scottish
chroniclers did not disdain to make use of the lay-smith's
craft, as a help to history, long after the Iceland skald had
been succeeded by the Saga-writer, and the flowery recitative
of an unclerkly age superseded by the terser narrative of the
parchment scribe. The art is as old as Odin and the gods,
if indeed it be not older, and these its creations. But its
golden age had passed ere Paganism began to give way before
Christianity, and the specimens we have in this Saga are
mostly of the period of its decadence and by inferior skalds.
Yet it is significant of the esteem in which the art continued
to be held by the settlers in the Orkneys, that we find Earl
Sigurd honouring Gunnlaug Ormstunga with princely gifts,
Arnor Jarlaskald enjoying the special favour and friendship
of Earl Thorfinn, and Earl Rognvald, the founder of the
cathedral, courting for himself the reputation of an accomplished skald.

But though we can thus trace to some extent the author-
ship of the unwritten materials from which the Saga was
framed, there is nothing to show where or by whom it was

written. There is proof, however, that it was known in Iceland in the first half of the thirteenth century. Its earlier chapters, down to the division of the Earldom between Thorfinn and Brusi, are incorporated into the Olaf Saga of Snorri Sturluson, and are there cited as from the " Jarla Saga," or Saga of the Earls. It must therefore have been in existence as a completed work before 1241, the date of Snorri's death. The compiler of the Fagrskinna, which is shown by internal evidence to have been written between 1222 and 1225, also quotes from it, by the title of " Jarla Sagan." The closing chapters of the Orkneyinga Saga, in its present form, recording the burning of Bishop Adam, could not have been written before 1222 ; but, as it is stated in the last chapter that the terrible retribution exacted by the Scottish King for the murder of the Bishop was still in fresh memory, it may very well have been completed before 1225. No manuscript of the Jarla Saga is known to exist, and the original form of what is now called " The Orkneyinga Saga" is thus matter of conjecture. We know it only as the substance of its earlier chapters was given by Snorri previous to 1241, and in the expanded version of the Flateyjarbók, where it is pieced into the Sagas of Olaf Tryggvi's son and Olaf the Holy. The Flateyjarbók, however, is nearly a century and a half later than Snorri's work, having been written between the years 1387 and 1394.

The object of the present issue being simply to provide a plain, readable, and unadorned translation of the Orkneyinga Saga (which has been hitherto inaccessible to the English reader), it has been deemed advisable to adhere to the form of the Saga adopted by its first editor ˙ Jonæus, though not to Jonæus's text, which is by no means free from corruptions. The Christiania edition of the Flateyjarbók, printed literally from the manuscript, has afforded the means of rectifying the text where necessary; and the expanded version of the earlier chapters given in the Flateyjarbók has also been translated and inserted as an appendix, for the sake of the fuller details which it supplies of the earlier history of the Earldom. In one sense it might have been desirable to have compiled a text which would have given the fullest history of the Orkney Earls, but this would not have been the " Orkneyinga Saga." It would have necessitated the collection and critical collation of all the passages in all the Sagas and early writings relating to the history of the Northmen in Scotland—a work which has long been in progress in abler hands, and under more favourable auspices.

The Introduction, however, has been compiled with a view to supplement the Saga narrative, as well as to furnish a continuation of the history of the Earldom down to the time when it ceased to form part of the Norwegian dominions. Some account of the islands previous to the Norse invasion, and a few notices of their antiquities and ecclesiastical remains, as well as of the existing traces of the Norsemen, seemed requisite to supplement the notes in illustration of the text. Chronological and Genealogical Tables have been added to facilitate reference; and on the maps of Scotland and of the island-groups which formed the Earldom proper are shown the names of the principal places mentioned in the Sagas as known to the Northmen.

In conclusion, I have to express my obligations to those kind friends who have aided me with their advice and assistance. To Dr. John Stuart, Dr. John Hill Burton, Sir Henry Dryden, Bart., and Colonel Balfour of Balfour and Trenaby, I am indebted for many valuable suggestions. To the first-named gentleman I am also under obligations for the use of the woodcuts of the symbols of the Sculptured Stones. The Society of Antiquaries of Scotland have generously contributed the woodcuts of the Bressay Stone, the Saverough Bell, and the Sword and Scabbard-tip; to the Society of Antiquaries of London I am indebted for the illustrations of the Stones of Stennis; to Mr. James Fergusson and Mr. John Murray for those of Maeshow; to Mr. Thomas S. Muir for the Dragon of Maeshow, the etchings of the churches of Weir and Lybster, and the ground-plans of the ancient churches; to Messrs. Chambers for the woodcut of Mousa; and to Dr Daniel Wilson and Messrs. Constable for those of the Brooch and Comb, illustrating the burial-usages of the Norsemen. The view of Egilsey church is from a photograph, for which I am indebted to Mr. George Petrie of Kirkwall, whose pleasant companionship in a pilgrimage among the localities described in the Saga is gratefully remembered. J. A.

NATIONAL MUSEUM
OF THE ANTIQUARIES OF SCOTLAND,
October 1873.

CONTENTS.

LIST OF ILLUSTRATIONS.

—◆—

SYLLABUS OF INTRODUCTION.

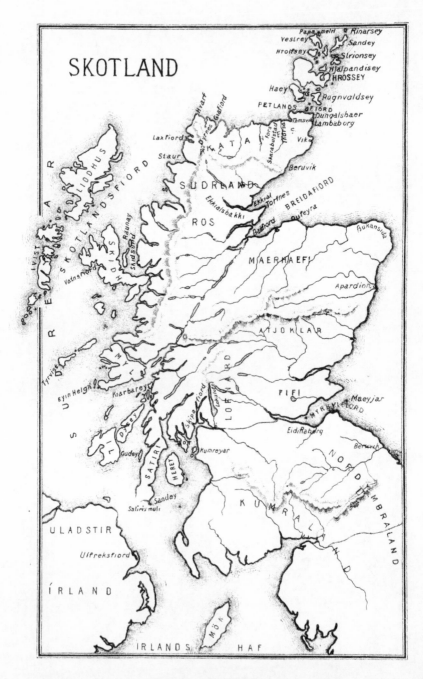

SKOTLAND

EDMONSTON & DOUGLAS, EDINBURGH.

INTRODUCTION.

———◆———

I. EARLIEST HISTORICAL NOTICES OF THE ORKNEYS.

THE historical notices of the Orkneys previous to the Norse occupation are few in number, and exceedingly obscure. We learn little more from the allusions of the Roman writers than that scarcely anything was known to them with certainty of these remote localities. It may be inferred, however, that the first wave of Celtic population that overspread the northern mainland of Britain must have gradually extended northward to the outlying Isles. The correspondence of the early remains found in the Islands with those of northern Scotland is of itself a striking testimony to the connection of their early population with the Celtic stock of the northern mainland of Scotland. We gather from these remains that the earliest population of the Islands, of which we have any reliable evidence, lived in the same manner as the natives of the northern mainland, fought with the same varieties of weapons of stone and bronze, erected the same forms of defensive structures, practised the same funereal rites, and constructed similar forms of sepulchral chambers, over which they piled the great mounds which are among the most striking features of an Orkney landscape.[1] The

---

[1] Writing of the barrows and cairns of Orkney, Captain Thomas states that at least 2000 might still be numbered. We have no estimate of the number in Shetland, but there also they are very numerous. Not less remarkable is the number of the early "dwellings of strength," of which Mousa is the type —huge edifices, constructed with amazing labour and wonderful skill. (See under Maeshow and Mousa.)

a

number and magnitude of these monuments and structural remains bear witness in a most remarkable manner to the activity, intelligence, and social organisation of the times that have no other record.

It is not until the middle of the 5th century of the Christian era that the early chronicles begin to cast occasionally a feeble and uncertain light upon the history of the northern isles. It is stated in the "Historia Britonum" of Nennius that the Saxon chiefs Ochtha and Ebissa, who came over with "forty keels" in the year 449, laid waste the Orkney Islands, and seized a great many regions beyond the Frisic Sea.[1] At that time, and for a long period previously (according to Nennius), the Picts had been in possession of the Orkneys. Whatever value may be attached to these statements as referring to events which took place 400 years before the author's own time, there can be no reason for discrediting his testimony when he says that the Picts continued in possession of the Orkneys in his day.[2]

Adamnan, in his Life of St. Columba, mentions that the saint being on a visit to Bruide Mac Meilcon, king of the Northern Picts, at his stronghold on the river Ness, requested the king to recommend to the *reguli* of the Orkneys (one of whom was then present, and whose hostages were then in the king's hands) that Cormac and the clerics who had accompanied him on a missionary voyage to the Orkneys should receive no harm ; and it is added that this was the means of saving them from a violent death. But if the authority and influence of the king of the Northern Picts extended to these islands in the reign of Bruide, it does not seem to have been effectual in protecting them from foreign invasion. Bruide Mac Meilcon died in 584, and some time before his death the new and rising power of the Dalriadic kings had made itself

---

[1] The Frisic Sea is supposed to mean the Firth of Forth.

[2] The "Historia Britonum" of Nennius (whoever he may have been) is believed, on what seems reliable evidence, to have been written about A.D. 858. (See the Irish Nennius, Irish Archæological Society, p. 18.)

felt as far as the Orkneys. In the Annals of Ulster there is a notice under the year 580 of an expedition against the Orkneys by Aedan, son of Gabran, seventh king of the Dalriad Scots, who, coming over from Ireland (then called Scotia) about the year 503, had established themselves in Argyle and the Western Highlands, and founded the kingdom of Dalriada. From the date of Aedan's expedition in 580 we have no mention of the islands in the native chronicles for a whole century, and the next entry, which occurs under the year 682, gives colour to the supposition that they may have been under Dalriadic rule in the interval. The record in 682 is simply, that the Orkneys were wasted by Bruide Mac Bile, the king of the Northern Picts, and apparently brought once more under the rule of the Northern Pictish kings.

II. EARLY CHRISTIANITY OF THE ISLANDS.

It is probable that both the island groups of Orkney and Shetland were visited at a very early period by wandering clerics of the Irish Church, whose missionary efforts contributed so much to the diffusion of Christianity in Scotland. But we have no record of an earlier visitation than that of the companions of St. Columba, although there are indications that between that time and the colonisation of the islands by the heathen Northmen, these Irish clerics were no strangers in any of the island groups.

The Irish monk Dicuil, who wrote his treatise "De Mensura Orbis Terrarum" in or about the year 825, states that "thirty years before that time some clerics had told him that they had lived in an island which they supposed to be Thule, where at the summer solstice the sun only hid himself behind a little hill for a short time during the night, which was quite light ; and that a day's sail towards the north would bring them from thence into the frozen sea." This island is obviously

Iceland. He then states that there are many other islands in
the northern British sea, which lie at the distance of two days
and two nights from the northern islands of Britain, in a
straight course, and with a fair wind and a full sail. "One
of these," he says, "a certain honest monk told me he had
visited one summer after sailing a day, a night, and another
day, in a two-benched boat." These appear to be the Shetland
Islands. Dicuil further states that "there are also some other
small islands, almost all divided from each other by narrow
sounds, inhabited for about a century by hermits proceeding
from our Scotia ;[1] but as they had been deserted since the
beginning of the world, so are they now abandoned by these
anchorites on account of the Northern robbers ; but they are
full of countless sheep, and swarm with sea-fowl of various
kinds. We have not seen these islands mentioned in the
works of any author." Here the reference to the "small
isles separated by narrow sounds" is distinctive of the Faroes,
of which the long narrow sounds are the peculiar physical
feature ; while the statement that they are full of countless sheep, taken in connection with the fact that the
Northmen named them "Sheep-isles" (Fær-eyiar), establishes the identity of the group which Dicuil describes.
The Faroes were colonised by "the Northern robbers," led
by Grim Kamban, in 825, the very year in which Dicuil
was writing.

The first Norwegian settlement was made in Iceland in
875, by Leif and Ingulf, who carried with them a number of
Irish captives; and the Landnamabók states that "before Iceland was colonised from Norway, men were living there whom
the Northmen called Papas ; they were Christians, and it is
thought they came over the sea from the west, for after them
were found Irish books, and bells, and crosiers, and other
things, so that one could see that they were Westmen : these
things were found in Papey, eastwards, and in Papyli." Again,

---

[1] Ireland was then called Scotia.

in the Islendingabók of Ari Frodi the same reason is assigned for the departure of the monks as is given by Dicuil. Ari Frodi also says, speaking of Iceland :— " Christian men were here then called by the Northmen *Papa*, but afterwards they went their way, for they would not remain in company with heathens ; and they left behind them Irish books, and bells, and pastoral staves, so that it was clear that they were Irishmen."

Thus by the concurrent testimony of Adamnan, the biographer of St. Columba, himself an abbot of the monastery of Hy ; of the Irish monk Dicuil, writing during the lifetime of the men who had fled from the Northern robbers ; and lastly, of the Icelandic historians themselves—it is established that the whole of the northern islands were visited by Christian teachers, and probably, in part at least, converted to the Christian faith, before they were overrun by the Norwegian invaders, and the new faith swallowed up in the rising tide of heathenism thrown upon their shores from the land of Odin and the Aser.

In the absence of all record we cannot expect to ascertain to what extent these early missionary settlements had succeeded in leavening the Celtic population of the islands of Orkney and Shetland with the Christian faith. But it seems probable that during the three centuries that intervened between the coming of Cormac in his coracle and the arrival of Harald Harfagri with his fleet of war galleys, the new faith had been firmly established and widely extended both in the northern mainland of Scotland and in the remoter isles.

The indications which point to a Christian occupation of the isles, of no inconsiderable extent and continuance, previous to their occupation by the Norsemen, are :—The dedications of the early ecclesiastical foundations ; the occurrence of monumental stones sculptured in the style peculiar to the earliest Christian monuments of the mainland of Scotland, and bearing inscriptions in the Ogham character ; the finding (as at Saverough and Burrian) of ecclesiastical bells of the square-sided form, peculiar to the early ages of the Church;

SQUARE-SIDED BELL FOUND AT SAVEROUGH, ORKNEY.

and the occurrence in the Norse topography of the islands of place-names indicative of the previous settlement of Celtic Christian priests.

The earliest dedications were probably those to St. Ninian and St. Columba, St. Brigid, and St. Tredwell. It may be significant that in the south parish of South Ronaldsay, where in all probability the companions of St. Columba would make their first landing in Orkney, there were no fewer than three chapels dedicated to him.[1]

---

[1] St. Ninian was commemorated at Dunrossness in Shetland (Sibbald's Description, 1711, p. 15); at Stove in South Ronaldsay, Orkney (Peterkin's Rentals, No. III.); at the north head of the bay of Wick in Caithness; and at Navidale in Sutherland. St. Columba's three chapels in South Ronaldsay were at Grymness, Hopay, and Loch of Burwick (Peterkin's Rentals, No. III. p. 86). There were also dedications to St. Columba in the islands of Sanday and Hoy in Orkney, at Olrig and Dirlet in Caithness, on Island Comb, at Tongue, and at Kilcalmkill in Sutherlandshire (Bishop Forbes's Calendar of Scottish Saints). St. Triduana, whose name has been corrupted into St.

The sculptured monuments furnish us with three collateral lines of inference, tending to the same conclusion. These inferences are derived from the inscriptions, the ornamentation, and the symbols of the monuments.

Two of these monuments bear inscriptions in the Ogham character, a style of cryptographic writing characteristic of the early inscribed stone monuments of Ireland, but occurring also in Cornwall, in Wales, and in Scotland. One of these two was found near the ancient church of Culbinsbrugh, in the island of Bressay in Shetland. It is a slab of chlorite slate, 4 feet in length, about 16 inches wide at the top, tapering to a little less than a foot at the bottom, and about 1¾ inch thick. It is sculptured on both sides in low relief, and the inscription is incised on the edges of the stone. On one of its sculptured faces it bears the Christian emblem of the cross, and among the figures sculptured on it are those of two ecclesiastics with pastoral staves (see Plates). The other inscribed stone was found by Dr. William Traill in the Pictish Tower or "Broch" of Burrian, in North Ronaldsay in Orkney. The inscription scratched on it has not yet been deciphered. It also bears the Christian emblem of the cross. The association of the cross with these Ogham inscriptions[1] points

Tredwell and St. Trudlin (the Tröllhæna of the Saga), had dedications in Papa Westray in Orkney (Martin's and Brand's Descriptions), and at Kintradwell in Sutherlandshire. It seems also, from the narrative of Bishop John's mutilation in the Saga, that there was a dedication to her near Thurso. St. Brigid had chapels in Stronsay and Papa Stronsay in Orkney. But it is impossible to tell how many of these early religious sites had similar dedications, as scarcely a tithe of those that are known have preserved their names. Brand and Sibbald both mention the fact that in their time there were still recognisable the sites of 24 chapels in the island of Unst, 21 in the island of Yell, and 10 or 11 in the island of Fetlar : 55 religious foundations in the three most northerly islands of the Shetland group. The Christian period of the Norse occupation is marked by dedications showing the influence of the Crusades or of the national religious feeling. The dedications to the Holy Cross, St. Mary, St. Peter, St. Lawrence, St. Olaf, and St. Magnus, are probably all of this period.

[1] Unfortunately, the readings of these inscriptions which have been attempted are far from satisfactory. The Shetland and Orkney specimens are

THE BRESSAY STONE.
Showing one side and Ogham inscription on edge.

THE BRESSAY STONE.
Showing the other side and Ogham inscription on edge.

to a period anterior to the Norse occupation of the islands.

In examining the characteristics of the art of these monumental stones, we are guided to similar conclusions. The Bressay stone bears none of the symbols peculiar to the Scottish monuments, and in its artistic features it comes nearer to some of the Irish than to the general style of the Scottish sculptures. It is sculptured in low relief, while all the Orkney examples are merely incised. But some of the forms of their ornamentation are also characteristic of the art of the illuminated Irish manuscripts of the 7th and 8th centuries, and others are equally characteristic of the art of the bronzes of what has been styled the late Celtic period.

The Scottish sculptured monuments scattered over the territory ranging from the Forth to the Orkneys are characterised by a peculiar set of symbols of unknown significance, which are often associated with the Christian emblem of the cross.[1] The symbol which is of most frequent occurrence, and which may therefore be said to be the most characteristic of the period of the monuments, is a crescent conjoined with what has been called a double sceptre, as represented in the first figure of the accompanying Plate.

This characteristic symbol occurs on a sculptured slab which was found built into St. Peter's Church in South Ronaldsay, and which had evidently formed part of a monument older than the church. It occurs also on the slab found at Firth, on the mainland of Orkney. Most singularly, it occurs on the phalangial bone of an ox which was found in the Broch of Burrian along with the slab previously described

in different styles of the Ogham writing, and the whole subject of the reading and interpretation of the inscriptions in this character is beset with difficulties of no ordinary kind. One rendering of the Bressay inscription makes it "the cross of Natdod's daughter here," and on the other edge of the stone, "Benres of the sons of the Druids here ;" while the language is supposed to be a mixture of Celtic and Icelandic. (Sculptured Stones of Scotland, vol. i. p. 30.)

[1] Sculptured Stones of Scotland (Spalding Club), by John Stuart, LL.D., *passim.*

SYMBOLS ON THE SCULPTURED STONES OF SCOTLAND.

as bearing an Ogham inscription and a peculiar form of cross.
It occurs associated with the same form of cross on the ela-
borately-sculptured stone at Ulbster in Caithness. We have
this crescent symbol also associated with the cross on the
inscribed stone of St. Vigeans in Forfarshire. This stone
bears the only inscription which is known to have been left
to us in the Pictish language :—[1]

DROSTEN	IPE	VORET	ELT	FORCUS
"Drost,	son of	Voret,	of the race of	Fergus,"

and is believed to refer to that Drost, king of the Picts, who
fell at the battle of Blathmig, according to the Annals of
Tighearnac, in A.D. 729.

The indications afforded by the Norse topography of the
Islands, if taken in connection with the passages previously
quoted from the Landnamabók and the Islendingabók of Ari
Frodi regarding the origin of the names Papa and Papyli in
Iceland, require only to be mentioned. The most obvious of
these are the frequency with which the name Papa[2] occurs
both in the topography of Orkney and Shetland, and the
occurrence of such names as St. Ninian's Isle in Shetland,
Rinansey (Ringan's-ey, St. Ninian's Isle) in Orkney, Daminsey,
now Damsey (St. Adamnan's Isle), and Enhallow (Eyin-Helga,
Holy Isle), given, we must suppose, intelligently by the
Norsemen.

[1] Sir James Simpson's reading of the inscription, given in the Sculptured
Stones of Scotland, vol. ii. p. 71.

[2] In Orkney we have the islands of Papa Westray and Papa Stronsay (the
Papey meiri and *Papey minni*, or greater and lesser Papa of the Saga), Paplay
in South Ronaldsay, Paplay in the parish of Holm, and Papdale, near Kirkwall, in the Mainland. In Shetland we have the isles of Papa—Papa Stour
(*Papey stora*) and Papa Little (*Papey litla*), and Papill in the islands of Unst
and Yell. Papa Stronsay, Papa Westray, and Paplay, in the Mainland of
Orkney, are mentioned in the Saga. Papa Stour occurs in a deed of A.D.
1229 (Diplom. Norveg. i. 89), Papill in Unst in a deed of A.D. 1360 (Ibid.
iii. 310), and a "Sigurdr of Pappley" is mentioned in the agreement between
Bishop William of Orkney and Hakon Jonson, May 25, 1369 (Ibid.
i. 404).

Thus, at the very starting-point of their recorded history, we find indications of Christianity, with suggestions even of its civilisation and its art shedding their benign influence over the isles.

III. ARRIVAL OF THE NORTHMEN, AND ESTABLISHMENT OF THE EARLDOM OF ORKNEY AND CAITHNESS.

The earliest notice we have of the visits of the Northmen to the shores of Britain occurs in the Anglo-Saxon Chronicle under the date A.D. 787 :—

" In this year King Beorhtric took Eadburh, King Offa's daughter, to wife. And in his days first came three ships of Northmen from Hæretha-land ; and then the reeve rode thereto, and would drive them to the king's vill, for he knew not what they were, and they there slew him. These were the first ships of Danish men that sought the land of the English race."

As they came from Hæretha-land, now Hordaland, on the west coast of Norway, they were Norwegians, not Danes.

The Irish Annals and the Welsh Chronicles agree in representing the first inroads of the Norsemen on the Irish coasts as having commenced in the year 795. In 798 they plundered Inispatrick of Man and the Hebrides ; in 802, and again in 806, they ravaged Iona, slaying in the latter year sixty-eight of the monastic family there. In 807 they established themselves on the mainland of Ireland ; and a few years afterwards we find a Norseman making Armagh the capital of his kingdom.

In 852, Olaf the White, a chieftain descended from the same family as Harald Harfagri, conquered Dublin, and founded the most powerful and permanent of the Norse kingdoms in Ireland.

By the victory of Hafursfiord in 872, Harald Harfagri made himself sole monarch of Norway. Large numbers of the wealthy and powerful odallers, whom he had dispossessed of their territorial possessions, fled to the islands of Orkney and Shetland, which, for a full century previous to this time, had been well known to the Norsemen as the viking station of the western haf—the rendezvous of the Northern rovers, who swept the coasts of the Hebrides and swarmed in the Irish Seas. Being fugitives from their country, and outlaws of the new kingdom which Harald had succeeded in establishing in Norway, they settled themselves permanently in the islands. Then they turned their haven of refuge into a base of operations for retaliatory warfare, harrying the coasts of Norway during the summer months, and living at leisure in the islands during winter on the plunder. At length King Harald, irritated by their incessant ravages, collected a powerful fleet, and visiting Shetland, Orkney, and the Hebrides, in succession, he swept their coasts clear of the plunderers, subduing the whole of the Northern and Western islands as far south as Man.

In this expedition Ivar, a son of Rognvald, Earl of Moeri, was killed.[1] In order to recompense Rognvald for the loss of his son, King Harald bestowed on him the territory of the subjugated isles of Orkney and Shetland, with the title of Earl of the Orkneys. Harald seems to have dealt similarly with the Hebrides, but his conquest of the vikings in these remote isles was not so complete as in the Orkneys. Ketil Flatnef (Flat nose), who, according to the Laxdæla Saga, had emigrated to the Hebrides because he could not resist King Harald in Norway, had married his daughter Aud to Olaf the White, the powerful king of Dublin, and had established himself in a kind of independent sovereignty in the Hebrides ; and though he seems to have migrated from them to Iceland in consequence of King Harald's expedition, the continued hostility to King Harald's rule is evinced by the fact that the second earl whom he sent to the Hebrides, Asbjorn Skerablesi, was slain by two relatives of Ketil Flatnef, his wife and daughter taken captive, and the latter sold as a

---

[1] There is a cairn in Sanday called Ivar's Knowe, which may be his burial mound.

slave. Rognvald, however, returned to his own Earldom in Norway, and made over his newly-acquired possessions to his brother Sigurd, the "first earl" of the Saga.

IV. THE EARLDOM IN THE NORSE LINE, 872-1231.

Thorstein the Red, son of Olaf the White, king of Dublin, came then to the north, and allying himself with Earl Sigurd, they crossed over to the mainland of Scotland, and subdued Caithness and Sutherland as far as Ekkialsbakki, and afterwards carried their conquests into Ross and Moray. In this invasion Earl Sigurd killed Maelbrigd the buck-toothed (Melbrigda tönn), a Scottish maormor of Ross or Moray; and having tied his head to his saddle-bow, "the tooth," which was very prominent, inflicted a wound on his leg, and the wound inflaming caused the death of the earl, who was hoylaid (buried in a mound or cairn) on Ekkialsbakki."[1] After his death, Thorstein the Red reigned as king over the conquered districts of Scotland, which at that time, says the Landnamabók,[2] comprehended "Caithness and Sutherland, Ross and Moray, and more than the half of Scotland." The Laxdæla Saga[3] says that in his engagements with the Scots Thorstein was always successful, "until at length he became reconciled with the King of the Scots, and obtained possession of the half of Scotland, over which he became king." But he was shortly afterwards slain in Caithness by the treachery of the Scots; and after his death Aud, his mother, migrated to Iceland. Previous to her departure she had given Groa, the daughter of Thorstein, in marriage to Duncan, earl or maormor of Duncansby in Caithness. Thus the Norse earl-

---

[1] Olaf Tryggvason's Saga, Flateyjarbók, cap. 180, in the Appendix; and Ynglinga Saga, Heimskringla, cap. 22. Earl Sigurd's grave-mound, on the estuary of the Oykel (Ekkialsbakki), was known in the 12th century as *Siwardhoch*, or Sigurd's How, and is still identifiable in the modern Cyderhall. (See the note on Ekkialsbakki, p. 107 of the Saga.)

[2] Landnamabók, cap. ii.   [3] Laxdæla Saga, cap. iv.

dom of Caithness passed for a time into the family of one of its native chiefs. But by the subsequent marriage of Grelauga, the daughter of Duncan and Groa, with Thorfinn Hausakliuf, son of Torf-Einar, Earl of Orkney, the Scottish earldom was again added to the earldom of the Isles.

While Thorstein the Red ruled on the northern mainland of Scotland, Guttorm, the son of Sigurd Eysteinson, had succeeded to the Orkney earldom on the death of his father, but after having held it for one year he died childless.

Meantime, when Rognvald, Earl of Moeri, heard in Norway of the death of his brother Sigurd, he obtained a grant of the earldom of Orkney from King Harald for his own son Hallad. Hallad found the Islands so much infested by vikings that he soon gave up the earldom in disgust, and returned to Norway, preferring the life of a farmer to that of an earl.[1]

Then Rognvald sent another son, Einar, to take possession of the earldom. Einar was a man of a different stamp from Hallad. He soon made his power felt among the western vikings, and freed his possessions entirely from their ravages. The sons of Harald Harfagri, Halfdan Halegg and Guthrod, grew up to be men of great violence. One spring they went north to Moeri and burnt Earl Rognvald in his own house with sixty of his men. Halfdan Halegg then sailed west to Orkney to dispossess Einar of the earldom, but having allowed himself to be surprised by Einar, he was captured in Rinansey, and killed by having a blood-eagle cut on his back.[2] Harald Harfagri came west, and fined the Orkneys in sixty marks of gold for the death of his son. Earl Einar offered to the Bœndr[3] that he would pay the money on condition that he should have all the odal possessions in the islands—a condition to which they agreed the

---

[1] Olaf Tryggvason's Saga, Flateyjarbók, cap. 180, in Appendix.

[2] This was done by hewing the ribs from the backbone, and tearing out the heart and lungs.

[3] Bœndr, the odal landholders. (See note on this word, cap. i. of the Saga.)

more readily, says the Saga, "that all the poorer men had but small lands, while those who were wealthy said they would redeem theirs when they pleased." [1] But the odal lands remained in the possession of the earl till Einar's great-grandson, Sigurd Hlodverson, was obliged to buy the assistance of the odallers against the Scots when hard pressed by the Scottish earl Finleik.[2]

When Einar died he left three sons, two of whom, Arnkell and Erlend, were killed with King Erik Bloodyaxe in England. The third, Thorfinn Hausakliuf, married Grelauga, daughter of Duncan, earl of Duncansbay, and thus reunited in the Norse line the two earldoms of Orkney and Caithness. Earl Thorfinn Hausakliuf left five sons. Arnfinn, the eldest, who was married to Ragnhild, a daughter of King Erik Bloodyaxe, was killed by his wife at Myrkhol (Murkle) in Caithness. She then married Havard, his brother. She soon tired of him, and instigated Einar Klining, his sister's son, to kill him. Havard fell in the fray at Stennis, and was buried there.[3] Ragnhild had promised to marry Einar if he killed her husband Havard. When the deed was done, however, she refused to perform her promise, and instigated another Einar, by the promise of her hand, to slay Einar Klining. This he did, but again Ragnhild was faithless. Then she married Liot, the third son of Earl Thorfinn Hausakliffer, and brother of the two husbands whom she had already had and slain. Meanwhile Skuli, a fourth brother, had gone to Scotland and obtained an earl's title for Caithness from the King of Scots.[4] He was defeated by Liot, and slain in the Dales of Caithness, and thus Liot became sole earl of Caithness and Orkney. He fell in battle with a native chieftain, named Magbiod[5] in the

---

[1] Olaf Tryggvason's Saga, Flateyjarbók, cap. 183, in Appendix.

[2] Finleik has been conjectured to be Finlay, the father of Macbeth.

[3] Olaf Tryggvason's Saga, Flateyjarbók, cap. 184, in Appendix.

[4] Ibid. cap. 185.

[5] This is probably the Celtic name Maelbrigd. Though it is suggestive of Macbeth, the date is too early for Macbeth MacFinlay.

Sagas, at Skida Myre[1] (Skitten) in Caithness, and was succeeded in the earldom by Hlodver, the last of the five brothers.

Earl Hlodver married Audna, the daughter of the Irish king Kiarval. He died shortly after his accession to the earldom, and was buried at Hofn (Huna) in Caithness.[2] His son Sigurd, sometimes called "the Stout," succeeded him. He is said to have been a mighty warrior, and to have driven the Scots completely from Caithness.[3] But he was not left in undisturbed possession of his Scottish earldom. The Scottish earl or maormor, Finlay (MacRuari ?) invaded Caithness and gave him battle at Skida Myre, where his uncle Liot had fallen before another Scottish maormor not long previously. Finlay had so large a force that there were no less than seven Scotsmen to one of Sigurd's men, and the Orkneymen who were with Earl Sigurd were unwilling to fight against such odds. Then Sigurd offered to restore to the Bœndr. their allodial lands, which they had resigned to Earl Einar, his great-grandfather. By this means, more than by the charmed raven-banner made for him by his Irish mother, he obtained the victory. "After this," says the Njal Saga,[4] "Earl Sigurd became ruler over these dominions in Scotland, Ross and Moray, Sutherland and the Dales" (of Caithness), which seem also to include the old Strathnaver. But his troubles with the Scots were not yet over. Caithness was invaded by two Scottish maormors, called Hundi and Melsnati in the Saga.[5] A battle took place at Duncansbay, in which Melsnati was slain, but Hundi fled, and the Norsemen, learning that another

---

[1] The locality of Skida Myre has been identified by Munch with the Loch of Scister, in the parish of Canisbay. It seems rather to be indicated by the modern Skitten, as the name formerly applied to the great tract of moorland in the north-west corner of the parish of Wick, now generally known as the Moss of Kilmster.

[2] Olaf Tryggvason's Saga, Flateyjarbók, cap. 186, in Appendix.

[3] "He kept Caithness by main force from the Scots." (See Appendix, p. 209.)   [4] Njal Saga, cap. lxxxvii.

[5] Njal Saga, loc. cit. This Hundi should be the father of the Kali Hundason of the subsequent narrative.

Scottish earl, Malcolm, was assembling an army at Duncansbay, gave up the pursuit and returned to Orkney. Afterwards
Sigurd became reconciled to Malcolm, King of the Scots, and
obtained his daughter in marriage.

But the most notable event in the life of Earl Sigurd was
that which befel him as he lay in the harbour of Osmondwall
shortly after his accession to the earldom. Olaf Tryggvason,
King of Norway, returning from a western cruise, happened
to run his vessels into the same harbour, as the Pentland
Firth was not to be passed that day. On hearing that the
earl was there he sent for him on board his ship, and told
him, without much parley, that he must allow himself to be
baptized, and make all his people profess the Christian faith.
The Flateyjarbók says that the king took hold of Sigurd's boy,
who chanced to be with him, and drawing his sword, gave
the earl the choice of renouncing for ever the faith of his
fathers, or of seeing his boy slain on the spot. In the position in which he found himself placed, Sigurd became a
nominal convert, but there is every reason to believe that the
Christianity which was thus forced upon the Islanders was
for a long time more a name than a reality. Nearly twenty
years afterwards we find Earl Sigurd bearing his own raven-
banner "woven with mighty spells," at the battle of Clontarf,
against the Christian king Brian ; and Sigurd's fall was made
known in Caithness by the twelve weird sisters (the Valkyriar
of the ancient mythology) weaving the woof of war :— [1]

> " The woof y-woven
> With entrails of men,
> The warp hardweighted
> With heads of the slain."

An incident which occurred just before he set out for
Ireland gives a striking illustration of the fierce manners of
the times. King Sigtrygg, who had come from Dublin to
obtain Earl Sigurd's aid, was being entertained at the Yule-

[1] Njal Saga, cap. clvi.

feast in Earl Sigurd's hall in Hrossey (the Mainland of
Orkney), and was set on the high seat, having Earl Sigurd on
the one side and Earl Gilli, who had come with him, on the
other. Gunnar Lambi's son was telling the company the
story of the burning of Njal and his comrades, but giving an
unfair version of it, and every now and then laughing out
loud. It so happened that as, in answer to an inquiry of
King Sigtrygg's how they bore the burning, he was saying
that one of them had given way to tears, one of Njal's friends,
Kari by name, who had just arrived in Orkney, chanced to come
into the hall. Hearing what was said, Kari drew his sword, and
smote Gunnar Lambi's son on the neck with such a sharp blow
that his head spun off on to the board before the king and the
earls, so that the board was all one gore of blood, and the earls'
clothing too. Earl Sigurd called out to seize Kari and kill
him, but no man stirred, and some spoke up for him, saying
that he had only done what he had a right to do, and so Kari
walked away, and there was no hue and cry after him.

The battle of Clontarf, in which Earl Sigurd fell, is the
most celebrated of all the conflicts in which the Norsemen
were engaged on this side of the North Sea. "It was at
Clontarf, in Brian's battle," says Dasent, "that the old and
new faiths met in the lists face to face for their last struggle,"
and we find Earl Sigurd arrayed on the side of the old faith,
though nominally a convert to the new. The Irish account
of the battle[1] describes it as seen from the walls of Dublin,
and likens the carnage to a party of reapers cutting down a
field of oats. Sigurd is described as dealing out wounds and
slaughter all around—"no edged weapon could harm him,
and there was no strength that yielded not, and no thickness
that became not thin before him." Murcadh, son of Brian
Borumha, was equally conspicuous on the side of the Irish.
He had thrice passed through the phalanx of the foreigners,
slaying a mail-clad man at every stroke. Then perceiving

[1] War of the Gaedhil with the Gaill, p. 191.

Sigurd, he rushed at him, and by a blow of his right-hand sword, cut the fastenings of his helmet, which fell back, and a second blow given with the left-hand sword cut into his neck, and stretched him lifeless on the field. In the Njal Saga the incidents connected with Earl Sigurd's death are differently related. His raven-banner, which was borne before him, was fulfilling the destiny announced by Audna, when she gave it to him at Skida Myre, that it would always bring victory to those before whom it was borne, but death to him who bore it. Twice had the banner-bearer fallen, and Earl Sigurd called on Thorstein, son of Hall of the Side, next to bear the banner. Thorstein was about to lift it, when Asmund the White called out, " Don't bear the banner, for all they who bear it get their death." " Hrafn the Red !" cried Earl Sigurd, " bear thou the banner." " Bear thine own devil thyself," said Hrafn.[1] Then said the earl, " 'Tis fittest that the beggar should bear the bag," and with that he took up the banner, and was immediately pierced through with a spear. Then flight broke out through all the host.

When the news of Earl Sigurd's death reached Scotland King Malcolm gave the earldom of Caithness to Thorfinn, his daughter's son by Sigurd, then only five years of age, and Sumarlidi, Brusi, and Einar, Sigurd's sons by his former marriage, divided the Orkneys between them. Sumarlidi soon died, and Einar got his portion. Einar made himself unpopular by the violence with which he exacted his services

---

[1] Hrafn the Red, whose denunciation of the raven-banner as the earl's devil may not altogether be accounted for by the fervour of his Christianity, was chased into the river, where he was in danger of being drowned by the rising tide. In this emergency he made a vow as follows :—" Thy dog, Apostle Peter, hath run twice to Rome, and he would run the third time if thou gavest him leave." The Irish Chronicle states that the full tide in Dublin Bay on the day of the battle coincided with sunrise, and that the returning tide in the evening aided in the destruction of the defeated foreigners. The date assigned by the Chronicle for the battle is Good Friday, 23d April 1014. It has been found by astronomical calculation that the full tide that morning did coincide with sunrise—a remarkable attestation of the authenticity of the narrative.

from the Bœndr for his viking expeditions, and was killed by
Thorkell Fostri (Aumundi's son) at Sandwick, in Deerness.
Brusi then took possession of the whole earldom of the
Orkneys, as Thorfinn had that of Caithness. Thorfinn, however, claimed a share of the Islands, and as he had the assistance of his grandfather Malcolm, the King of Scots, Brusi felt
himself unable to cope with him. He therefore went to
Norway to negotiate with King Olaf Haraldson for a grant
of the whole of the earldom of the Islands. Thorfinn followed
him on the same errand, but the king was more than a match
for them both, and the result was that he gave each a third of
the Islands, declaring the third which had belonged to Earl
Einar to be forfeited to himself for the murder of his friend
and henchman Eyvind Urarhorn, whom Einar had slain in
revenge for Eyvind's helping the Irish king Conchobhar against
him at Ulfreksfiord. After Thorfinn's departure, however, he
gave Brusi to understand that he was to have the forfeited third
of the earldom, as well as his own third, to enable him to hold
his own against Thorfinn. An arrangement was afterwards
made between Brusi and Thorfinn that the latter should
receive two-thirds of the Islands on condition of his undertaking the defence of the whole, as they were at that time
much exposed to the predatory incursions of Norse and
Danish vikings.

When Thorfinn's maternal grandfather, King Malcolm,
died, Kali Hundason [1] took the kingdom in Scotland. He
attempted to exact tribute from Thorfinn for his dominions in
the north of Scotland, and failing in this he sent his sister's
son, Moddan, into Caithness, giving him the title of Earl.
Thorfinn was supported by the inhabitants, however, and after
an unsuccessful attempt to establish himself in Caithness, Moddan returned to King Kali with the news that Thorfinn was
plundering in Ross and Sutherland. King Kali embarked a considerable force in eleven ships at Beruvik (apparently Berriedale
on the southern frontier of Caithness), and sent Moddan north-

---

[1] See the account of him in the Saga, cap. v. and note.

wards by land with another division of his army, intending
to enclose Thorfinn in the north-east corner of Caithness, and
attack him from two sides at once. Thorfinn, however, was
aware of the trap laid for him, and retired to the Islands.
There Kali came up with him off Deerness, in Orkney, and a
fierce battle took place, in which Kali was defeated. He fled
southwards, and Thorfinn, following him, obliged him again to
give battle at Baefiord, where he was again defeated, while
Thorkell Fostri fell upon Moddan at Thurso and slew him.
Then, say the Sagas, Earl Thorfinn overran Scotland as far
south as Fife, burning and slaying, and subduing the land
wherever he went. By these conquests he became the most
powerful of all the Earls of Orkney.

Rognvald Brusison was in Norway when he heard of his
father's death, and being odal-born to his father's third of the
Islands, and having received from King Magnus Olafson a
grant of that third which King Olaf had declared forfeited to
himself for Eyvind Urarhorn's murder, he went west to the
Orkneys, prepared to maintain his rights against the claims
of Thorfinn, who had taken possession of the whole. An
amicable arrangement was made between the kinsmen, and
they joined their forces for viking forays upon the Hebrides,
venturing even upon an extensive foray in England during
the absence of Hardicanute in Denmark. After an eight
years' alliance, however, discord broke out between the kinsmen, and in a sea-fight in the Pentland Firth, off Rauda
Biorg,[1] in Caithness, Rognvald was defeated and fled, and
Thorfinn reduced the whole of the Islands. Rognvald went
to Norway, and stayed some time with King Magnus. Then
he came west to the Islands in a single ship, and surprising
Thorfinn in a house on the Mainland of Orkney, he set fire to
it. Thorfinn broke down part of the wall of the house and
leapt out, carrying his wife Ingibiorg in his arms, and
escaped through the smoke. Rognvald, believing that

---

[1] Rattar Brough, a little to the east of Dunnet Head, seems to be the
modern form of Rauda Biorg.

Thorfinn had perished, took possession of the Islands.
Thorfinn, who had got secretly over to his dominions in
Caithness, returned shortly afterwards, and surprising
Rognvald in a house on Papa Stronsay, burnt the house and
all who were in it, except Rognvald, who sprang over the
heads of the men who surrounded him, and got away in the
darkness. He concealed himself among the rocks by the
shore, but was discovered by the barking of his dog, and
slain by Thorkell Fostri. Thus Thorfinn was again sole ruler
of the Orkney earldom, as well as that of Caithness. He
went to Norway to make his peace with King Magnus, who
was foster-brother to Earl Rognvald, and therefore would seek
vengeance for his death. At that time Magnus was at war
with Swein Ulfson, King of Denmark. While he lay with
his fleet at Seley two war-ships rowed up to the king's
vessel, and a man in a white cloak went straight aboard, and
up to the quarter-deck, where the king sat at meat. Saluting
the king, the man reached forth his hand, took a loaf from
the table, broke it, and ate of it. The king handed the cup
to him when he saw that he had broken bread at his table,
and then he learned that it was Earl Thorfinn, who, having
broken his bread and drunk from his cup, was, for the present
at least, safe from his vengeance, according to the ancient
laws of hospitality. He deemed it wise, however, to take his
departure without having obtained a formal reconciliation.
King Magnus died shortly afterwards, and was succeeded by
his uncle Harald Hardradi. Thorfinn again went to Norway
on hearing of King Magnus' death, and effected a reconciliation with King Harald, so that he was now established in the
earldom of Orkney by consent of the over-lord, the King of
Norway.

From Norway he went to Denmark, visiting King Swein
at Aalborg, and proceeded thence through Germany on a
pilgrimage to Rome, where he obtained absolution for all
his deeds. After his return from Rome it is said that he
turned his mind more to the government of his dominions

and the welfare of his people than he had previously done in his career of conquest. He built Christ's Kirk in Birsay, and established there the first bishop's see in the Orkneys. He died in 1064, having been Earl, by the Saga account, for "seventy winters," and the most powerful and wide-landed of all the Earls of the Orkneys. After his death, as the Saga states, his widow Ingibiorg was married to King Malcolm Canmore,[1] and became the mother of Duncan, whom, however, the Scottish historians have always represented as a bastard.

Thorfinn was succeeded by his two sons, Paul and Erlend, who were with King Harald Hardradi in his unfortunate expedition to England. After the battle of Stamford Bridge, in which King Harald fell, the Orkney earls were allowed to go home by the victorious Harold Godwinson, and they ruled their dominions jointly in great harmony till their sons grew up to manhood, when there began to be discord between the families. Hakon, the son of Paul, was of a turbulent and overbearing disposition. He seems to have had a lingering attachment to the Pagan faith of his forefathers, for, while in Sweden (which was longer in being converted to Christianity than Norway), he is said to have sought out the Pagan spaemen to learn his future from them. Coming to Norway he tried hard to induce King Magnus Barelegs to undertake an expedition to the Orkneys and the Western Isles, hoping that the king would conquer the Islands for the glory of the conquest, and hand them over to him, as Harald Harfagri had given them to Rognvald, Earl of Mœri. He was more successful than he anticipated. King Magnus, fired with the love of conquest, did make the expedition, but he deposed Paul and Erlend, and carried them to Norway, placing his own son Sigurd, a mere child, over the Orkneys.

Although the Saga speaks as if there had been only one expedition by King Magnus to Scotland, there were in reality

---

[1] See the Saga account, cap. xxiii. and note. The dates do not bear out the statement that Thorfinn was Earl for seventy years.

three. Fordun [1] states that when Donald Bane, Duncan, and Edgar, were struggling for the kingdom on the death of Malcolm in 1093, King Magnus was ravaging the gulfs of the Scottish seaboard, and it is stated in the Saga [2] that he assisted Murcertach in the capture of Dublin in 1094. In his second expedition in 1098 he carried off the Earls Paul and Erlend, and made his own son Sigurd Earl of Orkney. Munch surmises that the motives of this expedition were two-fold—to secure his power in the Orkneys, and to assist his protégé Donald Bane, who had again usurped the crown of Scotland on the death of Duncan in 1095, and was in 1097 hard pressed by Edgar with an English army. King Magnus took with him from the Orkneys Magnus Erlend's son (after-wards St. Magnus), and proceeded southwards to the Hebrides, where he ravaged Lewis, Skye, Uist, Tiree, and Mull, sparing Iona on account of its sanctity. The Saga says that he opened the door of the little church of Columkill (St. Oran's chapel), and was about to enter, but stopped suddenly, closed the door, forbade any one to enter, and gave the inhabitants peace. Then he went on to Isla and Kintyre, and thence to Man and Anglesea, where he fought the battle with the two Hughs, Earls of Chester and Shrewsbury. On his return northward he caused his vessel to be drawn across the isthmus of Tarbert, in imitation of the fabulous sea-king Beite, of whom a similar story is told. He returned to Norway in 1099, and during the next two years was occupied with the Swedish war. In 1102 he returned to the west, married his son Sigurd to Biadmynia, the daughter of Murcertach, and fell in a skirmish with the Irish in Ulster in 1103. He was buried in St. Patrick's church in Down. [3]

Sigurd, the son of King Magnus, remained Earl of the Orkneys until his father's death, when he succeeded to the throne of Norway.

Hakon Paul's son, and Magnus Erlend's son, then suc-

---

[1] Fordun, v. 24.   [2] Saga Magnus Berfoetts, Heimskringla, cap. xxv.
[3] Chron. Manniæ, Munch's edition, p. 59.

ceeded to the earldom, and held it jointly until Magnus was murdered in Egilsay by Hakon on the 16th April, A.D. 1115.[1]

After the murder of Magnus, Hakon became sole earl. He went on a pilgrimage to Rome and the Holy Land, and after his return became a good ruler, and was so popular " that the Orkneymen desired no other rulers than Hakon and his issue."

Earl Hakon left two sons, Harald and Paul (the silent). Harald, who had succeeded to the earldom of Caithness, which " he held from the King of Scots," was in some way unintentionally put to death by his mother Helga and her sister Frakork. As the Saga tells the story, he met his death by insisting on putting on a poisoned shirt which the sisters intended for his half-brother Paul, who, on Harald's death, became sole Earl of the Orkneys.

A new claimant arose, however, in the person of Kali, son of Kol, a nobleman resident at Agdir, in Norway, who had married a sister of Earl Magnus the saint. Kali received from King Sigurd the gift of half the Orkneys, which had belonged to his uncle Magnus, and his name was changed from Kali Kolson to Rognvald, because his mother said that Rognvald Brusison was the most accomplished of all the Earls of Orkney, and thought the name would bring her son good fortune.

Rognvald had many romantic adventures in the prosecution of his attempt to obtain possession of half of the earldom held by Paul, which are detailed at length in the Saga. At last he was advised by his father Kol to make a vow to St. Magnus, that if he should succeed in establishing himself in the Orkneys he would build and endow a "stone minster" at Kirkwall, dedicated to St. Magnus, " to whom the half of the earldom rightly belonged." The vow was made, and Rognvald's next expedition was successful. He landed in Shetland, and by a dexterous stratagem the beacons on Fair Isle and in the Orkneys were made to

---

[1] See the account of his death in the Saga, cap. xxxix. His feast days were 16th April and 13th December, the former commemorating his death, and the latter the removal of his relics from Birsay by Bishop William. (Den Norske Kirkes Historie af R. Keyser : Christiania, 1856, p. 162.)

give a false alarm of his descent upon the Orkneys, so that when he did land there he was unopposed. Then he secured the intervention of the bishop, and an agreement that he should have half the Islands was concluded between him and Earl Paul. Shortly thereafter Earl Paul was captured by Swein Asleifson, a notable leader at that time in the Islands, and the last and greatest of the Orkney vikings. Swein carried the earl off in his vessel, and, landing him on the southern shore of the Moray Firth, delivered him into the safe keeping of Maddad, Earl of Athole,[1] who was married to Margaret, a sister of Earl Paul. What became of the earl is not known, "but this," says the Saga, "is well known, that he came never again to the Orkneys, and had no dominions in Scotland." Swein Asleifson returned to Orkney, and by the joint consent of Earl Rognvald, Bishop William of Orkney, and Bishop John of Athole, Harald, the son of Maddad, earl of Athole, was made Earl, along with Rognvald, though he was at that time a child of only five years old. This arrangement was afterwards confirmed by a meeting, held in Caithness, of the Bœndr and chiefs of the Orkneys and Caithness.

The Earls Rognvald and Harald visited King Ingi by invitation at Bergen, and there Earl Rognvald met with Eindridi Ungi, a returned Crusader, and became possessed by a strong desire to visit the Holy Land. On his return voyage to Orkney, Earl Rognvald was shipwrecked at Gulberwick in Shetland, and narrowly escaped with his life. Bishop William strongly approved of his project to go on a pilgrimage to the Holy Land, and agreed to accompany him. Accordingly he went back to Norway to organise the expedition, and returned to the Orkneys followed by a large number of Jorsala-farers— mostly adventurers of very indifferent character, if we are to judge by their turbulent and lawless behaviour during their stay in the Orkneys, where they spent the winter previous to

---

[1] The Earls of Athole seem at this time to have occupied the *rath* or fortress at Logierait. It is mentioned in one of the Scone charters as the capital of the earldom in the 12th century. (Lib. Eccles. de Scon, p. 35.)

their departure for the East. Early in the spring of the year 1152 Earl Rognvald called a Thing-meeting of the inhabitants of the Islands, and told them of his purposed voyage, announcing that he was to leave the sole government in the hands of Harald during his absence, and asking them all to obey him and help him faithfully as their lawful lord. The summer was far advanced before he sailed, but he had a prosperous voyage, the adventures of which are detailed in the Saga ; and after visiting Jerusalem and bathing in the Jordan, he returned by way of Constantinople, Durazzo, Apulia, and Rome, and so overland to Norway, the whole expedition occupying about three years.

In the same summer that Earl Rognvald left the Orkneys on his pilgrimage, King Eystein came from Norway with a large force, and seizing Earl Harald Maddadson as he lay at Thurso with a single ship, made him pay a ransom of three marks of gold, and swear fealty to him for Orkney and Shetland. Earl Maddad of Athole was now dead, and Margaret, the mother of Earl Harald, had come to the Orkneys. Erlend, the son of the Earl Harald (Slettmali), who was killed by the poisoned shirt, had set up his claim to half the earldom after Rognvald's departure. His cause was favoured by King Eystein, and espoused by Swein Asleifson, and Earl Harald was obliged to make peace by taking oath to allow Erlend to remain in possession of the Islands, an arrangement which was afterwards confirmed by a Thing-meeting of the Bœndr of the Orkneys, Earl Rognvald's claim to his share of the Islands being, however, reserved. Earl Harald (Maddadson) was thus denuded of all power in the Islands. He fled across to Caithness, but after a time he returned to the Orkneys with four ships and a hundred men, and after an unsuccessful attempt to surprise Erlend[1] he was obliged to abandon the enterprise for a time. Meanwhile, Erlend had carried off Harald's mother Margaret (who seems to have been still a

[1] This was the occasion in which he and his men spent the Yule-feast day in the Orkahaug, which seems to be Maeshow. See the Saga, cap. xci.

beautiful woman, though of very indifferent character), and
fled with her to the island of Mousa in Shetland, where they
fortified themselves in the old Pictish tower or borg of Mousa,
which about two centuries before had given shelter during a
whole winter to a pair of lovers from Norway, under circumstances somewhat similar.[1] Harald pursued them, and laid
siege to the borg, which could not be taken by assault, but
the two earls came to a mutual understanding, and the siege
was abandoned. Erlend married Margaret, and the same
summer he and Harald went each on a visit to Norway to
meet Earl Rognvald on his return from the Holy Land.

Erlend succeeded in making an alliance with Earl Rognvald. Earl Harald was not aware of this till he returned
from Norway, and heard the news in Orkney. He and
Rognvald met at Thurso, and a skirmish took place between
their respective followers, in which thirteen of Rognvald's
men were slain, but by the efforts of their mutual friends the
two earls were brought to an agreement of peace. Erlend
and his faithful ally Swein Asleifson surprised the squadron
of the two earls at Scapa, taking fourteen ships, and putting
both the earls to flight. They crossed over to Caithness
during the night, each in a separate boat, and returning
some time after with a fresh force, they surprised Erlend in
Damsey, and slew him. Then they made peace with
Erlend's old ally, Swein Asleifson, although this was not
effected without some difficulty. Harald and Rognvald then
ruled the two earldoms jointly, and apparently in great
harmony, until the death of the latter in 1158. Rognvald
was slain at Calder, in Caithness, by Thorbiorn Klerk, the
former friend and counsellor of Earl Harald, who had been
made an outlaw by Earl Rognvald for a murder committed
in Kirkwall, following on a series of acts of violence.[2]

---

[1] See the notice from the Saga of Egill Skalagrimson, in the chapter on
Mousa.

[2] Some years after his death Earl Rognvald was canonised, but his name is
not commemorated in any of the dedications now remaining in the Islands.

Earl Harald Maddadson now became sole ruler of the earldoms of Orkney and Caithness. But by his second marriage he had allied himself with Hoarflad (Gormlath), daughter of Malcolm MacHeth, the so-called Earl of Moray, ex-bishop Wimund, and pretender to the Scottish throne, and consequently there could be no pacific relations between him and King William the Lion. The events of this period are somewhat confusedly told in the chronicles, but it seems probable that Harald was one of the six earls who rebelled against King Malcolm in 1160, in order to place William of Egremont, grandson of Duncan, on the throne,[1] and that he also supported Donaldbane, the son of William who aspired to the throne, and from 1180 maintained himself in Moray and Ross, till he was slain at the battle of Macgarvey, 1187.[2] When Harald Ungi, son of Eirik Slagbrellir, by Ingigerd (or Ingirid), daughter of Earl Rognvald, appeared as a rival claimant to the earldom of Orkney, having received from King Magnus Erlingson a grant of his grandfather's share of the Islands, King William embraced his interests, and gave him a grant of half of Caithness, which was thus taken from Earl Harald. Then Earl Harald became involved in difficulties with his other suzerain, the reigning King of Norway, through the expedition of the Eyarskeggiar or partisans of Sigurd, son of Magnus Erlingson, whom they endeavoured to place upon the throne in opposition to King Sverrir. Sigurd's cause was largely espoused by the Orkneymen, and the expedition (which was organised and fitted out in Orkney) did much mischief in Norway. Earl Harald was obliged to present himself before King Sverrir in Bergen. He went from Orkney accompanied by Bishop Bjarni. In presence of a great assembly in the Christ's Kirk garth, the earl confessed his fault, saying that he was now an old man, as his beard bore witness ; that he had bent the knee before many kings, sometimes in closest friendship, but oftener in circumstances

---

[1] Munch, Chron. Manniæ, p. 84.　　　　[2] Fordun's Annals, xvi.

of misfortune; that he had not been unfaithful to his
allegiance, although some of his people might have done that
which was contrary to the king's interests; and that he had
not been always able to rule the Orkneys entirely according
to his own will; and that now he came to yield up himself
and all his possessions into the king's power. So saying, he
advanced, and casting himself to the earth, he laid his head at
King Sverrir's feet. The king granted him pardon, but took
from him the whole of Shetland,[1] "which never after that
formed part of the Norwegian earldom of Orkney," though
after the time of the Saga-writer, Shetland as well as Orkney
was granted to Henry St. Clair in 1379 by King Hakon
Magnusson, the second of that name.

Yet though humiliated in this manner, and stripped of a
great part of his dominions, Earl Harald, according to Hoveden, dared to contest the possession of Moray with King
William, instigated no doubt by his wife, in whose right
alone he could have had any feasible claim to its possession.

Roger de Hoveden, chaplain to Henry II., a contemporary
chronicler, thus records the events that followed :—[2]

"In the same year (1196) William, King of Scots, having
gathered a great army, entered Moray to drive out Harald
MacMadit, who had occupied that district. But before the
king could enter Caithness, Harald fled to his ships, not
wishing to risk a battle with the king. Then the King of
Scots sent his army to Turseha (Thurso), the town of the
aforesaid Harald, and destroyed his castle there. But Harald,
seeing that the king would completely devastate the country,

---

[1] From this time till 1379 Shetland passed into the immediate possession
of the crown of Norway. So we find in 1312-1319, that King Hakon Magnusson grants to the Mary-Kirk in Oslo (Christiania), for the completion of the
fabric of the kirk, "all our incomes of Hjaltland and the Faroes, so that those
who have charge of the kirk's building and fabric every year shall render account thereof to our heirs, and when the fabric is altogether completed, then
shall the foresaid revenues of Hjaltland and the Faroes revert to the crown."
(Nicolaysen, Norske Fornlevninger, p. 426.)

[2] Chronica Rogeri de Hoveden (Rolls Ed.), iv. pp, 10, 12.

came to the king's feet and placed himself at his mercy, chiefly because of a raging tempest in the sea, and the wind being contrary, so that he could not go to the Orkneys ; and he promised the king that he would bring to him all his enemies when the king should again return to Moray. On that condition the king permitted him to retain a half of Caithness, and the other half he gave to Harald, the younger, grandson of Reginald (Rögnvald), a former Earl of Orkney and Caithness. Then the king returned to his own land, and Harald to the Orkneys. The king returned in the autumn to Moray, as far as Ilvernarran (Invernairn), in order to receive the king's enemies from Harald. But though Harald had brought them as far as the port of Lochloy near Invernairn, he allowed them to escape ; and when the king returned late from hunting, Harald came to him, bringing with him two boys, his grandchildren, to deliver them to the king as hostages. Being asked by the king where were the king's enemies whom he had promised to deliver up, and where was Thorfinn his son, whom he had also promised to give as a hostage, he replied, ' I allowed them to escape, knowing that if I delivered them up to you they would not escape out of your hands. My son I could not bring, for there is no other heir to my lands.' So, because he had not kept the agreement which he had made with the king, he was adjudged to remain in the king's custody until his son should arrive and become a hostage for him. And because he had permitted the king's enemies to escape, he was also adjudged to have forfeited those lands which he held of the king. The king took Harald with him to Edinburgh Castle, and laid him in chains until his men brought his son Thorfinn from the Orkneys ; and on their delivering him up as a hostage to the king, Harald was liberated.

"So Harald returned to Orkney, and there remained in peace and quiet, until Harald the younger, having received a grant of the half of the Orkneys from Sverrir Birkebein, the King of Norway, joined himself to Sigurd Murt, and many

other warriors, and invaded Orkney. Harald the elder, being
unwilling to engage with him in battle, left the Orkneys and
fled to the Isle of Man. He was followed by Harald the
younger, but Harald the elder had left Man before his arrival
there, and gone by another way to the Orkneys with his fleet,
and there he killed all the adherents of the younger Harald
whom he found in the Islands. Harald the younger returned
to Caithness to Wick, where he engaged in battle with Harald
the elder, and in that battle Harald the younger and all his
army were slain. Harald the elder then went to the King of
Scots, on the safe conduct of Roger and Reginald, the bishops
of St. Andrews and Rosemarkie, and took to the king a large
sum in gold and silver for the redemption of his lands of
Caithness. The king said he would give him back Caithness
if he would put away his wife (Gormlath), the daughter of
Malcolm MacHeth, and take back his first wife, Afreka, the
sister of Duncan, Earl of Fife, and deliver up to him as a
hostage Laurentius his priest,[1] and Honaver the son of Inge-
mund, as hostages. But this Harald was unwilling to do;
therefore came Reginald, son of Sumarlid, King of Man and
the Isles, to William, King of Scots, and purchased from him
Caithness, saving the king's annual tribute."

Reginald, being supplied with auxiliary forces from Ireland
by his brother-in-law, John of Courcy, overran Caithness,
and, returning home, left the conquered earldom in charge of
three deputies. Harald procured the murder of one of them,

---

[1] In the Chronicle of Melrose, under the date 1175, it is stated that
"Laurentius, Abbot in Orkney, was made Abbot of Melrose." But as his death
is recorded in the year 1178, the priest here mentioned by Hoveden must
have been a different person, though of the same name. At the same time, as
this passage shows that Earl Harald had a hird-priest named Laurentius, it is
not improbable that the so-called Orkney abbot, who was made abbot of
Melrose, may also have been Harald's family or court priest. Being himself
the son of a Scottish earl, and allied by marriage first with the family of the
Earl of Fife, and subsequently with the MacHeths, and having, moreover,
such close relations with the abbey of Scone, it is not unlikely that he may
have had Scottish priests about his family in preference to those of Norwegian
extraction.

and then, coming over from Orkney with a strong force, landed at Scrabster, where the bishop met him and endeavoured to mollify him. But Harald had a special grudge against Bishop John, which added to his rage at what he considered the defection of his Caithness subjects. The bishop had refused to collect from the people of Caithness a tax of one penny annually from each inhabited house, which Earl Harald had some years previously granted to the papal revenues. Accordingly he stormed the " borg " at Scrabster, in which the bishop and the principal men of the district had taken refuge, slew almost all that were in it, and caused the bishop to be blinded and his tongue to be cut out.[1] The two

---

[1] So says the Saga. Fordun says that the use of his tongue and of one eye was in some measure left him. The letter of Pope Innocent, addressed to the Bishop of Orkney, prescribing the penance to be performed by the man who mutilated the bishop, only mentions the cutting out of the tongue. It is as follows :—

"We have learnt by your letters that Lomberd, a layman, the bearer of these presents, accompanied his earl on an expedition into Caithness ; that there the Earl's army stormed a castle, killed almost all who were in it, and took prisoner the Bishop of Caithness ; and that this Lomberd, as he says, was compelled by some of the earl's soldiery to cut out the bishop's tongue. Now because the sin is great and grievous, in absolving him, according to the form of the church, we have prescribed this penance for satisfaction of his offence, and to the terror of others :—That he shall hasten home, and barefooted, and naked, except breeches, and a short woollen vest without sleeves, having his tongue tied by a-string, and drawn out so as to project beyond his lips, and the ends of the string bound round his neck, with rods in his hand, in sight of all men, walk for fifteen days successively through his own native district, the district of the mutilated bishop, and the neighbouring country ; he shall go to the door of the church without entering, and there, prostrate on the earth, undergo discipline with the rods he is to carry ; he is thus to spend each day in silence and fasting until evening, when he shall support nature with bread and water only ; after these fifteen days are passed he shall prepare within a month to set out for Jerusalem, and there labour in the service of the Cross for three years ; he shall never more bear arms against Christians ; for two years he shall fast every Friday on bread and water, unless by the indulgence of some discreet bishop, or on account of bodily infirmity, this abstinence be mitigated. Do you then receive him returning in this manner, and see that he observe the penance enjoined him." (Epist. Innoc. III. Lib. iii. No. 77 ; Diplom. Norvegicum, vii. 3.)

remaining deputies of King Reginald fled to the King of Scots,
whose first act was to take revenge on Harald's son Thorfinn.
He was blinded and castrated after the barbarous manner of
the times, and died miserably in the dungeon of Roxburgh
Castle. King William, then collecting a great army, marched
north to Eysteinsdal on the borders of Caithness in the spring
of 1202. Though Harald had collected a force of 6000 men,
he felt himself unable to cope with the king, and was obliged
to sue for peace, which was obtained on the hard condition of
the payment of every fourth penny to be found in Caithness,
amounting to 2000 marks of silver.

Earl Harald's career was now drawing to a close. He
died in 1206, at the advanced age of seventy-three, having
had the earldom for twenty years jointly with Earl Rognvald,
and forty-eight years after Rognvald's death.

His sons John and David succeeded him, and ruled jointly
for seven years, when David died and John became sole Earl
of Orkney and Caithness. The most notable event of his time
was the burning of Bishop Adam at Halkirk in Caithness.

Bishop Adam was a man of low birth. According to the
Saga he was a foundling, and had been exposed at a church
door. Previous to his consecration to the see of Caithness,
in 1214, he had been Abbot of Melrose.[1] He arbitrarily
increased the exaction of the bishop's scat to such an extent
that the populace rose in a body, and proceeding tumultuously
to Halkirk, where he was residing, demanded abatement of the
unjust exactions. Earl John, who was in the neighbourhood
at the time, declined to interfere, and the exasperated populace,
finding the bishop indisposed to treat them more liberally, first
killed his adviser, Serlo, a monk of Newbottle, and then burnt
the bishop. In the quaint language of Wyntoun—

> " Thre hundyre men in cumpany
> Gaddyrt on hym suddanly,
> Tuk hym owt quhare that he lay
> Of his chawmyre befor day,

---

[1] Chron. de Mailros, p. 114 ; see also p. lxxxi. *infra.*

Modyr naked hys body bare ;
Thai band hym, dang hym, and woundyt sair
In-to the nycht or day couth dawe.
The monk thai slwe thare, hys falawe,
And the child that in hys chawmyr lay,
Thare thai slwe hym before day.
Hymself bwndyn and wowndyt syne
Thai pwt hym in hys awyn kychyne,
In thair felny and thare ire
Thare thai brynt hym in a fyre."

The Saga tells that when the tidings of this outrage
reached King Alexander he was greatly enraged, and that
the terrible vengeance he took was still fresh in memory
when the Saga was written. Fordun states that the king
had the perpetrators of this deed mangled in limb and
racked with many a torture. The Icelandic Annals are more
precise. They say that he caused the hands and feet to be
hewn from eighty of the men who had been present at the
burning, and that many of them died in consequence.

With this tragic and ill-omened event the chequered
history of the line of the Norse Earls draws to a close. Earl
John sought to clear himself from the guilt of complicity in
the murder of the bishop by the testimony of " good men "
that he had no hand in it ; but seeing that he had neither
assisted the bishop nor sought to punish his murderers, he
was heavily fined by King Alexander, and deprived of part
of his Scottish earldom. Subsequently he had an interview
with the king at Forfar, and bought back his lands. In the
summer of 1224 he was summoned by King Hakon to
Norway, having fallen under suspicion of a desire to aid the
designs of Earl Skule against Hakon's power in Norway ;
and after a conference with the king at Bergen he returned
to Orkney, leaving his only son Harald behind him as a
hostage. In 1226 Harald was drowned at sea, probably on
his passage home from Norway. In 1231, Earl John having
become involved in a feud with Hanef Ungi, a commissioner
whom King Hakon had sent over to the Orkneys, Snækoll

Gunnason, grandson of Earl Rögnvald (Kali Kolsson), and
Aulver Illteit, they attacked him suddenly in an inn at
Thurso, set fire to the house, and slew him in the cellar,
where he had sought to conceal himself.

Thus the ancient line of the Norse Earls, that had ruled
the Orkneys since 872—a period of 350 years—became
extinct, and the earldom passed into the possession of the
house of Angus.

V. The Earldom in the Angus Line—1231-1312.

On the failure of the line of the Norse Earls by the death
of Earl John in 1231, King Alexander II. of Scotland, in
1232, granted the earldom of North Caithness to Magnus,[1]
the second son of Gilbride, Earl of Angus. Sutherland, or
the southern land of Caithness, was now made a separate
earldom, and given to William, son of Hugh Freskyn, who
was thus the first of the Earls of Sutherland.

Magnus seems to have been confirmed in the earldom of
Orkney by the King of Norway; but from this time the
notices of Orkney and its earls in the Icelandic or Norwegian
records are so few and obscure, that but little is to be
gathered from them. The Iceland Annals, however, record
the death of Magnus, Earl of Orkney, in 1239.

In the Diploma of Bishop Thomas Tulloch, drawn up
circa 1443,[2] it is stated that this Magnus was succeeded by

---

[1] Magnus, son of the Earl of Angus, appears among those present at the
perambulation of the boundaries of the lands of the Abbey of Aberbrothock
on 16th January 1222 (Regist. Vet. de Aberbrothock, p. 163); but he seems
to have been Earl of Angus as well as of Caithness at the date after mentioned.
A charter of King Alexander II. to the chapel of St. Nicholas at Spey, dated
2d October 1232, is witnessed by M. Earl of Angus and Kataness (Regist.
Moraviense, p. 123).

[2] The title prefixed to the translation of this document by Dean Gule,
made for William Sinclair of Roslin, in 1554, calls it:—"A Diploma or
Deduction concerning the Genealogies of the ancient Earls of Orkney, drawn
up from the most authentic records, by Thomas, Bishop of Orkney, with the
assistance of his clergy and others, in consequence of an order from King Eirik

Earl Gilbride, to whom succeeded Gilbride his son, who held both the earldoms of Orkney and Caithness in Scotland. The Annals only notice one Gilbride, whom they call "Gibbon, Earl of Orkney." His death is placed in the year 1256.

According to the Diploma, Gilbride had one son, Magnus, and a daughter, Matilda. This Magnus is mentioned in the Saga of Hakon Hakonson as accompanying the ill-fated expedition of that monarch against Scotland in 1263. "With King Hakon from Bergen went Magnus, Earl of Orkney, and the king gave him a good long-ship." Pilots had previously been procured from the Orkneys, and the fleet, after being two nights at sea with a gentle wind, put into Bressay Sound in Shetland, where they remained nearly half a month. Then they sailed for the Orkneys, and lay for some time in Elwick Bay, opposite Inganess, near Kirkwall. Then they moved round South Ronaldsay, and lay some time in Ronaldsvoe, while men were sent over to Caithness to levy a contribution from the inhabitants,[1] of which the scald sings that "he imposed tribute on the dwellers on the Ness, who were terrified by the steel-clad exactor of rings." Ordering the Orkneymen to follow him as soon as they were ready, the king sailed south to Lewis and Skye, where he was

of Denmark, Sweden, and Norway, to investigate the rights of William Sinclair to the earldom." But in the document itself King Eirik is spoken of as "our former lord of illustrious memory," and the date is evidently erroneous. It is probably to be assigned to about 1443. It was first printed by Wallace in 1699, and subsequently by Jonæus in the appendix to the Orkneyinga Saga in 1780 ; by Barry in his History of the Orkneys in 1805 ; in the Bannatyne Miscellany, 1848 ; and by Munch in his Symbolæ, Christiania, 1850.

[1] Among the documents found in the King's Treasury at Edinburgh in 1282, were the letters addressed by the King of Norway (presumably Hakon) to the inhabitants of Caithness. The inhabitants of Caithness seem to have been also obliged by the Scottish King to give hostages for their fealty to him. In the accounts of Laurence Grant, Sheriff of Inverness, for the year 1263, there is a charge of £15 : 6 : 3 for the expenses of twenty-one hostages from Caithness, at the rate of one denarius (penny) for each per day for twenty-five weeks, "and then they were set at liberty." (Compota Camerarium Scotiæ, i. p. 31.)

joined by Magnus, King of Man. The fleet, which now
consisted of more than a hundred vessels, for the most part
large and all well equipped, was divided into two squadrons,
one of which, consisting of fifty ships, plundered the coasts
of Kintyre and Mull, rejoining King Hakon at Gigha. A
detached squadron now plundered Bute, and the fleet cast
anchor in Arran Sound, from which King Hakon sent
Gilbert, Bishop of Hamar, and Henry, Bishop of Orkney,
with three other envoys, to treat for peace with the Scottish
King. The negotiations failed, and soon after the fleet was
disabled by a storm, and the power of the Norwegian King
utterly broken in the battle of Largs. King Hakon, gathering together the shattered remnants of his fleet and army,
retired slowly northwards, meeting with no impediment
until they arrived off Durness, in Sutherlandshire, when the
wind fell calm, and the fleet steered into the sound, where
seven men of a boat's crew, who had been sent ashore for
water, were killed by the Scots. In passing through the
Pentland Firth one vessel went down with all on board in
the " Swelkie," a dangerous whirlpool in certain states of the
tide, and another was carried by the current helplessly
through the Firth, and made straight for Norway. King
Hakon laid up his fleet in Midland Harbour and Scapa Bay.
He then rode to Kirkwall, and lay down to die. He was
lodged in the bishop's palace, and after having been confined
to his bed for some days, he recovered so much that he
attended mass in the bishop's chapel, and walked to the
cathedral to visit the shrine of St. Magnus. But there came
a relapse, and he was again laid prostrate. He caused the
Bible and Latin books to be read to him to beguile the
tedium of the sick bed, until he was no longer able to bear
the fatigue of reflecting on what he heard ; and then he
desired that Norwegian books should be read to him night
and day—first the Sagas of the Saints, and then the
Chronicles of the Kings, from Halfdan the Black through
all the succession of the Kings of Norway. Then he set his

affairs in order, caused his silver plate to be weighed out to
pay his troops, and received the sacrament. He died at
midnight on Saturday, 15th December 1263. On Sunday
the corpse, clothed in the richest garments, with a garland on
the head, was laid in state in the upper hall of the palace.
The king's chamberlains stood round it with tapers, and all
day long the people came to view the remains of their king.
The nobles kept watch over the bier through the night; and
on Monday the royal remains were borne to St. Magnus'
Cathedral, where they lay in state all that night. On
Tuesday they were temporarily interred in the choir of the
church, near the steps leading to the shrine of St. Magnus.
Before his death the king had given directions that his body
should be carried east to Norway, and buried beside the
remains of his father and his relatives in Bergen. In the
month of March the corpse was exhumed and conveyed to
Scapa, where it was placed on board the great ship in which
he had sailed on the unfortunate expedition to Largs, and taken
to Bergen, where it was interred in the choir of Christ's Church.

Magnus Gilbride's son, who was Earl of Orkney at the
time of King Hakon's expedition, died (according to the
Annals) in 1273.

He was succeeded by a son of the same name. The
Annals have the entry under the year 1276 :—" Magnus, King
of Norway, gave to Magnus, son of Earl Magnus of Orkney,
the title of Earl, at Tunsberg." He appears also as Earl of
Orkney in the document, dated 5th February 1283, declaring Margaret, the Maiden of Norway, the nearest heir to the
Scottish throne.[1] The death of Earl Magnus, Magnus' son, is
recorded in the year 1284,[2] along with that of Bishop Peter
of Orkney and Sturla the Lawman. The Diploma states that
he died without issue, and was succeeded by his brother John
in the earldom of Orkney and Caithness.

John, as Earl of Caithness, appears in 1289 as one of the

---

[1] Acta Parl. Scot., vol. i. p. 82.
[2] Iceland Annals, *sub anno.*

signatories to the letter addressed by the nobles to King
Edward of England proposing that the young Prince Edward
should marry Margaret, the Maid of Norway. His name also
occurs in the list of those summoned to attend the first
parliament of Baliol. He swore fealty to King Edward at
Murkle in Caithness, in 1297.

King Eirik of Norway in 1281 had married the Scottish
princess Margaret, daughter of Alexander III. She died in
1283, leaving one daughter, Margaret, "the Maid of Norway,"
who became sole heiress to the crown of Scotland, and in
1289 was formally betrothed to Prince Edward of England.
She died at sea off the coast of Orkney,[1] on her way to Scotland, in September or October 1290. There is no record of
the circumstances of her death,[2] but we learn from a letter

[1] The Scala Cronica says off the coast of Buchan. "One Master Weland,
a clerke of Scotlande, sent yn to Norway for Margaret, dyed with her by
tempeste on the se cumming oute of Norway to Scotland yn costes of
Boghan." (Scala Cronica, Mait. Club, pp. 110, 282.) Wyntoun says she was
"put to dede by martyry," and assigns as the reason that the Norwegians
would not have one who was of another nation and a female to be heir to the
throne of Norway, though their laws allowed it. He had probably heard the
story of the "false Margaret." (See p. lii.)

[2] In the Wardrobe Rolls of King Edward I. (1290) the following payments
occur :—" Sept. 1.—To Lord Eli de Hamville going by the king's orders with
the Lord Bishop of Durham towards Scotland to meet the messengers of the
King of Norway and the princess, and was to return with the news to the
king. To John Tyndale, the messenger from the Bishop of St. Andrews, who
brought letters from his master to the king concerning the rumours of the
arrival of the Princess of Scotland in Orkney—by gift of the king, xxsh. To
William Playfair, messenger of the Earl of Orkney, who brought letters to
our Lord the King, on the part of Lord John Comyn, concerning the reported
arrival of the Scottish Princess in Orkney—by gift of the king, xiiish. 4d."
There is also a detailed account of the expenses of two messengers who
left Newcastle on the 15th September, were at Haberdene on the 23d, at the
Meikle Ferry in Sutherland on the 30th, where they met the messengers from
Scotland, then proceeded by Helmsdale and Spittal to Wick, which they
reached on the 4th October. They left Wick on the 6th October, and arrived
at Norham on the 21st November. On the 13th May of the following year
(1291) Earl John of Orkney had a safe conduct to come to King Edward till
the 24th June, when the earl would doubtless communicate to the king all
that he knew of the princess's death.

of Bishop Audfinn of Bergen,[1] written twenty years after the event in connection with the case of the false Margaret, who was burned at Bergen in 1301 (as will be detailed hereafter), that her remains were brought back to Bergen in charge of the Bishop (most probably of the Orkneys) and Herr Thore Hakonson, whose wife, Ingibiorg Erlingsdatter, was Margaret's attendant on the voyage. In 1293 Eirik married Isabel, who is styled in the Iceland Annals "daughter of Sir Robert, son of Robert, Earl of Brus."[2] It appears that on the 24th of July of that year King Edward gave permission to Robert Bruce, Earl of Carrick, the father of Isabella Bruce, to go to Norway,[3] and to remain there for a time ; and Munch, the Norwegian historian, conjectures that he had then brought over his daughter, and stayed till the marriage took place,[4] and that King Eirik may have hoped by this alliance to bring the crown of Scotland once more into the possession of a branch of his own royal line. In 1297 Isabella bore him a daughter named Ingibiorg. King Eirik died 13th July 1299, and was succeeded by his brother Hakon (Magnusson).

John, Earl of Orkney, seems to have gone to Norway to take the oath of allegiance to King Hakon immediately after his accession, for we find in the Icelandic Annals that he was betrothed to King Eirik's daughter in 1299. The statement is explicit, and though it may seem strange to us that an infant scarcely two years of age should be betrothed to a man of forty, Munch makes the remark that such unlikely contracts were by no means so unusual in those days as to

[1] This letter was dated 1st February 1320, and the substance of it is given by Suhm, vol. xii. p. 29. It does not seem to be known from the original document however, but from a later "paraphrase," as Munch calls it, preserved in the Royal Library at Stockholm. (Det Norske Folks Historie, vol. iv. part 2, p. 348.)

[2] Under the date 1293 the following entry occurs in the Chronicle of Lanercost : — "Dominica etiam post festum Sancti Martini (Nov. 15) desponsata est filia Roberti de Carrick regi Norwagiae Magno." (Chron. de Lanercost, p. 155.) Magnus is plainly a mistake for Eirik, the son of Magnus, who reigned from 1280 to 1299. [3] Rymer's Fœdera, Syllabus I. p. 114.

[4] Det Norske Folks Historie, vol. iv. part 2, p. 202.

oblige us to discredit the statement. In fact, we find this same King Hakon betrothing his own daughter when an infant of one year to a man who, though he was much younger than Earl John, was nevertheless a full-grown man. But Earl John seems to have died shortly after the betrothal, for we find that Ingibiorg was betrothed anew in 1311, and John's successor in the earldom appears on record in 1312, with Ferquhard, Bishop of Caithness, witnessing the confirmation by King Robert I. and Hakon V. (at Inverness, 28th October) of the prior treaty executed at Perth, 6th July 1266, between King Alexander III. and Magnus IV. (the son of the unfortunate Hakon), by which the Kings of Norway ceded for ever the Isle of Man and all the other islands of the Sudreys, and all the islands in the west and south of the great Haf, except the isles of Orkney and Shetland, which were specially reserved to Norway. In consideration of this the King of Scotland became bound to pay to the King of Norway and his heirs for ever an annual sum of 100 merks, within St. Magnus' church, in addition to a payment of 4000 merks to be paid within the space of four years.

It was about the time of Earl John's visit to the court of King Hakon, on the occasion above referred to, that there occurred in Norway one of the most extraordinary instances of imposture on record. A woman appeared in Bergen, in 1300, declaring that she was the princess Margaret, daughter of King Eirik, and heiress to the crown of Scotland, who was believed by all in Norway and in Britain to have died off the coast of Orkney some ten years previously. She had come over in a ship from Lubeck,[1] and her story was that she had been "sold" or betrayed by her attendant Ingibiorg Erlingsdatter, in the interest of certain persons who wished her out of the way, and had falsely given her out for dead. Although her appearance and circumstances were strongly against the credibility of her story, it seems to have taken a strong hold of the popular mind, and not a few of the clergy and the higher classes, possibly influenced by political

[1] Munch, Det Norske Folks Historie, vol. iv. part 2, pp. 195, 344.

motives, appear to have given her countenance. She was a married woman, and was accompanied by her husband, a German. She is described by Bishop Audfinn as being well up in years, her hair was greyish, and partially whitened with age, and to all appearance she was at least twenty years older than the date of King Eirik's marriage with Margaret of Scotland, and consequently about seven years older than King Eirik himself, who was but thirteen when he was married. "Yet," says Munch, "though the king's daughter Margaret had died in the presence of some of the best men of Norway, though her corpse had been brought back by the bishop and Herr Thore Hakonson, to King Eirik, who himself had laid it in the open grave, satisfied himself of the identity of his daughter's remains, and placed them in the Christ's Kirk by the side of her mother's;—though this woman, in short, was a rank impostor, yet she found many among the great men to believe her story, and not a few of the priests also gave her their countenance and support. That this German woman, purely of her own accord, should have attempted to personate the princess Margaret ten years after her death, and should have ventured to appear publicly in Norway on such an enterprise, seems hardly credible. It is more likely that she may have been persuaded to it by some parties perceiving in her a certain personal resemblance, who schooled her in the story she must tell to give her personation an air of reality." King Hakon was away from Bergen, and no action was taken in regard to her case until he returned in the early part of the winter of 1301. It was natural that he should wish personally to see and examine the impostor, and confront her with the princess's attendants, especially to hear the testimony of Ingibiorg Erlingsdatter, before deciding on anything. There is no record of the trial, but soon after the king's arrival the "false Margaret" was burnt at Nordness in Bergen, as an impostor, and her husband was beheaded. As she was being taken through the Kongsgaard gate to the place of execution, she is reported to have said—" I remember well when I as a child was taken through this self-same gate to be carried to Scotland. There was then in the High Church of the Apostles an Iceland priest, Haflidi [1] by name, who was the court priest of my father King Eirik ; and when the clergy ceased singing, then Sir Haflidi struck up with the 'Veni Creator,' and the hymn was sung out to the end just as I was being taken on board the ship." Notwithstanding the manifest nature of the imposture she was regarded by the multitude as a martyr ; a chapel was erected on the spot where she suffered, and the number of pilgrimages made to it increased to such an extent that Bishop Audfinn interfered and forbade them.[2]

Earl John's successor in the earldom of Orkney and Caithness was his son Magnus, the fifth of the name, and last of the Angus line. He first appears on record in 1312 in the treaty between King Robert Bruce and Hakon Magnusson, concluded at Inverness. In 1320, as Earl of Caithness and Orkney, he subscribed the famous letter to the Pope, asserting the independence of Scotland.[3] It seems as if he had been

[1] Haflidi Steinson died nearly nineteen years after this as priest of Breida-bolstad in Iceland. The Iceland Annals, recording his death in 1319, recount the story as if this were the real Margaret (whose death they record in 1290), and add that "to this Haflidi himself bore witness when he heard that this same Margaret had been burnt at Nordness." (See Wyntoun's Statement, p. l, note 1.)

[2] On the 2d April 1320 Bishop Audfinn writes to the Archbishop that on the 1st February he had issued a prohibition against the bad custom of making pilgrimages to Nordness, and offering invocations to the woman who had been burnt many years ago for giving herself out as King Eirik's daughter. He also complains to the archbishop that opposition had been offered to the reading out of the prohibition in the Church of the Apostles of Bergen. (Munch, Det Norske Folks Historie, iv. part 2, p. 348.)

[3] This noble document was signed by eight earls and thirty-one barons of Scotland, at the abbey of Aberbrothock on the 6th April 1320. After asserting the legitimate claims of King Robert the Bruce, and narrating his struggles in the cause of Scottish independence, it goes on to say that " If he were to desist from what he has begun, wishing to subject us or our kingdom to the King of England or the English, we would immediately endeavour to expel him as our enemy, and the subverter of his own rights and ours, and make another king who should be able to defend us. For so long as a hundred remain alive, we never will in any degree be subject to the dominion of the English. Since

dead in 1321, for in a document addressed by King Robert Bruce to the "ballivi" of the King of Norway in Orkney, and dated at Cullen, 4th August 1321, he complains that Alexander Brun, "the king's enemy," convicted of *lese majestatis*, had been received into Orkney and had been refused to be given up, though instantly demanded by "our ballivus in Caithness, Henry St. Clair." He was certainly dead in 1329, for in that year Katharina, as his widow, executes two charters in her own name as Countess of Orkney and Caithness, by which she purchases from the Lord High Steward (Drottset), Herr Erling Vidkunnson, certain lands in Rognvaldsey, including the Pentland Skerries.[1] In one of these documents she speaks of Earl John as he from whom her husband had inherited his possessions which he left to her, thus corroborating the statement of the Diploma that Magnus was the son of John.[2]

VI. THE EARLDOM IN THE STRATHERNE LINE—1321-1379.

The Diploma states that the earldom now passed by lineal succession to Malise, Earl of Stratherne, Magnus V. having left no male issue. In 1331 Malise, Earl of Stratherne, possessed lands in Caithness,[3] doubtless in right of his wife, probably a daughter of Magnus V. Malise fell in the

not for glory, riches, nor honour, we fight, but for liberty alone, which no good man loses but with his life." The duplicate, preserved in the General Register House, is printed in facsimile in the National Manuscripts of Scotland, published under the superintendence of the Lord Clerk Register.

[1] The lands are those of Stufum, Kuikobba, Klaet, Thordar, Borgh, Leika, Lidh, Haughs-æth and Petland-Sker. (Diplom. Norvegicum, ii. 146.)

[2] Munch, in his Genealogical Table of the Earls of Orkney, makes Katharina to be the daughter of Earl John (following Douglas' Peerage of Scotland), and Magnus to be a son of Malcolm of Caithness, whom he conjectures to have been a son of the first Magnus. But in a note on this subject in the second series of his History, he acknowledges the mistake, referring to this document in proof of Magnus' descent from Earl John. (Det Norske Folks Historie, Anden Afdeling, vol. i. p. 317.)

[3] An entry in the Chamberlain Rolls for that year mentions the dues of the fourth part of Caithness, which the Earl of Stratherne had. (Comp. Camer. Scot. i. p. 235.)

battle of Halidon Hill in 1333, and was succeeded by his son, also named Malise, who became heir to the three earldoms of Stratherne, Caithness, and Orkney.

Malise (the younger) styles himself Earl of Stratherne, Caithness, and Orkney, in a document dated at Inverness in 1334,[1] in which he grants his daughter Isabella in marriage to William, Earl of Ross, granting her also the earldom of Caithness failing heirs male of himself and his wife Marjory.[2]

William, Earl of Ross, succeeded his father Hugh, who fell at Halidon Hill in 1333, but it is stated that he was not confirmed in the earldom for three years, on account of his absence in Norway.[3]

It seems that Earl Malise must have passed over to Norway about the same period, in all probability to obtain formal investiture of the earldom of Orkney from the Norwegian King Magnus, and William, Earl of Ross, may have accompanied his father-in-law. There is no record of Malise's movements, but we learn incidentally that he had betaken himself to his northern possessions,[4] when he lost the earldom of Stratherne, which was declared forfeited by King Edward and given to John de Warrenne, Earl of Surrey. It is stated that Malise, apparently seeking to preserve the

---

[1] This document is not not now to be found, but Mr. Cosmo Innes says (Lib. Insule Missarum, p. xliii) that he made a note of its purport as given above in the Dunrobin charter-room. Sir Robert Gordon, in his Genealogy of the Earls of Sutherland (p. 49), gives the purport of the document in precisely similar terms, but says that it is dated 28th May 1344. Sir James Balfour, in his Catalogue of the Scottish Nobility, also gives 1344. The confirmation of this contract by David II. is recorded as a "confirmation of a contract of marriage betwixt Malisius, Earl of Stratherne, Caithness, and Orkney, and William, Earl of Ross." (Robertson's Index of Missing Charters, p. 51.)

[2] There is also on record a confirmation by Robert I. of a charter of the lands of Kingkell, Brechin, to Maria (Marjorie ?) de Stratherne, spouse of Malise of Stratherne. (Robertson's Index, p. 19.)

[3] Chronicle of the Earls of Ross, Mis. Scot., vol. iv. p. 128.

[4] There is an entry in the Chamberlain Rolls, in 1340, in regard to a payment by Johannes More, "pro terris de Beridale in Cattania, de quibus dicit se hereditarium infeodari per comitem de Strathern et per Regem confirmari." (Comp. Camerar. Scot. i. p. 265.)

earldom in a branch of his own family, gave one of his daughters in marriage to John de Warrenne, and that King David then declared the earldom forfeited,[1] and bestowed it on his nephew, Maurice de Moravia,[2] son of Sir John de Moravia of Abercairny, who had married Malise's sister Mary.[3]

Malise appears to have made an effort to recover the earldom of Stratherne in 1334. In that year King Edward, by a letter dated 2d March, directed Henry de Beaumont, Earl of Boghan, not to allow any process to be made before him respecting the earldom of Stratherne forfeited for treason by Earl Malise. He also wrote a letter of the same date to Edward Balliol, stating that he has heard that Malise, Earl of Stratherne, claims the county of Stratherne, which he had granted to John de Warenne, Earl of Surrey, and requesting Balliol to act with deliberation.[4]

The Diploma states that Malise was first married to Johanna, daughter of Sir John Menteith, and that by her he had a daughter Matilda, married to Wayland de Ard. But there is a record of a confirmation by Robert I. (1306-1329) of a grant of the lands of Carcathie (Cortachy) in Forfarshire, and half of Urkwell in the earldom of Stratherne, by Malise, Earl of Stratherne, to his wife Johanna, daughter of the late John de Monteith.[5] As Malise the younger only became

[1] Sir James Balfour (Catalogue of the Scottish Nobility) says:—" This Earl Malisius was forfaulted by King David II. for alienating the earldom of Stratherne to the Earl of Warrenne, an Englishman, the king's enemy, and all his possessions annexed to the crown." Sir Robert Gordon says that the charter by King David granting the earldom of Stratherne to Maurice Moray is dated the last day of October 1345.

[2] A dispensation granted by Pope Benedict XII. in July 1339 for the marriage of Maurice de Moravia with Johanna, widow of John, Earl of Athole, styles her Countess of Stratherne. (Theiner's Monumenta, p. 275.) Maurice fell at the battle of Durham in 1346. Johanna, Countess of Stratherne, in her widowhood executed a charter in favour of Robert of Erskine and his wife, Christian of Keith, her cousin, which is confirmed by Robert, Steward of Scotland and Earl of Stratherne in 1361. (Chartulary of Cambuskenneth, Grampian Club, p. 255.)　　[3] Third Report of Com. on Hist. MSS. p. 416.

[4] Rymer's Fœdera, Syllabus i. p. 272.

[5] Robertson's Index of Charters, pp. 18, 34.

Earl of Stratherne on the death of his father in 1333, if the confirmation be correctly ascribed to Robert I., this must refer to the Malise who was earl previous to 1333, and who had a daughter Matilda contracted to Robert de Thony in 1293, "being not yet in her 20th year." [1]

The Diploma further states that Malise (the younger) was married the second time to a daughter of Hugh, Earl of Ross, consequently a sister of William, Earl of Ross, who married Malise's daughter Isabella. From the deed of 1334 we learn that Malise's wife's name was Marjory. In a deed of 1350 we find William, Earl of Ross, styling his sister Marjory Countess of Caithness and Orkney,[2] and with her consent appointing his brother Hugh his heir in the event of his own death without male issue. From this it would appear that Malise was then dead. He must have been dead before 1353, when his son-in-law, Erngils Suneson, obtained the title of Earl of Orkney from the King of Norway. He is mentioned as dead in 1357 and 1358,[3] and the Earl of Ross is then said to have entered to his lands in Caithness, doubtless in right of his wife Isabella, and in terms of that deed of 1334 previously noticed.[4]

---

[1] Hist. Doc. Scot. i. p. 394.

[2] Balnagown Charters, Orig. Paroch. ii. 487.

[3] Robert Stewart, Seneschal of Scotland and Earl of Stratherne, certifies that, in his court held at Crieff, 8th May 1358, he had seen read and confirmed the charters granted to the abbot and convent of Inchaffray of the annual of 42 marcs of the thanage of Dunyne, given by the former earls of good memory—Malise the first and Malise the second, his predecessors. (Liber Insula Missarum, p. 55.) Et. nihil hic de terris quondam Malesii infra comitatu Cathanie quia comes de Ross se intromittit de eisdem. (Comp. Camerar. Scot., an. 1357, i. p. 320.) That the second Malise of Robert Stewart's deed is the last Malise who was Earl of Stratherne seems to be shown by another deed of Robert Stewart, dated in 1361, in which, as Seneschal of Scotland and Earl of Stratherne, he grants to James Douglas the lands of Kellor in Stratherne, "which the late Malise gave." In the confirmation of this grant by Eufamia, Countess of Moray and Stratherne, he is styled "the late Malise of good memory." (Regist. Honoris de Morton, ii. pp. 60, 86.)

[4] See page lvi.

While Malise was in Norway and Sweden two of his daughters had been married to Swedish noblemen—one to Arngils [1] or Erngisl, son of Sune Jonsson, and another to Guttorm Sperra.[2] On the death of Malise, or shortly thereafter, Erngisl Suneson claimed his wife's share of the earldom. In the year 1353 we find him executing a deed on the 10th April as plain Erngisl Suneson, and on the 6th May thereafter his signature appears to a document drawn up at Vagahuus concerning the queen's dowry, occupying the foremost place among the nobles of Norway, and with the title of Earl of Orkney.[3] Although the Diploma states that he held only his wife's share of the earldom, it is plain from this document that he must have received the title of Earl of the Orkneys from the King of Norway. He soon became involved with the Swedish party in favour of King Eirik of Pomern, and in 1357 King Magnus sequestrated his estates in Norway, and declared his title forfeited. His right to the earldom would have lapsed with the death of his wife, who died childless before 1360.[4] Nevertheless he continued to style himself Earl of Orkney during his lifetime.[5] He died in 1392.

On the sequestration of Erngisl's rights by the king, a certain Duncan Anderson, who appears to have been a Scotchman, and probably agent for Alexander de Ard, the son of Matilda, called the eldest daughter of Malise, issued a manifesto, notifying to the inhabitants of Orkney that he has

[1] Called in the Diploma "Here Ginsill de Swethrik," for "Erengisle de Suecia." He was lawman of Tisherad in Sweden in 1337.

[2] In the Diploma he is called "quodam Gothredo, nomine Gothormo le Spere"—*Gothredo* being a misreading for *Gothricio*, "a native of Gothland." (Munch, Symbolæ, p. 55.)

[3] Munch, Norske Folks Historie, 2d series, i. p. 595.

[4] In 1360 he grants certain lands to the monastery of Calmar for the souls of his deceased wives, Meretta and Annot or Agneta, the latter being probably Malise's daughter, as the name is not a common one in Sweden.

[5] He styles himself "Comes Orchadensis" in a deed of 4th March 1388. (Diplom. Norvegicum, v. 246.)

the true and legitimate heir of Earl Malise, the former Earl
of Orkney, under his guardianship ; that this heir has now
the full and undeniable right to the earldom ; and that, as
he has heard that the King of Norway has recently sequestrated the revenues of the earldom, he warns the inhabitants
not to allow these revenues to be taken furth of the land till
the true heir be presented to them, which will be ere very
long, if the Lord will. The inhabitants, who seem to have
been somewhat disquieted by the missive, sent a representation on the subject to the court of Norway. It would seem
that a representation must have been made by the court of
Norway to the Scottish King regarding the troubling of the
islands by the claimants or their friends in Scotland, for
an edict was issued by King David from Scone, in 1367,
forbidding any of his subjects, of whatever rank or condition,
to pass into Orkney, or frequent its harbours, on any other
errand than that of lawful commerce.

In 1375, King Hakon of Norway granted the earldom of
Orkney for a single year till next St. John's Day to Alexander
de Ard,[1] naming him, however, in the document not as Earl
but simply as Governor and Commissioner for the King, and
declaring, in the document addressed to the Islanders, that
this grant is given provisionally until the said Alexander shall
establish his claim to the earldom. He seems not to have
been regarded with much favour by the king, for this grant
was not renewed, and in 1379 Henry St. Clair and Malise
Sparre preferred their claims to the earldom.

Alexander de Ard had succeeded to the earldom of Caithness by the law and custom of Scotland, in right of his mother
as heir to Earl Malise. In 1375 he resigned the castle of
Brathwell (Brawl), and all the lands in Caithness or any other
part of Scotland which he inherited in right of his mother,
Matilda de Stratherne, to King Robert II., who bestowed them
on his own son, David Stewart.

Earl David Stewart appears in 1377-78 as Earl Palatine

---

[1] Diplom. Norvegicum, ii. 337-339.

of Stratherne and Caithness. King Robert III. gave the earldom of Caithness to his brother, Walter Stewart, of Brechin, who held it till about 1424. He then resigned it to his son Alan, who was slain at Inverlochy in 1431. The earldom reverted to his father, who in 1437 was forfeited for his share in the murder of King James I. The earldom remained in possession of the crown till 1452, when it was granted by King James II. to Sir George Crichtoun, Admiral of Scotland. On his death in 1455 King James granted the earldom of Caithness to William St. Clair, then Earl of Orkney, in whose line it has continued till the present day.

VII. The Earldom in the Line of St. Clair—1379-1469.

The genealogical questions connected with the succession of the St. Clairs of Roslin to the earldom of Orkney are involved in apparently inextricable confusion.

So early as 1321 we find a Henry St. Clair acting as the "ballivus" of King Robert Bruce in Caithness,[1] and in 1364 we also find a Thomas St. Clair installed at Kirkwall as the "ballivus" of the King of Norway, an Alexander St. Clair, and a Euphemia de Stratherne, styling herself one of the heirs of the late Malise, Earl of Stratherne.[2]

The Diploma states explicitly that one of the four daughters of Malise, Earl of Stratherne,[3] by his wife Marjory, daughter of Hugh, Earl of Ross, was married to William St. Clair. This must be William St. Clair, son of the Sir William

---

[1] See the document dated at Cullen, 4th August 1321, quoted on p. lv, *supra*.

[2] In a deed executed at Kirkwall, 20th January 1364, by which Bernard de Rowle resigns to Hugh de Ross (brother of William, Earl of Ross) the whole lands of Fouleroule in Aberdeenshire, the witnesses are John de Gamery and Symon de Othyrles, canons of Caithness ; Euphemia de Stratherne, one of the heirs of the late Malise, Earl of Caithness ; Thomas de St. Clair, "ballivus regis Norvagie ;" and Alexander St. Clair. (Regist. Aberdonense, i. 106.)

[3] Sir James Balfour calls her Lucia. She is also called Lucia by William Drummond, author of the "Genealogie of the House of Drummond, 1681," but in neither case is any documentary authority cited. Camden says the eldest daughter.

St. Clair who fell with the Douglas in Spain fighting against the Saracens in 1330.[1] The Diploma goes on to narrate that Henry St. Clair, the son of William St. Clair and this daughter of Malise, succeeded to the earldom of Orkney apparently in right of his mother. We know from the deed of investiture that his accession to the earldom took place in 1379.

In a charter of 1391 Earl Henry names his mother Isabella St. Clair. It is usually said that his father, William St. Clair, married Isabella, daughter of Malise, Earl of Stratherne. But, as we have seen from the deed of 1334, Isabella was married to William, Earl of Ross, not to William, Earl of Roslin. Yet it appears from the deed of 1391 that Henry's mother's name was Isabella, and though he does not style her a daughter of Malise, the terms of the document imply that she was heiress to lands in Orkney and Shetland. The Diploma only mentions one of the Earls Malise, and it may be that the Isabella whom William St. Clair married was the daughter of the elder and sister of the younger Malise of Stratherne.

If he had married one of the four daughters of the younger Malise it seems unaccountable why he did not claim his wife's portion of the earldom. We find that the representatives of the other sisters were claimants, and that one of them, Erngisl Suneson, actually received his wife's share, and enjoyed the title of Earl of Orkney, while Alexander de Ard is said to have succeeded to the earldom of Caithness in virtue of a similar claim, and had his rights to the earldom of Orkney so far recognised by the King of Norway on the forfeiture of Erngisl Suneson. The Earl of Ross, as we have seen, also succeeded to the share falling to his wife Isabella. But no claim seems to have been made for the Isabella who is said to have been married to William St. Clair. If she had been a daughter of the younger Malise it can scarcely be doubted that such a claim would have been made, and if made, established as readily as that of the other

[1] Barbour's Bruce (Spald. Club), p. 482.

sisters. William St. Clair was alive in 1358, five years after the claim of the sister married to Erngisl Suneson had been made good, and one year after Erngisl's title to the earldom had been declared forfeited.

But a more fatal objection to the statement of the Diploma, that William's wife was a daughter of the younger Malise, arises from the fact that in the attestation by the Lawman and Canons of Orkney in favour of James of Cragy (1422) it is expressly certified that Henry Sinclair was himself married to a daughter of the younger Malise, styled "Elizabeth de Stratherne, daughter of the late reverend and venerable Malise, Earl of Orkney," and that by her he had a daughter, Margaret, who was married to James of Cragy. The Diploma, on the other hand, states that Henry was married to Janet Haliburton, daughter of Walter Haliburton of Dirleton, and by her had a son Henry, who succeeded him. It is quite possible, however, that both these statements might be true, the attestation in favour of James of Cragy having no reason to mention the second wife, and the Diploma having no special reason to mention the first wife in connection with the succession which it derives through the mother, making her, moreover, such a remarkable instance of longevity that she survived her husband, her son, and all her younger sisters, and all their sons and daughters, and became sole heiress to the earldom after Earl Henry's death, although he left a son who ought to have succeeded him, but who, according to the Diploma, succeeded to her, his grandmother.

In whatever way these apparently contradictory statements are to be reconciled, the statement of the Diploma that Henry St. Clair was the first of the line who enjoyed the title of Earl of Orkney is undoubtedly borne out by the records. In the summer of 1379 he passed over to Norway and received formal investiture from King Hakon of the earldom of Orkney and also of the lordship of Shetland,[1]

---

[1] Munch's Norske Folks Historie, 2d series, vol. ii. p. 96. See also the deed of investiture, which is printed at length in the Diplomatarium Norvegicum, vol. ii. pp. 353-358.

which, since the time of its forfeiture to King Sverrir by Earl
Harald Maddadson, had been in the possession of the crown
of Norway. The conditions on which he accepted the earldom
are set forth at length in the deed of investiture, and con-
trasting them with the semi-independence of the ancient earls
a recent writer has remarked that they left him little more than
the lands of his fathers.[1] Although the Earls of Orkney
had precedence of all the titled nobility of Norway, and
their signatures to the national documents stand always after
the Archbishops, and before the Bishops and nobles, though
the title was the only hereditary one permitted in Norway
to a subject not of the blood royal, yet it was now declared
to be subject to the royal option of investiture. The earl
was to govern the Islands and enjoy their revenues during
the king's pleasure, but he was taken bound to serve the
king beyond the bounds of the earldom, with a hundred
men fully equipped, when called on by the king's message ;
he was to build no castle or place of strength in the Islands,
make no war, enter into no agreement with the bishop, nor
sell or impignorate any of his rights, without the king's express consent ; and moreover he was to be answerable for
his whole administration to the king's court at Bergen. At
his death the earldom and all the Islands were to revert to
the King of Norway or his heirs, and if the earl left sons
they could not succeed to their father's dignity and possessions
without the royal investiture. At the following Martinmas

---

[1] Balfour, Oppressions of Orkney (Maitland Club), p. xxvi. Such was not
the opinion of Father Hay, the panegyrist of the St. Clairs of Roslyn. He
says that " Henry, prince of Orknay, was more honoured than any of his ances-
tres, for he had power to cause stamp coine within his dominions, to make laws,
to remitt crimes ;—he had his sword of honour carried before him wheresoever he
went ; he had a crowne in his armes, bore a crowne on his head when he constituted laws ; and, in a word, was subject to none, save only he held his lands
of the King of Danemark, Sweden, and Noraway, and entred with them, to
whom also it did belong to crowne any of those three kings, so that in all
those parts he was esteemed a second person to the king." (Genealogie of the
St. Clairs, p. 17.) Father Hay's romances receive no countenance whatever
from the deed of investiture.

he was taken bound to pay to the king 1000 English nobles.[1] It was part of the compact also that Malise Sperra, son of Guthorm Sperra, should depart from all his claims to the earldom in right of his mother;[2] and he left with King Hakon, as hostages for the due fulfilment of his share of the contract, the following from among his friends and followers :— William Daniel, knight, Malise Sperra, and David Crichton.

But King Hakon died in the year after Earl Henry's investiture, and the events that took place in the Orkneys during the reign of King Olaf, his successor, are entirely unknown to the Norwegian chroniclers. Earl Henry seems neither to have courted the favour of his suzerain nor to have stood in awe of his interference. He built the castle of Kirkwall in defiance of the prohibition contained in the deed of his investiture, and seems to have felt himself sufficiently independent to rule his sea-girt earldom according to his own will and pleasure.

The fact that King Hakon's investiture of Earl Henry took him bound not to enter into any league with the bishop nor to establish any friendship with him without the king's express consent, shows us that the bishop was then acting in opposition to the king and the representatives of the civil power. The likelihood is that Earl Henry found this

---

[1] About £333 sterling.

[2] Father Hay states (Genealogie of the St. Clairs, p. 17) that Henry St. Clair "married Elisabeth Sparres, daughter of Malesius Sparres, Prince of Orkney, Earl of Kaithness and Stratherne, through which marriage he became Prince of Orkney." But Malise Sperra never had any connection with the earldoms of Caithness or Stratherne. In another place, p. 33, he says that Sir William Sinclair (who fell fighting with the Saracens in Spain in 1330) "was married to Elizabeth Sparre, daughter to the Earle of Orkney, and so by her became the first Earl of Orkney of the Saintclairs. His name was Julius Sparre. He is also reputed Earl of Stratherne and Caithness." But this is manifestly a tissue of impossibilities. He seems to have copied the last statement from the Drummond MS. (1681), where the additional statement is made that Elizabeth's mother was Lucia, daughter of the Earl of Ross. (Genealogie of the House of Drummond : Edinburgh, 1831, p. 237.) Both writers seem to have confounded Malise, Earl of Stratherne, with his daughter's son, Malise Sperra.

opposition of the bishop favourable to his own design of
making himself practically independent, and represented it
as the excuse for the erection of the castle of Kirkwall,
contrary to the terms of his agreement with the crown. Munch
attributes the discord to the growing dislike of the Norwegian
inhabitants of the Islands to Scotsmen, whose numbers had
been long increasing through the influence of the Scottish
family connections of the later earls. Whatever may have
been its origin, the end of it was that in some popular com-
motion, of which we have no authentic account, the bishop was
slain in the year 1382.[1]

Malise Sperra appears to have endeavoured to establish
himself in Shetland[2] in opposition to Earl Henry. He had
seized, it is not stated upon what grounds, the possessions in
Shetland which had belonged to Herdis Thorvaldsdatter, and
of which Jón Hafthorson and Sigurd Hafthorson were the
lawful heirs. It seems as if a court had been about to be
held by the earl to settle the legal rights of the parties concerned. The court would be held at the old Thingstead, near
Scalloway, but a conflict took place, the dispute was terminated
by the strong hand, and Malise Sperra was slain.[3] As a
number of his men were slain with him, it seems probable
that he had been the aggressor. As both he and the earl are
among those who were present at the assembly of nobles at
Helsingborg, on the accession of King Eirik of Pomern in
September 1389, and the Iceland Annals place the death of
Malise Sperra in this same year, it is probable that the earl

[1] Iceland Annals, *sub anno.* Munch, Det Norske Folks Historie, 2d
series, vol. ii. p. 106.

[2] He seems to have held lands in Banffshire. In the Chamberlain Rolls,
1438, there is an entry of a receipt of £9 from James M'fersane for the land
formerly belonging to Malis Speir, knight in the Sheriffdom of Banff, remaining in the king's hands. (Diplom. Norvegicum, i. 366.)

[3] The Iceland Annals, under the date 1389, have the following entry :—
"Malise Sperra slain in Hjaltland, with seven others, by the Earl of Orkney.
He had previously been taken captive by him. From that conflict there
escaped a man-servant who with six men in a six-oared boat got away safely to
Norway."

landed in Shetland on his way home from Norway for the express purpose of seeing justice done in the cause of the heirs of Thordis.   In 1391, by a deed executed at Kirkwall (and subsequently confirmed by King Robert III.), he dispones the lands of Newburgh and Auchdale in Aberdeenshire,[1] to his brother David for his services rendered, and in exchange for any rights he may have to lands in Orkney and Shetland, derived from his mother Isabella St. Clair.   In 1396 a deed was executed at Roslin by John de Drummond of Cargyll, and Elizabeth, his wife, in favour of Henry, Earl of Orkney, Lord Roslyn, "patri nostro," by which they renounce in favour of the earl's male issue, and for them and their heirs, all claims to the earl's lands "infra regnum Norvagie." [2]

The Diploma states that after the death of the first Henry St. Clair, his mother, the daughter of Malise,[3] came to Orkney, and, outliving all her sisters and all their sons and daughters, became the only heiress of the earldom.   It is added that of this thing there were faithful witnesses still living who had seen and spoken with the mother of Henry the first.

Her grandson Henry, son of the first Henry, succeeded to the earldom, but there seems to be no record of his investiture

---

[1] Diplom. Norvegicum, ii. 401.   Regist. Mag. Sigill. 196.

[2] This deed is said by Robert Riddell to be in the Perth Charter-chest.   A copy of it is in one of his MS. note-books in the Advocates' Library.   See also Robertson's Index of Charters, p. 128.   The "double" of this deed is said by William Drummond (1681) to have been given to him by a friend, and the substance of it is given by him as follows :—"Sir John Drummond and his lady Elisabeth Sinclair oblige themselves to a noble and potent Lord, Henry, Earle of Orkney, Lord Roslin, their father, that they nor their aires shall never claime any interest or right of propertie to any lands or possessions belonging to the said earle or his aires lying within the kingdome of Norroway, so long as he or any air-male of his shall be on lyfe to inherit the same ; bot if it happen (which God forbid) the said earle to die without any air-male to succeed to him, then it shall be lawful for them to claim such a portion of the aforesaid lands as is known by the Norwegian laws to appertain to a sister of the family.   Sealled at Rosline 13th May 1396."   (Genealogie of the House of Drummond, p. 91.)

[3] Henry himself had married a daughter of Malise.   See page lxiii.

by the Norwegian king. In 1404 he was entrusted with the guardianship of James I., and on his way to France with the young prince, for whose safety it was judged necessary that he should be removed from Scotland, he was captured by the English off Flamborough Head, and retained some time in captivity.[1] In 1412 he went to France with Archibald Douglas to assist the French against the English.[2] In 1418 John St. Clair, his brother, swears fealty to King Eirik at Helsingborg for the king's land of Hjaltland, and becomes bound to administer the Norse laws according to the ancient usage, and it is stipulated that at his death Shetland should again revert to the crown of Norway.[3] It seems from this that Earl Henry must have been dead in 1418, though Bower in his continuation of Fordun says that he died in 1420.[4] A dispensation was granted for his widow's marriage in 1418.[5]

Henry was succeeded by his son William, the last of the Orkney earls under Norwegian rule. But the investiture of the new earl did not take place till 1434, and for a period of fourteen years the administration of the Islands was carried on by commissioners appointed by King Eirik.

On the death of Earl Henry, Bishop Thomas Tulloch was appointed commissioner in 1420. He swore fealty to King Eirik in the church of Vestenskov in Laland, undertaking the adminstration of the Islands according to the Norsk law-book and the ancient usages.[6] On 10th July 1422 he

---

[1] Father Hay says that he escaped through the instrumentality of one John Robinsone, indweller at Pentland, one of his tenants, who went to the place where his master was confined and played the fool so cunningly that he was allowed access to the prison, and so found means to convey the earl out in disguise. (Genealogie of the St. Clairs, p. 81.)

[2] Balfour's Annals, i. 148.

[3] Diplom. Norvegicum, ii. 482.   [4] Fordun, Scotichron. xv. cap. 32.

[5] Douglas' Peerage. The Diploma says nothing of his wife, but he is said to have married Egidia Douglas, daughter of Lord William Douglas, and Egidia, daughter of Robert II. (Extracta ex Cronicis Scocie, p. 200.)

[6] Diplom. Norvegicum, ii. 489. This document is endorsed—"Biscop Thomes breff af Orknoy, at han skal halde Orknoy til myn herres konnungens hand, oc hans effterkommende, oc lade him with Noren lagh."

received as a fief from the king "the palace of Kirkwall and pertinents, lying in Orkney, in Norway, together with the lands of Orkney and the government thereof."[1]

In 1423 the administration of the Orkneys and Shetland was committed to David Menzies of Wemyss by King Eirik. In 1426 a complaint was sent to the king by the inhabitants, setting forth that they had been subjected to oppression and wholesale spoliation during the period of his administration.[2] Among the accusations preferred against him it was asserted that he diminished the value of the money by one-half, that he threw the Lawman of the Islands into prison unjustly, and illegally possessed himself of the public seal and the law-book of the Islands, which the Lawman's wife had deposited on the altar of the Church of St. Magnus for their security ; that he exacted fines and services illegally and with personal violence, and was guilty of many other illegal acts of tyrannical oppression.

The government of the Islands seems to have been again entrusted to Bishop Tulloch[3] until 1434, when the young earl received his formal investiture.[4]

William, the last of the Orkney earls under Norwegian rule, succeeded to his father Henry, and received investiture on terms nearly similar to those imposed upon his grandfather. Moreover, he was to hold for the king and his successors the castle of Kirkwall, which his grandfather had built without the king's consent. He had taken the title

---

[1] Diplom. Norvegicum, ii. 498. This document is endorsed—" Item biscop Thomes aff Orknoy bref um Kirkwaw slot i Orknoy, oc um landet oc greves-chapet ther samestads."

[2] This document is printed at length in Torfæus, pp. 179-182 ; in Balfour's Oppressions of Orkney (Maitland Club), pp. 105-110 ; and also in the Norse language of the time in the Diplomatarium Norvegicum, ii. 514.

[3] Torfæus, Hist. Orc. 182. The document of which Torfæus here gives a copy, however, is that of the 31st year of the reign of King Eirik (1420), previously noticed, and refers not to the bishop's second appointment but to his first.

[4] Torfæus, p. 183.

before he received investiture from King Eirik, for in 1426 he appears as Earl of Orkney on the assize at Stirling, for the trial of Murdoch, Duke of Albany.[1] In 1435, as Lord High Admiral of Scotland, he had command of the fleet that conveyed the Princess Margaret to France. In 1446 he was summoned by the Norwegian Rigsraad to appear at Bergen on next St. John's Day,[2] to take the oath of allegiance to King Christopher, the successor of Eirik of Pomern. In 1460 the king's commissioners in Kirkwall certify to King Christian I. that John of Ross, Lord of the Isles, has for a long time most cruelly endeavoured to depopulate the Islands of Orkney and Shetland by burning the dwellings and slaying the inhabitants, and that in these circumstances Lord William St. Clair, the Earl of Orkney and Caithness,[3] had been prevented from coming to the king.[4] On 28th June 1461 Bishop William of Orkney writes to the king from Kirkwall excusing the earl for not having come to take the oath of allegiance, because in the month of June of that year he had been appointed one of the regents of the Kingdom of Scotland on account of the tender years of the prince (King James III.), and therefore was personally resident in Scotland. The bishop also repeats the complaint against John of Ross, Lord of the Isles, and the bands of his Islesmen, Irish, and Scots from the woods, " who came in great multitudes in the month of June, with their ships and fleets in battle array, wasting the lands, plundering the farms, destroying habitations, and putting the inhabitants to the sword, without regard to age or sex." [5] Tradition still points in several parts of the Islands to " the Lewismen's graves," probably those of the invaders who were killed in their plundering expeditions through the Islands.

On the 8th September 1468 a contract of marriage was signed between James III. of Scotland and Margaret,

---

[1] Balfour's Annals, i. 155.   [2] Diplom. Norveg. vii. 430.

[3] He had received a grant of the earldom of Caithness from King James II. 28th August 1455, as formerly mentioned, p. lxi.

[4] Diplom. Norvegicum, v. 599.   [5] Ibid. v. 605.

daughter of King Christian I. of Denmark, Sweden, and Norway, by which, after discharging the arrears of the tribute due by Scotland for Man and the Hebrides,[1] King Christian engaged to pay a dowry of 60,000 florins with his daughter, stipulating for certain jointure lands (including the palace of Linlithgow and the castle of Doune), and her terce of the royal possessions in Scotland if left a widow. Of the dowry 10,000 florins were to be paid before the princess's departure, and the Islands of Orkney were pledged for the balance of 50,000 florins. Only 2000 florins of the 10,000 promised were paid, and the Islands of Shetland were pledged for the remainder. The amount for which the whole of the Islands of Orkney and Shetland were thus impignorated was 58,000 florins of 100 pence each, or about £24,000.

In 1471 King James III. gave William, Earl of Orkney, the castle and lands of Ravenscraig in Fife in exchange for all his rights to the earldom of Orkney, and an Act of Parliament was passed on the 20th of February of the same year annexing to the Scottish Crown "the Erledome of Orkney and Lordship of Schetland, nocht to be gevin away in time to cum to na persain or persainis, excep alenarily to ane of the king's sonnis of lauchful bed."

VIII. THE BISHOPRIC OF ORKNEY—1060-1469.

The origin of the bishopric of Orkney is involved in obscurity. Its early history is complicated by the fact that there were two if not three distinct successions of bishops, only one of which is recognised by the Norse writers.

The Saga statement regarding the origin of the bishopric unfortunately is lacking in precision. It is stated that Earl Thorfinn built Christ's Kirk in Birsay, apparently after his return from his pilgrimage to Rome, and that the first bishop's see in the Orkneys was established there. Taking this in

---

[1] These islands had been ceded by Norway to Scotland in 1266 on condition of an annual payment of 100 merks, which at this time had fallen into arrear for 26 years.

connection with the statement that William the Old, who was bishop in 1115, when St. Magnus was murdered, was the first bishop, the inference would be that the bishopric was erected in his time. The statement regarding his tenure of office for sixty-six years is scarcely credible ; but supposing it to be the fact, as he died in 1167, we obtain 1102 as the date of the erection of the bishopric.

On the other hand, Adam of Bremen states[1] that Thorolf was the first Bishop of Orkney, and that he was consecrated by Adalbert, Archbishop of Hamburg, in the middle of the 11th century,[2] and that another bishop named Adalbert succeeded him. Now, as William the Old was not consecrated before 1102, if there was a bishop in Earl Thorfinn's time (the date of his death being 1064), it must have been this Thorolf. If Thorolf was consecrated in the middle of the 11th century, it was probably before Earl Thorfinn's death in 1064. But it seems that the see was vacant or unoccupied before 1093.

It appears from a letter of Lanfranc, Archbishop of Canterbury (1070-1089), that Earl Paul of Orkney had sent to him a cleric whom he wished to be consecrated a bishop, and Lanfranc orders Wulstan, Bishop of Worcester, and Peter, Bishop of Chester, to go to York and assist the archbishop there at the consecration. This must refer to the Earl Paul, son of Thorfinn, who with his brother Erlend was carried to Norway by King Magnus on his second expedition to the west in 1098, and neither of them ever returned. The name of this bishop is not given in Lanfranc's letter. But the English writers[3] mention that in the end of the 11th century a cleric named Ralph was consecrated Bishop of Orkney by Thomas,

---

[1] His words imply that it was by request of the Orkneymen themselves that Adalbert sent them preachers "extremi venerant Islani, Gronlani, et Orchadum legati petentes ut prædicatores illuc dirigeret, quod et fecit."

[2] Keyser, Den Norske Kirkes Historie, i. 158 ; Torfæus, i. 160 ; Munch, Det Norske Folks Historie, ii. p. 216 ; Grub's Eccles. Hist. i. 252.

[3] Twysden, Decem Scriptores, pp. 1709-13.

Archbishop of York. Thomas was archbishop from A.D. 1070 to 1100. It is mentioned that when the right of the Archbishop of York to consecrate Turgot Bishop of St. Andrews was asserted in 1109, it was proposed that he should do it by the assistance of the (English) Bishops of Scotland and of Orkney. Anselm, Archbishop of Canterbury (1092-1107), wrote[1] to Earl Hakon Palson, exhorting him and his people to obey the bishop " whom now by the grace of God they had."

A second bishop, named Roger, was consecrated by Gerard, who was Archbishop of York in the beginning of the 12th century, from 1100 to 1108.

A third bishop, named Ralph, previously a presbyter of York, said to have been elected by the people of Orkney, was consecrated by Archbishop Thomas, the successor of Gerard. It is this Ralph who figures in the accounts of the battle of Northallerton, 1138. Pope Calixtus II. and Pope Honorius II. addressed letters to the Norwegian Kings, Sigurd and Eystein, in favour of Ralph.[2] In the letter of Pope Honorius it is expressly stated that another bishop had been intruded in the place of Ralph. This must refer to William the Old, whom the Sagas make bishop from the year 1102.

The explanation of all this seems to be that the Archbishops of Hamburg and York both tried in vain to secure the right of consecrating the Bishops of Orkney; the former on the ground that as the successors of St. Anschar they were primates of the Scandinavian churches, and the latter on the same ground on which they claimed the right to consecrate the Bishop of St. Andrews—viz. that their jurisdiction extended to the whole of Scotland and the Isles. In the appendix to Florence of Worcester's Chronicle,[3] written in the beginning of the 12th century, it is said that " the Archbishop of York had jurisdiction over all the bishops north of the Humber,

[1] Printed in the Notes and Illustrations to the Scala Cronica (Maitland Club), p. 234.

[2] Monasticon Anglicanum, vi. p. 1186.

[3] Flor. Wig. Chron. Monum. Hist. Britann. p. 644.

and all the bishops of Scotland and the Orkneys, as the Archbishop of Canterbury had over those of Ireland and Wales. Meantime, however, the Norwegians made their own bishops, and these, having obtained possession of the see, were the real bishops of Orkney, though the others might enjoy the empty title.

Thus WILLIAM THE OLD was the first of the actual bishops of Orkney of whom we have distinct record. As the Saga and the Saga of St. Magnus both state explicitly that he held the bishopric for sixty-six years, and the Annals place his death in 1168, he must have been consecrated in 1102. The see, which was first at Birsay, where Earl Thorfinn erected the Christ's Kirk,[1] was removed to Kirkwall on the erection of the Cathedral, 1137-52. He went with Earl Rögnvald to the Holy Land in 1152. When Pope Anastasius erected the metropolitan see of Trondheim in 1154 he declared the Bishop of Orkney one of its suffragans, and Bishop William's canonical rights were thus implicitly recognised. He died in 1168; and in 1848, when certain repairs were being executed on the cathedral, his bones were found enclosed in a stone cist thirty inches long and fifteen inches wide, along with a bone object like the handle of a staff, and a leaden plate, inscribed in characters apparently of the 13th century :—

HIC REQUIESCIT WILLIALMUS SENEX, FELICIS MEMORIÆ,
PRIMUS EPISCOPUS.

The position in which the bones were found in the choir seems to indicate that they must have been moved from their previous resting-place. Bishop William's bones, and the cist which contained them, were carted away with the rubbish when the church was re-seated in 1856.[2] The leaden plate and bone object which were found in the cist are

---

[1] The name Christ's Church, says Munch, was only given to a cathedral church.

[2] Sir Henry Dryden's Notices of Ancient Churches in Orkney, in the *Orcadian*, 1867.

preserved in the Museum of the Society of Antiquaries of Scotland.

WILLIAM II., the second bishop, is only known from the entry of his name in the list of bishops[1] (1325), and the entry of his death under the year 1188 in the Icelandic Annals.

BJARNI, son of Kolbein Hruga (who built the castle on the island of Weir), was the third bishop. His mother, Herborg, was a great-granddaughter of Earl Paul.[2] Bjarni himself was a famous poet, and to him is ascribed the *Jomsvikinga-drapa*—the Lay of the Jomsburg Vikings.[3] A bull of Pope Innocent III., dated at the Vatican, 27th May 1198,[4] is addressed to him in connection with the refusal of Bishop John of Caithness to collect an annual tribute in his diocese, as noticed hereafter.[5] It appears from a deed of his in the Chartulary of the monastery of Munkalif at Bergen that he possessed lands in Norway, as well as his patrimonial lands in Orkney and castle in the island of Weir. By that deed he gives to the monastery, "for the souls of his father (Kolbein Hruga), his mother, his brother, his relations and friends," the lands called *Holand*, near the Dalsfiord, north of Bergen. It is curious thus to find in authentic records a mortification of lands to a church in Norway to provide masses for the soul of a man who is now known in his own former home in Orkney only as *Cobbie Row*, "the giant," or "goblin" of the castle, which he built and inhabited. Bishop Bjarni was present with John, Earl of Orkney, at the great assembly of nobles at Bergen,[6] in 1223, and died shortly thereafter.

JOFREYR, the fourth bishop, was consecrated in 1223 according to the Annals. There was a Jofreyr, Dean of Tunsberg, present at the same assembly in Bergen above

---

[1] Munch's Catalogue of the Bishops of Orkney, Bannatyne Miscellany, iii. 181.   [2] See the Saga, p. 126.

[3] Fornmanna Sögur, vol. vi.   [4] Diplom. Norvegicum, vii. p. 2.

[5] See page lxxx.   [6] Hakonar Saga hins gamla, Flateyjarbók, iii. 52.

referred to, and as the name is a very uncommon one, it is probable that he is the same who was made Bishop of the Orkneys. He seems to have been long an invalid, for, by a bull dated at Viterbo, 11th May 1237,[1] Pope Gregory IX. enjoins Sigurd, Archbishop of Nidaros (Drontheim), to move Bishop Jofreyr of Orkney, who had been paralytic and confined to bed for many years, to resign office, or, if he was unwilling to resign, to provide him with a wise and prudent helper. Jofreyr retained the see, however, for ten years after this. The Annals place his death in 1247.

HENRY (I.) was the fifth bishop. A papal dispensation for the defect of his birth, by Pope Innocent IV., is dated 9th December 1247.[2] He was then a canon in the Orkneys. He was with King Hakon's expedition in 1263, and died in 1269.

PETER, the sixth bishop, was consecrated in 1270. A brief of his,[3] dated at Tunsberg, 3d September 1278, grants forty days' indulgence to those in his diocese who contribute in aid of the restoration of St. Swithin's cathedral at Stavanger, which had been destroyed by fire. He died in 1284.

DOLGFINN, the seventh bishop, was consecrated in 1286. Nothing is known of him but the name. He died, according to the Annals, in 1309.

WILLIAM (III.) was the eighth bishop. He was consecrated in 1310. At the Provincial Council held at Bergen, in 1320, there were several complaints made by the archbishop against William, Bishop of Orkney.[4] Kormak, an

---

[1] Diplom. Norvegicum, vii. p. 13. [2] Ibid. i. 32.

[3] Keyser, Den Norske Kirkes Historie, ii. 210. Torfæus Hist. Orc., p. 172.

[4] Diplom. Norvegicum. The Chron. de Lanercost, under the date 1275, incidentally notices a Bishop of Orkney, named William, who related many wonderful things of the islands under Norwegian rule, and specially of Iceland. Munch supposes him to have been one of the titular bishops consecrated at York, and suggests that he may have been the author of the curious fragment of a Chronicon Norvegiæ preserved in the Panmure transcript, along with the transcript of the Diploma of the succession of the Earls of Orkney, printed at Christiania, 1850. (Munch, Symbolæ, pp. 2, 18 ; Det Norske Folks Historie, iv. part 1, p. 678 ; Chron. de Lanercost, p. 97.)

archdeacon of the Sudreys, and Grim Ormson, prebendary of Nidaros, had been sent by the archbishop on a visitation of the diocese of Orkney, and had reported that William had squandered the property of the see, that he had bestowed the offices of the church on foreigners and apostates, that he had compromised his dignity as a prelate of the church by participation in the boisterous pastime of hunting and other unseemly diversions, that he had been careless and lukewarm in the exercise of his spiritual office, and had not sought out those who practised idolatry and witchcraft, or who were heretics or followed ungodly ways.   Moreover, he had imprisoned Ingilbert Lyning, a canon of Orkney, whom the archbishop had sent to make inquiry into the collection of the Peter's pence, and had deprived him of his prebendary and all his property.   He had also clandestinely appropriated to himself during fifteen years a portion of the church dues, amounting to the value of 53 marks sterling, and he had refused to permit the removal of the corpse of a woman from Orkney, although her will had been that she should be interred in the cathedral of Trondheim.   He was suspended in the following year (1321) by the archbishop, but in 1324 we find him assisting at the consecration of Laurentius, Bishop of Hole.[1] By a deed,[2] dated at Bergen, 9th September 1327, he mortgages his dues of Shetland to his metropolitan, Eilif, Archbishop of Nidaros, for the payment of 186 marks sterling, which he should have paid the archbishop for six years' teinds. By another document of the same year,[3] Bishop Audfinn of Bergen requests Bishop William of Orkney to assist his priest Ivar in the collection of the *Sunnive-miel*—a contribution which the inhabitants of Shetland had paid from old time to the shrine of St. Sunniva at Bergen.   The date of this bishop's death has not been ascertained.

WILLIAM (IV.), ninth bishop, succeeded him, sometime

---

[1] Keyser, Den Norske Kirkes Historie, ii. 216.
[2] Diplom. Norvegicum, vii. p. 134.   [3] Ibid. p. 134.

after the year 1328. There is extant an agreement between him and Hakon Jonsson, dated at Kirkwall, 25th May 1369.[1] The next mention we have of him is the entry in the Annals, under the date 1382—"Then was heard the mournful tidings that Bishop William was slain in the Orkneys."

WILLIAM (V.), tenth bishop, appears only in a record of the time of King Robert III. of Scotland. Munch supposes that he may have been the William Johnson who appears as Archdeacon of Zetland, in a Norse deed dated at Sandwick in Shetland, March 4, 1360.

HENRY (II.), eleventh bishop, according to Torfæus, appears in a record of 1394.

JOHN, twelfth bishop, appears in the Union Treaty of Calmar in 1397.

PATRICK, thirteenth bishop, appears in an Attestation by the Lawman of Orkney, two canons of the church of St. Magnus, and four burgesses of Kirkwall, of the descent and good name of James of Cragy, laird of Hupe.[2] He is otherwise unnoticed, but as he is there referred to by his canonical title, and the many losses, injuries, and disquietudes which he endured at the hands of his adversaries, are specially alluded to, there seems to be no doubt that he held the bishopric between the death of John and the incumbency of Thomas de Tulloch.

THOMAS de Tulloch, fourteenth bishop, first appears in existing records in 1418. He seems to have been previously Bishop of Ross.[3] On 17th June 1420, at the church of Vestenskov in Laland, he gives his pledge to King Eirik and his successors, and undertakes that he will hold the crown lands of Orkney committed to him, for the Kings of Norway,

---

[1] Among the persons mentioned in this record are Sir Richard of Rollisey (Rousay), Sir Christen of Sanday, John of Orkney, Sigurd of Pappley, John of Dunray (Downreay in Caithness). The title "sir" is equivalent to our "reverend." (Diplom. Norvegicum, i. 308.)

[2] Printed from the Panmure transcript in the Miscellany of the Spalding Club, vol. v. p. 257.

[3] Theiner, Vetera Monumenta, p. 376.

promising at the same time to give law and justice to the people of Orkney according to the Norsk law-book and the ancient usages.[1] In 1422 he receives the palace and pertinents of Kirkwall—"thet slot oc faeste Kirkqwaw liggende j Orknoy j Norghe meth landet Orknoy," etc.—as a fief from King Eirik. A record of the set of the threepenny lands of Stanbuster, in the parish of St. Andrews, executed by him on 12th July 1455, and confirmed by his successor in 1465, is preserved at Kirkwall. His death took place before 28th June 1461, when we find his successor in office.[2]

WILLIAM (VI.) de Tulloch, the last bishop during the dominion of Norway in the Orkneys, was bishop in June 1461, and tendered his oath of allegiance in 1462.

A bull of Pope Sixtus IV., dated at the Vatican, 17th August 1472, placed the see of the Orkneys under the metropolitan Bishop of St. Andrews.

IX. THE BISHOPRIC OF CAITHNESS—1150-1469.

The Bishopric of Caithness appears to have been co-extensive with the older earldom, comprehending Caithness and Sutherland as far south as Ekkialsbakki or the Kyle of Sutherland. In later times the cathedral church was at Dornoch.[3] But it would seem as if the episcopal see had at one time been at Halkirk (called in the Saga Há Kirkiu, or the High Kirk), near Thurso, where we find the bishops frequently residing. The date of the erection of the bishopric is unknown.

ANDREW is the first bishop who appears in authentic records. About the year 1153 King David granted to him

---

[1] See page lxix. Both these documents are printed at length in the second volume of the Diplomatarium Norvegicum, and are exceedingly curious specimens of the language of the time. [2] Diplom. Norveg. v. 605.

[3] There was a monastery at Dornoch before the death of Earl Rögnvald in 1158. King David of Scotland addressed a missive to Rögnvald, Earl of Orkney, and to the Earl of Caithness (Harald Maddadson), and to all good men in Caithness and Orkney, requesting them to protect the monks living at Durnach in Caithness, their servants and their effects, and to see that they sustained no loss or injury. (Regist. de Dunfermelyn, p. 14.)

the lands of Hoctor Comon,[1] and about the same time he himself gave a grant of the Church of the Holy Trinity of Dunkeld to the monks of Dunfermline.[2] About the year 1165 he and Murethac, his clerk, are witnesses to a charter of Gregory, Bishop of Dunkeld, confirming the said gift. About the year 1181 he is a witness to the grant by Earl Harald Maddadson to the see of Rome of a penny annually from every inhabited house in Caithness, which brought his successor, Bishop John, into such trouble.[3] He is also a witness to the remarkable document engrossed in the Book of Deer, by which King David I. declares the clerics of Deer to be free from all lay interference and undue exaction, "as it is written in their book, and as they pleaded at Banff and swore at Aberdeen."[4] The Chronicle of Mailros records his death at Dunfermline on 30th December 1185. He seems to have been a learned man, and was much about the court of David I. He is said to have been the author of part of the curious treatise "De Situ Albaniæ," attributed to Giraldus Cambrensis.

JOHN, second bishop, succeeded him. He seems to have refused to exact from the inhabitants the papal contribution of one penny annually from each inhabited house in Caithness granted by Earl Harald, for in a bull[5] dated at the Vatican, 27th May 1198, Pope Innocent III. enjoins Bishop Bjarni of Orkney and Bishop Reginald of Ross to compel Bishop John to give up his opposition to its collection on pain of the censure of the Church. About this time also Caithness had been taken from Harald by King William the Lion, with whom he was involved in hostilities, and given over to Reginald Gudrodson, the petty king of the Hebrides. Hence, on Harald's recovery of his possessions in 1202, he was so exasperated that he took vengeance on the bishop[6] by blind-

---

[1] Regist. de Dunfermelyn, p. 14.   [2] Ibid. p. 74.

[3] Diplom. Norveg. vii. p. 2.

[4] The Book of Deer (Spald. Club), p. 95.

[5] Diplom. Norvegicum, vii. p. 2.

[6] See page xliii, and also the account of these transactions in the Saga, cap. cxv.

ing him and cutting out his tongue, and inflicted severe punishments on the people, whom he held to have been guilty of rebellion. Bishop John appears to have survived his mutilation till 1213.

ADAM, third bishop, was consecrated in 1214 by Malvoisin, Bishop of St. Andrews. He was a foundling exposed at a church door, but he had been Abbot of Melrose previous to his appointment to the see of Caithness. In 1218 he went with the Bishops of Glasgow and Moray on a pilgrimage to Rome. He seems to have been of an opposite disposition to that of his predecessor, who suffered martyrdom in the cause of his people. It was an old custom in Caithness that the husbandmen paid the bishop a *spann* of butter for every twenty cows. Bishop Adam exacted the contribution first for every fifteen, and at length for every ten cows. Exasperated by these exactions, the people rose in a body and came to him at Halkirk, where in the tumult a monk of Newbottle named Serlo was killed and the bishop himself burned in his own kitchen. A letter of Pope Honorius III., dated in January 1222, and addressed to the Scottish bishops of the time, is extant in the archives of the Vatican,[1] in which, after commending King Alexander for his promptitude and zeal in avenging Bishop Adam's murder, he goes on to tell that, having learned from their letters what a horrible crime, what a detestable deed had been committed, his spirit quailed and his heart trembled and his ears tingled as he realised the daring atrocity of the deed. "Your letters," he says, "have informed us that a dispute having arisen between Adam, Bishop of Caithness, of adorable memory, on the one part, and his parishioners on the other, concerning the tithes and other rights of the Church, and these matters having been submitted to the king himself by the mediation of certain ecclesiastics, with consent of the bishop, and the king being absent in England, his parishioners, moved with anger against him because he upheld the cause of his Church against them, fell on their pious pastor like raven-

---

[1] Printed in Theiner's Vetera Monumenta, p. 21.

ing wolves, on their father like degenerate sons, and on their
Lord Christ like emissaries of the devil, stripped him of his
clothing, stoned him, mortally wounded him with an axe, and
finally killed and burned him in his own kitchen." The letter
concludes with an injunction to excommunicate all concerned
in the murder. The bishop's body was interred in the church
at Skinnet, and is said to have been subsequently removed to
Dornoch in 1239.[1] The Saga states that the fearful vengeance
taken by King Alexander II. for the murder of the bishop
was still fresh in memory in the writer's time ; and we learn
from the Annals that "the Scottish king caused the hands and
feet to be hewn from eighty men who had been present at the
burning, so that many of them died."

GILBERT de Moravia, fourth bishop, had been Archdeacon
of Moray previous to his elevation to the see of Caithness in
1223. He built the cathedral at Dornoch, and his charter of
constitution[2] is still extant in the record-room at Dunrobin
Castle. For many years there had been an intimate connection between the diocese of Caithness and the abbey of
Scone,[3] and in the constitution of his cathedral Bishop
Gilbert named the Abbot of Scone one of the canons. The
fourteen churches assigned to the prebends were those of Clyne,
Dornoch, Creich, Rogart, Lairg, Farr, Kildonan, and Durness,
in Sutherland ; and Bower, Watten, Skinnet, Olrig, Dunnet,
and Canisbay, in Caithness. Golspie and Loth, Reay,
Thurso, Wick, and Latheron, were reserved to the bishop.

---

[1] Chron. de Mailros, pp. 139, 150.

[2] Printed in the Miscellany of the Bannatyne Club, vol. iii.

[3] The bones of St. Fergus, the patron saint of Caithness, were deposited
in the abbey of Scone. Harald Maddadson, Earl of Orkney and Caithness,
granted a mark of silver yearly to the canons of Scone for the souls of himself and wife, and the souls of his predecessors. The grant is witnessed by his
son "Turphin." The Abbot of Scone obtained a royal precept from King
Alexander II. addressed to the sheriffs and bailies of Moray and Caithness, for
the protection of the ship of the convent when on its voyages within their
jurisdiction. The Abbey of Scone was proprietor of the church of Kildonan,
which, with its chapels and lands, was confirmed to the canons of Scone by
Pope Honorius III. in 1226. (Liber Ecclesie de Scon, pp. 37, 45, and 67.)

He seems to have been a man of mark in his time. He built the " Bishop's Castle" at Scrabster, and was made keeper of the king's castles in the north.[1] He seems also to have been the first discoverer of gold in Sutherlandshire, for Sir Robert Gordon states that he " found a mine of gold in Duriness, in the lands belonging to his bishoprick." He died at Scrabster in 1245, and was afterwards canonised. His relics were preserved in the cathedral church at Dornoch, and continued to be held in reverence down to the middle of the 16th century. In a record of the year 1545 it is stated that the parties compearing before Earl John of Sutherland in the chapter-house of the cathedral at Dornoch made oath by touching the relics of the blessed Saint Gilbert. He is the only bishop of Caithness, except Bishop Adam, whose death is recorded in the Icelandic Annals. The entry is under the year 1244 :—" Death of Gilibert, bishop in Scotland."

WILLIAM, fifth bishop, was his successor. In 1250 he appears among the other Scottish bishops in a document addressed to Alexander III. concerning the liberties of the Church. He died in 1261 or 1262.

WALTER de Baltrodin, a canon of Caithness, was chosen as his successor. Pope Urban IV. in 1263 addressed a letter [2] to the bishops of Dunkeld, Brechin, and Ross, setting forth that his election had not been proceeded with according to canonical form, but as it had been unanimous, and in consideration of the poverty of the Church, and the expense of making such long journeys to distant places, he enjoins them to prefer the said Walter to the bishopric if they find that he is not disqualified by defect of birth or otherwise. He died before 1274. On his death, Nicolas, Abbot of Scone, was chosen as his successor, but rejected by the Pope.[3]

ARCHIBALD, Archdeacon of Moray, was chosen on the rejection by the Pope of Nicolas, Abbot of Scone. The Pope's

---

[1] Sir Robert Gordon mentions a tradition that he was the builder of the noble castle of Kildrummy, in Mar.

[2] Theiner, Vet. Mon. Hib. et Scot. p. 89.   [3] Ibid. p. 104.

letter confirming his election mentions R., the Dean,
Patrick, the treasurer, and Roger de Castello, canon of
Caithness, as the parties by whom he was nominated. In
his time Boyamund de Vitia was commissioned by Pope
Gregory X. to collect a special subsidy in aid of the crusade,
and his accounts furnish us with the names of a number of
the churches in the diocese of Caithness and the amounts
contributed.[1]

Bishop Archibald must have been dead before 1279, for in
that year the Pope addressed a letter to the Bishops of St.
Andrews and Aberdeen,[2] setting forth that the see of Caithness being vacant, the chapter had proceeded to the election
of R., the Dean of Caithness, and had constituted Henry
of Nottingan [3] (in Caithness) their procurator to obtain confirmation of the said election, and that the said Henry, in the
Pope's presence, had confessed that the said dean had a son
thirty years old or more, and that he was said to have
another, although he (Henry of Nottingan) did not believe
it ; and, moreover, that he had been stricken with paralysis,
and was old and debilitated. The bishops are enjoined to use
their influence to oblige him to resign.

ALAN de St. Edmund, eighth bishop, was an Englishman,
elected by the influence of Edward I. of England. In 1290

---

[1] There was collected in the year 1274—From Olric (Olrig), 2 marcs ;
Dinnosc (Dunnet), 32s. 4d. ; Cranesby (Canisbay), 40s. ; Ascend (Skinnet),
5s. 4d. ; Haukyrc (Halkirk), 14s. 2d. ; Turishau (Thurso), 26s. 7d. ; the
chapel of Haludal (Halladale), 9s. 4d. ; Lagheryn (Latheron), 27s. 10d. ;
Durness, 14s. 8d. There was collected in the year 1275—Laterne (Latheron),
32s. ; Cananby, 32s. ; Thorsau, 2 marcs ; the chapel of Helwedale (Halla-
dale), 9s. 4d. ; Ra (Reay), 9s. 4d. ; Haukyrc (Halkirk), 13s. 9d. ; Olric
(Olrig), 2 marcs ; the church of Scynand (Skinnet), 18s. 8d. ; the church of
Dunost (Dunnet), 2 marcs ; Keldoninave (Kildonan), 2 marcs. The personal
contributions include one from Magister H. de Notingham—doubtless the
Notingham near Forse which still bears the name unchanged. (Theiner,
Vet. Monum. pp. 112, 115.)

[2] Theiner, Vetera Monumenta, p. 124.

[3] Henry of Nothingham was a canon of Caithness in 1272. (Lib. Eccles.
de Scon, p. 85.)

he signs the letter addressed to that king, proposing a marriage between the Maid of Norway and the young Prince
Edward. Alan was a favourite with King Edward, and was
made Chancellor of Scotland in 1291. In that year a writ[1]
was addressed by the king to Alexander Comyn, keeper of
the royal forest of Ternway, in Moray, ordering him to give
Bishop Alan 40 oaks suitable for material for the fabric of
the cathedral church of Caithness, which the king had
granted for the souls of Alexander, King of Scotland, and
Margaret, his queen, the sister of King Edward. Bishop
Alan died in 1291, and on his death King Edward ordered
the Bishops of St. Andrews and Glasgow to commit the
vacant cure to some cleric in the king's allegiance.[2] The
fulfilment of this mandate is not on record, but we learn
from the letter of Pope Boniface VIII.[3] addressed to Bishop
Adam in 1296, that on the death of Alan the chapter of
Caithness had chosen the Archdeacon of Caithness, whose
name is given as I(oannes?) to be his successor, but because
the election had not been in canonical form it was not confirmed by the Pope, who preferred to the vacant diocese
Adam, then precentor of the church of Ross.

ADAM, ninth bishop, as we learn from the Pope's letter
above mentioned, was not elected in the usual way, but preferred by the Pope and consecrated by the Bishop of Ostia.
The letter addressed by the Pope[4] "to the chapter of Caithness, to the people of the district and diocese of Caithness,
and to our dearest son in Christ the King of Scots," in 1296,
announces his preferment, and the reasons that led to it.
He died at Sienna very shortly after the date of this letter.[5]

ANDREW, abbot of the Cistercian monastery of Cupar,[6] was
now preferred to the see of Caithness; and because, "on account
of the wars that are imminent in those parts, and the dangers
of the way, which is long and perilous, it is impossible for

---

[1] Rotuli Scotiæ, vol. i. p. 6.   [2] Ibid. vol. i. p. 7.
[3] Theiner, Vet. Monum. p. 161.   [4] Ibid.   [5] Ibid. p. 163.   [6] Ibid.

him to approach the apostolic seat for consecration," a mandate was addressed to the Bishops of Aberdeen, Glasgow, and Ross, to give him consecration.

FERQUHARD, Bishop of Caithness, appears in 1310, among the other bishops of Scotland, acknowledging Robert Bruce as King of Scotland. In 1312, along with Magnus, Earl of Caithness and Orkney, he attests the payment of 100 marks sterling (the annual tribute payable for the Hebrides) by King Robert Bruce to the King of Norway, in St. Magnus' Cathedral, Kirkwall. He was dead and the see vacant in 1328.[1]

NICOLAS, a deacon, was bishop-elect in 1332.[2]

DAVID was the next bishop, but of him we have no record except that he was dead before 1340.[3]

ALAN, Archdeacon of Aberdeen, was confirmed as Bishop of Caithness in 1341 by Pope Benedict XII.[4] He died in 1342.

THOMAS de Fingask was elected on the death of Alan, and his confirmation by Pope Clement VI. is dated in November 1342.[5] He is witness to a writ by William, Earl of Ross, in 1355, declaring the abbey of Ferne exempt from all the king's taxes.[6] He appears as witness to a deed with Ingelram of Caithness, Archdeacon of Dunkeld, in 1359.[7] He died at Elgin in 1360, and was buried in our Lady's aisle of the chanonry church of Elgin, under the bishop's seat.

MALCOLM is the next bishop of whom we have any authentic account.[8] His confirmation by Pope Urban V. is dated

---

[1] Comp. Camerar. Scot. i. 25-26.

[2] See a paper by Joseph Robertson, Proc. Soc. Antiq. Scot. vol. ii. p. 31, *note.* [3] Theiner, Vet. Monum., p. 276.

[4] Ibid. [5] Ibid. p. 277. [6] Origines Parochiales, ii. 485.

[7] Regist. Morav. p. 368.

[8] There is a writ of Pope Innocent VI., dated in May 1360, preferring Thomas to be bishop of the "Ecclesia Cathayensis," and ordering him to repair to his diocese on being consecrated by the Bishop of Preneste. It appears from subsequent documents, however, that he was obstructed and interfered with by the bishops of Limerick, Ardfert, and Clonmacnoise, who laid many charges of criminal and illegal proceedings against him, asserting

Feb. 21, 1369.[1]   A bull of Pope Gregory XI., dated at Avignon in March 1376, confirms to Dr. William of Spynie the chanonry and prebendary of the church of Orkney, which had become vacant by the preferment of Malcolm to be Bishop of Caithness.[2]

ALEXANDER appears as Bishop of Caithness in 1389, when, along with Alexander, Bishop of Ross, and Adam, Abbot of Kinloss, he takes part in the settlement of a dispute between the Earl and Bishop of Moray.[3]   He appears by proxy at the provincial synod held at Perth in 1420.[4]

ROBERT was bishop in 1434, and his successor WILLIAM, who appears as bishop in 1449, was still in office at the period of the transference of the Orkneys from the Norwegian to Scottish rule, in 1469.

X. ANCIENT CHURCHES OF ORKNEY.

" The Cathedral of St. Magnus," says Worsaae, " is incontestably the most glorious monument of the time of the Norwegian dominion to be found in Scotland."   "It is," says Peterkin, " one of the two cathedral churches in Scotland remaining entire, and is, therefore, a national monument, interesting from its antiquity, its beauty, and the rarity of such relics in this part of the empire."   Nothing conveys to the mind of the stranger visiting Kirkwall a more vivid impression of the ancient importance of this quaint little town, which has been the capital of the Orkneys for at least 800

---

that the " Ecclesia Cathayensis" was a parochial and not a cathedral church, and the Pope appointed George, Archbishop of Cashel, to report on the matter. Owing to the death of the archbishop the report was not made, and the remit was renewed by the successsor of Pope Innocent VI. to the Bishop of Lismore. It is not clear whether this was a preferment to the see of Caithness following on the death of Thomas de Fingask, or a series of mistakes.   See Theiner's Vetera Monumenta, pp. 316, 318, 324.

[1] Theiner, Vetera Monumenta, p. 333.

[2] Diplom. Norvegicum, vii. p. 309.   [3] Regist. Morav. p. 200.

[4] Regist. Episc. Brechinensis, p. 39.

years, than the grandeur of its cathedral, and the imposing aspect of the ruins of the palaces of the Bishops and Earls of Orkney.

The Saga tells how the erection of the cathedral was undertaken by Earl Rögnvald II. (Kali Kolson), in fulfilment of a vow which he had made to build and endow a splendid stone minster in Kirkwall in honour of St. Magnus, his mother's brother, from whom he derived his right to a share of the earldom of the Orkneys. He won the earldom in the year 1136, and the erection of the cathedral was commenced under the superintendence of his father Kol, in 1137, and carried on until the earl's means failed. By agreement with the odallers, a mark for each ploughland in the islands was contributed for the purpose of carrying on the work, and this brought in money enough to enable the erection of the church to be proceeded with.

The cathedral, as it now stands, however, is by no means the work of Earl Rögnvald's time, although the portion built by him is still clearly distinguishable. "The church," says Sir Henry Dryden,[1] "as designed and partly built in the time of Kol (father of Earl Rögnvald), was of the same width as at present, but possibly one bay shorter at the west end. There can be little doubt that the choir terminated in an apse, which began about half-way along the great piers in front of the subsequent altar steps, and extended as far as the line of those steps. The builders, having laid out the whole church, carried up the choir and its two aisles and the transepts to the eaves, and built the piers of the central tower." The architectural history of the structure, however, is puzzling. "Though I spent eighteen weeks at the cathedral," says Sir Henry in a letter to Mr. Worsaae, "and have thought over the thing many times, I cannot make out the history of the building to my own satisfaction. There is no doubt that there is a great

[1] For the details of the structure by Sir H. Dryden, see the Transactions of the Architectural Institute of Scotland, 1869-73. See also Billings' Baronial and Ecclesiastical Antiquities, 1848; and Worsaae's Danes and Northmen, 1852.

Sᵗ MAGNUS CATHEDRAL KIRKWALL from the South east

deal of copying in it, *i.e.* of building at one time in the style of another." [1] The chief interest of the structure lies in the fact that it was built by a Norwegian earl, and designed and superintended by the Norwegian Kol, who had the principal oversight of the whole work. It is significant of their community of origin that the oldest portions of St. Magnus show traces of the same peculiarities of style which are found in the nearly contemporary but somewhat older Norman churches in Normandy, the home of the Christian descendants of the Vikings who followed Hrolf the Conqueror, son of Rögnvald, Earl of Moeri.

The cathedral was erected for the express purpose of receiving the relics of St. Magnus, but we have no record of their transference to the new church. There is reason to believe that they had been brought to Kirkwall before the erection of the cathedral was begun, and, though it is not so stated, it may be inferred that on their removal from Christ's Church in Birsay, they were deposited in the church of St. Olaf at Kirkwall, and remained there for some years until the cathedral was ready to receive them. It seems probable that it is to the church of St. Olaf that Kirkwall owes its name of *Kirkiu-vagr*, the Creek of the Kirk. This name does not occur in the Saga before the time of Earl Rögnvald Brusison, who is said to have resided there, and it is most likely that the church of St. Olaf was built by him in memory of his foster-father, King Olaf the Holy. Earl Rögnvald was in the battle of Stiklestad (1030) in which the warrior saint of Norway fell, and being his foster-son he was more likely than any of the subsequent earls to dedicate a church to his memory. We are told in the Saga [2] that the relics of St. Magnus were exhumed by Bishop William twenty years after his death and placed in a shrine at Christ's Kirk. Shortly thereafter,

---

[1] Sir Henry Dryden recognises the following styles in the building:—1st style, 1137 to 1160 ; 2d style, 1160 to 1200 ; 3d style, 1200 to 1250 ; 4th style, 1250 to 1350 ; 5th style, 1450 to 1500. (Guide to St. Magnus' Cathedral by Sir H. Dryden, Daventry, 1871.)

[2] Magnus Helga Saga (edidit Jonæus : Hafniæ, 1780), pp. 536, 538.

f

says the Saga, St. Mágnus appeared in a dream to a man who
lived in Westray, by name Gunni, and ordered him to tell
Bishop William that he (St. Magnus) wished to go out of
Birgisherad and east to Kirkwall. Gunni was afraid to do
so lest he should excite the wrath of Earl Paul, whose father
had been the murderer of St. Magnus. The following night
St. Magnus again appeared to him, ordering him to disclose
his dream whatever the consequences might be, and threaten-
ing him with punishment in the life hereafter if he disobeyed.
Struck with terror, Gunni went to the Bishop and told him
in the presence of Earl Paul and all the congregation. Earl
Paul, it is said, turned red with anger, but all the men there
united in requesting the bishop to proceed at once to carry
the wishes of St. Magnus into execution. So the bishop went
east to Kirkwall with the relics, accompanied by a great con-
course of people, and "placed them in a shrine upon the altar
of the church which then was there," and which could have
been no other than St. Olaf's,[1] seeing that the building of the
cathedral was not commenced until after Earl Paul had been
carried off to Athole by Swein Asleifson. The Saga of St.
Magnus adds that there were then few houses in the town,
but that after the relics of St. Magnus had been transferred
thither the town rapidly increased.

Earl Rögnvald (II.) himself was buried [2] in the cathedral in
1158. In the winter of 1263 the remains of King Hakon

---

[1] The present church of St. Olaf's, which is not older than the 16th century, and is said by Wallace to have been built by Bishop Reid, in all probability stands on the site of the older one. The veneration of St. Olaf extended
both to Scotland and England. There was a church dedicated to him at
Cruden, and among the articles enumerated in an inventory of the treasury
of the cathedral of Aberdeen in 1518, there is "a small image of St. Olaf of
silver decorated with precious stones."—(Regist. Episc. Aberdonense, ii. p. 172.)

[2] Neale, in his Ecclesiological Notes (p. 116), states that Earl Rögnvald's
remains were first interred in the church of Burwick, South Ronaldsay, but
gives no authority for the statement. The Saga, on the other hand, states
expressly that his remains were taken to Kirkwall, and interred in the cathedral. It is not likely that the founder of the cathedral would have been interred anywhere else.

Hakonson were deposited in the cathedral previous to their removal to Bergen. Worsaae states that the remains of the Princess Margaret, the Maid of Norway, were interred in the cathedral in 1290, and the local tradition is to the same effect, but there is no authority for the statement. The princess's remains were taken back to Norway and buried in the High Church of Bergen by King Eirik, beside the remains of her mother.[1]

EGILSEY CHURCH, on the little isle of Egilsey, is interesting from the suggestions of its connec-

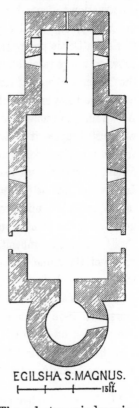

tion with the earlier Christianity of the islands previous to the Norse invasion.

The church stands on the highest ground of the island, on the west side, and is a conspicuous object in the landscape from all sides. It consists of chancel and nave, but differs from all the existing churches in the islands in having a round tower rising at the west end of the nave. It is of small size, the nave being 30 feet long by 15½ feet in breadth inside, and the chancel 15 feet long by 9½ feet in breadth. The chancel is vaulted, and the walls are about 3 feet thick. The tower, which seems to have been built with the nave, is 7 feet diameter inside, and is now 48 feet high, the walls being about 3½ feet thick. It is stated that about 15 feet were taken

EGILSHA S.MAGNUS.

off the height to prevent its falling.[2] The only two windows in

---

[1] See p. liii, antea.

[2] In the engraving given of this church by Hibbert, the church and tower are both represented as covered by a stone roof, that of the tower being a conical cap resembling the usual termination of the Irish Round Towers.

the nave that are original are round-headed and 3 feet high, with jambs splaying inwards from 8½ to 33 inches wide, and having no external chamfer. Two windows in the chancel are exactly similar but smaller. Over the chancel vault there is a small chamber lighted by a flat-headed window 18 inches high.

Its original dedication is unknown,[1] and there is nothing to fix the date of its erection with absolute certainty.

"The church of Egilsey," says Munch, "is shown by its construction to have been built before the Northmen arrived in Orkney, or, at all events, to belong to the more ancient Christian Celtic population ; both its exterior and its interior show so many resemblances to the old churches in Ireland of the 7th and 8th centuries, that we are compelled to suppose it to have been erected at that time by Irish priests or *Papas*. As we find no remains of any similar churches on the islands,[2] we must suppose it to have been the first of the few on the thinly inhabited isle-group. The island on which it stood might, therefore, very justly be called ' Church isle.' But the Irish word *Ecclais* (church), derived from the Latin *Ecclesia*, might easily be mistaken by our forefathers for Egils, the genitive of the man's name Egil."

If we could unhesitatingly adopt Munch's view of the origin of the name Egilsey, it might be safely assumed that this was the church which gave its name to the island, as no other ecclesiastical site is known within its bounds. The Norsemen were heathens down to the time of the Christian-ising cruise of King Olaf Tryggvason in A.D. 1000, and not very hearty in their Christianity for a long time after that. The church could not have been built, therefore, between 872

---

[1] In Jo. Ben's description of the islands (1529) it is said that the church of Egilsey was dedicated to St. Magnus. But as he adds that St. Magnus was born in Egilsey, and brought up there from his infancy, and that he gave a piece of ground to his nurse, on which she made an underground house with all its furniture of stone, it is plain that he is merely repeating the absurd tra-ditions of the time.

[2] There were three towered churches in Shetland (see p. ci.)

EGILSEY CHURCH, from the South east

(from a Photograph)

and the accession of Earl Thorfinn in 1014.   Nor is it likely to have been erected during Thorfinn's minority, for he was only five years old when his father fell fighting under a heathen banner at Clontarf.   The Saga tells that Thorfinn built Christ's Church in Birsay, and made it the first bishop's see in the Orkneys.   If he, or any of his successors previous to the death of St. Magnus, had erected such a notable structure as that of Egilsey, it would probably have been recorded. There was a church in Egilsey in 1115 when St. Magnus was murdered, and the only question is whether it was the present church.   Its resemblances to the Irish churches of the 7th and 8th centuries are not sufficiently definite and determinative to enable us to assign to it unhesitatingly an Irish origin; while, on the other hand, the resemblance to the round-towered churches of Norfolk suggests that it may have been of Scandinavian origin.   But there is nothing in the architecture of the building either to fix the date of its erection or to determine the questions of Celtic or Scandinavian origin with any degree of certainty.[1]

The CHURCH OF ORPHIR is one of the few circular churches in Britain, built in imitation of the church of the Holy Sepulchre at Jerusalem.   The crusades were the means of importing this form into the ecclesiastical architecture of the west.   A few of these round churches remain in Denmark, and, like those of England, they are mostly of the 12th century.[2]

---

[1] "Its style of architecture," says Sir Henry Dryden, "discarding certain indications of an earlier date, prevents our assigning to it a date later than the beginning of the 12th century. When we contrast it with the Kirkwall Cathedral begun in 1137, we are forced to give an earlier date than that to Egilsey, and this opinion is corroborated by the churches at Orphir and Brough of Birsay.—(Ruined Churches in Orkney and Shetland, in the *Orcadian* of 1867.)

[2] Those in Britain are Cambridge, consecrated in 1101; Northampton, about 1115; Maplestead, 1118; the Temple Church, London, 1185; the small Norman church in Ludlow Castle, and the Earls' Church at Orphir in Orkney—the only example in Scotland. "The round churches at Cambridge, Northampton, and London," says Ferguson, "were certainly sepulchral, or erected in imitation of the church at Jerusalem" (History of Architecture,

All that remains of this interesting structure is merely the semicircular chancel and about 9 feet of the walls of the circular nave on either side, as shown in the annexed ground-plan. It is described in the Old Statistical Account as having been a rotundo, 18 feet in diameter and 20 feet high, two-thirds of which were taken down to build the present

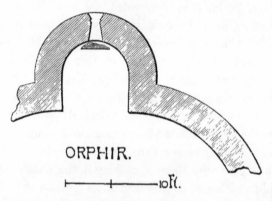

ORPHIR.

parish church. The curvature of the part of the walls still remaining would give a diameter of 18 to 19 feet. The semi-circular chancel is 7 feet wide and a little more than 7 feet deep. The walls are well built of yellow Orphir freestone. The only remaining window is a small one in the east end of the chancel, 30 inches high, having a semicircular head, and the jambs splaying inwards from 10½ inches to 20 inches wide. It has a groove for glass.

The Rev. Alex. Pope of Reay, who visited Orphir in 1758, has given a description of "The Temple of Orphir, or Gerth House," but there is little to be gathered from it, and the measurements as given [1] are evidently wrong. He states,

ii. p. 60). Wilson, on the other hand, supposes that the early dry-built bee-hive houses of the Western Islands may have served as a model for some of the earliest Christian oratories, of which that at Orphir, he remarks, is an interest-ing example (Prehistoric Annals, ii. p. 369). But there is no analogy what-ever between the architectural features of Orphir and those of the beehive houses, nor has it any resemblance to the earlier oratories and chapels of the Western Isles.

[1] Pope's Translation of Torfæus (Wick, 1866), p. 108.

however, that extensive remains, supposed to be those of the Earls' Palace at Orphir, had been discovered in excavating the foundations of the neighbouring farm-buildings. Indications of these, and of an extensive refuse-heap, are still to be seen.

The church of Orphir is first mentioned in the Saga in connection with Earl Paul Hakonson's residence at Orphir. The church is there referred to as a splendid structure, and it is not spoken of as recently erected, or as having been built by Earl Paul. But Earl Hakon, his father, who had made a pilgrimage to Rome and the Holy Land, is said in the Saga to have brought back relics which he would doubtless deposit in the church at Orphir, where he seems to have resided. The probability is that the church was built by him after his return from his pilgrimage, perhaps as an expiatory offering for the murder of his cousin, St. Magnus. Earl Hakon died in 1122, and three out of the six round churches in Britain had been built before that time.

CHRIST'S CHURCH in Birsay is the first church of which we have any record in the Saga, and, so far as we know, the first church erected in the Orkneys after the conversion of the Norwegian inhabitants to Christianity. It was built by Earl Thorfinn some time about the middle of the 11th century. Earl Thorfinn made a pilgrimage to Rome about the year 1050, and it is likely that Christ's Church would be built after his return to Orkney, or between 1050 and 1064, the date of his death. It was the seat of the bishopric previous to the erection of the cathedral of St. Magnus, and William the Old, who was the first (actual) bishop, lived to see the bishopric transferred to Kirkwall some time after 1137.

It is doubtful whether any recognisable traces of the original Christ's Church now remain. Neale says, "The parish church, which contains some fragments of old work, seems to have been the famous Christ's Church built by Earl Thorfinn." But it does not seem at all likely that any portion of the existing parish church can be as old as the middle of the 11th century. There are remains of an older church, how-

ever, beside it, which are still known as the Christ's Kirk, and
Mr. George Petrie, who has made a ground-plan of the structure (of which only part of the foundation remains), has ascertained that it had an apse at the east end.

The CHURCH OF WEIR, on the island of the same name,

WEIR.

consists of chancel and nave, the
extreme length exteriorly being 36
feet, and the width 18½ feet. The
nave is 19 feet by 13 feet inside, and
the chancel little more than 7 feet
square. The door is in the west end,
having parallel jambs with no rebate.
The doorway has a semicircular head,
roughly arched with thin slaty stones
set on edge, the arch being set a
little back on the imposts.[1] There
are two windows on the south side
of the nave, only one of which appears to be original. It is flat-headed,
22 inches high and 8 inches wide,
the jambs splaying inwards to a
width of 27 inches. The chancel arch, of which a representation is given in the accompanying plate, is exactly like
the doorway. There is one window in the south side, which
seems to have been round-headed, 27 inches high by 11
inches wide.

Of this chapel Mr. Muir says,[2] "Excepting that at Lybster,
in Caithness, the entrance to the chancel is the most diminutive,
not of primitive date, I have ever seen, the total height being

---

[1] Sir H. Dryden says this mode of putting on the arch was probably
resorted to in order to give a support to the centre on which the arch was
built. This seems highly probable, and in some cases it would seem as if the
original supports still remain in the shape of two long thin slabs resting on
the imposts on either side and meeting in the centre of the arch. See the
engraving of the doorway in St. Mary's Church, Kilbar, Barra, in Mr. Muir's
Characteristics of Old Church Architecture, p. 230.

[2] Caithness and Part of Orkney, an Ecclesiological Sketch, by T. S. Muir,
p. 25.

only 4 feet. In plan, size, and general expression, Weir and Lybster are remarkably alike, and in all probability both buildings are the work of the same period, though Lybster is perhaps fully the older of the two." Sir Henry Dryden also remarks the similarity of the chapels of Weir and Lybster, and adds "Probably Weir is of the 12th or 13th century, but the characteristics are not decisive enough to approximate more closely to its date."

It is most probable that this chapel[1] was built by Bishop Bjarni, the son of Kolbein Hruga, who built the castle on the island of Weir, as recorded in the Saga. Bjarni was bishop from 1188 to 1223, and would probably reside on his paternal estate in Weir when not required by the duties of the episcopate to be in Kirkwall. This period answers to the indications afforded by the architectural characteristics of the building, and we have no record of any other person who was likely to have erected a chapel on this little island. The fact that it is still called "Cobbie Row's Chapel" points to its connection with Kolbein Hruga's family.

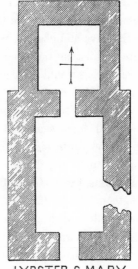

LYBSTER S. MARY

├────┼────┼──── 15ft.

The CHURCH AT LYBSTER[2] (Reay), in Caithness, corresponds in style and plan so closely to the church of Weir that it may be described here briefly. There is no other church in Caithness of any antiquity which demands special notice. Ecclesiastical sites of early date are thickly scattered over the county, but the ruins of the buildings themselves have suffered so much that there is scarcely an architec-

---

[1] From an expression of Jo. Ben's it would seem to have been dedicated to St. Peter :—"Weir, insula est parva, Petro Apostolo dicata."

[2] This church, which was called St. Peter's in 1726, is called St. Mary's by Mr. Muir.

tural feature left to guide us to conclusions as to their date. The church at Lybster is fortunately an exception. It consists of chancel and nave, slightly larger than Weir, and very rudely constructed. There is a doorway with inclined jambs in the west end, of which a representation is given in the accompanying plate ; but Mr. Muir notices as a singular feature of the building that there are nowhere traces of windows, although all the elevations except the east one, which is broken down to a little below the gable line, remain nearly entire. The entrance to the chancel is of the same form as the doorway, having inclined jambs. "With regard to even the probable age of this building," says Mr. Muir, "I would not like to venture an opinion. The diversified shapes and sizes of the stones, and the primitive form and smallness of the entrances to the nave and chancel, would suggest extreme earliness of date ; whilst, on the other hand, the refined character of the ground-plan would indicate a period of time not more remote than the 12th century."

ST. PETER'S CHURCH, on the Brough of Birsay, a holm of about 40 acres, separated from the mainland by a channel about 150 yards wide, and dry at low water, consists of nave, chancel, and apse, all well defined, and apparently built at the same time, the material being a grey whinstone. The total length of the building is 57 feet. The nave is 28 feet by 15½ inside, and the chancel about 10 feet square. There is but one doorway, in the west end of the church. It has parallel jambs without any rebate for a door.[1] There are

[1] Sir Henry Dryden remarks that the same mode of making doorways is to be seen in the chapels at Lybster in Caithness, at Weir, at Linton in Shapinsay, Uyea in Shetland, and in some of the early oratories in Ireland, and suggests the question—Were there doors in these churches, and if so, where were they placed and how were they hung ? "It is known," he adds, "that in many cottages in old time the door was an animal's hide hung across the opening, and probably this may have been the case in these unrebated church entrances." The custom of closing the entrances to the places of worship by a skin or heavy curtain survives in the East to the present day. The "veil of the Temple," covering the entrance to the Holy of Holies, is a familiar illustration of this ancient custom among the Jews.

Chancel Arch of Church at Weir

Doorway in West end of Church at Lybster, Reay

the remains of a window in the north wall, 3 feet high by
10½ inches wide, square-headed, and splaying both internally
and externally to a width of 22½ inches. Only the foundations of the apse remain. The floor was originally level to
the end of the apse, but subsequently there had been a reredos
which blocked off the apse, and then there were steps to the
altar, some portion of which still remains. A stone projec-
tion or "seat," 14 inches high and the same in width, runs
all round the nave. In the north-east and south-east corners
are two circular spaces, 5½ feet in diameter, in one of which
are the remains of a spiral stone staircase. In all probability the church was twin-towered, like many of the Scandinavian churches dating from the 13th century. Barry
states that this church was dedicated to St. Peter, but the dedication seems to have been unknown in the locality [1] in 1627.

There are the remains of a chapel similarly situated on
the Brough of Deerness, at the east end of the Mainland.
The Brough of Deerness is an outlying rock, nearly 100 feet
high, and covered with green sward on the top. The chapel
stands near the centre of the area, and is surrounded by a
stone wall enclosing an area of about 60 feet by 45. The
chapel, which is a smaller and ruder building than that
on the Brough of Birsay, is a simple parallelogram of
not more than 17 feet by 10 inside, the walls being from
3 to 4 feet thick. The doorway is in the west end, and there
are the remains of a window in the east end, but the heads
of both are gone. Around the chapel there are the foundations of about a score of stone-built huts scattered irregularly over the area of the Brough. They are irregularly
built, with a tendency towards the rectangular form, the
walls being from 2½ to 3 feet thick. Several of them are
nearly as long as the church, but not so wide, the internal

---

[1] The minister of Birsay in 1627 says :—"There is likewise ane litill holm
within the sea callit the Brughe of Birsay, quhilk is thocht be the elder sort to
have belongit to the reid friaris, for there is the foundation of ane kirk and
kirkyard there as yet to be seen."—Peterkin's Rentals, No. III., p. 98.

area measuring about 18 feet by 6. Low[1] states that in his time, notwithstanding the difficulty and danger of the access to the Brough, "even old age scrambled its way through a road in many places not six inches broad, where certain death attended a slip." Jo. Ben, in 1529, mentions that people of all classes and conditions were in the habit of climbing up to the top of the Brough on their hands and knees to visit the chapel called the "Bairns of Brugh;" and when they had reached the top, "on their bended knees and with hands joined they offered their supplications with many incantations to the Bairns of Brugh, throwing stones and water behind their backs, and making the circuit of the chapel twice or thrice." There is still a fine spring on the Brough, which doubtless had the reputation of a "holy well" in connection with these superstitious practices. The Brough was fenced with a strong stone wall toward the land side in Low's time, and from this and the remains of the huts he concludes that it had been a rock fort subsequently converted into a sanctuary by the ecclesiastics.

The old parish church of Deerness, of which Low has preserved three sketches (one of which is engraved in Hibbert's Shetland), had the peculiarity of being twin-towered, as the church on the Brough of Birsay seems also to have been, and as many of the Scandinavian churches dating from the 13th century were.[2] Low describes it as having a vaulted chancel at the east end, of which the twin towers rose from each corner. The tower on the south-east corner of the chancel was entered by a doorway opening from the chancel (in the same manner as the one at Brough of Birsay), and a spiral staircase led to a small apartment or vestry between the towers, on the second storey. From this apartment was the entrance to the other tower.

---

[1] Low's Tour through Orkney and Zetland, MS. in the possession of David Laing, Esq.

[2] See the article on "The Twin-towered Churches of Denmark," by J. Kornerup, in the Aarboger for Nordisk Oldkindighed for 1869, p. 13.

There were three towered churches in Shetland—St. Laurence in West Burra, St. Magnus at Tingwall, and Ireland Head, but, like the old church of Deerness, they have long disappeared, and there is no description of them more precise than the casual notices of Low and Brand. It is not even quite clear whether they were single-towered or twin-towered. If single-towered they may have been examples of the rare form of which Egilsey is now the only remaining instance.

XI. MAESHOW AND THE STONES OF STENNIS.

Maeshow, the Orkahaug of the Saga, is connected in such an interesting way with the Norse history of the Isles that it is necessary to notice briefly its most peculiar features.

It stands about a mile to the north-east of the great stone ring of Stennis. Its external appearance is that of a truncated conical mound of earth, about 300 feet in circumference at the base and 36 feet high, surrounded by a trench 40 feet wide. Nothing was known of its internal structure till the year 1861, when it was opened by Mr. Farrer, M.P.,[1] but the common tradition of the country represented it as the abode of a goblin, who was named "the Hogboy,"[2] though no one knew why. When excavated, the mound was found to cover a great cairn of stones, in the centre of which was a chamber about 15 feet square, the walls of which still remained entire to a height of 13 feet. A long low passage led from the west side of the chamber to the exterior of the mound, a distance

---

[1] Detailed accounts of the excavation, with translations and facsimiles of the inscriptions of Maeshow, have been given in a privately-printed work by Mr. Farrer, and in a work published by the late Mr. John Mitchell. An account of the structure of Maeshow, with notices of the inscriptions, is given by Dr. John Stuart, secretary to the Society of Antiquaries of Scotland, in their Proceedings, vol. v. p. 247. A notice, with readings of the inscriptions, by Dr. Charlton, is given in Archæologia Æliana, vol. vi. p. 127 (1865). See also the splendid work on The Runic Monuments of Scandinavia and England, by Professor George Stephens, Copenhagen, 1866-68.

[2] Hogboy is the Norse word *Haug-bui*, the tenant of the *haug*, how, or tomb—a hoy-laid dead man, or the goblin that guards the treasures buried in the how. (Ordbog det Norske Gamle Sprog, *sub voce*.)

of about 54 feet, and on the other three sides of the chamber there were small cells or *loculi* entered by openings in the walls about 2½ feet square at a height of about 3 feet above the floor.

Structurally, Maeshow belongs to a class of chambered sepulchral cairns of common occurrence in the north of Scot-

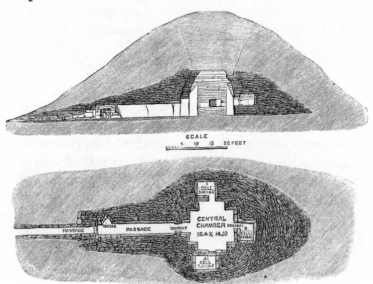

Plan and Section of Maeshow.

land, but to a special variety of that class which is peculiar to the Orkneys.[1] These chambered tombs occur in groups in certain places, thus suggesting the probability that, as in the great royal cemeteries of early times in Ireland, they may have been for centuries the gathering places of the tribes and the burying-places of their kings.

But the most interesting fact connected with Maeshow was the discovery that a large number of Runic inscriptions

---

[1] The leading specific feature of the Orkney group of chambered cairns is the formation of small cells or loculi off the principal chamber. The Caithness group is distinguished by the tricameration of the chamber, and the Clava group by having a circular or oval chamber undivided and unfurnished with *loculi*.

had been scratched on the stones of the interior walls of the chamber. It was evident, from the height at which the inscriptions occurred, as well as from indications of the weathering of the stones previous to their being inscribed, that when the runes were cut the chamber was roofless and partially

View of Chamber in Maeshow.

filled up with rubbish. The form of the letters of which the inscriptions are composed is that of the later class of Norse Runes, "which," says Professor Munch, "are never older than A.D. 1100 at least." The majority of the inscriptions are such as men seeking the shelter or concealment of the "broken how" might scribble from mere idleness. One gives the Runic alphabet. A number of others are simple memoranda consisting of the name of a man and the statement that he "hewed this" or "carved these runes." But one of the longer inscriptions supplies the important information that "the Jorsala-farers broke open the Orkahaug in the lifetime of the blessed earl." This seems to imply that the inscription was carved after the death of " the blessed earl" Rögnvald, or subsequent to 1158. The Jorsala-farers who accompanied him from Norway in 1152 remained a considerable time in Orkney before the expedition was ready, and as we learn from the Saga their conduct during that time was such as would naturally result from the enforced idleness of a numerous body of rough and uncontrolled adventurers. The

RUBBING FROM MAESHOW TUMULUS.

"breaking of a how" in the hope of finding treasure was a common exploit among the Northmen. It seems to have been done sometimes also as a proof of courage, for the bravest were not altogether void of superstitious fears. From another part of the inscription we gather that the Jorsala-farers who broke the Orkahaug were disappointed in the hope of finding treasure, as it had been previously carried away. In all probability they were not the first who had been tempted by the magnitude of the monument to try the venture. On one of the buttresses, long slabs inserted in the corners of the chamber, is carved a cross, and on another a dragon, similar in style to that in the tomb of King Gorm the Old at Jellinge in Denmark, and bearing also some resemblance to one sculptured on the Runic stone dug up in St. Paul's Churchyard, London, and to another at Hunestad in Scania. The tomb of King Gorm is dated about the middle of the 10th century. Rafn assigns the stone dug up in London to about the middle of the 11th century; while the Hunestad example is assigned to about 1150, which is close on the date of Earl Rögnvald's expedition to the Holy Land, which brought the Jorsala-farers to Orkney.

Among the names thus carved on the stones of Maeshow are those of Ingibiorg, Ingigerd, Thorer, Helgi, Ingi, and Arnfinn. All these are names of persons who are mentioned in the Saga as living in Earl Rögnvald's time, and several of whom were closely connected with him. Ingigerd, his daughter, was married to Eric Slagbrellir, and they had a daughter named Ingibiorg. Helgi was a particular friend of Earl Rögnvald's. Arnfinn was taken prisoner by Earl Harald the morning after he and his men had spent the Yule-feast day at Orkahaug on his way to surprise Earl Erlend.[1] There is nothing, however, to identify any of these names with certainty as the names of the persons mentioned in the Saga. But the fact that the name Orkahaug, which only occurs once in the Saga, is not known to occur anywhere else except in the inscription carved on the walls of Maeshow, referring to the breaking open of the tumulus, is interesting in more ways than one. It shows that the Norsemen were ignorant of the origin of the tumulus, which they knew only as the Orka-haug[2] or "mighty how." In one of the inscrip-

---

[1] See Chap. xci.

[2] The first part of the word seems analogous to the last part of our own Carling-wark, indicating astonishment at the amount of labour required for the rearing of such a structure.

tions the writer assigns its construction to the sons of Lodbrok, which is equivalent to saying that its origin was quite unknown [1] to them.

About a mile to the south-west of Maeshow, and scattered over the ness or tongue of land separating the loch of Stennis from the sea, is a remarkable group of stone circles and tumuli.[2] The largest of the circles, the "Ring of Brogar," having a diameter of 366 feet, encloses an area of 2½ acres.

Ring of Brogar, from the south-west.

It is surrounded by a trench 29 feet broad and 6 feet deep. Within the enclosure thirteen stones of the great circle still remain standing, the stumps of thirteen more are visible, and ten are lying prostrate. The original number of the stones, says Captain Thomas, on the presumption that they were placed at nearly equal distances apart, would have been sixty, so that twenty-four have been entirely obliterated. The highest stone stands almost 14 feet above the surface of the ground, and the lowest is about 6 feet, the average being from 8 to 10 feet. It is difficult to realise the amount of laborious effort expended in the construction of a work like this, which does not appeal to the eye like the magnitude of the great mounds

---

[1] In his recent work on Rude Stone Monuments of all Countries (London : John Murray, 1872), Mr. Ferguson suggests that Maeshow may have been erected for Earl Havard, who fell at Stennis about A.D. 970. But apart from its Celtic structural character, if it had been Earl Havard's tomb his countrymen could scarcely have so completely forgotten the fact in the short space of 200 years.

[2] The most detailed account of these is to be found in an elaborate paper on the Celtic Antiquities of Orkney, by Captain F. W. L. Thomas, R.N., in the Archæologia, vol. xxxiv.

around it. But when one reflects on what is implied in the
transportation and erection of these great stones, and the
excavation of a ditch round them of 10 yards wide, 2 yards
deep, and 366 yards long, it loses none of its magnificence in
comparison with the more imposing monuments.

The smaller circle, called the "Ring of Stennis," is more
clearly monumental than the Ring of Brogar, as it contains

Ring of Stennis and Cromlech, from the northward.

the remains of a cromlech within it. It seems to have consisted originally of twelve stones placed round the circumference of a circle of about 100 feet in diameter, and surrounded by a deep and broad trench with a circumscribing
mound, now nearly obliterated. Only two stones of the circle
remain standing, and a third lies prostrate. Peterkin states

Ring of Stennis, from the westward.

that some were thrown down and removed by the tenant of
the adjoining lands in 1814. The cromlech is also thrown
down, but one of the supports of the massive capstone is still
standing, and the capstone, which lies beside it, is 9 feet long
by 6 feet broad.

The Ring of Bookan is a circular space 136 feet in

diameter, surrounded by a trench 44 feet broad and 6 feet deep. There are upwards of twenty tumuli, some of them very large, in the immediate vicinity.

In the Saga of Olaf, Tryggvi's son, Stennis is mentioned as the place where Havard, eldest of the five sons of Earl Thorfinn Hausakliuf, was slain in battle with his sister's son Einar. The Saga says:[1]—"Havard was then at Stæinsnes in Hrossey. There it was they met, and there was a hard battle, and it was not long till the Earl fell. The place is now called Havard's *teigr*." Teigr is an individual's share, or allotment, of the tun or town-land, and the expression might be taken to mean rather that Havard was buried by simple inhumation than that there was a cairn or tumulus raised over him, in which case it would have been known as Havard's How. But the name of Havard was never connected with the great tumulus known as Maeshow, and if he was buried in a tumulus at all, it is more likely that his corpse was burnt with the customary ceremonies of that heathen time and his ashes placed in a great stone urn. The grave-mounds of the Viking period in Norway prove this to have been then the common practice. Such a mound, enclosing such an urn, was opened at Stennis by Mr. Farrer, M.P., in 1853. This tumulus, if not Havard's, was apparently Norse, and being the largest in the neighbourhood of Stennis, must have been that of a person of great distinction.

The fact that the Norsemen at this early period (about A.D. 970) called this place Steins-ness, shows that it was known to them, only as it is to us, as the ness of the monumental stones. If they had had anything to do with the erection of any of these monuments, in all probability we should have had some incidental record of the fact in one or other of the Sagas.

[1] Flateyjarbók (Christiania, 1860-68), vol. i. p. 225. See the translation in the Appendix, p. 208.

XII. MOUSA AND THE PICTISH TOWERS.

The little island of Mousa (the Mosey of the Saga), lying off the Mainland of Shetland, is interesting as containing the best preserved specimen of the "towers of defence," which were the strongholds of the native inhabitants previous to the Norse invasion.

The tower of Mousa, of which a view is here given, consists of a circular dry-built wall, 15 feet thick at the base, enclosing an area or circular court 30 feet in diameter, and open to the sky, so as to admit light to the ranges of windows which open from the galleries towards the interior. The doorway leading through the wall into this interior court is the only opening to the outside of the tower. From the court other openings in the wall give access to small ovoid chambers in the thickness of the wall on the ground-floor, and to a stair which ascends to the upper galleries. Above the chambers on the ground-floor the wall is carried up hollow, or rather there are two concentric walls with a space of about 3½ feet between them, which is divided into storeys or galleries by horizontal courses of transverse slabs, which bind the two walls together. Thus each of these courses of horizontal slabs forms the roof of the gallery beneath it, and serves as a floor to the one above it.

These singularly-constructed towers were once thickly planted over the whole of the northern mainland of Scotland, as well as over the most of the Northern and Western Isles.[1] A number of them have been excavated of late years, and the results of these excavations[2] furnish us with interesting evidences of the conditions of life among the people who lived in them. The relics that have been obtained from them have no connection as a class with those that are usually found in the cisted graves and chambered tombs of earlier times.[3] But judging from the general character of their included remains, the people who lived in these towers were possessed of a considerable degree of civilisation. There is abundant evidence that they were not only expert hunters and fishers, but that they kept flocks and herds, grew grain and ground it by hand-mills,[4] practised the arts of spinning and weaving, had ornaments of gold of curious workmanship, and were not unskilled workers in bronze and iron. Their pottery was rude, but not ruder than the pottery manufactured and used for common or domestic purposes in some of the islands of Scot-

---

[1] The following enumeration of the known sites of the "Pictish Towers," Borgs, or Brochs, will give some idea of their number and distribution. In Shetland there are, in the island of Unst, 7 ; in Whalsay, 3 ; in Yell, 9 ; in Fetlar, 4 ; in Mainland and its outlying islets, 51 ; in Foula, 1—total, 75. In Orkney, in the island of North Ronaldsay, 2 ; in Papa Westray, 2 ; in Westray, 5 ; in Sanday, 9 ; in Eday, 1 ; in Stronsay, 3 ; in Shapinsay, 1 ; in Gairsay, 1 ; in Rousay, 3 ; in Mainland, 35 ; in South Ronaldsay, 4 ; in Hoy, 1 ; in Hunday, 1 ; in Burray, 2—total, 70. In Caithness, 79. In Sutherland, 60. In Lewis and Harris, 38. In Skye, 30. (For detailed descriptions of Mousa, and many others of these Towers, and lists of their sites, so far as known, see the Archæologia Scotica, "Transactions of the Scottish Society of Antiquaries," vol. v.)

[2] Detailed accounts of these are printed in the Proceedings and Transactions of the Society of Antiquaries of Scotland.

[3] No instance of a flint arrow-point, a flint celt, a polished stone axe, or perforated stone hammer, has yet been found in a Broch or "Pictish Tower."

[4] As the people of the islands did universally to a comparatively recent period, and as in some of the islands they do to this day.

land within the present century. It is true that silver denarii of the Roman Emperors Antoninus, Trajan, and Vespasian, have been found in the outbuildings connected with the Broch or "Pictish Tower" of Lingrow at Scapa in Orkney; but it is to be noticed that upwards of 4000 of these Roman denarii have been found in Scandinavia, where the Romans never were, and found so often associated with relics of the Viking period as to suggest that they were carried thither some centuries after their dates.

The Tower of Mousa, Moseyjar-borg, is twice mentioned by the Saga writers. The earliest notice occurs in the Saga of Egill Skalagrimson, the warrior-poet, and refers to a period about A.D. 900. It is there stated that Bjorn Brynulfson, fleeing from Norway with Thora Roald's daughter, because his father would not allow him to celebrate his marriage with her, was shipwrecked on the island of Mousa, landed his cargo, and lived in the Borg through the winter, celebrating his marriage in it, and afterwards sailed for Iceland. The second notice of Mousa,[1] singularly enough, occurs on an occasion somewhat similar to this, when Earl Erlend Ungi fled from Orkney with Margaret, the widow of Maddad, Earl of Athole, and was besieged in the Borg by Earl Harald (Maddadson), who was displeased at the prospect of having Erlend for a step-father.

XIII. Remains of the Northmen.

Turning from the pages of the Saga to the scenes of the events which it records, we find, both in the topography and traditions of the localities, and in the customs and characteristics of the people, abundant evidence of the substantial truth of the narrative.

The range of territory possessed and occupied by the Norsemen may still be distinguished on the map of Scotland by the prevalence of Norse place-names. In Shetland and

---

[1] See the Saga, p. 161.

Orkney the topography is altogether Norse. In Caithness and Sutherland there is a core of Celtic topography in the central mountain districts, while the Norse names spread out through the valleys, forming a broad fringe along the seaboard, and occupying the whole angle of lowland Caithness. But south of Ekkialsbakki they rapidly thin out, and finally disappear, with a few outlying instances, in Moray. The permanent dominions of the Northmen in the mainland of Scotland were limited to the earldom proper, the southern boundary of which was the Kyle of Sutherland. The Saga says they conquered the country as far south as Ekkialsbakki; and though they sometimes extended their power over parts of Ross and Moray, and even made a raid on one occasion as far south as Fife, they made no permanent lodgment south of the Moray Firth, and their presence in Ross has but slightly affected the topography between the Kyle of Sutherland and the Beauly Firth.

In the Hebrides the Norse names, though much disguised by contact with the Celtic, still form a considerable if not a preponderating element in the topography, and their old Norse name, " Sudreyar," still survives in the title of the Bishop of Sodor and Man. Along the western seaboard of the Scottish mainland, from Cape Wrath to the Mull of Kintyre, the Northmen have left their traces more sparsely, but very distinctly, upon the topography. In Bute, Arran, and the Cumbraes, and on the shores of the Solway Firth, the topography also shows the influence of the Northern element, exerted during the existence of the Norse " Kingdom of Man and the Isles."

There are many remnants of the older usages[1] in the peculiar local customs; and in the characteristics of the people of the Northern Isles there are also, of necessity, many striking resemblances to those of the Scandinavian race. The elucidation of these, however, would lead into a field far too wide to

---

[1] Scat still remains the Orkney grievance. "Scalds" were got rid of in the 17th century, having been then solemnly abolished by the kirk-session of Kirkwall, on pain of 40s. penalty and four hours in the cuckstool, as slanderers and persons offensive to their neighbours.

be entered on here. The language of the early colonists, which must have survived as long as the Islands were governed "according to the Norse law-book and the ancient usages," seems to have died out rapidly after they were transferred to Scottish rule. Yet Jo. Ben found it existing in Rendal in Orkney in 1529 ; and it is stated[1] that in 1593 a clergyman, named Magnus Norsk, who was ordained to a Shetland parish, went to Norway to learn the Norse language, in order to qualify himself for his ministry, because the Shetlanders at that time understood no other tongue. Even so late as 1774, Low found people in Foula who could repeat the Lord's Prayer in Norse, and he gives thirty-five stanzas of an old Norse ballad which he took down from oral recitation. In the Faroe Isles a large number of these ballads and metrical tales have been collected.[2] There can be no doubt that they were equally common in the neighbouring island groups, but no literary antiquary possessed of the requisite knowledge seems to have visited Shetland and Orkney in time to rescue them from oblivion.

The curious literary fragment, taken down phonetically by Low, who was completely ignorant of the language, is plainly akin to the old Scandinavian *Kœmpeviser*. The story is based on the *Sörlathattr*, one of the scenes of which is laid in the island of Hoy. The main incidents of the older poem

---

[1] Fasti Eccles. Scot. v. p. 441. This statement must be taken *cum grano salis*. There can be no doubt, however, that the old language was in use in Shetland at that date. The latest known document in the Norse language, written in Shetland, is dated 1586, and among those mentioned in it is " Mons Norsko minister i Jella"—Magnus Norsk, minister in Yell. (Mem. de Soc. Antiq. du Nord, 1850-60, p, 96.)

[2] See Lyngbye's Faeroiske Qvæder, with Muller's Introduction : Randers, 1822. The old man, William Henry, of Guttorm, in Foula, from whom Low took down the Shetland ballad, spoke to him of " three kinds of poetry used in Norn and recited or sung by the old men—viz., the Ballad, the Vysie or Vyse, now commonly sung to dancers, and the simple song. By the account he gave of the matter, the first seems to have been valued chiefly for its subject, and was commonly repeated in winter by the fireside ; the second seems to have been used in public gatherings, now only sung to the dance ; and the third at both." (Low's MS.)

are as follow :—Hedin, a prince of Serkland, had sworn mutual brotherhood with Hogni, King of Denmark. Nothing occurred to disturb their friendship until Hogni went on a war expedition. Hedin, wandering in the woods, fell in with a sorceress, from whom he received a magic philtre to enable him to win the love of Hilda, Hogni's daughter. The result was that he ran off with her in a splendid ship belonging to Hogni, and made for Serkland. When Hogni came home he set off in pursuit, and came up with them at the island of Hoy. There they both landed with their men, and a furious battle commenced. Odin (who enjoyed a good fight) cast a spell upon the combatants, so that they were obliged to fight on without ceasing, until a Christian should come who should have the hardihood to mingle in the fray, of which Hilda was doomed to be all the time an agonised spectator. At last Olaf Tryggvi's son came to the Orkneys, and Ivar Liomi, one of his men who landed in Hoy, went into the fight and broke the spell, killed Hedin and Hogni, and bore off the prize.[1]

The story of the Shetland ballad is that Hiluge, a young nobleman at the court of Norway, made love to the king's daughter Hildina, and was rejected by her, though her father supported his pretensions to her hand. When the king and Hiluge were away at the wars, an Earl of Orkney came to Norway, and found such favour with Hildina that she consented to fly with him to the Orkneys. When the king and Hiluge returned and discovered what had happened in their absence, they set sail, with a great host, in pursuit of the fugitives. Hildina persuaded the earl to go unarmed to meet her father, and ask for his pardon and peace. The king was pleased to forgive him, and to grant his consent to their union.

---

[1] In the Stockholm edition of Snorro's Edda, it was Hilda, by her enchantments, who raised the slain, as fast as they fell, to renew the combat, and the episode of Ivar Liomi and the Christian additions do not occur. Allusions to Hogni's daughter Hilda occur in the stanzas of Eyvind Skaldaspiller (Saga of Harald Harfagri, cap. 13), and in those of Einar Skalaglum (Harald Grafeld's Saga, cap. 6, and Olaf Tryggvason's Saga, cap. 18).

But now Hiluge, by artfully working on the king's mind, stirs up his latent wrath against the earl, and induces him to revoke his consent. The result is, that he decides that Hiluge and the earl shall meet in single combat, and fight it out to the death of one or other. Hiluge was victorious ; and, not content with the death of his enemy, he cut off his head and cast it into Hildina's lap with taunting words. Hildina answered his taunts boldly, and conceived a bloody revenge. But she must now follow him to Norway, where he renewed his courtship. Ere long she seemed to relent, and gave him her promise, but besought her father to grant her this boon, that she herself should fill out the first wine-cup at the bridal. Her request was granted. The guests came, the feast was set, and Hildina filled up the wine-cups for them. The wine was drugged, and they were all cast into a deep sleep, from which nothing could awake them. Hildina now caused her father to be carried forth, and set fire to the house. Hiluge, awaking in the midst of the burning, cried out for mercy. Hildina replied that she would give him the same mercy as he had given to her earl, and left him to perish in the flames.

The dialect of the ballad resembles that which prevailed in Norway in the middle of the 15th century, but presents several peculiarities of local origin. The allusions in it to St. Magnus show that it cannot be older than the 12th century in its present form, although the story of Hedin and Hogni, on which it appears to have been founded, belongs to the heathen time.

Looking at the number of Runic monuments in the island of Man,[1] and the beauty of their workmanship, it certainly seems surprising that none of these characteristic works of northern art should have survived in the Orkneys.[2] Previous

[1] For descriptions and readings of these see Munch's Chronicon Manniæ, Christiania, 1860 ; Cumming's Runic and other Monumental Remains in the Isle of Man, London, 1857 ; and Worsaae's Danes and Northmen, London, 1852.

[2] It is no less singular to find a Rune-inscribed stone so far up the valley of the Spey as Knockando in Morayshire. See Sculpt. Stones of Scotland, i. p. 61.

to the discovery of the inscriptions in Maeshow, the only
Rune-inscribed monument known within the
bounds of the ancient earldom was the stone
in the churchyard of Crosskirk, Northmavine,
Shetland, described by Low, which reads
(according to his imperfect copy) "Bid pray
for the soul of ——," and consequently
belongs to the Christian time. That there
were similar monuments in other places, however, is shown by the recent discovery of a
Runic fragment at Aithsvoe, Cunningsburgh,
Shetland.[1] It is a mere fragment of the ter-
minal part of a monumental inscription, incised on the edge of the stone, consisting of
the letters KVIMIK, which Professor Stephens
reads as the concluding part of the customary
formula, "—— hewed me," *i.e.* carved this stone.

But perhaps the most interesting and suggestive remains of the Northmen are those
that have been from time to time recovered
from the soil which they made their own
—the relics which were actually possessed by
the men and women of the Saga time ; the
weapons they used, and the ornaments they
wore. In the grave-mounds of the heathen
period, the warrior Viking still lies as he was
laid, with his shield at his shoulder, and his
sword ready to his hand.

The sword here figured, which is of a distinctively Scandinavian type, was dug up
in making the railway near Gorton, in
Morayshire, and is now in the museum of the Society of

---

[1] This fragment, which is now in the museum of the Society of Antiquaries
of Scotland, is figured and described by Professor George Stephens of Copenhagen, in the " Illustreret Tidende " for 20th July 1873, and will be included
in the third volume of his great work on the Runic monuments of Scandinavia
and England, now preparing for the press.

Antiquaries of Scotland. It is 35 inches in length, of excellent workmanship, damascened along the centre of the blade, and the pommel and recurved guard are beautifully inlaid with silver. A number of fragments of shield-bosses and broken swords, from Orkney graves, are also in the museum. The swords are chiefly of the older form, with straight guard and massive square or triangular pommel. In one of the

interments at Westray the scabbard-tip here figured was found, and in others the bones of the dog and horse were found along with the human skeleton, indicating the continuance in Orkney of the sepulchral rites which prevailed in the heathen time in Norway.

For at least a century and a half after the establishment of the Norse earldom in Orkney and Shetland, the heathen Norsemen practised the burial customs which they had brought with them from Norway. Sigurd, Eystein's son, the first Earl of Orkney, was buried in a cairn on Ekkialsbakki, (and his grave-mound was known as Sigurd's How (*Siward-hoch*) in the 12th century,[1]) and Torf Einar caused his men to rear a cairn over the remains of Halfdan Hálegg, the son of Harald Harfagri, whom he offered to Odin in Rinansey.

A vivid picture of the ceremonies attending the burial of a Norse chief of the 10th century is preserved in the narrative of an eye-witness, in the work of an Arab geographer;[2] and

---

[1] See the note at p. 107 of the Saga.

[2] "Description by Ahmed Ibn Fozlan (an eye-witness) of the ceremonies attending the incremation of the dead body of a Norse chief, written in the early part of the 10th century. Translated from Holmboe's Danish version of the Arabic original, with notes on the origin of cremation and its continuance, by Joseph Anderson, Keeper of the Museum." Printed in the Proceedings of the Society of Antiquaries of Scotland, vol. ix.

all its details are amply confirmed by the contents of the grave-mounds of the period. Ahmed Ibn Fozlan, being in the country on the upper part of the Volga (then occupied by the Norsemen), as ambassador from the Caliph Al Moktader (A.D. 907-932), resolved to see for himself whether what he had heard of their burial customs was true. A great chief among the Norsemen had just died, and Ibn Fozlan describes, with curious minuteness of detail, the strange things he witnessed on the occasion. He gives a most characteristic picture of the drinking habits of the Northmen. "This nation," he says, "is much given to wine and drink, by day and night, and it is not uncommon for one or another of them to die with beakers in their hands. When a chieftain dies, his family ask his maids (concubines) and men-servants, ' Which of you will die with him ?' One of them will say, ' I,' and by this promise he is bound, and cannot revoke it. If he should desire to do so, he is not permitted." It is mostly the maids who are willing to be thus sacrificed, says Ibn Fozlan, and on this occasion it was one of them who offered to die with her lord. She was accordingly given in charge to the other servants, who were to indulge her in every wish till the day of her sacrifice ; and he adds, that "every day she drank, sang, was lively and merry." Meantime the dead man had been laid in a temporary grave, and strong drink, fruits, and musical instruments placed beside him, as if to relieve the tedium of his confinement until the completion of the preparations for the funeral rites. A splendid suit of clothing was prepared for him, his ship was hauled up on the strand, and placed on four posts erected for the purpose. A bed was prepared in the midst of the deck, with a tent-like canopy over it, and covered with gold-embroidered cloth. In the preparation of this bed there comes on the scene an old hag, "whom they called the dead man's angel." It was she who took charge of the making of the dead man's clothing and all needful arrangements, and she it was also who was to put the girl to death. " I saw her," says Ibn Fozlan ; " she was sallow and stern." While the " dead man's angel " was arranging the bed, the multitude were away at the temporary grave, disinterring the corpse. They clothed him in the rich garments provided for the occasion, and then bore him to the ship, where he was laid in state under the canopy. " So they laid him on the mattress, and stayed him up with pillows, then brought the strong drink, the fruits, and odoriferous herbs, and set them by his side, placing bread, meat, and onions also before him. Then came a man forward with a dog, hewed it into two portions, and cast them into the ship. So brought they all the dead man's weapons and laid them by his side. Then they led forth two horses, made them run till they were covered with sweat, then hewed them in pieces with the sword, and cast the flesh into the ship. So also they brought forth two oxen, hewed them in pieces, and cast them into the ship. Next they came with a cock and hen, slew them, and cast them also into the ship." In the meantime the woman who was to die kept going backwards and forwards in and out of the tent. At last they led her away to an object which they had made in the form of the framework of a door—two posts, with a cross piece on the top, or, as is suggested, a substitute for a trilithon. " She set her feet on the palms of men's hands, stepped up on the frame, and said some words in their tongue, after which they made her stand down. Then they lifted her up a second and third time, and she went through the same ceremony. Now they handed her a hen, the head of which she cut off and cast away, but the body they cast into the ship. I asked my interpreter what it was that the woman had said. He answered, she said the first time, ' Lo ! I see my father and my mother ;' the second time, ' Lo ! here I see seated all my deceased relations ;' the third time, ' Lo ! here I see my master seated in paradise—paradise, beautiful and green, my master surrounded by his men and his menials ; he calls for me ; bring me to him.' Thereupon they conveyed her to the ship. She took the bracelets from her arms, and gave them to the crone whom they called 'the dead man's angel;' and the rings from her ankles, and gave them to the two young girls who had attended her, and who were 'the dead man's angel's daughters.' Then came men with shields and staves, and brought her a beaker of strong drink. She sang a song, and drank it out. Folk said to me that she thereby took leave of her friends. They reached her a second beaker. She took it, and sang a long time. The old hag bade her hasten to empty it, and go into the tent where her dead master was. I watched her; she was out of herself. In attempting to go into the tent she stuck by the head in the space between the tent and the ship. The old hag caught hold of her by the head and dragged her in with her, while the men commenced to beat their shields with the staves, that her shrieks might not be heard, and so frighten other girls, and make them unwilling to die with their lords." The sequel is too horrible to be given as it stands in the old Arab's plain-spoken narrative. A cord was finally wound round her neck, at the ends of which two men pulled, while the "dead man's angel" stabbed her to the heart with a broad-bladed knife. Then the relatives of the dead man set fire to the pile. A storm that was just beginning to rage fanned the flames, and drove them aloft to a great height. A Norseman who was standing by said to Ibn Fozlan "You Arabs are fools. You take the man whom you most have loved and honoured, and put him down into the earth, where vermin and worms devour him. We, on the contrary, burn him up in a twinkling, and he goes straight to paradise." After the pile was consumed to ashes they raised a great mound over the spot, and set up on it a pillar made of a tree-trunk, on which they carved the names of the dead man and of their king.

The burial usages, however, were not always the same. Great men were buried with the pomp and ceremony befitting their rank, while meaner men were simply reduced to ashes and inhumed in a clay urn, or in a stone pot, not unfrequently in the stone cooking-kettle that had served them when in life.[1] This burial in stone urns, or in cooking vessels of steatite, is of common occurrence in the grave-mounds of the Viking period in Norway, and is also not unfrequently found in Orkney and Shetland.

Associated with such burials in Norway there are occasionally found the peculiar brooches which are characteristic of the later Pagan time.[2] Although they occur perhaps more frequently with unburnt burials, they link on with the custom of cremation. Thus they afford a valuable index to the chronology of these remains in Scotland, because the Pagan period of the Scandinavian occupation may be said to be limited to the time between the expedition of Harald Har-

fagri and the battle of Clontarf (872-1014). These brooches are found in Scandinavian graves of this period, in Scotland, England, Ireland, Normandy, Russia, and Iceland—in short, wherever the heathen Vikings effected a settlement. In Scotland they have been found in various places—in Sutherland, in Caithness, in Orkney, in the Hebrides, and even in remote St. Kilda. The specimen here figured, which is now

---

[1] A large number of these stone kettles, made of steatite, and furnished with iron "bows," exactly like those of our modern cast-iron pots, are preserved in the Christiania Museum, filled, as they were found, with the burned bones of the former owners. Sometimes the sword of the owner is found twisted and broken, and laid on the top of the bones.

[2] There are upwards of 400 of these brooches in the museum at Stockholm, nearly half as many in Christiania, and a large number in Copenhagen.

in the Museum of the Society of Antiquaries of Scotland, is one of a pair found in a stone cist on a mound which covered the remains of a " Pictish Tower" at Castletown in Caithness.[1] They are usually found in pairs, one near each shoulder of the skeleton. This corresponds with the statement of an ancient Arab writer, that the Norse women used to wear such brooches in pairs on their breasts.[2]

The most remarkable discovery of these characteristic Scandinavian interments that has hitherto occurred in Scotland was made in the island of Westray, Orkney, in 1849, by Mr. William Rendall.[3] A number of graves were found in the sandy links near Pierowall (the Hofn of the Saga), in some of which were swords and shield-bosses, indicating that the skeletons were those of men. But in one a pair of tortoise or shell-shaped brooches and a trefoil ornament were the only objects found with the skeleton. In another, a pair of these brooches were found on the breast, and a pair of combs, of the

form here figured, lay on either side of the neck, apparently as they had fallen out of the hair. In a third, a pair of brooches, a pair of combs, and a bronze pin, were found. It appears from these examples that the brooches undoubtedly belonged to women, and that the warriors were usually buried with sword and shield and "panoply of war ;" and, as we read in Ibn Fozlan's account, the dog and the horse of the deceased appear also to have been sacrificed at the grave, and

---

[1] The other one is in the museum at Copenhagen, and is figured in Worsaae's Danes and Northmen, p. 255.

[2] Mem. de la Soc. Antiq. du Nord, 1840-44, p. 79.

[3] For full details of this remarkable group of interments, see Wilson's Prehistoric Annals of Scotland, vol. ii. p. 303, and Journal of the British Archæological Association, vol. ii. p. 329.

interred with him, in Orkney as well as on the banks of the Volga.

But we meet with few memorials of the daily life of the Norsemen beyond those which have been buried with them in the early period of their occupation of the Islands. Christianity abolished the custom of burying such relics with the dead, and for the remains of the Christian period we must look to the yet unexcavated sites of the *skális* and homesteads of which we read in the Saga. It would be equally interesting to the archæologist, and instructive to the historian, to be able to compare the relics from such sites as those of Kolbein Hruga's castle in Weir, the castle of which Blán was the keeper in Damsey, or the *skáli* of Swein Asleifson at Langskail in Gairsay, with the extensive collections obtained in recent years from the "Pictish Towers" of Orkney, which have given us such suggestive glimpses of the domestic life of the period preceding the Norse occupation.

It gives a curious feeling of reality to the ancient legends when we can thus handle the blades and bucklers of which we read such stirring stories, and remember that it was because the Norse sword was then the longest, and the Norse arm the strongest, that we now read the earliest chapters of the history of northern Scotland in the guise of an Iceland Saga.

CHRONOLOGICAL TABLE.

795. First appearance of the Norse Vikings in the Western Seas. They plunder the Isle of Rachrin.

798. Invasion of the Isle of Man by the Norsemen. Inispatrick burned.

802. I Columbkill burned by the Norsemen.

806. I Columbkill again plundered by the Norsemen, and sixty-eight men of the monastery slain.

807. First invasion of the mainland of Ireland by the Norsemen.

815. Turgesius (Thorkell ?), chief of the invading Northmen, establishes himself as king of the foreigners in Ireland, making Armagh the capital of the kingdom.

824. Bangor, in the north of Ireland, the seat of the monastery of St. Comhgall, burned, and the bishop and clergy slain by the Northmen.

843. Union of the Picts and Scots under Kenneth M'Alpin, founder of the Scottish dynasty.

853. Arrival of Olaf the White in Ireland. He seizes Dublin, establishes himself there as king, makes an expedition to Scotland, and besieges and takes Dumbarton.

872. Harald Harfagri becomes sole King of Norway ; makes an expedition against the western Vikings, who have established their viking station in Orkney, drives them from their haunts, and subdues Shetland, Orkney, the Hebrides, and Man. He gives Orkney and Shetland, as an earldom of Norway, to Rögnvald, Earl of Mœri, father of Hrolf (Rollo), the conqueror of Normandy.

875. Earl Sigurd Eysteinson, who had received the earldom of Orkney from his brother Rögnvald, Earl of Mœri, forms an alliance with Thorstein the Red, son of Olaf the White, King of Dublin. They invade the northern mainland of Scotland, and subdue Caithness and Sutherland as far as Ekkialsbakki. Thorstein the Red is shortly afterwards killed in Caithness ; and Earl Sigurd dies, and is buried under a cairn at Ekkialsbakki.

A.D.

893. Einar (Torf Einar) slays Halfdan Hálegg, one of the sons of Harald Harfagri, and buries him under a cairn in North Ronaldsay.

933. Death of Harald Harfagri. Eirik Bloodyaxe, his son, becomes King of Norway. About this time the name "Scotia" and "Scotland," previously applied to Ireland, is first given to North Britain, which had formerly been called Caledonia, Pictavia, or Alban.

950. Fall of King Eirik Bloodyaxe, and of Arnkell and Erlend, sons of Torf Einar, and Earls of Orkney, in battle in England.

963. Thorfinn Hausakliuf Earl of Orkney. The sons of Eirik Bloodyaxe arrive in Orkney.

980. Sigurd Hlodverson becomes Earl of Orkney.

986. I Columbkill plundered by the Norsemen, and the abbot and fifteen of the clerics slain.

992. Olaf Tryggvi's son, while on a roving expedition, is baptized by a hermit in the Scilly Isles.

995. Olaf Tryggvi's son becomes King of Norway, and immediately establishes Christianity by the strong hand. Returning from a western cruise, on his way to Norway he finds Earl Sigurd Hlodverson by chance at Osmondwall in the Orkneys, and obliges him to profess Christianity, and to promise to establish the true faith in the Orkneys.

1000. Fall of King Olaf Tryggvi's son at the battle of Swalder in Norway.

1014. Battle of Clontarf, near Dublin, in which Sigurd Hlodverson, Earl of Orkney, fell. Thorfinn, his son, is made Earl of Caithness and Sutherland by Malcolm II., King of Scots, his maternal grandfather.

1015. Olaf Haraldson (afterwards St. Olaf) becomes King of Norway.

1018. Battle of Ulfreksfiord, in which Earl Einar is vanquished by Eyvind Urarhorn and King Conchobhar.

1019. Einar (Wrymouth), Earl of Orkney, slain by Thorkel Fostri at Sandwick, in Deerness, Orkney.

1020. The Earls Thorfinn and Brusi acknowledge the suzerainty of King Olaf the Holy over the Orkneys.

1028. Olaf the Holy driven from Norway by Canute the Great, King of England and Denmark.

1030. Fall of King Olaf the Holy at the battle of Stiklestad.

1034. Death of Malcolm II., King of Scots. According to the Saga, "Kali Hundason takes the kingdom," and according to the Scottish historians Duncan I. succeeds to the throne in Scot-

A.D. land. Mission of Einar Thambarskelfir and Kalf Arneson to Russia to offer their aid to Magnus, son of King Olaf the Holy, to obtain the throne of Norway.

1035. Magnus the Good, son of Olaf Haraldson (the Holy), succeeds to the throne of Norway, and Rognvald Brusison becomes Earl of Orkney.

1039. Duncan I., King of Scots, slain by Macbeth, who becomes king.

1047. Magnus the Good dies in Denmark, and is succeeded by Harald Sigurdson, surnamed Hardradi.

1050. Einar Thambarskelfir and the sons of Endridi slain in Norway by Harald Hardradi.

1054. Macbeth defeated by Malcolm (Canmore), son of Duncan.

1057. Malcolm Canmore crowned at Scone.

1064. Death of Thorfinn Sigurdson, Earl of Caithness and Orkney. He is succeeded by his sons Paul and Erlend, and his widow, Ingibiorg (according to the Saga) is married to Malcolm Canmore.

1066. Fall of King Harald Sigurdson (Hardradi) at the battle of Stamford Bridge, near York, in which Harald Godwinson was victor. His son Olaf (Kyrre) and the Orkney Earls, Paul and Erlend, who were with him in the battle, receive peace from the conqueror and liberty to return to Orkney. Olaf Kyrre succeeds to the throne of Norway.

1067. Malcolm Canmore marries Margaret, sister of Edgar Atheling.

1093. Malcolm Canmore killed at Alnwick. Death of King Olaf Kyrre, and accession of Magnus Barelegs to the throne of Norway. He makes an expedition to the west, ravages the Scottish coasts, and assists Muirceartach in the capture of Dublin.

1098. King Magnus makes a second expedition to the west, seizes the Earls of Orkney, Paul and Erlend, and sends them both to Norway (where they died); places his own son, Sigurd, over the Orkneys ; and overruns the Hebrides, Kintyre, and Man.

1103. Magnus, King of Norway, slain in Ireland. His son, Sigurd, goes from Orkney to Norway, and succeeds to the kingdom jointly with his brothers Eystein and Olaf. Magnus Erlendson (St. Magnus), and Hakon, Paul's son, succeed to the earldom of Orkney.

1106. Accession of Alexander I. to the throne of Scotland.

1107. King Sigurd (Magnusson) sets out on a pilgrimage to Jerusalem, which occupies him for three years. He is thenceforth called Sigurd, the Jorsala-farer.

1115. Magnus Erlendson (St. Magnus) slain in Egilsay by his cousin Hakon, Paul's son.

A.D.

1124. Death of Alexander I., and accession of David I., King of Scots.

1130. Death of King Sigurd, the Jorsala-farer, and accession to the throne of Norway of King Harald Gilli, an illegitimate son of King Magnus Barelegs, from the Hebrides.

1136. Harald Gilli slain by Sigurd Slembidiakn. Rognvald (Kali) Kolson obtains the earldom of Orkney from Earl Páll, son of Hakon, who is carried off to Athole by Swein Asleifson.

1139. Death of Sigurd Slembidiakn. Visit of Bishop John of Athole to Orkney. Harald Maddadson, son of Maddad, Earl of Athole, shares the earldom of Caithness and Orkney with Earl Rognvald (Kali).

1151. Earl Rognvald and Erling Skakki leave Norway to prepare for their pilgrimage to Jerusalem. The Jorsala-farers winter in Orkney.

1152. Earl Rognvald leaves the Orkneys on his pilgrimage to Jerusalem. King Eystein comes to Orkney from Norway, and seizing Earl Harald Maddadson at Thurso obtains from him an acknowledgment of his suzerainty over the Orkneys.

1153. Death of David I., King of Scotland, and accession of Malcolm the Maiden.

1155. Earl Rognvald returns from Palestine. Erlend Ungi receives Rognvald's mother, Margaret, in marriage, and is shortly afterwards slain by the Earls Rognvald and Harald.

1158. Earl Rognvald slain at Calder in Caithness by Thorbiorn Klerk. Earl Harald becomes sole ruler of Caithness and Orkney.

1165. Malcolm the Maiden dies at Jedburgh, and is succeeded by King William the Lion.

1168. Death of William the Old, first Bishop of Orkney.

1176. Magnus Erlingson becomes King of Norway. Harald Ungi (son of Eirik Slagbrellir by a daughter of Earl Rögnvald) receives from King Magnus the title of earl and half of the Orkneys, and from King William the Lion half of Caithness, and is subsequently defeated and slain in Caithness by Earl Harald Maddadson.

1184. Magnus Erlingson, King of Norway, slain by King Sverrir, who succeeds him.

1188. Death of William II., Bishop of Orkney.

1192. Canonisation of Rognvald (Kali), Earl of Orkney, who was killed by Thorbiorn Klerk.

1194. The Eyjarskeggiar collect forces in Orkney, and attempt to place Sigurd, son of Magnus Erlingson, on the throne of Norway, but are defeated, and nearly all slain, by King Sverrir at Floruvogr, near Bergen.

A.D.

1195. Earl Harald Maddadson, compromised by this expedition, goes to Norway with Bishop Bjarni, lays his head at the king's feet, saying that he is now an old man, and entirely in the king's power. He is pardoned by King Sverrir, but on condition of forfeiting to the crown of Norway the whole of Shetland, which does not again form part of the domain of the Norwegian Earls of Orkney till 1379.

1202. King William the Lion marches north to Eysteinsdal on the borders of Caithness, with a great army, to take revenge for the mutilation of Bishop John, and the expulsion of the deputies of Rognvald Gudrodson from Caithness by Earl Harald. Harald purchases peace by a payment of 2000 merks.

1206. Death of Earl Harald Maddadson. He is succeeded by his surviving sons, John and David. Thorfinn, his eldest son, died in Roxburgh Castle, where he was confined as a hostage, and had been mutilated by King William the Lion.

1214. Death of King William the Lion, and accession of Alexander II. to the throne of Scotland. Death of David, son of Harald Maddadson. His surviving brother John becomes sole Earl of Orkney and Caithness.

1222. Burning of Bishop Adam at Halkirk in Caithness, by the enraged peasantry. The King of Scots caused the hands and feet to be hewed from a number of those who were present at the burning, and many of them died in consequence.

1223. Death of Bishop Bjarni, and consecration of Jofreyr to the see of the Orkneys.

1231. Earl John slain at Thurso. The line of the ancient Norwegian Earls of Orkney having become extinct by his death, King Alexander II. creates Magnus, son of Gilbride, Earl of Angus, Earl of Caithness, and separating Sutherland into another earldom, gives it to William, son of Hugh Freskyn.

1239. Death of Magnus, Earl of Caithness and Orkney.

1243. Death of Gilbert, Bishop of Caithness.

1247. Death of Jofreyr, Bishop of Orkney.

1249. Death of Alexander II., King of Scots, at Kerrera, Argyllshire.

1256. Death of Gilbride II., Earl of Orkney.

1263. Expedition of King Hakon Hakonson, of Norway, to Scotland; he is defeated at Largs, and dies at Kirkwall.

1266. Cession of the Hebrides and Man to Scotland by treaty between Magnus IV., King of Norway, and Alexander III., King of Scotland.

1273. Death of Magnus, son of Gilbride, Earl of Orkney.

A.D.

1276. Magnus, son of Magnus, made Earl of Orkney by King Magnus Hakonson, at Tunsberg.

1281. Marriage of King Eirik Magnusson to Margaret, daughter of King Alexander II. of Scotland.

1283. Death of Margaret, Queen of Norway.

1284. Margaret, infant daughter of Eirik, King of Norway, recognised as heiress to the Scottish throne. Death of Magnus Magnusson, Earl of Orkney.

1286. Death of King Alexander III. of Scotland.

1289. Betrothal of the Princess Margaret, the Maiden of Norway, to Prince Edward of England.

1290. Death of Margaret, the Maiden of Norway, off the coast of Orkney, on her way to Scotland.

1293. Marriage of King Eirik Magnusson of Norway to Isabella, daughter of Robert Bruce, Earl of Carrick.

1300. Appearance at Bergen of the false Margaret, a German woman who gave herself out as the " Maiden of Norway," daughter of King Eirik and Queen Margaret, stating that she had been " sold " by Ingibiorg Erlingsdatter, and spirited away by parties who had an interest in her disappearance.

1301. The false Margaret is burnt as an impostor at Nordness in Bergen, and her husband beheaded.

1310. Death of John, Earl of Orkney.

1312. Treaty of Perth (1266) renewed at Inverness.

1314. Battle of Bannockburn.

1333. Battle of Halidon Hill. Death of Malise, Earl of Stratherne.

1334. Forfeiture of the earldom of Stratherne, and marriage of Isabella, daughter of Malise, Earl of Stratherne, Caithness and Orkney, to William, Earl of Ross. Malise goes to Norway.

1353. Erngisl Suneson, son-in-law of Malise, Earl of Stratherne, made Earl of Orkney.

1375. King Hakon grants the earldom of Orkney for one year to Alexander de Ard, who resigns all his lands in Caithness to King Robert II.

1379. Henry St. Clair made Earl of Orkney and Shetland by King Hakon Magnusson, at Marstrand.

1382. Bishop William of Orkney slain.

1389. Malise Sperra slain near Scalloway by Henry, Earl of Orkney.

1392. Death of Erngisl Suneson.

1397. Union Treaty of Calmar, by which Denmark, Sweden, and Norway, were made one kingdom.

1400 (circa). Death of Earl Henry St. Clair.

1418 (circa). Death of Earl Henry (II.) St. Clair.

A.D.

1420. Bishop Thomas Tulloch made commissioner in the Orkneys for
  the King of Norway.

1423. David Menzies of Wemyss made commissioner in the Orkneys
  for the King of Norway.

1434. William St. Clair made Earl of Orkney.

1468. Contract of marriage between King James III. of Scotland and
  Margaret, Princess of Denmark, and impignoration of the
  islands of Orkney and Shetland for the Princess's dowry.

GENEALOGICAL TABLES.

I. THE NORSE LINE OF THE EARLS OF ORKNEY.

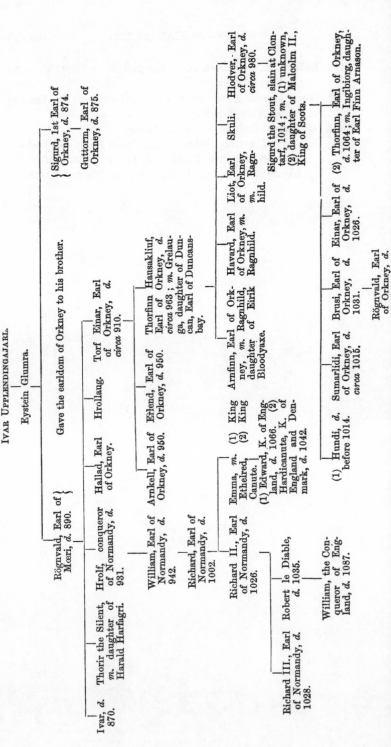

THORFINN, EARL, m. Ingibiorg Arnason.

Paul, Earl of Orkney, d. 1098; m. daughter of Hakon Ivarsson.

Erlend, Earl of Orkney, d. 1098; m. Thora, daughter of Sumarlidi Ospakson.

Hakon, Earl of Orkney, d. circa 1122.

Thora.

Herbiorg.

Ragnhild.

Magnus, Earl of Orkney, slain 1115, canonised 1135.

Erling, slain in Ireland.

Gunnhild, m. Kol, Kali's son.

Cecelia, m. Isak.

Harald Slettmali, d. circa 1127.

Margaret, m. (1) Maddad, Earl of Athole; (2) Erlend Ungi.

Ingibiorg Ragna, m. Sigurd of Westness.

Paul, Earl of Orkney, carried off to Athole by Swein Asleifson.

Rögnvald (Kali Kolsson), Earl of Orkney, d. 1158, canonised 1192.

Ingirid, m. Jon Petrsson.

Sigrid.

Herborg, m. Kolbein Hruga.

Ingigerd, m. Eirik Slagbrellir.

Bjarni, Bishop of Orkney.

Ingibiorg, m. Olaf, King of the Sudreyar.

Harald Maddadson, made Earl of Orkney 1139; d. 1206; m. (1) Afreka, sister of Duncan, Earl of Fife; (2) Gormlath, daughter of Malcolm MacHeth.

Harald Ungi, Earl of Orkney, d. circa 1198.

Magnus Mangi, d. 1184.

Rögnvald.

Ingibiorg.

Elin.

Ragnhild, m. (1) Lifolf Skalli, (2) Gunni Andreson.

Snaekoll Gunnison.

Gudrod, King of Man.

Ragnhild, m. Sumarlid of Argyle and the Isles.

Erlend Ungi, Earl of Orkney, d. 1156.

Rögnvald Gudrodson, d. 1229.

Reginald, Dugald, Angus.

(1.) Thorfin, d. in Roxburgh Castle 1201.

Margaret.

Helena.

Hakon.

David, Earl of Orkney, d. 1214.

John, Earl of Orkney, d. 1231, leaving no male issue.

Gunhild.

Herborg.

Langlif.

(2) Henry, Earl of Ross.

II. THE ANGUS LINE OF THE EARLS OF ORKNEY.

GILBRIDE, Earl of Angus, married a sister or daughter of John, Earl of Orkney, son of Harald Maddadson.

Magnus II., Earl of Orkney and Caithness, *d.* 1239.

Gilbride I., Earl of Orkney and Caithness.

Gilbride II., Earl of Orkney and Caithness, *d.* 1256.

Magnus III., Earl of Orkney and Caithness, *d.* 1275.　　Matilda.

Magnus IV., Earl of Orkney and Caithness, *d.* 1284.

John, Earl of Orkney and Caithness, *d. circa* 1310.

Magnus V., Earl of Orkney and Caithness, *m.* Katharina, *d. circa* 1320.

Margaret, *m.* Simon Fraser, who fell at Halidon Hill, 1333.

Isabella (?) *m.* Malise, Earl of Stratherne, who fell at Halidon Hill, 1333.

III. THE STRATHERNE LINE OF THE EARLS OF ORKNEY.

MALISE, Earl of Stratherne, *m.* Isabella (?), daughter of Magnus, Earl of Orkney.

Isabella (?) *m.* to Sir William St. Clair of Roslin.

Malise, Earl of Stratherne, Caithness, and Orkney, *m.* (1) Johanna, daughter of Sir John Menteith ; (2) Marjory, daughter of Hugh, Earl of Ross ; *d. circa* 1350.

Matilda, *m.* to Wayland (?), de Ard. Alexander de Ard.

Isabella, *m.* to William, Earl of Ross, in 1334.

Agnetta, *m.* to Arngils or Erngisl Suneson, who was made Earl of Orkney 1353.

(?) *m.* to Guttorm Sperra. Malise Sperra, slain at Scalloway by Earl Henry St. Clair, 1389.

Elisabeth, *m.* to Henry St. Clair, Earl of Orkney.

IV. THE ST. CLAIR LINE OF THE EARLS OF ORKNEY.

WILLIAM ST. CLAIR of Roslin *m.* Isabella (?), daughter of Malise, Earl of Stratherne.

David.

Henry, made Earl of Orkney 1379 ; *m.* (1) Elisabeth, daughter of Malise (the younger), Earl of Stratherne, Caithness, and Orkney ; (2) Janet, daughter of Walter Haliburton of Dirleton ; and *d. circa* 1400.

Margaret, *m.* to James of Cragy.

Elisabeth, *m.* to John de Drummond.

Henry, Earl of Orkney, *m.* Egidia Douglas, daughter of Lord William Douglas ; *d. circa* 1418.

John.

William, Earl of Orkney, exchanged his rights to the Earldom of Orkney for the lands of Ravenscraig, 1471.

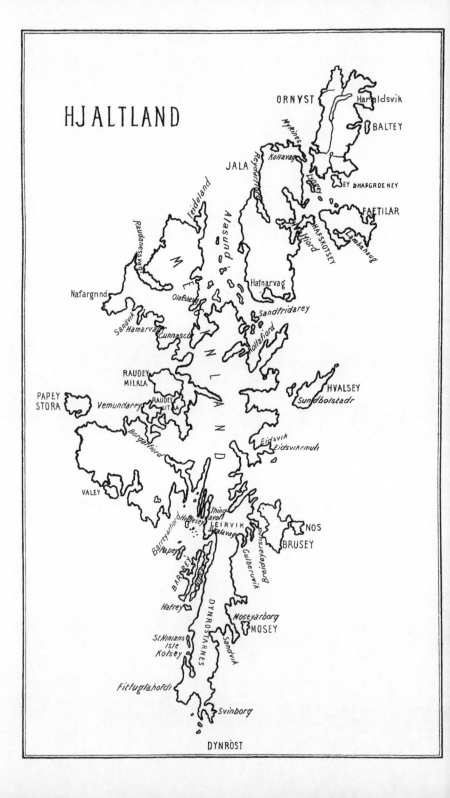

HJALTLAND

ORNYST
Haraldsvik
BALTEY

JALA
Mykines
Kollavag
Reydarfirth

Teideland
Alasund

EY DHAFGROE NEY
FAETILAR

WHAFSKOTSEY
Multfiord
Lambahaug

Raudanessvag

Hafnarvag

Nafargrind
Olafsberg
Sandfridarey

Sandvik
Hamarvagi
Cunnascit
Hollafiord

RAUDEY
MILKLA
HVALSEY
Sundbolstadr

PAPEY
STORA
Vemundarey
RAUDEY
LITLA

Borgarfiord
Eidsvik
Eidsvikrmuli

VALEY

Thing
vavoll
Oth.Olesey
LEIRVIK
Scalavag
NOS
BRUSEY
Barreyarfiord
Gulberwik
Papey
BARREY

Hafrey
DYNROSTARNES
Moseyarborg
MOSEY
St.Ninians
Isle
Kolsey
Sandvik

Fitfuglahofdi
Svinborg

DYNRÖST

ORKNEYAR.

FRIDAREY
(Fair Isle)

about 30 miles N: of
Rinansey

PAPEY
MEIRI
Trollhaena
Kirkja.

RINANSEY

Nautaland
Rekavik
Hofn

VESTREY

Vestfiord

Hreppisnes

FÆREY
EIDEY

KALFR

Ivarshaug
SANDEY

Hellisnes

HROLFSEY
Skebrohead
EVINHELGA
Vesthes
ERJUSUND

Brugh of
Birsay

Ghrists
Kirk
BIRGISHERAD
Birgisá
H R O S S
M e g
Rennadal

EGILSEY

VIGR

GAREKSEY

Hofsnes
Lyngholm

PAPEY MINNI

STRIONSEY

Gja
HJALPANDISEY

Aurridafiord
DAMSEY
Carnes
HELLISEY

Ellidavik
Tanskarunes

AUSTRSKER

Steinsnes
Kirkiuvag
n Knarrarstad
Hafnarvag
Orfiara
Medallands
-hofn

Skalpeid
oGeitaberg

Dyrsund
Sandvik
Dyrnes

Dyrnesmuli
o Brugh of
Deerness

KOLBEINSEY

Straumsnes

GRIMSEY

KALFEY
FÆREY
FLOTEY

Upoland

Rekavik

HAEY

GLUMSHOLM
HUNDEY

Papuli

BORGAREY

Hauesseid
Rognaldsvoe
Papuli.
ROGNVALDSEY
Widivag
Bardsvik
Thordarekra

Vageland

Asmundarvag

SVINEY

P E T L A N D S F I O R D

PETLAND SKER.

Raudabiorg

hofn
STRAUMSEY

Thorsa.

Dungalsbaer

Dungalsnes

Myrkhol

Thrasvik
Lambaborg

ORKNEYINGA SAGA.

CHAPTER I.

OF THE EARLS.

IT is said that' the Orkney Islands were colonised in the days of Harald the Fairhaired,[1] but previously they were a station for Vikings.[2]

The first Earl of the Orkneys was called Sigurd. He was the son of Eystein Glumra (the loud-talking), and brother of Rögnvald, Earl of Moeri.[3]

After Sigurd his son Guttorm ruled one year.

Torf-Einar,[4] son of Earl Rögnvald, succeeded him. He was a man of great power, and was Earl a long time. Hálfdán Hálegg[5] (high-legs) made an expedition against Torf-Einar, and drove him from the Orkneys. Einar returned, and slew Hálfdán in Rinansey.[6] Thereupon King

---

[1] The events narrated in this chapter are told with greater fulness of detail in the extracts from the Flateyjarbók given in the Appendix.

[2] *Vikinga-boeli*, a vik-ing station, or haunt of the sea-rovers, who harried the coasts wherever they could find plunder. From *vik*, a bay or creek, are formed the nouns *viking*, denoting the species of plundering, and *vikingr*, denoting a person engaged in it.

[3] Moeri, a province of Norway, lying southwards of Drontheim (Saga of Harald Harfagri, cap. x). The word signifies a plain bordering on the sea.

[4] "He was called Torf-Einar because he cut peat for fuel." (See Appendix).

[5] A son of Harald Harfagri.

[6] Rinansey, North Ronaldsay. Munch suggests that the form Ronansey implies its derivation from St. Ronan or Ninian, and that the name is therefore older than the Norse colonisation. St. Ninian is often called St. Ringan, and Ringansey seems quite a probable derivation of Rinansey.

B

Harald brought an army over to the Orkneys. Then Einar fled to Scotland. King Harald made the Orkneymen swear oaths of fealty to him for themselves and all their possessions. The Earl and King Harald were afterwards reconciled. He became the King's man, and held the land as a fief from him. He had, however, no tribute to pay, as there was much predatory warfare then in the islands; but he paid the king sixty marks of gold[1] (once for all). After this, King Harald made a raid on Scotland, as is told in the Glumdrapa.[2]

After Torf-Einar, Arnkell, Erlend, and Thorfinn Hausa-kliúf (skull-splitter), his sons, succeeded him. In their days Eirik Blódöx[3] (bloody axe) came over from Norway, and the Earls were his vassals. Arnkell and Erlend fell in battle,[4] but Thorfinn governed the land and became an old man. His sons were Arnfid, Hávard, Lödver, Ljót, and Skúli; their mother was Grélaug, daughter of Earl Dungad (Duncan) in Caithness.[5] Her mother was Gróa, daughter of Thorstein the Red.

In the days of Earl Thorfinn the sons of Eirik Blódöx

[1] This is represented in the Saga of King Harald as a fine exacted by Harald for the death of his son, and paid by the Earl for the *bœndr* or freeholders who surrendered their odal lands to him in consideration of being freed from this payment (see Appendix).

[2] A poem by Thorbiorn Hornklofe, quoted in the Saga of Harald Harfagri.

[3] Son and successor of Harald Harfagri.

[4] They fell in battle in England, with King Eric Bloodyaxe, and "five kings," as told in the Saga of Hakon the Good. The place where this battle was fought has not been satisfactorily identified.

[5] Dungad, called also Dungal, was a native chieftain, Maormor, or "Jarl," in the north-east corner of Caithness, who seems to have considered the policy of conciliation preferable to that of resistance, judging from the intimate relations he formed with the foreigners, marrying the daughter of one, and giving his daughter in marriage to another, of the chiefs of the invaders. His *bœ* or hamlet of residence became on this account so well known to the Norsemen, that they named the district of Dungalsbae (now Duncansbay) by it, and spoke of the headland (now Duncansbay Head) on which it was situated, as Dungalsness, or Duncan's cape. The supposed remains of his castle were seen by Pennant in 1796, and are described by him as the ruins of a circular building, in all probability one of the "burghs" or circular towers so common in the north of Scotland, which seem to have been the defensive habitations of the native Celtic or Pictish population of the period between the 6th and 9th or 10th centuries. It is now a green mound. From the Session Records of the parish it appears that the district retained its ancient name of "Dungasby" down to the beginning of the last century, when it first appears as Duncansbay, and to

arrived from Norway, when they had fled from Earl Hákon, and they did many deeds of violence in the islands. Earl Thorfinn died on a sickbed, and his sons, of whom there are extensive histories, succeeded him. Lödver survived his brothers, and ruled the land alone. His son was Earl Sigurd the Stout; he was a powerful man, and a great warrior.

In his days Olaf, Tryggvi's son, returning from a viking expedition to the west, came to the Orkneys with his men, and seized Earl Sigurd in Rörvág,[1] as he lay there with a single ship. King Olaf offered the Earl to ransom his life on condition that he should embrace the true faith and be baptized; that he should become his man, and proclaim Christianity over all the Orkneys. He took his son Hundi or Hvelp (whelp) as a hostage, and left the Orkneys for Norway, where he became King; and Hundi stayed with him some years, and died there.

After that Earl Sigurd paid no allegiance to King Olaf. He married the daughter of Malcolm, King of Scots,[2] and their son was Earl Thorfinn; his elder sons [by a former marriage] were Sumarlidi, Brúsi, and Einar.

this day it is called "Dungsby" by the older inhabitants. The name of the adjacent district of Canisbay, now applied to the whole parish, is similarly derived from *Conan's bœ*. It appears between 1223 and 1245 as Canenesbi (Sutherland Charters), and in Blaeu's Atlas, the MS. maps of which were drawn (*circa* 1620), by Mr. Timothy Pont, the minister of the adjacent parish of Dunnet, it is marked Conansbay. These two, Duncan and Conan, are the only native chieftains of Caithness at the time of the Norse invasion whose names have come down to us, probably because they were the only ones who held friendly relations with the invaders.

[1] In the Saga of Olaf, Tryggvi's son, it is said that Earl Sigurd lay at Asmundarvag, now Osmundwall, in the south end of the island of Hoy. There is a place called Roray on the west side of the island, which might be the ancient Rörvag.

[2] Munch (Chronicon Manniæ, p. 46) alludes to the mistake so common among the historians of Scotland to confound the *two* Malcolms, and to make one of them, as if one Malcolm only (Malcolm II.) reigned from 1004 to 1034. Though this theory has been ingeniously supported from a Norse point of view, it is at variance with the concurrent testimony of the early Scottish Chronicles. The Saga is the only authority for this marriage; but admitting its testimony on this point to be unassailable scarcely necessitates the repudiation of the authority of the Scottish Chronicles on the question of the succession. (Compare Skene's Highlanders, cap. 5; Robertson's Scotland under her Early Kings, vol. ii. p. 447; and Fordun (Skene's edition), text and notes.)

Five years after the death of King Olaf, Tryggvi's son,[1]
Earl Sigurd went to Ireland. He set his elder sons over
his domains, and sent Thorfinn to the King of Scots, his
mother's father. While on this expedition Sigurd was
killed in Brian's battle;[2] and as soon as the news came to
the Orkneys his sons Sumarlidi, Brúsi, and Einar, were
accepted as Earls, and they divided the islands among them,
each taking one third.

Thorfinn was five winters old when their father fell.
When the King of Scots heard of the Earl's death he
bestowed Caithness and Sutherland upon his grandson, with
the title of Earl, and gave him men to rule the domain along
with him. Earl Thorfinn was very precocious in the
maturity of all his powers. He was of large stature and
strong, but ungainly. As he grew up it soon became apparent that he was avaricious, harsh, and cruel, yet a very
clever, man.

The brothers Einar and Brúsi were different in their dispositions.. Brúsi was clever and fond of company, eloquent
and beloved. Einar was stubborn and taciturn, disagreeable
and avaricious, yet a great warrior. Sumarlidi was like
Brúsi in his disposition. He was the eldest, and the most
short-lived of the brothers. He died on a sickbed.

After his death Thorfinn demanded his share of [Sumar-
lidi's portion of] the Orkneys, although he already had
Caithness and Sutherland which had belonged to his father
Sigurd. This Einar considered to be much more than a
third of the Orkneys, and he would not give up any part of
them to Thorfinn. Brúsi, however, consented to give up
his share [of the portion belonging to Sumarlidi], saying that
he did not covet more of the land than his own proper third.
Then Einar took possession of two shares of the islands.
He became then a powerful man, and had a large number
of retainers. In the summer he made war expeditions,
calling out great levies of his men from their homes;
but these expeditions were not always successful, and the

---

[1] Olaf, Tryggvi's son, fell at the battle of Svoldr, A.D. 1000.
[2] The battle of Clontarf, A.D. 1014 (see the Introduction). The Iceland
Annals say that he held the earldom for sixty-two years, so that he must have
become Earl in A.D. 952; but Munch makes his true period to be 980-1014.

Bœndr[1] began to grow tired of them, but the Earl exacted all his services with violence, and did not suffer any one to speak against them. He was indeed a man of the greatest violence. Then there arose great scarcity in the islands on account of the labour and large expense to which the Bœndr were thus subjected. However, in the parts belonging to Brúsi there were good seasons and easy life, and he was greatly liked by the Bœndr.

CHAPTER II.

OF AMUNDI AND THORKEL.

THERE was a powerful and wealthy man, by name Amundi, who lived in Hrossey,[2] at Sandvik on Laufandaness. He

---

[1] The word *Bóndi* (pl. *Bœndr*), literally "a resident " or "dweller," has no English equivalent, although the form remains in the words "husband"and husbandman," (hus-bondi, house-dweller or house-master). The Bœndr were freeholders by odal tenure, proprietors of the lands which they had inherited by succession from the original "land-takers." "In the primitive form of Scandinavian society," says Balfour, in his Odal Rights and Feudal Wrongs, "land was the only wealth, its ownership the sole foundation of power, privilege, or dignity. As no man could win or hold possession without the strong arm to defend it, every landowner was a warrior, every warrior a husbandman. King Sigurd Syr tended his own hay harvest, and Sweyn of Gairsay and Thorkel Fostri swept the coasts of Britain or Ireland while the crops which they and their rovers had sown grew ready for their reaping." The use of the ancient term survived in Orkney till 1529, as we learn from the description by Jo. Ben, that in the parish of Rendale the people saluted each other with "Goand da boundæ " (i.e. *godan dag bondi !*") instead of the "Guid day, gudeman," of the Scottish vernacular. Among the documents found in the king's treasury at Edinburgh in 1282, was one entitled "A quit-claiming of the lands of the *bondi* of Caithness for the slaughter of the Bishop,"— viz. Bishop Adam, who was burned at Halkirk in 1222 by the "*bondi*," exasperated by his exactions. Although the word is Icelandic, it has been retained in the translation as a convenient term to designate the class, in preference to such periphrastic renderings as "farmer-lairds," "peasant proprietors," or "peasant nobles," as are usually employed.

[2] Hrossey (Horse Isle) was the name given by the Norsemen to the mainland of the Orkney group. The Sandvik here mentioned as the residence of Amundi and Thorkel can only be the Sandvik (now Sandwick) on Deerness. When Thorfinn drew his vessels in under Deerness before he was attacked by Kali Hundason (cap. v.), he sent to Thorkel asking him to collect men and come to his assistance. Thorkel's residence could not therefore have been far from Deerness, although the mention of Laufandaness is somewhat suggestive of Lopness in Sanday.

had a son, by name Thorkel, who was the most accomplished man in all the Orkneys.

One spring the Earl called out the Bœndr as usual, but they murmured greatly, and brought their grievances before Amundi, and asked him to say a good word for them to the Earl. He replied that the Earl was not disposed to listen to advice, and it would be of no avail to ask him to do this, as he and the Earl were such good friends ; he further said that, from what he knew of his own temper and that of the Earl, there was great danger that they might become enemies, and he would have nothing to do with the matter. Then they asked Thorkel, and he was very reluctant, although at last he yielded to their solicitations, but Amundi thought he had been too rash to promise.

When the Earl held a meeting (Thing) [1] Thorkel spoke on behalf of the Bœndr. He begged the Earl to spare the people, and told him of their distress. The Earl answered blandly, and said he would give great weight to Thorkel's words. " I had intended," he said, " to take out six ships, but now I shall not take more than three; but thou, Thorkel, do not ask this of me a second time."

The Bœndr were very grateful to Thorkel for his assistance, and the Earl made an expedition during the summer, and again in the autumn.

Next spring the Earl again called out his men, and held a meeting with the Bœndr. Thorkel spoke again on their behalf, and begged the Earl to spare them. The Earl became wroth, and said that for his speech the lot of the Bœndr should be far worse than before. Then he became so mad with rage, that he said that one or other of them should not leave the meeting unhurt, and immediately dissolved the meeting.

When Amundi heard what Thorkel and the Earl had said to each other, he bade his son go abroad, and Thorkel went to Earl Thorfinn in Caithness. He stayed there a long

---

[1] The Things were local or general assemblies for determining by public agreement the course that should be pursued with reference to matters affecting the common weal or the public peace. All odal-born freemen (not under outlawry) had an equal voice, and king, earl, or common bondi, met on the thingstead on equal terms, as thingmen.

time, and became foster-father to the Earl, who was still young. From that time he was called Thorkel Fóstri, and became a man of great repute. Other men of note and influence fled from the Orkneys on account of Earl Einar's violence; some to Earl Thorfinn, some to Norway, and some to other countries.

When Earl Thorfinn came to man's estate, he sent to his brother Einar, and demanded from him what he considered his share of the Orkneys. Einar was not inclined to divide his possessions: so, when Earl Thorfinn heard this, he called out men from Caithness, and set out for the Orkneys. When Earl Einar had news of this, he collected an army, with the intent to defend his possessions. Earl Brúsi also collected an army, and went to meet them, and tried to reconcile them; and peace was made on condition that Thorfinn should have one-third of the Orkneys as his own proper share.

Then Brúsi and Einar joined their portions, on the footing that the latter should rule them and defend them for both, and that he who survived the other should inherit his portion. But this compact was thought unfair, as Brúsi had a son, by name Rögnvald, and Einar had no son. Thorfinn appointed his own deputies to manage his possessions in the islands, but he himself lived for the most part in Caithness.

In the summer Einar went on expeditions to Ireland, Scotland, and Bretland (Wales). One summer, when ravaging Ireland, he fought in Ulfreksfiörd[1] with Konufögr,[2] an Irish king, and was defeated, with a heavy loss of men. The next summer Eyvind Urarhorn[3] (bull's horn) came from Ireland

---

[1] Ulfreksfiord seems to have been the Norse name of Lough Larne, which in a document of the reign of the Irish King John (A.D. 1210) is styled *Wulvricheford* (Worsaae's Danes and Northmen, p. 311). It is suggestive of the identification of this Lough as the scene of Earl Einar's defeat, that Norse burials have been discovered at Larne. One of these is described in the Crania Britannica, pl. 56. The form of the iron sword found buried with the skeleton, having a short guard and triangular pommel, establishes its Norwegian character.

[2] Konufögr is plainly the Norse form of the Irish Conchobhar. Severa Irish kings of this name are mentioned in the Annals.

[3] Eyvind Urarhorn was a Lenderman (or Baron) of King Olaf Haraldson. He had gone to Ireland to King Conchobhar previous to Einar's expedition, and had assisted the Irish against the Orkneymen. The Saga of Olaf Haraldson says that Earl Einar was much displeased with the Northmen who had

on his way to Norway, and being overtaken by a violent gale, he turned his ships into Asmundarvág,[1] and lay there for a while. When Earl Einar heard this, he went thither with many men, seized Eyvind, and caused him to be killed, but gave quarter to most of his followers. They went to Norway in the autumn, and when they met King Olaf,[2] they told him of Eyvind's murder. He said little about it, but it was afterwards found that he considered this a great loss and a serious offence against himself, though he never said much about things with which he was displeased.

Earl Thorfinn sent Thorkel Fóstri to collect his revenues, but Earl Einar regarded it as chiefly owing to Thorkel that Earl Thorfinn had come into [his possessions in] the Islands. Thorkel left the islands suddenly, and went to Ness (Caithness). He told Earl Thorfinn that he had become aware that Earl Einar had intended to kill him, if his relatives and friends had not given him warning. "And now," he added, "I will avoid the risk of having such a meeting with the Earl as shall bring matters to a crisis between us, and I will go farther away, where his power does not reach me."

Thorfinn persuaded him to go to King Olaf, in Norway, and spend the winter with him in great friendship; "for you will," he said, "be highly esteemed wherever you come among noble men; but I know your temper and that of the Earl to be such that you will not long refrain from hostilities.

Thorkel then prepared for his departure, and in the autumn he went to Norway to visit King Olaf, and spent the winter with him in great friendship. The King often sought Thorkel's advice, because he considered him a wise man and a weighty counsellor, and such was the truth. In telling of the Earls, the King found that he was very partial, a great friend of Thorfinn, and an enemy of Earl Einar. Early in the spring the King sent a ship with a message to

been in the battle on the side of the Irish king, and seized this opportunity of wreaking his vengeance on Eyvind, their leader.

[1] Asmundarvag, now Osmundwall, in the south end of the island of Hoy. The termination *vágr* usually becomes *wall*, as Kirkiuvagr, which in the modern form is Kirkwall.

[2] Olaf Haraldson, surnamed "the Holy," and afterwards known as St. Olaf, who became king in the year 1015.

Earl Thorfinn, asking him to come and see him; and the Earl did not put off the journey, for protestations of friendship had accompanied the message.

CHAPTER III.

THORKEL SLAYS EARL EINAR.

THORFINN went east to King Olaf in Norway, where he was well received, and spent the summer there; and when he prepared to go westward again, King Olaf gave him a large and excellent war-ship, fully equipped. Thorkel Fóstri went with the Earl, who gave him the ship in which he had come from the west in the summer. The King and the Earl parted great friends.

In the autumn Earl Thorfinn came to the Orkneys. When Earl Einar heard of it, he stayed with many men in his ships. Brúsi went to meet the two brothers, and tried to reconcile them; and once more they made peace and confirmed it with oaths. Thorkel Fóstri should be pardoned, and be a friend of Earl Einar, and each of them should give the other a banquet, and the Earl should first come to Thorkel at Sandvik.[1]

When Einar came, he and his men were most sumptuously treated, yet the Earl was not cheerful. The banqueting hall was a large one, with doors at each end. When the Earl was going away, Thorkel was to accompany him, and he sent men to examine the way by which they were to go. When they returned, they said they had discovered three divisions of armed men in ambush, and were certain that foul play was intended. Upon hearing this, Thorkel delayed starting, and called his men together. The Earl asked him to make himself ready, and said it was now time to go. Thorkel replied that he had many things to see to, and kept going out and in.

There were fires on the floor, and Thorkel walked about, and once when he entered by one of the doors he was followed by an Icelander, by name Hallvard, from the east of

---

[1] Now Sandwick, in Deerness.

Iceland, who shut the door after him. As Thorkel passed between the fire and where the Earl sat, the latter said : " Are you ready now ? "

Thorkel replied : " I am ready now," and struck the Earl a blow on the head, so that he fell forward on the floor.

Hallvard said : " I never saw people with so little presence of mind as you who are here. Why do you not take the Earl out of the fire ? "

With his axe he again struck the Earl on the back of the head, and pulled him towards the bench. Then Thorkel and his men walked out quickly by the door opposite to that by which he had entered, and there, outside the door, were the rest of his men fully armed.

The Earl's men took hold of their master and found that he was dead. They were too much stupified to take revenge, as the thing was done so suddenly, and no one expected such a deed from Thorkel; besides, the Earl's men were mostly without arms, and many of them were good friends of Thorkel's before. Thus Thorkel had to thank his good fortune that he enjoyed a longer life.

The Earl's men went away, and Thorkel to his ship. In a few days, shortly after the beginning of the winter, he left for the east, and arrived safely in Norway. He went immediately to see King Olaf, who received him very graciously, and felt much pleasure at his deed; and with him Thorkel spent the winter.

CHAPTER IV.

OF EARL BRUSI.

AFTER the death of Earl Einar, Earl Brúsi took possession of that portion of the domain which had belonged to his brother (Einar), for there had been many witnesses to the compact which they had made. Thorfinn thought it right that they should each have one-half of the Islands, yet Brúsi had two-thirds that year. Next year Thorfinn demanded one-half, to which Brúsi did not consent, and they had many meetings about it. Their friends tried to settle matters between them, but Thorfinn would not take anything less than half of the Islands.

Brúsi said : " I was satisfied with that third part which I inherited from my father, and no one claimed it from me, and I have inherited a second third after my brother according to a lawful agreement; and although I am unable to contend with you, brother, I will have recourse to other means than giving up my lands and title at present."

Thus the meeting ended. But Brúsi saw that he had no strength to hold his own against Thorfinn, because he had much larger possessions, and, besides, some hope of assistance from his- grandfather, the King of Scots. He therefore resolved to go to Olaf, King of Norway, taking with him his son Rögnvald, who was then ten years old. The King received him well, and he told him his business and explained to him how matters stood between him and his brother, and begged his assistance to keep his possessions, offering in return his full friendship.

The King replied by stating that Harald the Fairhaired had reserved to himself all odal rights [1] in the Orkneys, and that the Earls since that time always held those lands as fiefs, and never as their own.

" It is a proof of this," he said, " that when Eirik Blód-öx and his sons were in the Orkneys, the Earls were their vassals ; and when Olaf, Tryggvi's son, my kinsman, came there, your father, Earl Sigurd, became his man. Now, I have succeeded to the entire heritage of Olaf, Tryggvi's son. I will give you the islands as a fief, on condition that you become my man, and then I will try whether my help will not be of more avail to you than the

---

[1] In the Saga of Harald Hárfagri it is stated (cap. vi.) that " King Harald made this law over all the lands he conquered, that all the odal possessions should be his, and that the Bœndr, both great and small, should pay him land-dues for their possessions." Thus he put an end to odal right, in its pure and simple form at least, wherever he extended his authority; and the Bœndr, thus taxed and deprived of their odal rights, complained, with justice, that they were changed from a class of proprietary nobles into a class of tributary tenantry. Having assumed the ownership of the earldom of Orkney as his own by conquest, his heirs became the odal-born lords of Orkney, while the Earls were theoretically the liegemen of the Kings of Norway, though having also an odal right to the earldom which the royal prerogative could not set aside.

aid and assistance of the King of Scots to your brother
Thorfinn.   But if you will not accept these terms, I will try
to recover the possessions and dominion which my kinsmen
have inherited and possessed there in the west."

The Earl considered these words thoughtfully, and sought
the advice of his friends as to whether he should consent to
King Olaf's terms and become his man.   " I do not see," he
said, " how matters will go with me at our parting if I refuse,
because the King has made an unequivocal claim, and regards
the Islands as his property.   Now, considering his great
power, and the circumstance that we are here, he will have
no scruples in making my case such as he likes."

Thus, although the Earl had objections to both alternatives, he resolved to give up all, himself and his dominions,
into the King's power.   Then King Olaf asserted his suzerainty over all his hereditary possessions, and the Earl
became his man, and confirmed this compact with oaths.

Earl Thorfinn heard that his brother Brúsi had gone east
to King Olaf to solicit his assistance ; but as he had himself
seen the King before, and secured his friendship, he thought
that his case had been well prepared there, and he knew that
many would advocate his cause.   Nevertheless, he resolved
to prepare to go to Norway as quickly as possible, intending
that he should arrive there very nearly at the same time with
his brother, so that he might see the King himself before his
brother had concluded his business.   This, however, turned
out otherwise than the Earl intended, for he did not see King
Olaf until the treaty between Earl Brúsi and the King was
fully concluded ; and he did not know that Earl Brúsi had
given up his dominions until he came to the King.

At their first interview the King made the same claim
to the dominion of the Orkneys which he had made before
to Earl Brúsi ; and he made the same request of Thorfinn—
namely, that he should acknowledge the King's suzerainty
over his portion of the islands.

The Earl gave a courteous answer to this demand, saying :
" I consider your friendship of great importance ; and if you
think you require my assistance against other chiefs, you
have well deserved it ; but I cannot well pay you homage,
as I am already an Earl of the King of Scots, and his vassal."

But when the King found from these words that the Earl wished to avoid the claims which he had put forward, he said : " If you will not become my man, there is the other alternative—viz., that I place that man over the Islands whom I choose. But I wish you to promise me with oaths not to claim those lands, and to leave him in peace whom I place over them. Now, if you will not accept any of those conditions, he who governs the land will say that hostilities may be expected from you, and in that case you must not think it strange if a dale meets a hill."[1]

The Earl answered by requesting time to consider these matters. The King gave him time, and permission to consult with his friends ; but then the Earl asked the King for a further delay to the next summer, so that he· might go home; "for," said he, " my counsellors are at home, and my judgment is not yet mature on account of my age." The King told him to make his choice.

Thorkel Fóstri was with the King at the time, and he sent a message to the Earl secretly, telling him that whatever else his intentions were he should not think of parting with the King without being reconciled to him for the present, as he had got him in his power. Now the Earl thought there was no alternative but to let the King have his will, although he did not consider it by any means a desirable thing to relinquish all hope of his patrimony, and to promise with oaths to leave those in undisturbed possession of his dominions who had no hereditary right to them. But because he was not certain about his departure (if he refused), he chose to submit to the King, and to become his man, as Brúsi his brother had previously done.

The King perceived that Thorfinn was a man of much stronger will than Brúsi, and distrusted him therefore more. He saw that Thorfinn would think himself sufficiently powerful, with the aid of the King of Scots, though he broke this treaty; and the King was sagacious enough to perceive that, while Brúsi agreed to everything sincerely, and made only such promises as he intended to keep, Thorfinn agreed cheerfully to everything, while at the same time he had resolved within himself what course he would take ; and

---

[1] If like meets like, or if you be met in the same spirit as you come.

though he made no objections to anything which the King proposed, yet the King suspected that he intended to act upon their agreements afterwards in his own way.

CHAPTER V.

OF THE EARLS BRUSI AND THORFINN.

WHEN King Olaf had considered all these matters, he had a general meeting summoned by the blowing of a trumpet, to which the Earls were also called.

The King said: "I will now make publicly known the treaty between me and the Earls of the Orkneys. They have acknowledged my suzerainty over all the Orkneys and Hjaltland (Shetland), promising to become my men, and confirming these their promises with oaths. In return, I will give to Brúsi one-third of the land, and to Thorfinn another third, which they had before; but the last third, which belonged to Earl Einar, I adjudge to be forfeited to me, because he slew Eyvind Urarhorn, my henchman[1] and beloved comrade. Of this portion I will dispose as I shall think fit; and I make it a condition with you, my Earls, that you be reconciled to Thorkel Amundi's son concerning your brother Einar's slaying, and I wish to act as an arbitrator between you if you agree to this."

The Earls consented to this, as to everything else which the King proposed. Then Thorkell stepped forward and submitted his case to the King's decision, after which the meeting was dissolved. King Olaf awarded a weregild[2] for Earl Einar as for three Lendermen; one-third, however, should be remitted in consideration of the Earl's guilt.

Earl Thorfinn asked permission to depart, and when he had obtained it, he made himself ready in great haste. One day, when all was ready, and the Earl was drinking on board his ship, Thorkel, Amundi's son, came and laid his head

---

[1] The word is *hirdman*. The hirdmen were the King's bodyguard.

[2] The *manbote* (or fine for manslaughter) for every Norwegian Lenderman or Baron was fixed at 6 marks of silver, by the Older Gula-thing.

on the Earl's knees, and asked him to do with it what he liked.

The Earl said : "Why do you do this ?   We are reconciled according to the King's arbitration ; arise."

He rose and said : "I will abide by the King's arbitration concerning differences between me and Brúsi ; but, as far as you are concerned, I leave everything to you.   Although the King has reserved for me possessions and safety in the Orkneys, I am so well acquainted with your disposition that I know it would be impossible for me to go there unless I have your confidence ; and I will promise you never to go to the Orkneys, whatever the King says."

The Earl replied slowly, and said : "Would you rather have me to adjust our affairs than abide by the King's decision ?   If so, I make it the first condition that you shall go with me to the Orkneys, and remain with me, and not leave me except with my permission ; that you shall be in duty bound to defend my land, and to do everything I wish to have done while we are both alive."

Thorkel replied : "I leave this to you, like everything else that concerns me."   Thereupon he submitted his case to the Earl's decision.

The Earl said he would fix the money payment [for his brother's death] afterwards, and received oaths from Thorkel according to their agreement ; and Thorkel prepared to go with him.   The Earl left as soon as he was ready, and he and King Olaf never met afterwards.

Earl Brúsi remained behind, and prepared for his departure more leisurely.   Before he left, King Olaf had an interview with him, and said : "I think it advisable to make you my confidential agent in the western parts.   I intend to give you two-thirds of the islands, which you had before, because I do not wish you to have less power, now that you are my man, than you had before ; and as a pledge of my good faith, I will keep your son Rögnvald with me.   I see that with two-thirds of the land and my assistance you may well hold your own against Earl Thorfinn.

Brúsi was thankful for two-thirds of the land.   He stayed a little while yet before he left, and came west to the Islands (the Orkneys) in the autumn.   His son Rögnvald

remained with King Olaf.   These facts are mentioned by
Ottar Svarti (the swarthy) :

> Readily these noble people
> Will obey thee as thy subjects.
> Use your power with moderation ;
> Hjaltlanders ! your fame is well known.
> Till we had thee, fierce in battle,
> To these eastern shores, there was not
> Any prince on earth who conquered
> Those far distant western islands.

When the brothers Thorfinn and Brúsi came west to the
Islands, Brúsi took possession of two-thirds of the domain,
and Thorfinn of one, but he was all the time in Caithness, in
Scotland, and placed deputies over the islands.   Brúsi alone
had to defend them, for they were in those times very much
exposed to the ravages of Norwegians and Danes, who called
there on their viking expeditions to the west, and plundered
in the outlying parts.   Brúsi made complaints to his brother
Thorfinn on account of his not contributing anything to the
defence of the Orkneys or Hjaltland (Shetland), although he
received his full share of all the land-dues and revenues.
Then Thorfinn proposed to Brúsi to take two-thirds of the
Islands, undertaking the defence of the whole, and leave
Brúsi one-third.   Although this division did not take place
immediately, yet it is said in the History of the Earls that
it did take place, and that Thorfinn had two-thirds of the
Islands, and Brúsi one-third, when Canute the Great conquered
Norway, after the flight of King Olaf.

King Olaf, Harald's son, received no homage from Earl
Thorfinn after he made the treaty with him and Brúsi.

Earl Thorfinn now became a powerful chief.   He was
a man of very large stature, uncomely, sharp-featured, dark-
haired, and sallow and swarthy in ·his complexion.   Yet
he was a most martial-looking man, and of great energy;
greedy of wealth and of renown; bold and successful in
war, and a great strategist.   He was five years old when
he received the title of Earl and the revenues of Caithness
from King Malcolm,[1] his grandfather, and fourteen when he
went forth from his own territory on maritime expeditions,

---

[1] Malcolm II., King of Scotland.

and attacked the possessions of other chiefs. So says
Arnór Jarlaskáld (the Earls' poet) :

> By the prince in storm of helmets
> Was the sword's edge deeply crimsoned.
> Scarcely fifteen, the great-hearted
> Sought renown on fields of battle,
> Ready to defend his own land,
> Or to ravage in another's.
> Under heaven a braver leader
> Ne'er was found than Einar's brother.

Earl Thorfinn was greatly supported by the King of
Scots. This assistance being so near, it much increased
his power in the Orkneys.

The King of Scots died after the reconciliation of the
brothers. Karl Hundason[1] took the kingdom in Scotland.
He considered Caithness to belong to him, as to the former
kings, and demanded tribute from it as from other places.
Thorfinn, however, did not think his inheritance from his
mother's father large, though he had Caithness; and besides,
according to his own opinion, it had been given to him first;
he was therefore unwilling to pay any tribute. Thus they
became open enemies, and made war on each other. King
Karl wished to appoint a chief, by name Moddan, over
Caithness; he was his sister's son, and he gave him the
title of Earl. Then Moddan went down from Scotland and
collected forces in Sutherland.

[1] The identity of Karl or Kali Hundason is one of the historical puzzles
which exercise the ingenuity of modern historians. Supposing the Saga name
of this individual to be a Norse corruption of the name of a Scottish king, it
resembles none more nearly than that of Culen Induffson, the Culen Mac
Induff of the *Chronica Pictorum*. But if Kali Hundason be intended for
Culen Induffson, the dates do not agree by more than sixty years. On the
other hand, supposing the events here narrated to be of the period assigned to
them by the Saga, Kali Hundason ought to be Duncan, son of Crinan, Abbot
of Dunkeld, who was the grandson and successor of King Malcolm Mac Kenneth. But Fordun states that Duncan's succession was a peaceful one. It is
not to be overlooked, however, that Earl Thorfinn was also a grandson of
Malcolm Mac Kenneth ; and if we could account for the discrepancy as to the
name given by the Saga, the war between the two grandsons of the deceased
monarch might readily be accounted for. For full details of the specula-
tions regarding the identity of Kali Hundason, see Skene's Highlanders of
Scotland, cap. v. ; the Irish version of "Nennius" (Irish Archæological
Society), Appendix, p. 78 ; Robertson's Scotland under her Early Kings, vol.
ii. p. 477 ; and Munch's Norske Folks Historie, vol. i. pt. 2, p. 854.

When Earl Thorfinn heard of this, he gathered together an army in Caithness. Thorkel Fóstri also came to Earl Thorfinn from the Orkneys with many men, and their united forces were somewhat more numerous than those of the Scots. When the Scots knew this they hesitated in their invasion, and returned to Scotland. Earl Thorfinn subdued Sutherland and Ross, and plundered far and wide in Scotland, and returned again to Caithness, and Thorkel went back to the Islands ; their men also returned home. Earl Thorfinn stayed at Dungalsbæ, in Caithness, where he had five warships and followers numerous enough to man them.

Moddan came to find King Karl (at Beruvik)[1] and informed him of his unsuccessful expedition. The King became very angry at his land being plundered, and started immediately with eleven war-ships and a numerous army. He sailed northward along Scotland, after having despatched Moddan to Caithness a second time with many troops. Moddan went by land, and it was intended that he should make the attack from that side, so that Earl Thorfinn might be placed between the two armies.

Now, it is to be told of King Karl that he did not stop until he arrived at Caithness, and he and Earl Thorfinn were not far from each other. Thorfinn went on board his ships, and sailed out on the Pentland Firth, intending to go to the Orkneys; and so near were they that King Karl

[1] The words "at Beruvik" in Jonæus's edition are not in the Flateyjarbók. Two places of this name are mentioned in the Saga. One of these is plainly Berwick-on-Tweed (cap. xcii.) The locality of the other (which must be the "Beruvik" of this passage) is fixed by the statement in cap. xciv., where it is said that Earl Rögnvald was then in Sutherland celebrating the marriage of his daughter with Eirik Slagbrellir ; and when word was brought to him that Harald had come to Thurso, he rode with a number of his followers "from Beruvik to Thurso." It has been conjectured that the place here indicated was *Caistal a Bharruick*, an old square tower situated on an eminence near Kirkiboll, on the east side of the shore of the Kyle of Tongue (*Orig. Parochiales*, vol. ii. p. 717). Judging from the context, however, it seems more likely that it may have been the *vik* or inlet at the mouth of the water of Berriedale (Berudal), on the southern border of Caithness, where there are also the ruins of an old square tower—the Castle of Berriedale. This agrees with the statement that King Kali, sailing *northward* from Beruvik, saw the sails of Thorfinn's ships going towards Deerness, as he sailed into the mouth of the Firth from the east. Had Kali come from the Kyle of Tongue, he would have sailed *east*, and Thorfinn would have seen and intercepted him from Duncansbay.

saw their sails as he sailed into the Firth from the east, and
immediately sailed after them. Earl Thorfinn directed his
course to the east of the Orkneys, intending to go to Sandvik.[1] He moored his ships on the east side of Dyrness, and
immediately sent word to Thorkel to collect troops.

Earl Thorfinn arrived at Dyrness late in the evening;
but as soon as it was daylight next morning, King Karl
came upon them unawares with eleven war-ships. There
were only two alternatives—one to run on shore, and leave
the ships with all their valuable contents to the enemy; the
other was to meet the King, and let fate decide between
them. Earl Thorfinn exhorted his men, and ordered them
to have their arms ready. He said he would not flee, and
told them to row briskly towards the enemy. Then both
parties fastened their ships together. Earl Thorfinn addressed his men, advising them to be smart and to make
the first attack fiercely, and saying that few of the Scotsmen
would be able to make a stand. The fighting was long and
fierce. Arnór Jarlaskáld says:

> Once, off Dyrness, to the eastward,
> Came King Kali in a mail-coat
> Famous for its strength and brightness;
> But the land was not defenceless,
> For, with five ships, nothing daunted,
> Scorning flight in warlike temper,
> Valiantly the Prince went forward
> 'Gainst the King's eleven vessels.

> Then the ships were lashed together—
> Know ye how the men were falling?
> All their swords and boards were swimming
> In the life-blood of the Scotsmen;
> Hearts were sinking—bowstrings screaming,
> Darts were flying—spear-shafts bending;
> Swords were biting, blood flowed freely,
> And the Prince's heart was merry.

Now Earl Thorfinn incited his men to the utmost, and
a fierce conflict ensued. The Scots in the King's ships
made but a feeble resistance before the mast, whereupon
Thorfinn jumped from the quarter-deck, and ran to the fore-

---

[1] Now Sandwick, in Deerness, Orkney.

deck, and fought fiercely.   When he saw the crowd in the
King's ships getting thinner, he urged his men to board
them.   King Karl, perceiving this, gave orders to his men
to cut the ropes, and get the ships away instantly; to take
to their oars, and bear away.   At the same time Thorfinn
and his men fastened grappling-hooks in the King's ship.
He called for his banner to be borne before him, and a great
number of his men followed it.   King Karl jumped from
his ship into another vessel, with those of his men who
still held out; but the most part had fallen already.   He
then ordered them to take to their oars ; and the Scots took
to flight—Thorfinn pursuing them.   Thus says Arnór:

> Never was a battle shorter;
> Soon with spears it was decided.
> Though my lord had fewer numbers,
> Yet he chased them all before him ;
> Hoarsely croaked the battle-gull, when
> Thickly fell the wounded king's-men ;
> South of Sandwick swords were reddened.

King Karl fled all the way south to Breidafiord,[1] where
he went on shore, and collected an army anew.   Earl Thorfinn went back after the battle, when Thorkel Fóstri came
to him with a numerous army.   They then sailed south to
Breidafiord in pursuit of King Karl, and when they came to
Scotland they began to plunder.   Then they were told that
Earl Moddan was at Thurso, in Caithness, with a large
army.   He had sent to Ireland for men, because he had
there many relatives and friends, and he was waiting for
these troops.   Then it was thought advisable that Thorkel
should go to Caithness with a portion of the army; but
Thorfinn remained in Scotland, and plundered there.
Thorkel went secretly, because all the inhabitants of Caithness were true and faithful to him ; and no news went of
his journey till he came to Thurso by night, and surprised
Earl Moddan in a house, which they set on fire.   Moddan
was asleep in an upper storey, and jumped out; but as he
jumped down from the stair, Thorkel hewed at him with a
sword, and it hit him on the neck, and took off his head.

[1] Broad Firth—the Moray Firth.

After this his men surrendered, but some escaped by flight. Many were slain, but some received quarter.

Thorkel did not stay there long, but went to Breidafiord, bringing with him all the men he had been able to collect in Caithness, Sutherland, and Ross. He met Earl Thorfinn in Moray, and told him what he had done in his expedition, for which he received hearty thanks from the Earl, and there they both stayed for a while.

CHAPTER VI.

OF THE ORKNEYMEN.

Now it is to be told of King Karl that he went to Scotland after the battle with Earl Thorfinn, and collected an army as well from the south as the west and east of Scotland, and all the way south from Satiri (Kintyre); the forces for which Earl Moddan had sent also came to him from Ireland. He sent far and near to the chieftains for men, and brought all this army against Earl Thorfinn. They met at Torfnes,[1] on the south side of Bæfiord. There was a fierce battle, and the Scots were by far the most numerous. Earl Thorfinn was among the foremost of his men; he had a gold-plated helmet on his head, a sword at his belt, and a spear in his hand, and he cut and thrust with both hands. It is even said that he was foremost of all his men. He first attacked the Irish division, and so fierce were he and his men, that the Irish were immediately routed, and never regained their position. Then King Karl had his standard brought forward against Earl Thorfinn, and there was the fiercest

---

[1] Torfness, the scene of the final conflict between Earl Thorfinn and Kali Hundason, is here described as on the south side of Bæfjord, and by Arnor, the Earls' skald, as south of Ekkial, the river Oikel, which gave its name to Ekkiálsbakká, or the district along the banks of the Oikel and its estuary—the Kyle of Sutherland—which formed the march between the territory of the Norse earls and Scotland. Torfness may thus be conjectured to be Tarbatness, although we have nothing to fix the locality more definitely. Bæfiord, in this case, would be the wider portion of the Dornoch Firth. Munch suggests that the seemingly French name of Beaufort Castle may be a corruption of Bæfiord (which in that case would be the Beauly Frith); but in all probability the name Beaufort is what it seems to be, and much more modern.

struggle for a while; but it ended in the flight of the King; and some say he was slain.   Thus Arnór Jarlaskáld:

> Reddened were the wolf's-bit's edges
> At a place—men call it Torfness;—
> It was by a youthful ruler
> This was done, upon a Monday.
> Pliant swords were loudly ringing
> At this War-Thing, south of Ekkial,
> When the prince had joined in battle
> Bravely with the King of Scotland.

> High his helm the Lord of Hjaltland
> Bore amid the clang of weapons;
> In the battle ever foremost,
> Reddened he his gleaming spear-point
> In the wounds it gave the Irish.
> Thus my lord his mighty prowess
> Showed beneath his British buckler—
> Taking many warriors captive;
> Hlodver's kinsman burnt the country.

Earl Thorfinn drove the fugitives before him through Scotland, and subdued the country wherever he went, and all the way south to Fife.   Then he sent Thorkel Fóstri away with some of his men.   When the Scots heard that the Earl had sent away some of his men, those that had submitted to him meant to attack him.   As soon, however, as he was aware of their treachery, he called his men together and went to meet them; but when they knew he was prepared, they hesitated to make the attack.   Earl Thorfinn resolved to give battle to the Scots as soon as he met them; but they had not the manliness to defend themselves, and ran away into woods and deserted places; and when he had pursued the fugitives, he called his men together, and said he would burn the whole district, and thus pay the Scots for their treachery. Then the Earl's men went over hamlets and farms, and burnt everything, so that scarcely a hut was left standing. Those of the men whom they found they killed, but the women and old people dragged themselves into woods and deserted places, with wailings and lamentations.   Some of them they drove before them, and many were taken captives.   Thus says Arnór Jarlaskáld:

> Fast the flames devoured the homesteads ;
> Lives that day were in great peril ;
> Fire the Scottish kingdom ravaged—
> All reduced to smoking ashes ;
> Great the mischief done that summer
> By the mighty Slaughter-Teacher ;
> Three times were the luckless Scotsmen
> By the Prince completely vanquished.

After this Thorfinn went through Scotland to the north, till he reached his ships, and subdued the country wherever he went, and did not stop till he came to Caithness, where he spent the winter; but every season after this he went out on expeditions, and plundered in the summer time with all his men.

CHAPTER VII.

OF THE FAMOUS DEEDS OF EARL THORFINN.

EARL THORFINN made himself famous in the Orkneys by entertaining his own men and many other men of note throughout the winter, so that no one had to go to inns— providing food and drink at his own charges, in the same manner as chiefs in other countries, Kings, and Earls entertain their henchmen and guests at Christmas time.   About this time Earl Brúsi died, and Earl Thorfinn took possession of all the islands.   But of Rögnvald, Brúsi's son, it is said that he was in the battle of Stiklastad[1] when King Olaf was killed.   Rögnvald escaped, with other fugitives, and carried away King Olaf's brother, Harald Sigurdson, who was dangerously wounded, and brought him to a small Bondi to be cured; but he himself crossed the Kjöl,[2] and went to Jamtaland, and thence to Sweden to see King Onund.   Harald stayed with the Bondi until he had recovered from his wounds. The Bondi then gave him his son as an attendant, and he

---

[1] In which King Olaf Haraldson (the Holy) was killed, A.D. 1030.

[2] The Kjölen mountains, part of the range separating Norway from Sweden.

went through Jamtaland to Sweden secretly. At their
parting, which took place in a certain copse, Harald sang :

> Though now thus here and there I'm hunted
> Through the covert—small's the honour,
> Who knows but that far and wide yet
> Some day shall my name be famous ?

Harald met Rögnvald in Sweden, and they went both
of them east to Gardariki (Russia), along with many others
who had been with King Olaf. They did not stop till they
came east to King Jarizleif, in Hólmgard ; [1] and he received them most heartily for the sake of King Olaf the
Holy. He took them both, as well as Erling, Rögnvald's
son, into his service as defenders of his country.

CHAPTER VIII.

MAGNUS, OLAF'S SON, ACCEPTED KING OF NORWAY.

RÖGNVALD, Brúsi's son, remained in Gardariki (Russia) when
Harald, Sigurd's son, went to Mikligard (Constantinople); he
had the defence of the frontier in summer, and spent the
winters in Hólmgard. The King as well as the people
esteemed him highly. Rögnvald was a man of large stature
and great strength, and one of the handsomest men in appearance, and his accomplishments were such that his equal
was hardly to be found. Arnór Jarlaskáld says that he
fought ten battles in Gardar:

> So it happened that ten battles
> Fought the soldier fierce in Gardar.

Einar Thambarskelfir and Kálf Arnason brought Magnús,
Olaf's son, from Gardariki (Russia). Rögnvald met them in
Aldeigiuborg.[2] He had nearly made an attack on Kálf before
he had informed him of their business. Einar said that
Kálf repented of (his share in) the great crime of having

---

[1] Hólmgard, now Novogorod, formerly Cholmogori, in Russia, which the
Northmen called Gardariki.

[2] The town of Ladoga, which Rurik, the first King of Russia, made his
capital in the 9th century. It is now a mere hamlet.

deprived King Olaf the Holy of his life and kingdom, and
that he now wished to make amends to his son Magnús.
He further told Rögnvald that Kálf wished to place Magnús
on the throne, and support him against the Vikings in the
pay of the Canutes. By this Rögnvald was softened, and
now Einar Thambarskelfir asked him to go with them up to
Hólmgard, and introduce them and their business to King
Jarizleif. He should tell him that the Norwegians were so
disgusted with the rule of the Canutes, but most of all with
Alfifa,[1] that they would prefer any hardships to serving them
longer; and then he should ask King Jarizleif to permit
Magnús, Olaf's son, to become their chief. When they came
there, Rögnvald, Queen Ingigerd,[2] and many of the noblemen,
pleaded their cause. King Jarizleif was unwilling to trust
Magnús into the hands of the Norwegians, because of their
treatment of his father. At last, however, they succeeded
so far that twelve of the noblest men made oaths to the effect
that their offers were sincere; but King Jarizleif trusted
Rögnvald so much that he did not require him to swear.
Kálf promised King Magnús with an oath that he would
accompany him both within his kingdom and out of it, and
do everything to support his power and to secure his safety.
Thereupon the Norwegians accepted Magnús as their King,
and swore fealty to him.

Einar and Kálf stayed in Hólmgard till after Christmas.
Then they went down to Aldeigiuborg (Ladoga), and procured
ships. As soon as the sea was open in the spring, Rögnvald,
Brúsi's son, made himself ready to go with King Magnús.
They went first to Sweden, then to Jamtaland, crossed the
Kjöl, and came to Veradal. When King Magnús came to
Thrándheim, all the population submitted to him. Then he
went down to Nídarós,[3] and was accepted King of the whole
country at the Eyrar-Thing. After this came the dealings
of King Magnús and King Sveinn.

[1] Alfifa, queen of Canute the Great.
[2] Ingigerd, daughter of King Olaf of Sweden, was married to King Jarizleif. She stipulated that Rögnvald should accompany her to Russia, and he
received the town and earldom of Ladoga (Aldeigiuborg).
[3] Nídarós, now the town of Drontheim, so called from its being situated
at the mouth of the river Nid.

CHAPTER IX.

ROGNVALD ASKS MAGNUS FOR LEAVE TO GO TO THE ISLANDS.

WHEN Rögnvald, Brúsi's son, came to Norway, he heard of
the death of his father Brúsi, and at the same time, that Earl
Thorfinn had taken possession of the whole of the Islands.
Then he wished to visit his odal possessions, and asked King
Magnús to permit him to go. The King saw that it was
necessary for him to go, and willingly gave him permission.
At the same time, he gave him the title of Earl, and three
war-ships well equipped. He also gave him a grant of that
third part of the Orkneys which King Olaf had possessed,[1]
and had given to his father Brúsi. At last King Magnús
promised his foster-brother his full friendship, adding that
his assistance should be at his service whenever he required
it. Thus they parted the best of friends.

CHAPTER X.

OF ROGNVALD'S VOYAGE.

EARL ROGNVALD sailed for the Orkneys, and went first to the
estates which his father had possessed. Thence he sent
messengers to his kinsman, Earl Thorfinn, and asked for that
third part (of the Islands) which had belonged to his father.
He also requested them to tell him that he had obtained
from King Magnús a grant of that third which had belonged
to King Olaf. He therefore demanded two-thirds, if it was
the pleasure of his kinsman Thorfinn. At this time Thorfinn had great quarrels with the Irish and the inhabitants of
the Sudreyar (Hebrides), and felt himself greatly in want of
assistance. He therefore gave Rögnvald's messengers the
following reply :—That Rögnvald should take possession of
that third which rightly belonged to him. "As for the
third which Magnús calls his own," he said, "we gave that
up to King Olaf the Holy because we were then in his

---

[1] King Olaf adjudged Earl Einar's third of the islands to be forfeited for
the slaying of Eyvind Urarhorn. (See cap. v.)

power, but not because we thought it just. I and my kinsman Rögnvald will agree all the better the less we talk of
that third, which has been long enough a cause of dispute.
But if Rögnvald wishes to be my faithful friend, I consider
those possessions in good hands which he has for his pleasure
and for the good of us both. His assistance will soon be of
greater value to me than the revenues which I derive from
them."

Upon this the messengers returned, and said he had
yielded up to Rögnvald two-thirds on condition that they
should be allies, as it was right they should be, on account
of their relationship. Rögnvald said, however, that he did
not demand more than what he considered his own; but as
Thorfinn had so willingly given up the lands, he would indeed
assist him, and be his firm friend, which was but natural, as
they were so nearly related. Accordingly Rögnvald took
possession of two-thirds of the islands.

CHAPTER XI.

THE BATTLE OF THE KINSMEN THORFINN AND ROGNVALD.

EARLY in the spring Thorfinn sent word to his kinsman
Rögnvald, and asked him to go out with him on an expedition, bringing as many men as he could. As soon as
Rögnvald received this message, he collected together as
many men and vessels as he could, and when he was ready
he went to meet Earl Thorfinn, who was also ready with his
band. He received his kinsman Rögnvald very well; and
they joined their forces. During the summer they plundered in the Sudreyar (Hebrides), and in Ireland, and in
Scotland's Fiord;[1] and Thorfinn conquered the land wherever
he went. They had a great battle at a place called Vatnsfiord.[2] It began early in the morning, and the kinsmen
gained the victory. This is mentioned by Arnór Jarlaskáld :

---

[1] *Skotlandsfiord*, Scotland's Firth, was the name given to the channel between the Hebrides and the mainland of Scotland. (See cap. xxx.)

[2] Vatnsfiord, probably Loch Vattin, an arm of the sea branching off Loch
Bracadale, in Skye.

Know ye that place, Vatnsfiord ?
There was I in greatest danger ;
Marks are there of my Lord's doings,
He who tries the strength of warriors.
Forth the people quickly carried
From the ships the shields of many ;
Then was heard the dismal howling
Of the gray wolf o'er the corpses.

After this battle they returned to the Orkneys, and stayed at home during the winter. Thus eight winters passed that Earl Rögnvald had two-thirds of the islands without any objection on the part of Earl Thorfinn. Every summer they went out on war expeditions, sometimes both together, sometimes separately, as Arnór says :

The chief beloved did many deeds.
Everywhere there fell before him
Irishmen, or British people ;
Fire devoured the Scottish kingdom.

The kinsmen agreed very well whenever they met ; but when bad men went between them dissensions often arose. Earl Thorfinn dwelt for the most part in Caithness, at·the place called Gaddgedlar,[1] where Scotland and England (?) meet.

[1] Gaddgedlar.—This passage has given rise to a variety of conjectures. None of the explanations which have yet been offered are free from difficulties. Munch (*Chronicon Manniæ*, p. 46) says that, considering the situation of Caithness, and how well the author of the saga must have known it, it becomes evident that between "Caithness" and "at the place" an *and* must have been dropped by the subsequent writer, who, living about A.D. 1380, and in Iceland (this part of the saga existing only in the *Codex Flateyensis*), might easily have dropped an *ok* (or the abbreviation thereof), not conscious of the great blunder he committed. He further adds that Gaddgedlar is evidently the Norse corruption of "Galwydia," Galloway. This explanation is open to the objections that, besides the improbability of Thorfinn having dwelt for the most part in Caithness and in Galloway, the latter place does not fit the description that there Scotland and England meet. The word *eingland*, signifying meadow, or strath land, may possibly have been used as a general term for "The Dales of Caithness," if it may not be supposed to be a mis-transcription of the word *eignarland*, meaning Thorfinn's own territory. Gaddgedlar might be the Norse pronunciation of the native word Gall-gael, applied to the mixed population of the districts where the Norse element had not entirely displaced the Celtic, or the border districts between the Norse earldom and the purely Celtic territory "where Scotland and his (Thorfinn's) own land meet."

CHAPTER XII.

OF EARL THORFINN'S WARFARE.

ONE summer Earl Thorfinn made war in the Sudreyar (Hebrides) and in Scotland. He had sent men into England to foray, and they carried away all the spoil they could find. But when the English became aware of the presence of the Vikings, they gathered together and attacked them. They took from them all the cattle, and killed all the men that were of any note, but sent back some of the reivers, and requested them to tell Earl Thorfinn how they had made the Vikings tired of plunder and rapine, to which they added many insulting words. Thereupon the reivers went to Earl Thorfinn and told him of their mishaps. He was greatly annoyed at the loss of his men, yet he said he could not then do anything, and that they would have to refrain at this time; but he said he was quite able to repay the Englishmen for their mockery, and would do so if he were well next summer.

CHAPTER XIII.

OF EARL THORFINN'S EXPEDITION TO ENGLAND.

AT that time Hardicanute was King of England and Denmark. Earl Thorfinn went to the Orkneys and spent the winter there. Early in the spring he called out a levy from all his domains, and sent word to his kinsman Rögnvald. Rögnvald assented, and called out men from all his possessions. Earl Thorfinn collected troops in Caithness and the Orkneys. He also had many from Scotland and Ireland, and from the Sudreyar (Hebrides), and with all these forces he sailed to England as he had promised. Hardicanute was in Denmark at the time. As soon as the Earls came into England they began to harry and plunder; but the chiefs whose duty it was to defend the land went to meet them with an army. There was a great and fierce battle, in which the Earls gained the victory. After this they plundered far and wide in England, slaying men, and burning the dwellings of the people. This is mentioned by Arnór:

Not forgotten was this battle
By the English, or men ever.
Hither came the rich ring-giver,
With his warriors, nearly doubled ;
Swords cut keenly ; under shield-boss
Rushed all Rögnvald's men together ;
Strong were all the old one's people.
South of Man did these things happen.

On the native land of Britons
Brought the Earl his banner forward ;
Reddened then his beak the eagle ;
Forward pressing hard his warriors,
Battle waxed, and men diminished ;
Fugitives were chased by victors ;
Blazed the fire, with red rays gleaming
Of the wood's foe, leaping heavenward.

Earl Thorfinn had two pitched battles in England. Besides, he had many casual encounters, and slew many people. He stayed there throughout the summer, and went back in autumn to the Orkneys for the winter.

CHAPTER XIV.

KALF FLEES TO THE ORKNEYS.

ABOUT this time Kálf Arnason was banished by King Magnús. He crossed the seas, and went to Earl Thorfinn, his brother-in-law. Thorfinn's wife was then Ingibiörg, the mother of the Earls (Paul and Erlend), and daughter of Earl Finn Arnason. There was great friendship between Kálf and Earl Thorfinn. The Earl had a great many of his men about him, which became very expensive to him. Then there were many who advised him not to leave two-thirds of the Islands to Rögnvald, since his own expenses were so large. Thereupon Earl Thorfinn sent men into the Islands to demand from Rögnvald that third portion which had belonged to Earl Einar Rangmuth (wry-mouth).

Upon receiving this message, the Earl (Rögnvald) consulted with his friends. Then he called Earl Thorfinn's
messengers, and told them that he had received that portion
of the Islands which they claimed as a fief from King Magnús, and that the King called it his patrimony. "It was
therefore," he said, "in the power of King Magnús to decide
which of them should have it; and he would not give it up
if the King wished him to retain it."

The messengers went away, and told these words to Earl
Thorfinn, adding that the third portion [which he had de-
manded] would certainly not be got without trouble. On
hearing this, Earl Thorfinn became very angry, and said that
it was unfair if King Magnús should have the inheritance of
his brother, adding that he had yielded to the demand more
because he was then in King Olaf's power than because it
was a just claim. "Now," he said, "I think Rögnvald does
not return me well my good will in having left him in quiet
possession for a time, if I am not to have the inheritance of
my brother now except by fighting for it." Now Earl Thorfinn became so enraged that he straightway sent men to the
Hebrides and to Scotland, and collected together an army,
making it known that he would march against Rögnvald,
and demand that without abatement which he had not got
when he asked peacefully for it.

When this was told to Earl Rögnvald, he called his
friends together, and complained to them of his kinsman
Thorfinn intending to come and make war on him. He
then asked what help they would offer him, saying that he
would not give up his own without a trial of strength.
But when he asked them to declare themselves, their
opinions were very different. Some spoke in favour of
Earl Rögnvald, and said that one could not be hard upon
him for not being willing to part with his possessions;
others again said it was excusable on the part of Earl Thorfinn to desire to have those possessions for a while which
Rögnvald had had before, and which had belonged to Earl
Einar. Further, they said it was the greatest foolishness for
Rögnvald to fight with such troops as he could get from two-
thirds of the Islands against Thorfinn, who had one-third,
with Caithness, a great deal of Scotland, and all the Hebrides

besides. There were also those who advised reconciliation.
They asked Earl Rögnvald to offer Earl Thorfinn one-half of
the Islands, so that they might still be friends, as it was meet
they should be, owing to their relationship. But when
Rögnvald found that their opinions were divided, and that
they all dissuaded him from resistance, he made known his
determination that he would not part with his possessions
by any arrangement, but that he would rather leave them for
a time, and go to King Magnús, his foster-brother, and see
what assistance he would give him to retain them. Then
he made ready, and went to Norway, and did not rest until
he came to King Magnús, and told him how matters stood.

The King received Earl Rögnvald very well, and invited
him to stay as long as he liked, and to receive such lands
from him as were sufficient to keep him and his men; but
Earl Rögnvald said he wished assistance to recover his possessions. King Magnús said he would certainly give him
such aid as he stood in need of. Rögnvald stayed a short
time in Norway, until he had made ready his expedition for
the Orkneys. He had a numerous and well-equipped army,
which King Magnús had given him. The King also sent
word to Kálf Arnason that he should have his estates restored to him, and be permitted to stay in Norway, if he took
Earl Rögnvald's part in his dispute with Earl Thorfinn.

CHAPTER XV.

BATTLE OFF RAUDABIORG.

EARL ROGNVALD sailed from Norway for the Orkneys, and
landed in Hjaltland (Shetland), where he collected men, and
went thence to the Orkneys. There he summoned his
friends to meet him, and obtained reinforcements. Earl
Thorfinn was in Caithness, and news soon reached him
of Earl Rögnvald's proceedings. He collected forces from
Scotland and the Sudreyar (Hebrides). Rögnvald immediately sent King Magnús's message to Kálf Arnason, who
apparently received very well all that the King had said.
Earl Rögnvald collected his army together in the Orkneys,

intending to cross over to Caithness, and when he sailed into
the Pentland Firth he had thirty large ships.   There he was
met by Earl Thorfinn, who had sixty ships, but most of them
small.   They met off Raudabiorg[1] (red cliff), and at once
prepared for battle.

Kálf Arnason was there also; he had six ships, all of
them large, but did not take part in the fight.

Now the battle began with the utmost fury, both Earls
encouraging their men.   When the fighting had thus continued for a while, the loss of men began to be heaviest on
Earl Thorfinn's side, the chief cause being the great difference
in the height of the ships.   Thorfinn himself had a large
ship, well equipped, in which he pressed forward with great
daring ; but when the smaller vessels were cleared, the Earl's
ship was attacked from both sides, and they were placed in
great danger.   Many of the Earl's men were killed, and
others dangerously wounded.   Then Earl Rögnvald commanded his men to leap on board ; but when Thorfinn perceived the imminent danger, he caused the ropes to be cut
with which his ship was fastened to the other, and rowed
towards the shore.   He had seventy dead bodies removed
from his ship, and all those who were disabled by wounds
went also on shore.   Then Thorfinn ordered Arnór Jarlaskáld, who was among the Earl's men and high in his

[1] Raudabiorg, or Red Headland, must be looked for in the neighbourhood
of Dunnet Head, where the red beds of the Old Red Sandstone form the distinctive feature of the coast.   A little to the east of Dunnet Head there is an
outlying crag named Brough of Rattar, or Rattar Brough—in all probability
a corrupted form of the old name Raudabiorg.   Still farther to the eastward,
where the burn of Rattar enters the Firth, are the ruins of an old "Pictish
tower," or broch—in old Norse, *borg*.   In its immediate vicinity is a little
promontory called Kirk o' Taing (*Kirkiu Tunga*, the Tongue, or Ness of the
Kirk), on which are the ruins of one of the small rudely-built chapels of the
early Christian time.   On the north side of the chapel the edges of a number
of stone cists are visible through the turf ; and from two of these, which were
dug up in cutting a drain in the spring of 1872, eight silver armlets of the
ancient penannular form were obtained.   These correspond exactly with the
armlets which formed part of the great hoard exhumed at Skaill, in Orkney,
on the opposite side of the Firth, with Cufic and Anglo-Saxon coins of the
tenth century—in all probability a hoard deposited by some of the vikings on
their return from a plundering expedition.   As Earl Thorfinn and his men
were Christians, it seems probable that, if the chapel was then in existence,
the bodies of the seventy slain in the fight off Raudabiorg, which were landed
here, would be buried in the consecrated ground attached to this chapel.

favour, to go on shore ; and on landing he sang these
verses :——

> This will I not hide from comrades,
> Though 'tis right one's chief to follow,
> Yet am I myself unwilling
> Thus to meet the son of Brúsi.
> When these Earls so fierce in battle
> Close in fight, then will our case be
> Hard beyond the case of most men
> In this trial of our friendship.

Earl Thorfinn selected the ablest of his men to man his
ship, and then he went to see Kálf Arnason, and asked his
assistance. He said that Kálf would not be able to buy
king Magnus's friendship, since he had already been banished,
and was therefore unable to keep the king's favour, even when
they were once reconciled. "You may be sure," he added,
"that if Rögnvald overcomes me, and he and King Magnus
become masters here in the west, you will not be welcome
in this quarter, but if I come off victorious you shall lack
nothing that it is in my power to give you. If we two keep
together we shall be a match for any one here in the west,
and I hardly think you will allow yourself to lie crouching
aside like a cat among stones while I am fighting for behoof
of us both. Moreover our ties are so close that it is more
seemly for us to aid each other, since you have no ties of
blood or affinity with our enemies."

When Kálf heard Thorfinn's persuasions he called his
men and gave orders to fall to and fight on the side of Earl
Thorfinn. Now Thorfinn and Kálf both rowed back to the
fight, and when they arrived Thorfinn's men were ready to
fly, and many of them had been slain. The Earl pushed his
ship forward against that of Earl Rögnvald, and a fierce fight
ensued. As is said by Arnór Jarlaskáld—

> Then I saw the two wealth-givers
> Hewing down each other's warriors.
> Fierce the fight was in the Pentland,
> As the sea swelled and the red rain
> Crimsoned all the yielding timbers,
> While from shield-rims sweat of hot blood
> Dripping, stained the warriors' garments.

Kálf attacked Rögnvald's smaller ships, and speedily cleared them, as there was a great difference in the height of the ships. When the hired troops from Norway saw the vessels beside them cleared they cut away their ship and fled. Then only a few ships remained with Earl Rögnvald, and the victory began to lean the other way. So says Arnór Jarla-skáld :—

> Then the prince so fierce in battle,
> Valiant kinsman of the Vikings,
> All the old land might have conquered
> With assistance of the Islesmen.
> Fewer were his slaughtered heroes ;
> But the chief's strong men in helmets,
> All the way to northern Hjaltland,
> Chased the weak and flying remnant.

And when the main portion of the troops had fled, Kálf and Earl Thorfinn attacked Earl Rögnvald's ship together, and then a great number of his men were slain. When he saw the imminent danger, and that he would not be able to overcome Thorfinn and Kálf, he had the cables cut, and fled.

It was now late in the day, and darkness was coming on. Earl Rögnvald stood out to sea the same night, and sailed for Norway, and did not stop till he found King Magnus, who received him well, as he had done before, and invited him to remain with him, and there he stayed some time.

CHAPTER XVI.

EARL THORFINN SUBDUES THE ISLANDS.

Now it is to be told of Earl Thorfinn that on the morning after the battle he sent boats to all the islands to search for the fugitives. Many were killed, and some were pardoned. Earl Thorfinn subdued all the Islands, and made all the inhabitants his subjects, even those who had sworn allegiance to Earl Rögnvald. Thorfinn then fixed his residence in the Orkneys, keeping a great number of men about him ; he imported provisions from Caithness, and sent Kálf Arnason to the Sudreyar (Hebrides), and ordered him to remain and maintain his authority there.

When Earl Rögnvald had stayed with King Magnus for some time, he said to the King that he wished to go back to the Islands. When the King heard this he said it was not wise, and advised him to remain until the winter had passed away and the sea was free from ice. Yet he said that he would give him as many men as he wanted, and a sufficient number of ships. Rögnvald in reply said that this time he would go without the King's men, adding that he could not lead an army against Earl Thorfinn without a great loss of men, as he had such extensive dominions in the west. "This time," he continued, "I intend to go to the west in a single ship, as well manned as possible; thus I expect there will be no news of us beforehand; and if I get to the Islands I shall take them by surprise, and then we may speedily gain such a victory as could hardly, if at all, be gained by a number of troops; but if they become aware of our movements we can still let the sea take care of us."

King Magnus said he might go as he pleased, and return to him when he wished.

After this Rögnvald made his ship ready, and selected the crew carefully. Several of King Magnus's henchmen went with him, and altogether he had a picked crew in his vessel. When they were ready they sailed out to sea and had a fair wind. This was early in the winter.

CHAPTER XVII.

RÖGNVALD COMES TO THE ISLANDS.

RÖGNVALD first came off the coast of Hjaltland (Shetland), and heard that Earl Thorfinn was in the Orkneys with few men, because he did not expect any enemies in the depth of winter. Rögnvald went straightway to the Orkneys. Earl Thorfinn was in Hrossey,[1] suspecting nothing. When Rögnvald arrived in the Orkneys, he went where he had heard that Earl Thorfinn was, and came upon him unawares, so that his presence was not known until he had secured all the doors of the house in which the Earl and his men

---

[1] The Mainland of Orkney.

were. It was in the night time, and most of the men were asleep, but the Earl was still sitting over his drink. Rögnvald and his men set fire to the house. When Earl Thorfinn became aware of the presence of enemies he sent men to the door to know who they were. They were told that it was Earl Rögnvald. Then they all leaped to their weapons, but they were unable to do anything in the way of defence, as they were all prevented from getting out. The house was soon in flames, and Earl Thorfinn said that permission should be asked for those to go out who were to receive quarter. When this was asked of Earl Rögnvald he permitted all the women and thralls to go out, but. he said that most of Thorfinn's henchmen would be no better to him alive than dead. Those who were spared were dragged out, and the house began to burn down. Earl Thorfinn bethought him of a plan, and broke down part of the woodwork of the house and leaped out there, carrying Ingibiörg, his wife, in his arms. As the night was pitch dark he got away in the smoke unperceived by Earl Rögnvald's men, and during the night he rowed alone in a boat over to Ness (Caithness). Earl Rögnvald burnt the house, with all who were in it, and no one thought otherwise than that Earl Thorfinn had perished there.

After this Rögnvald went over the Islands and took possession of them all. He also sent messages over to Ness (Caithness), and to the Sudreyar (Hebrides), to the effect that he intended to have all the dominions of Thorfinn, and nobody spoke against him. Earl Thorfinn was then in Caithness in hiding with his friends, and no news went abroad of his escape from the burning.

CHAPTER XVIII.

EARL RÖGNVALD SLAIN.

EARL Rögnvald resided in Kirkiuvág (Kirkwall), and brought there all necessaries for the winter ; he had a great number of men, and entertained them liberally. A little before Christmas the Earl went with a numerous following

into little Papey [1] to fetch malt for the Christmas brewing.
The evening which they stayed in the islands they sat a
long time round the fires to warm themselves, and he who
had to keep up the fires said they were running short of
fuel. Then the Earl made a slip of the tongue in speaking,
and said: "We shall be old enough when these fires are
burnt out," but he intended to have said that they would be
warm enough; and when he noticed his blunder he said:
"I made a slip of the tongue in speaking just now; I do
not remember that I ever did so before, and now I recollect
what my foster-father King Olaf said at Stiklastad when
I noticed a slip of the tongue which he made—namely, that
if it ever so happened that I should make a slip in my
speech I should not expect to live long after it. It may be
that my kinsman Thorfinn is still alive."

At that moment they heard that the house was surrounded
by men. It was Earl Thorfinn and his men. They set the
house on fire immediately, and heaped up a large pile before
the door. Thorfinn permitted all others to come out except
Earl Rögnvald's men, and when most of them had gone out
a man came to the door dressed in linen clothes only, and
asked Earl Thorfinn to lend a hand to the deacon; this man
placed his hands on the wall and sprang over it and over
the ring of men, and came down a great way off, and disappeared immediately in the darkness of the night. Earl
Thorfinn told his men to go after him, saying: "There went
the Earl, for that is his feat and no other man's." They
went away, and divided into parties to search for him.
Thorkel Fóstri with some others went along the beach, and

---

[1] The two Papeys, the great and the little (anciently Papey meiri and
Papey minni), now Papa Westray and Papa Stronsay, are both mentioned in
the Saga. Fordun, in his enumeration of the islands, has a "Papeay tertia,"
which is not now known. There are three islands in Shetland called Papey,
and both in Orkney and Shetland there are several districts named Paplay or
Papplay, doubtless the same as the Papyli of Iceland. Munch considers that
these names betray a Kelto-Christian origin. They probably indicate the
settlements of Irish ecclesiastics in the islands previous to the arrival of the
Northmen. The recent discoveries in Orkney of ecclesiastical bells of the
early square form, and of stone monuments with Ogham inscriptions (in one
case associated with a figure of the cross of an early form), seem to point to
the settlement of ecclesiastical communities in the islands at a very early
period. (See Introduction.)

they heard the barking of a dog among the rocks by the sea. Earl Rögnvald had had his favourite dog with him. Thorkel had the Earl seized, and asked his men to kill him, offering them a reward in money. But no one would do it. So Thorkel Fóstri slew Earl Rögnvald himself, as he knew that one of the two (Earls) must die. Then 'Earl Thorfinn came up, and did not find fault with the deed. They spent the night in the island, and all were killed who had accompanied Earl Rögnvald thither.

Next morning they took a barge and filled it with malt; then they went on board and ranged the shields which had belonged to Earl Rögnvald and his men along the bulwarks, neither had they more men in the barge than Rögnvald had had. So they rowed to Kirkiuvág (Kirkwall); and when those of Rögnvald's men who were there saw the vessel they thought it was Earl Rögnvald and his men returning, and they went unarmed to meet them. Thorfinn seized thirty of them and slew them; most of them were henchmen and friends of King Magnus. To one of the King's henchmen the Earl gave quarter, and told him to go east to Norway and tell King Magnus the tidings.

CHAPTER XIX.

EARL RÖGNVALD'S BURIAL.

THE body of Earl Rögnvald was brought to the larger Papey[1] and buried there. Men said that he was one of the most accomplished and best-beloved of all the Earls of the Orkneys; and his death was greatly lamented by all the people.

After this Earl Thorfinn took possession of the whole of the Islands, and no one spoke against him.

Early in the spring these tidings came east to Norway to King Magnus. He regarded the death of Rögnvald, his foster-brother, as a great loss, and said he would avenge him by and by, but just then he was at war with King Swein, Ulf's son.[2]

---

[1] Now Papa Westray.　　　　[2] King of Denmark.

CHAPTER XX.

EARL THORFINN COMES TO KING HARALD.

ABOUT this time King Harald, Sigurd's son,[1] King Magnus's uncle, arrived in Norway, and King Magnus gave him the half of the kingdom. One winter they called out men from the whole of Norway, intending to go south to Denmark, but while they lay in Seley[2] two war ships rowed into the harbour and up to King Magnus's ship. A man in a white cloak went from the [strange] ship, and along the [King's] ship, and up to the quarterdeck. The King sat at meat; the man saluted him, and taking up a loaf he broke it and ate of it. The King received his salutation, and handed the cup to him when he saw that he ate the bread. The King looked at him and said : " Who is this man ? "

" My name is Thorfinn," he said.

" Art thou Earl Thorfinn ? " said the King.

" So am I called in the west," he said, " and I am here with two ships of twenty benches, well manned considering our means, and I wish now to join in this expedition with you, if you will accept my assistance ; all my men and I myself are in God's power and yours, my lord, on account of my great misdeeds by which I have offended you."

In the meantime some men gathered together and listened to their conversation.

" It is true, Earl Thorfinn" (said the King), " that I intended, in case we should meet, that you should not have to tell of our parting, but now matters stand so that it does not become my dignity to have you slain, and you shall go with me now, but the terms of our reconciliation I will declare when I am more at leisure."

Earl Thorfinn thanked the King and returned to his ship. The King stayed a long time in Seley, and men gathered to him from Vík ;[3] for he intended to sail to Jut-

---

[1] Harald Sigurdson is the famous Harald Hardradi who afterwards fell at the battle of Stamford Bridge, near York, fighting against Harald Godwinson the Saxon King of England, in 1066.

[2] A small island off Lindesnes, in the south of Norway.

[3] The district round the head of the Christiania Fiord.

land when he obtained a fair wind.   Thorfinn was often in
conversation with the King, who treated him in a friendly
manner, and had him frequently present at his councils.

One day the Earl went on board the King's ship, and
went up to the poop.   The King asked him to sit down.
The Earl sat down, and they both drank together and were
merry.   A tall brave-looking man, dressed in a red
tunic, came to the poop and saluted the King, who received
his greeting graciously.   He was one of the King's henchmen.   He said : " I have come to see you, Earl Thorfinn."

" What is your business with me ? " said the Earl.

" I wish to know what compensation you intend to give
me for my brother who was killed by your orders out west
in Kirkiuvág (Kirkwall), along with others of King
Magnus's henchmen."

" Have you never heard," said the Earl, " that it is not
my wont to pay money for the men whom I cause to be
killed ? "

" I have nothing to do with how you have treated other
people, if you pay the manbote for him for whom it devolves
on me to seek compensation.   I also lost some money there
myself, and was shamefully treated.   It is more binding on
me than any one else to seek redress for my brother and
myself, and therefore I now demand it.   The King may
remit offences committed against himself, even if he thinks
it of no importance that his henchmen are led out and
slaughtered like sheep."

The Earl answered : " I understand it to be to my advantage here that I am not in your power.   Are not you
the man to whom I gave quarter there ? "

" True enough," said he, " it was in your power to have
killed me like the others."

Then the Earl said : " Now the saying proves true—' That
often happens to many which they least expect.'   I never
thought I should be so placed that it would be injurious
to me to have been too generous to my enemies ; but now
I have to pay for having given you quarter ; you would
not have denounced me to-day in the presence of chiefs if I
had caused you to be killed like your comrades."

The King looked at the Earl and said : " There it comes

out still, Earl Thorfinn, that you think you have killed too
few of my henchmen without compensation." While saying
this the king turned blood-red [with anger]. The Earl
started up and left the poop, and returned to his own ship,
and all was quiet during the evening. In the morning,
when the men awoke, a fair wind had sprung up, and they
rowed away from the harbour. The King sailed south to
Jutland with the whole fleet. In the earlier part of the day
the Earl's ship stood out farther to sea, and in the afternoon
he took a westerly course, and there is nothing to be told of
him till he arrived in the Orkneys, and resumed the government of his dominions.

King Magnus and Harald sailed to Denmark, and spent
the summer there. King Swein was unwilling to meet
them, and stayed in Skàney [1] with his army. That summer
King Magnus was seized with an illness of which he died;
but he had previously declared that he gave the whole kingdom of Norway to his uncle Harald.

CHAPTER XXI.

EARL THORFINN'S MESSAGE TO KING HARALD (HARDRADI).

EARL THORFINN now ruled the Orkneys and all his dominions.
Kálf Arnason was frequently with him. Sometimes he
made viking expeditions to the west, and plundered in
Scotland and Ireland. He was also in England, and at one
time he was the chief of the Thingmen.

When Earl Thorfinn heard of the death of King Magnus, he
sent men to Norway to King Harald with a friendly message,
saying that he wished to become his friend. When the
messengers reached the King he received them well, and promised the Earl his friendship. When the Earl received this
message from the King he made himself ready, taking from the
west two ships of twenty benches, with more than a hundred
men, all fine troops, and went east to Norway. He found the
King in Hördaland, and he received him exceedingly well,
and at their parting the King gave him handsome presents.

---

[1] Scania, the southern part of Sweden.

From thence the Earl went southwards along the coast to Denmark. He went through the country, and found King Svein in Alaborg;[1] he invited him to stay, and made a splendid feast for him. Then the Earl made it known that he was going to Rome ;[2] but when he came to Saxland he called on the Emperor Heinrek, who received him exceedingly well, and gave him many valuable presents. He also gave him many horses, and the Earl rode south to Rome, and saw the Pope, from whom he obtained absolution for all his sins.

Then the Earl returned, and arrived safely home in his dominions. He left off making war expeditions, and turned his mind to the government of his land and his people, and to the making of laws. He resided frequently in Birgishérad (Birsay), and built there Christ's Kirk, a splendid church ; and there was the first Bishop's see in the Orkneys.

Thorfinn's wife was Ingibiörg, [called] the mother of the Earls. They had two sons who arrived at manhood; one was called Paul, the other Erlend. They were men of large stature, fine-looking, wise, and gentle, more resembling their mother's relations. They were much loved by the Earl and all the people.

---

[1] Aalborg, in Jutland.

[2] Earl Thorfinn's pilgrimage to Rome took place most probably about the year 1050. King Magnus died in A.D. 1047, and some time must have elapsed before Thorfinn heard of his death. Then his messengers went to Norway, and returned ; and his own expedition was thereafter prepared. After visiting King Harald Hardradi in Norway, he stayed some time with Svend Estridson, the King of Denmark. Then he visited Henry III., Emperor of Germany, and would probably reach Rome soon after the accession of Pope Leo IX., who occupied the Papal throne from 1049 to 1055. As Macbeth, the only Scottish sovereign who ever visited the city of Rome, made his pilgrimage thither in the year 1050, and Thorfinn and he were close friends and allies, it is probable that they went together. (Compare Saga of King Harald Hardradi ; Wyntoun, vol. ii. pp. 468, 469 ; Marianus Scotus, in Mon. Hist. Brit., p. 604 ; Florence of Worcester ; Chron. de Mailros ; Ritson's Annals, vol. ii. p. 116 ; Skene's Highlanders, chap. v. ; Grub's Ecclesiastical History of Scotland, chap. xiii.)

CHAPTER XXII.

OF EARL THORFINN'S DEATH.

EARL THORFINN retained all his dominions to his dying day, and it is truly said that he was the most powerful of all the Earls of the Orkneys. He obtained possession of eleven Earldoms in Scotland, all the Sudreyar (Hebrides), and a large territory in Ireland. So says Arnór Jarlaskáld—

> Unto Thorfinn, ravens' feeder,
> Armies had to yield obedience
> From Thussasker [1] right on to Dublin.
> Truth I tell, as is recorded.

Earl Thorfinn was five winters old when Malcolm [2] the King of Scots, his mother's father, gave him the title of Earl, and after that he was Earl for seventy winters. He died towards the end of Harald Sigurdson's reign.[3] He is buried at Christ's Kirk in Birgishérad (Birsay), which he had built. He was much lamented in his hereditary dominions ; but in those parts which he had conquered by force of arms many considered it very hard to be under his rule, and [after his death] many provinces which he had subdued turned away and sought help from the chiefs who were odal-born to the government of them.[4] Then it soon became apparent how great a loss Thorfinn's death was to his dominions.

The following stanzas were made about the battle between Earl Rögnvald, Brùsi's son, and Earl Thorfinn:—

> Since the Earls have broken friendship
> Peace I can enjoy no longer.
> Feasts of corpses to the ravens

---

[1] This quotation from Arnór seems to have reference only to Thorfinn's conquests in Ireland. Doubtless the extent of these is considerably exaggerated. The Thussasker appear to be the outlying skerries off the S.E. of Ireland, still known as the Tuscar Rocks.

[2] Malcolm II., Mac Kenneth.

[3] Harald Sigurdson (Hardradi) was slain at Stamford Bridge in 1066, and Earl Thorfinn died in 1064.

[4] Transferred their allegiance to the native chieftains, to whom they belonged by hereditary right.

Each has in his turn provided.
Off the Islands were the blue tents
By the mighty rent asunder,
Dabbled were the foul birds' feathers
In red blood 'neath lofty branches.

Have ye heard how Kalfr followed
Finnr's son-in-law in battle ?
Quickly didst thou push thy vessels
'Gainst the Earl's ships on the water.
To destroy the son of Brúsi,
Thou, courageous ship's commander
Wast unwilling, but of hatred
Mindful, didst thou help Thorfinn.

When the Earls had joined in battle
Misery there was unbounded.
Thick and fast the men were falling
In the struggle ; sad the hour when
Nearer went the daring Eastmen
To the unexampled fire-rain.
In that battle off the Red Biorg
Many a noble man was wounded.

Swarthy shall become the bright sun,
In the black sea shall the earth sink,
Finished shall be Austri's labour,
And the wild sea hide the mountains,
Ere there be in those fair Islands
Born a chief to rule the people—
May our God both help and keep them—
Greater than the lost Earl Thorfinn.

CHAPTER XXIII.

OF THE EARLS PAUL AND ERLEND, AND GENEALOGIES.

Now the sons of Earl Thorfinn succeeded him. Paul was
the elder of the two, and he ruled for both of them. They
did not divide their possessions, yet they almost always
agreed in their dealings.

Ingibiörg, the mother of the Earls, was married to

Malcolm, King of Scots,[1] who was called Langháls (Longneck),
and their son was Duncan, King of Scots, the father of
William the excellent man; his son was called William
Odling (the Noble), whom all the Scots wished to have
for their King.[2]

Earl Paul, Thorfinn's son, married the daughter of Earl
Hákon, Ivar's son, by whom he had many children. They
had a son called Hákon, and a daughter called Thóra, who
was married in Norway to Haldór, son of Brynjólf Ulfaldi
(camel). Another son of theirs, named Brynjólf, married
Gyrid, Dag's daughter. A second daughter of Paul, called
Ingirid, was married to Einar Vorsakrák. Herbiörg was the
third daughter of Paul. She was the mother of Ingibiörg
Ragna, who was married to Sigurd of Westness; their sons
were Hákon Pík, and Brynjólf. Sigrid was a second
daughter of Herbiörg. She was married to Kolbein Hrúga
(heap). The fourth daughter of Earl Paul was Ragnhild,
who was the mother of Benidikt, the father of Ingibiörg, the

---

[1] This marriage is unknown in Scottish history, and rests on the authority
of the Sagas alone. Duncan is said by the Scottish historians to have been a
bastard, while the Sagas make him the legitimate offspring of Malcolm and
Ingibiörg, who must by this time have been old enough to be Malcolm's
mother. She was married to Earl Thorfinn before Kálf Arnason was banished
by King Magnus (cap. xiv.), which was some time between 1036 and 1041.
Earl Thorfinn died in 1064, seven years after King Malcolm was crowned at
Scone, in 1057. Malcolm's marriage with the Princess Margaret of England
took place in 1067, or less than three years after Ingibiörg became a widow.
Munch supposes that Ingibiörg must have died in childbed with Duncan, and
suggests that the fact that Duncan claimed the crown before Edgar, the son
of Malcolm by Margaret, may be taken as showing that he must have been
the offspring of a previous marriage. Macpherson (Wyntoun, vol. ii. p. 472),
while accepting the statement of the Saga, accounts for Duncan being called a
bastard from the circumstance that Malcolm's marriage with Ingibiörg was
within the degrees of propinquity forbidden by the canon law.

[2] This William Odling (the Noble) is William of Egremont (the boy of
Egremont), son of William Fitz Duncan, and consequently grandson of Duncan. The reference here to him as the person whom all the Scots wished to
have for their king is explained by the fact that, on the death of David I., by
the old Celtic law of succession, he became in the eyes of the Celtic population
the rightful heir to the throne; and his claims were supported by no fewer
than seven Earls, among whom were those of Strathern, Ross, and Orkney.
The insurrection was speedily put down, but the claim was subsequently
revived by Donald Bane Macwilliam, who, on the same principle, obtained the
support of the northern chiefs. (See Skene's Highlanders of Scotland for a
full account of the conflict between the feudal and the Celtic systems of
succession.)

mother of Erling Erkidiákn (archdeacon). Ragnhild had a
daughter, by name Berglíot, who was married to Hávard,
Gunnar's son. Their sons were Magnus, Hákon Kló (claw),
Dufniál, and Thorstein. All those were the families of
Earls and chiefs in the Orkneys, and all of them will be
mentioned in this Saga afterwards. The wife of Earl
Erlend, Thorfinn's son, was Thóra, the daughter of Sumarlidi,
Ospak's son ; the mother of Ospak was Thórdís, the daughter
of Hall of Sída (in Iceland). Their sons were Erling and
Magnus, and their daughters Gunnhild, and Cecilia, who was
married to Isak, and their sons were Indridi and Kol.
Erling had a natural daughter called Játvör ; her son was
Berg.

CHAPTER XXIV.

HERE IS TOLD OF THE DEATH OF KING HARALD AND HIS
DAUGHTER.

WHEN the brothers Paul and Erlend had succeeded to the
government of the Orkneys, King Harald Sigurdson (Hardradi) came from Norway with a large army. He first
touched Hjaltland ; from thence he went to the Orkneys,
and left there his Queen Ellisif, and their daughters Maria
and Ingigerd. From the Orkneys he had many troops ;
both the Earls went with him on the expedition. He went
from Orkney to England, and landed at a place called Klif-
land (Cleaveland), and took Skardaborg (Scarborough). Then
he touched at Hallarnes (Holderness), and had a battle there,
in which he was victorious. The Wednesday next before
Matthiasmas (20th September) he had a battle at Jórvík
(York) with the Earls Valthióf and Mórukári. Mórukári
was slain there.[1] Next Sunday the borg at Stamford-
bridge surrendered to him ; and he went on shore to
arrange the government of the town ; and there he left
his son Olaf, the Earls Paul and Erlend, and his brother-in-
law Eystein Orri. While he was on shore he was met by
Harald Gudinason (Godwinson) at the head of a numerous

---

[1] This is a mistake. Morkere was present at the battle of Hastings, and
he and Waltheof went afterwards to Normandy with William the Conqueror.

army. In that battle King Harald Sigurdson fell. After
the death of the King, Eystein Orri and the Earls arrived
from the ship, and made a stout resistance. There Eystein
Orri fell, and almost the whole army of the Northmen with
him.

After the battle King Harald (Godwinson) permitted
Olaf, the son of King Harald Sigurdson, and the Earls to
leave England, with all the troops that had not fled. Olaf
sailed in the autumn from Hrafnseyri [1] to the Orkneys. The
same day and at the same hour as King Harald fell, his
daughter Maria died, and it is said that they had but one life.

Olaf spent the winter in the Orkneys, and was very
friendly to the Earls, his kinsmen. Thóra, the mother of
King Olaf, and Ingibiörg, the mother of the Earls, were
daughters of two brothers. In the spring Olaf went to
Norway, and was made King along with his brother Magnus.

While the brothers (Paul and Erlend) ruled the Orkneys
they agreed extremely well a long time; but when their
sons came to manhood Erling and Hákon became very
violent. Magnus was the quietest of them all. They were
all men of large stature, and strong, and accomplished in
everything. Hákon, Paul's son, wished to take the lead among
his brothers; he considered himself of higher birth than the
sons of Erlend, as he was the daughter's son of Earl Hákon
Ivar's son, and Ragnhild, the daughter of King Magnus the
Good. Hákon wished his friends to have the lion's share of
everything before those who leant to the sons of Erlend, but
Erlend did not like his sons to be inferior to any in the
Islands. Matters went so far that the kinsmen could not be
together without danger. Then their fathers persuaded them
to compose their differences. A meeting was appointed,
but it soon became apparent that each [of the fathers]
was inclined to take the part of his sons, and therefore
they did not agree. Thus dissensions arose between the
brothers, and they parted without coming to an agreement,
which was by many considered a great misfortune.

[1] Fordun (v. cap. i.) records the landing of Macduff "at Ravynsore in
England." Camden mentions a place on Holderness, at the mouth of the
Humber, formerly called Ravensere. It no longer exists, having been de-
stroyed by the encroachments of the sea.

CHAPTER XXV.

A MEETING OF PEACE.

AFTER this well-disposed men interfered and tried to reconcile them. A meeting for reconciliation was appointed in Hrossey,[1] and at that meeting they made peace on the understanding that the Islands should be divided in two shares, as they had been between Thorfinn and Brúsi, and thus matters stood for a while.

When Hákon had arrived at the age of manhood he was continually on war expeditions. He became a very violent man, and greatly molested those who adhered to Erlend and his sons; and this went so far that they came to open enmity a second time, and attacked each other with numerous troops. Hávard, Gunnar's son, and all the principal friends of the Earls, consulted once more and tried to make peace between them. This time Erlend and his sons refused to make peace if Hákon remained in the Islands; and because their friends considered their quarrels so dangerous to themselves, they besought Hákon not to let the condition that he should leave the Islands for a time stand in the way of peace. Then, by the advice of good men, they became reconciled.

After this Hákon left the Islands, and first went east to Norway, and saw there King Olaf Kyrri (the quiet), and stayed with him for a while. This was towards the end of his reign. After that he went east to Sweden to King Ingi, Steinkel's son, who received him well. He found friends and kinsmen there, and was highly honoured on account of the esteem in which Hákon, his mother's father, was held. He had possessions from Steinkel, the King of the Swedes, ever since he was banished by King Harald, Sigurd's son, and became greatly beloved both by the King and the people. A second daughter's son of Earl Hákon, Ivar's son, was Hákon who was called the Norwegian; he was the father of King Eirík Spaki (the wise), who was King of Denmark after Eirík Eymuni (the ever-remembered).

[1] Now called the Mainland of Orkney.

E

Hákon remained in Sweden for a while, and was well
treated by King Ingi. But when some time had passed in
this way he felt so home-sick that he wanted to go west again
to the Islands. Christianity then was young, and newly
planted in Sweden. Many men still dabbled in ancient
lore, and were persuaded that by such means they were able
to ascertain future events. King Ingi was a good Christian
man, and loathed all those that meddled in ancient [super-
stitious] lore, and made strenuous efforts to abolish the evil
customs which for a long time had accompanied heathenism; but the chiefs and leading Bœndr murmured loudly
if they were reproved for their evil habits, and at last
matters went so far that the Bœndr elected another King,
Swein, the brother of the Queen, who permitted them to
make sacrifices, and was therefore called "Sacrificing Swein."
King Ingi had to flee from him to Western Gautland (Gothland); but their dealings ended thus, that King Ingi caught
Swein by surprise in a house, and burnt the house and
him in it. After this he subdued the whole country, and
uprooted many wicked customs.

CHAPTER XXVI.

OF THE WORDS OF THE SPAE-MAN.

WHEN Hákon, Paul's son, was in Sweden he had heard of a
man in that country who practised sorcery and spae-craft,
whether he used for those purposes witchcraft or other
magical arts. Hákon became very curious to see this man,
and anxious to know what he could ascertain about his
future. So he went in search of the man, and at last he
found him in a seaside district, where he went from one
feast to another, and foretold the seasons and other things to
the country people. When Hákon had found this man, he
inquired of him whether he would succeed in regaining his
dominions, or what other fortune awaited him. The spae-
man asked him who he was, and he told him his name and
family—that he was the daughter's son of Hákon, Ivar's son.
The spae-man then said: "Why should you ask foresight

or knowledge of the future from me ? You know well that your kinsmen have had little liking for such men as I am ; and yet it might be necessary for you to try to ascertain your fate from your friend, Olaf the Stout, in whom all your faith is placed ; but I suspect that he would not condescend to tell you what you are anxious to know, or else he may not be so mighty as you call him."

Hákon answered : "I will not reproach him, and I should rather think I was not worthy to learn wisdom from him, than that he was incapable ; so that I might learn from him for that matter. But I have come to you, because I thought that we had no reason to envy each other on account of virtue or religion."

The spae-man replied : "I am glad to find that you place your entire trust in me, and not in that faith which you and your kinsmen profess. Truly they who apply themselves to such things are strange men. They keep fasts and vigils, and believe that by such means they will be able to ascertain that which they desire to know ; but the more they apply themselves to these things, the less they ascertain of what they wish to know when it is most important to them to know it. But we undergo no bodily pains, yet we always obtain knowledge of those things which it is of importance to our friends not to be ignorant of. Now matters will go between us in this way, that I shall help you because I understand that you think you will rather obtain the truth from me than from the preachers of King Ingi, in whom he puts his entire trust. After three nights' time you shall come to me, and then we shall try whether I may be able to tell you any of the things you wish to know."

Upon this they parted, and Hákon stayed in the district. When three nights had passed, he went again to see the spae-man. He was in a certain house alone, and groaned heavily as Hákon entered. He passed his hand across his forehead, and said that it had cost him much pain to obtain the knowledge which Hákon desired. Hákon then said he wished to hear his future.

The spae-man said : "If you wish your whole fate unfolded, it is long to tell, for there is a great future in store for you, and grand events will happen at certain periods of

your life. I foresee that you will at last become the sole
ruler of the Orkneys; but you will perhaps think you have
long to wait. I also see that your sons will rule there. Your
next journey to the Orkneys will be a very eventful one,
when its consequences appear. In your days you will also
commit a crime,[1] for which you may or may not obtain
pardon from the God in whom you believe. Your steps go
farther out into the world than I am able to trace, yet I
think you will rest your bones in the northern parts. Now
I have told you what has been given me to tell you at this
time, but what satisfaction you may have derived from your
visit rests with yourself."

Hákon replied: "Great things you have foretold, if they
turn out to be true; but I think my fate will prove itself
better than you have said; and perhaps you have not seen
the truth."

The spae-man said he was free to believe what he liked
of it, but that such events would not the less surely come
to pass.

CHAPTER XXVII.

OF THE SCHEMES OF HAKON, PAUL'S SON.

AFTER this Hákon went to see King Ingi, and stayed with
him a short while. Then he obtained leave from the King
to depart. He went first to Norway to see his kinsman,
King Magnus, who received him very well. There he
heard that the government of the Orkneys was almost
exclusively in the hands of Earl Erlend and his sons, and
that they were greatly loved, but that his father Paul took
little part in the government. He also thought he could
perceive from conversations with men from the Orkneys,
who gave him a true account of the state of matters, that
the Orkneymen had no desire for his return home. They
were living in peace and quiet, and were afraid that Hákon's
return would give rise to disturbance and strife. When
Hákon was turning this over in his mind, he thought it
likely that his kinsmen would try to keep him out of his

---

[1] The reference here must be supposed to be to the murder of St. Magnus.

possessions, and that it would be dangerous for him if he did not go west with a numerous retinue.   Then he devised a scheme to induce King Magnus to put him into his possessions in the Orkneys.

CHAPTER XXVIII.

HAKON'S INTERVIEW WITH KING MAGNUS.

THIS was after King Magnus had put Steigar Thórir and Egil to death, and put down all opposition to his rule. Hákon was a sagacious man, and he thought he could understand from King Magnus's conversation that he was ambitious of grand undertakings, and covetous of the possessions of other rulers.   Hákon began to tell the King that it would be a princely feat to make an expedition to the west, and subdue the Islands, as Harald the Fairhaired had done.   He also said that if he established his power in the Sudreyar (Hebrides), he might easily make forays into Ireland and Scotland from them.   Then, having subdued the western countries, he might attack the English, with the help of the Northmen, and thus take revenge for his grandfather Harald, Sigurd's son.

When they were speaking about these things, it became evident that the King was pleased with this proposal, and said it was spoken like a nobleman, and quite according to his own mind.   "But I wish you not to be surprised, Hákon," said the King, "in case I shall be persuaded by your words to carry an army into the west, if I put forward a strong claim to the possessions there, without regard to the claims of any man."

When Hákon heard this suggestion, he was not so well pleased, because he suspected the real meaning of the King's words; and after this he no longer persuaded the King to go; neither was it required, for after their conversation, the King sent messages throughout his dominions to make known that he was soon to lead out an expedition, and then he made it known to the people that he was going to the west, whatever might be the result.   Preparations were

made for the expedition throughout the whole kingdom.
King Magnus took with him his son Sigurd, who was eight
winters old, and a hopeful boy.

CHAPTER XXIX.

THE WESTERN EXPEDITION OF MAGNUS BARELEGS.

WHEN the brothers Paul and Erlend ruled the Orkneys, King
Magnus came from Norway. He had a large army. Many
of his vassals followed him, among whom were Vidkunn
Jónsson, Sigurd Hrani's son, Serk from Sogn, Dag Eilif's
son, Skapti from Gizki, Ogmund, Finn and Thórd, Eyvind
Olnbogi (the King's High Steward), Kali, Snæbiörn's son
from Agdir, the son of Thorleif Spaki (the wise) who was
maimed by Hallfred, and Kol his son. Kali was a very
wise man, much esteemed by the king, and made verses well.

When King Magnus came to the Orkneys, he seized the
Earls Paul and Erlend, and sent them east to Norway, but
placed his son Sigurd over the Isles, and gave him counsellors. King Magnus went to the Sudreyar (Hebrides),
accompanied by Magnus and Erling, the sons of Earl Erlend,
and Hákon, Paul's son. But when King Magnus came to
the Islands, he began hostilities first at Liódhús (Lewis), and
gained a victory there. In this expedition he subdued the
whole of the Sudreyar, and seized Lögman, the son of
Gudröd, King of the Western Islands. Thence he went to
Bretland (Wales), and fought a great battle in Anglesea
Sound with two British chiefs[1]—Hugh the Stout and Hugh
the Bold. When the men took up their arms and buckled
for the fight, Magnus, Erlend's son, sat down on the foredeck,
and did not take his arms. The King asked why he did not

---

[1] "Hugh the Stout " was Hugh, Earl of Chester ; and "Hugh the Bold,"
Hugh of Montgomery, Earl of Salop. According to Ordericus Vitalis, King
Magnus came into the Menai Straits with only six ships, carrying a red shield
on the mast as a sign of peace and commercial intercourse. The Welsh King
Griffith was at that time engaged in war with the Norman Earls above mentioned, who had invaded his territories, and advanced as far as the Straits,
when the arrival of King Magnus gave an unexpected turn to the course of
events, in the death of the Earl of Montgomery, as here narrated.

do so. He said he had nothing against any one there, and would not therefore fight.

The King said: "Go down below, and do not lie among other people's feet if you dare not fight, for I do not believe that you do this from religious motives."

Magnus took a psalter and sang during the battle, and did not shelter himself. The battle was long and fiercely contested, and both swords and missiles were used. For a long time the result of the battle was doubtful. King Magnus shot from a bow, and a man from Hálogaland[1] was with him. Hugh the Bold fought valiantly. He had a suit of armour which covered him entirely, except his eyes. King Magnus ordered the man from Hálogaland to shoot at the same time as he did, and they shot both at once. One of the arrows struck the nose-piece of the helmet, and the other pierced the eye, and that was said to be the king's arrow.

CHAPTER XXX.

KALI'S DEATH.

AFTER Hugh's death the British (Normans) fled, and King Magnus obtained a great victory. He lost there many brave men, and many others were wounded. Kali had received many wounds, but none mortal. After the battle King Magnus sailed from the south along the coasts of Bretland and Scotland, having conquered all the Sudreyar and Anglesea, which is one-third of Bretland.

King Magnus had appointed Magnus, Erlend's son, as one of the waiters at his table, and he performed continually the duties of that office; but after the battle in Anglesea Sound the king showed that Magnus had incurred his serious displeasure. He had not been wounded, although he had not sheltered himself. During the night he stole away from the King, and hid himself for some time in the woods, while the King's men made a search for him. Magnus made his way to the court of Malcolm,[2] the King of Scots, and remained

---

[1] Hálogaland, the most northern part of Norway.

[2] The Saga writer (says Munch) has been here misled by the Scottish deno-

there a while. For some time he was with a certain bishop in Bretland. He was also in England; but he did not come to the Orkneys while King Magnus was alive.

King Magnus held northward, along the coasts of Scotland, and messengers came to him from Malcolm, the King of Scots, to ask for peace. They said that the King of Scots was willing to give him all the islands lying west of Scotland, between which and the mainland he could pass in a vessel with the rudder shipped. Thereupon King Magnus landed in Satiri (Kintyre), and had a boat drawn across the neck (isthmus) of Satiri,[1] he himself holding the helm, and thus he gained possession of the whole of Satiri, which is better than the best island of the Sudreyar, Man excepted. It is in the west of Scotland, and on the land side there is a narrow isthmus, across which vessels are frequently drawn. Thence King Magnus went to the Sudreyar, and sent his men into Scotland's Fiord.[2] They rowed in along one coast and out along another, and thus took possession of all the islands west of Scotland.

Then the King made it known that he was going to spend the winter in the Sudreyar, but gave permission to those who had most urgent business to go home. When the troops knew this, they all wished to go home, and murmured greatly at being longer detained. The King then held a council with his advisers, and looked at the wounds of his men. He saw

mination of the reigning monarch, Edgar MacMalcolm. Malcolm Canmore died in 1093, the year of King Magnus's first expedition to the west. The second expedition, which was in 1098, was the one in which he fought with the two Norman Earls in Anglesea Sound. The events of the two expeditions are here mixed up together, and the references to Malcolm Canmore do not synchronise with either. It is possible that the offer of the islands (as here mentioned) may have come to King Magnus from Donald Bane, the brother of King Malcolm, to secure the support of King Magnus in his attempt to retain the throne against Edgar, although the incident of the drawing of the boat across the isthmus may have taken place in the reign of Edgar. The "Fagrskinna" (p. 156) adds that King Malcolm of Scotland sent his daughter out to the Orkneys to be married to Magnus's son Sigurd, he being then nine and she five years of age, and that he left her in the Orkneys when he went to Norway. The author has confounded Malcolm with Mýrkiartan.

[1] Pennant mentions (1772) that not long previously it was customary for vessels of nine or ten tons to be drawn across the isthmus by horses, in order to avoid the dangerous and circuitous passage round the Mull.

[2] Scotland's Firth—the channel between the west coast of Scotland and the Hebrides.

Kali, and asked about his wounds. Kali said they did not
heal well, and that he did not know what the end would be.
The King asked for his advice. Kali said: " Is it not so
that your friends are now failing you ? " The King said he
did not think so. Kali asked him to hold a wapinschaw,
and thus to ascertain the number of his troops. This the
King did ; then he missed many men. This he told to Kali.
Then Kali sang :

> How do thy great chiefs repay thee
> For the bounties lavished on them ?
> Now, O King, of this make trial—
> On western currents ships are shaken.

The King replied :

> Surely it was in my folly
> That my wealth I gave to these men ;
> Yet my long ships, swiftly speeding,
> Still shall climb the chilly billows.

After this the King kept a watch to prevent men from
deserting.

When King Magnus was in the Sudreyar, he obtained
the hand of Biadmonia, the daughter of Mýrkiartan,[1] the son
of Thiálbi, the King of the Irish in Kunnáttir (Connaught),
for his son Sigurd, who was then nine winters old, and she
five. This winter Kali died from his wounds. Sigurd Sneis
(slice), Kali's kinsman, a Lenderman from Agdir, had fallen
in Anglesea Sound.

CHAPTER XXXI.

BIRTH OF KALI, SON OF KOL.

EARLY in the spring King Magnus left the Sudreyar, and
went first to the Orkneys, where he heard of the death of the
Earls. Erlend died in Nidarós,[2] and was buried there ; and
Paul died in Biörgvin (Bergen). Then King Magnus married
Gunnhild, the daughter of Earl Erlend, to Kol, Kali's son, in

---

[1] Muircearteach, grandson of Brian Boroimhe, King of Munster.
[2] Now Drontheim, so called because situated at the mouth of the Nid.

order to compensate him for (the loss of) his father. Her
dowry consisted of possessions in the Orkneys, including a
farm at Papul.[1] Some say that Erling, Erlend's son, fell in
Anglesea Sound, but Snorri Sturluson says he fell in Uladstir[2]
with King Magnus. At his wedding Kol became King
Magnus's vassal. Afterwards he went to Norway with the
King, and home to Agdir with his wife, and went to reside
at his estates there. Kol and Gunnhild had two children;
their son was called Kali, and their daughter Ingirid. They
were both very promising children, and brought up with
affectionate care.

CHAPTER XXXII.

SIGURD MADE KING.

WHEN Magnus had been king nine winters, he went to the
west, and made war in Ireland, and spent the winter in
Kunnáttir (Connaught). The next summer, on St. Bartho-
lomew's Day, he fell in Uladstir (Ulster). When Sigurd
heard in the Orkneys of the death of his father, he went
immediately to Norway, and was made king, along with his
brothers Eystein and Olaf. He had left the daughter of
the Irish king in the west.

One winter or two after the death of King Magnus,
Hákon, Paul's son, came from the west, and the kings
gave him an earl's title and possessions beseeming his birth.
Then he returned to the west and took possession of the
Orkneys. He had always accompanied King Magnus while
he was alive. He was with him in his expedition to Gaut-
land, which is mentioned in the song made about Hákon,
Paul's son.

CHAPTER XXXIII.

MAGNUS (ERLEND'S SON) OBTAINS THE TITLE OF EARL.

WHEN Earl Hákon had ruled the Orkneys for some time,
Magnus, the son of Earl Erlend, came from Scotland, and

---

[1] See note at p. 38.   [2] Ulster, in Ireland.

wished to take possession of his patrimony.   The Bœndr
were highly pleased with this, for he was beloved among them,
and had many kinsmen and connections who wished to help
him to his dominions.   His mother was married to a man
called Sigurd.   Their son was named Hákon Karl (man).
They had estates in Papul.   When Earl Hákon heard that
Earl Magnus had come to the Orkneys, he collected men
together, and refused to give up any part of the Islands.
But their friends tried to make peace between them, and at
last they succeeded so far that Hákon consented to give up
half of his dominions if the Kings of Norway approved of it.
Magnus went immediately to Norway to see King Eystein,
for King Sigurd had then gone to Jerusalem.[1]   King Eystein
received him exceedingly well, and gave up to him his patrimony, one-half of the Orkneys, with the title of Earl.
Thereupon Magnus went west to his dominions, and his kinsmen and friends and all the people were glad to see him back.
Through the kind offices of mutual friends, Magnus and
Hákon agreed very well.   So long as their friendship continued there were good times and peace in the Orkneys.

CHAPTER XXXIV.

OF EARL MAGNUS (ERLEND'S SON).

THE holy Magnus, Earl of the Islands, was a most excellent man.   He was of large stature, a man of a noble
presence and intellectual countenance.   He was of blameless
life, victorious in battles, wise, eloquent, strong-minded,
liberal and magnanimous, sagacious in counsels, and more
beloved than any other man.   To wise men and good he was
gentle and affable in his conversation; but severe and un-
sparing with robbers and vikings.   Many of those who
plundered the landowners and the inhabitants of the land
he caused to be put to death.   He also seized murderers and
thieves, and punished rich and poor impartially for robberies
and thefts and all crimes.   He was just in his judgments,

---

[1] King Sigurd, the Jorsalafarer, set out on his pilgrimage to Jerusalem in
1107.

and had more respect to divine justice than difference in the estates of men. He gave large presents to chiefs and rich men, yet the greatest share of his liberality was given to the poor. In all things he strictly obeyed the divine commands; and he chastened his body in many things, which in his glorious life were known to God, but hidden from men. Thus, he made known his intention to espouse a maiden of a most excellent family in Scotland, and having celebrated his marriage, he lived with her for ten winters free from the defilement of carnal lusts, for he was pure and spotless with regard to all such sins, and if he were tempted, he bathed in cold water, and prayed for divine assistance. Many other glorious virtues he exhibited to God himself, but concealed from men.

CHAPTER XXXV.

OF MAGNUS AND HAKON.

MAGNUS and Hákon ruled their lands and defended them for some time, the two agreeing very well. In a song made about them, it is said that they fought with a chief called Dúfniál, their third cousin, who fell before them. They also slew a famous man named Thorbiörn, in Borgarfiörd,[1] in Hjaltland. Other deeds of theirs are set forth in song, though not specially narrated here. When they had ruled the land for some time, it happened, as often is the case, that men of evil dispositions were found who destroyed their good understanding. Hákon was more disposed to listen to these miserable men, because he was very jealous of the popularity and greatness of his kinsman Magnus.

---

[1] Borgarfiord, the "fiord of the Borg," now Burra Firth, on the west side of the Mainland of Shetland, so named by the Norsemen on account of the "borg," or "Pictish tower," which still stands on the little holm of Hebrista, though greatly ruined. It is probable that the reason of Thorbiorn's connection with Borgarfiord was its affording him and his followers a shelter and defensive position in the borg. The old name Borgarfiord occurs in a document in the Norse language dated 1299. It is a record drawn up in the Lagthing of certain charges made against Herr Thorvald Thoresson, by a woman named Ragnhild Simonsdatter, who accuses him of malversation of the land-rents of Brekasettr. (*Diplom. Norvegicum*, vol. i. p. 81.) Harald of Borgarfiord in Shetland witnesses a document in 1498.

CHAPTER XXXVI.

OF EARL MAGNUS.

Two men with Earl Hákon are chiefly mentioned as being the worst in creating enmity between the two kinsmen. These were Sigurd and Sighvat Sokki (sock). Through the slander of wicked men this enmity went so far that the Earls gathered troops together and went to meet each other. Both went to Hrossey, where the Orkney Thingstead [1] was, and when they arrived there, both drew up their troops in battle array, and prepared to fight. There were both the Earls and all the chief men, many (of whom) were friends of both, and did all they could to make peace between them, showing much goodwill and virtuous disposition. This meeting was during Lent. But, as many well-disposed men joined themselves together to avert hostilities between them, and to assist neither of them against the other, they confirmed their reconciliation with oaths and shaking of hands.

Some time after this, Earl Hákon, with hypocrisy and fair words, appointed a day of meeting with the blessed Earl Magnus, so that their friendship and the newly-made peace should neither be disturbed nor destroyed. This meeting, which was to confirm their peace and reconciliation, should take place in the spring, in the Pasch week, in Egilsey.[2] Earl Magnus was well pleased with this arrangement, as he thought it was meant to confirm a sincere peace, without any suspicions, treachery, or covetousness. Each of them should

[1] The place where the Orkney Things were held is nowhere more particularly indicated. Stennis has been suggested, on the supposition that the great stone circle there would have been thus utilised by the Northmen. It does not appear, however, that the occasion on which Havard, son of Thorfinn Hausakliuf, was killed at "Steinsness" was a Thing meeting there, and this is the only occasion on which Stennis is mentioned in the whole of the Flateyjarbók. "Tingwale," in the parish of Rendale, occurs in the Orkney Land List of 1502. This seems to be the only trace of the old Thing-völl in Hrossey.

[2] Egilsey, in Jo. Ben's description of the Orkneys (1529) called "Insularum Ecclesia," is regarded by Munch as deriving its name not from the Norse proper name *Egil*, but from the Irish *Eaglais*, a church. "To this day," he says, "Egilsey contains a church shown by its construction to have been built before the Northmen arrived in Orkney, or at all events to belong to the more ancient Christian Celtic population. (See under "Egilsey" in the Introduction).

have two ships and an equal number of men (at the conference). Both swore to keep the peace, on conditions dictated
by the wisest men.

Immediately after Easter, preparations were made for the
meeting. Earl Magnus summoned all those whom he knew
to be best disposed to him, and most likely to make matters
smooth between them. He had two ships, and as many men
as had been agreed upon, and when he was ready he went
to Egilsey. As they were rowing in calm and smooth water,
a great wave rose under the ship, which was steered by the
Earl, and broke over it where he sat. His men wondered
very much at such an occurrence,—that a breaker should rise
in smooth water where no man could remember a breaker to
have arisen, and where the water was so deep. Then the
Earl said: "No wonder that you are surprised at this.
Indeed, I take this as a foreboding of my death. Perhaps
it will come to pass as was prophesied about Earl Hákon,
and this may be to prepare us for Hákon, my kinsman, not
dealing honestly with me at this meeting." The Earl's men
became very sorrowful when he spoke of his death being
near at hand, and begged him to take care of his life, and
not to trust himself to the good faith of Earl Hákon. Earl
Magnus answered: "Let us go this time, and let all that
depends on our journey be in God's will."

CHAPTER XXXVII.

EARL HAKON AND EARL MAGNUS.

Now it is to be told of Earl Hákon that he gathered together
a numerous army, and had many ships equipped as if for
battle. And when the troops were assembled, he made
known to his men that he intended that this meeting should
decide between him and Earl Magnus, so that both of them
should not rule over the Orkneys. Many of his men
approved of this plan, adding many wicked suggestions to
it, yet Sigurd and Sighvat Sokki counselled the worst things.

Then they began to row fast, and went along quickly.
Hávard, Gunnar's son, who was the friend and counsellor of

the Earls, and equally faithful to both, was on board the Earl's ship. Hákon had concealed this wicked plan from him, in which he would by no means have had any part. And when he knew that the Earl was so resolute in this wicked purpose, he jumped overboard, and swam to a certain uninhabited island.

Earl Magnus arrived first with his men at Egilsey, and when they saw Earl Hákon coming they perceived that he had eight war-ships. Then Earl Magnus suspected that he intended to act treacherously towards him. So he walked along the island with his men, and went into the church to pray. His men offered to defend him. The Earl replied : " I will not put your lives in danger for mine, and if peace cannot be established between us, let it be as God wills." His men now recognised the truth of his words, and as he foreknew the hours of his life—whether from his wisdom or from a divine revelation—he would neither fly nor avoid his enemies. He prayed devoutly, and had a mass sung for him.

CHAPTER XXXVIII.

THE OFFERS OF EARL MAGNUS.

HAKON and his men came up in the morning, and ran first to the church and ransacked it, but did not find the Earl. He had gone to another part of the island, to a certain hiding-place, accompanied by two men. But when the holy Earl Magnus saw that they searched for him, he called to them, and thus made known to them where he was, and said they need search no farther. And when Hákon saw him, he and his men ran thither with loud yelling and clangour of their weapons.

Earl Magnus was praying when they came up to him, and when he had finished his prayer he made the sign of the cross, and said firmly to Earl Hákon : " You did not act well, kinsman, when you broke your oaths, and it is highly probable that you were instigated to this more by the wickedness of others than your own. Now, I will make you three offers, that you may rather accept one of them than break your oaths, and slay me who am innocent."

Hákon's men asked what these offers were.

" The first is, that I shall go to Rome, or away to Jerusalem, and visit the holy places, taking with me two ships from the Orkneys, with the necessary equipment for the journey, and obtain benefits for the souls of us both. I shall swear never to return to the Orkneys."

This offer was promptly rejected.

Then said Earl Magnus : " Now, because my life is in your power, and I have offended against Almighty God in many things, you shall send me to Scotland, to our mutual friends, and keep me in custody there, with two men for companionship.   Make such provision that I shall not be able to escape from this custody."

This too was promptly refused.

Magnus then said : " There is yet one more offer which I will make, and God knows that I think more of your soul than of my own life, for it were better that you should do as I shall offer you than that you should take my life.   Let me be maimed as you like, or deprived of my eyes, and throw me into a dark dungeon."

Then said Earl Hákon : " This offer I accept, and I ask for no more."

But the chiefs started up and said to Earl Hákon : " One of you will we kill now, and from this day you shall not both rule the lands of the Orkneys."

Earl Hákon replied : " Slay him then, for I will rather have earldom and lands than instant death."

Thus their conversation was related by Höldbodi, a truthful Bondi in the Sudreyar, who was one of the two of Earl Magnus's men who were with him when he was taken.

CHAPTER XXXIX.

THE BEHEADING OF EARL MAGNUS.

THE worthy Earl Magnus was as cheerful as if he were invited to a banquet, and spoke neither words of offence nor anger. After these words had passed, he fell on his knees to pray, hiding his face in his hands, and shedding many tears before God. Then, when the holy Earl Magnus was thus doomed to death, Hákon ordered his banner-bearer, Ofeig, to slay the Earl, but he refused, with the utmost wrath. Then forced he Lífólf, his cook, to be the slayer of Magnus, but he began to weep aloud. "Weep not thus," said Earl Magnus, "for this is an honourable task. Be firm, and you shall have my clothing, according to the custom and laws of the men of old. Be not afraid, for you do this against your will, and he who forces you sins more than you."

When he had said this, he took off his tunic and gave it to Lífólf. Then he asked for permission to pray, which was granted to him. He fell upon the earth, and gave himself to God, offering himself as a sacrifice. He prayed not only for his friends, but also for his enemies and murderers, and forgave them, with all his heart, their offences against himself. He confessed his sins to God, and prayed that they might be washed from him in the shedding of his blood. He commended his spirit to God's keeping, and prayed that His angels might come to meet his soul and carry it into the rest of paradise. Some say that he took the sacrament when the mass was sung. Then, when God's friend was led to execution, he said to Lífólf: "Stand before me, and hew me a mighty stroke on the head, for it is not fitting that high-born lords should be put to death like thieves. Be firm, poor man, for I have prayed to God for you, that he may have mercy upon you." After that he signed the sign of the cross, and stooped under the blow, and his spirit passed into heaven.

CHAPTER XL.

THE SAINTSHIP OF EARL MAGNUS MADE MANIFEST.

THE place where Earl Magnus was slain was previously covered with moss and stones, but shortly afterwards his merits before God became manifest in this wise, that it became green sward where he was beheaded. Thus God showed that he had suffered for righteousness' sake, and had obtained the beauty and verdure of paradise, which is called the land of the living.

Earl Hákon did not permit his body to be brought to the church (for burial).

The day of Earl Magnus's death was two days after Tiburtiusmas (14th April). Then he had been seven winters Earl in the Orkneys along with Earl Hákon. Seventy-four winters had passed since the death of King Olaf. The Kings of Norway were at this time Sigurd, Eystein, and Olaf. It was one thousand and ninety-one winters after the birth of Christ.[1]

CHAPTER XLI.

THE EARL'S BODY BROUGHT TO CHURCH.

THORA, the mother of Earl Magnus, had invited both the Earls to a banquet after their meeting, and Earl Hákon went there after the murder of the holy Earl Magnus. Thóra herself served at the banquet, and brought the drink to the Earl and his men who had been present at the murder of her son. And when the drink began to have effect on the Earl,

---

[1] These dates are self-contradictory, and utterly irreconcilable. King Magnus Barelegs fell in Ireland in the year 1103 ; and it is stated in the Saga of Sigurd, the Jorsala-farer, that Hàkon, Paul's son, came to Norway to King Sigurd "a year or two after King Magnus's fall." The King gave him the earldom and government of the Orkneys, and he went back immediately to Orkney. Then it is added that four years after the fall of King Magnus—that is, in 1107—King Sigurd set out on his pilgrimage to Jerusalem. Now, it is mentioned in this Saga (cap. xxxiii.) that Earl Magnus went to Norway to see King Eystein, "for King Sigurd had then gone to Jerusalem." This must have been after 1107. King Eystein gave him his patrimony, one-half of the Orkneys. If his visit to Norway was in the year after King Sigurd's departure, as seems likely from the narrative, or in 1108, and "he had been seven winters Earl in the Orkneys along with Earl Hákon," this would bring the date of his death exactly to the year assigned in the Iceland Annals appended to the Flateyjarbók, or to 1115. The entry in the "Annalar" for that year is : "Pindr enn heilagi Magnus jarl i Orkneyium." Torfæus dates this event in 1110. The Saga of St. Magnus says he had been twelve winters Earl of the Orkneys jointly with Hákon, counting evidently from the vacancy of the earldom in 1103 by the accession of Sigurd, Magnus' son, then Earl of the Orkneys, to the throne of Norway. This also gives the date 1115.

then went Thóra before him and said : " You came alone here,
my lord, but I expected you both.   Now, I hope you will
gladden me in the sight of God and men.   Be to me in stead
of a son, and I shall be to you in stead of a mother.   I
stand greatly in need of your mercy now, and (I pray you
to) permit me to bring my son to church.   Hear this my
supplication now, as you wish God to look upon you at the
day of doom."

The Earl became silent, and considered her case, as she
prayed so meekly, and with tears, that her son might be
brought to church.   He looked upon her, and the tears fell,
and he said, " Bury your son where it pleases you."

Then the Earl's body was brought to Hrossey, and
buried at Christ's Kirk (in Birsay), which had been built by
Earl Thorfinn.

CHAPTER LXII.

THE MIRACLE-WORKING OF MAGNUS THE MARTYR.

SOON after this a heavenly light was seen above his burial-
place.   Then men who were placed in danger began to pray
to him, and their prayers were heard.   A heavenly odour
was frequently perceived above his burial-place, from which
people suffering from illness received health.   Then sufferers
made pilgrimages thither both from the Orkneys and Hjaltland, and kept vigils at his grave, and were cured of all their
sufferings.[1]   But people dared not make this known while
Earl Hákon was alive.

It is said of the men who were most guilty in the
murder of the holy Earl Magnus that most of them met
with a miserable death.

[1] A curious catalogue of cases in which diseased and infirm people were
miraculously restored to health and vigour, after paying their vows at the
shrine of St. Magnus, is given in the Magnus Saga.   These pilgrims mostly
came from Shetland.   Two of the cases are interesting as affording the earliest
notices of leprosy (líkthrá) in Shetland—a disease which seems to have continued in the Islands till towards the close of the last century.—(Sir James
Simpson's Archæological Essays—Leprosy and Leper Hospitals in Britain.)
These cases appear to have been overlooked by Sir James.   Schröder has published a curious Swedish version of the story of St. Magnus, in which the
account of his miracles is considerably varied.

CHAPTER XLIII.

THE MIRACLES WROUGHT BY THE BLESSED FRIEND OF GOD, MAGNUS.

WILLIAM was Bishop of the Orkneys at this time. He was the first bishop there. The bishop's seat was at Christ's Kirk in Birgishérad (Birsay). William was bishop for six winters of the seventh decade.[1] For a long time he disbelieved in the sanctity of Earl Magnus, until his merits became manifest to such a degree that God made his holiness grow the more conspicuous the more it was tried, as is told in the book of his miracles.

CHAPTER XLIV.

THE JOURNEY OF EARL HAKON TO THE SOUTH.

AFTER the murder of Earl Magnus, Hákon, Paul's son, took possession of all the Orkneys, and exacted an oath of fealty from all men, and took submission from those who had served Earl Magnus. He became a great chief, and made heavy exactions from those of Earl Magnus's friends who in his opinion had taken part against him.

Some winters after this he prepared to leave the country, and went to Rome. Then he also went to Jerusalem, according to the custom of the palmers, and brought away sacred relics, and bathed in the river Jordan. After that he returned to his dominions, and resumed the government of the Orkneys. He became a good ruler, and established peace throughout his dominions; he also made new laws for the Orkneys, which the landowners liked better than the

---

[1] That is for sixty-six years. As William died, according to the Icelandic Annals, in 1168, and was bishop in the year of St. Magnus's death, 1115, he was undoubtedly bishop for fifty-three years. That he was bishop for the long period of sixty-six years, as this passage seems to imply, may be open to some doubt. Munch supposes that the " seventh decade " may be an error for " sixth." This would place his consecration to the see of Orkney in 1112 ; but the Saga of St. Magnus says he was bishop sixty-six years.

former ones. Then he became so popular that the Orkney-men desired no other rulers than Hákon and his issue.

CHAPTER XLV.

GENEALOGICAL.

WHEN Earl Hákon ruled over the Orkneys there lived a noble and wealthy man, by name Maddan, at Dal (Dale), in Caithness. His daughters were Helga and Frákörk Thórleif. Helga, Maddan's daughter, was the concubine of Earl Hákon, and their son was Harald, who was called Sléttmáli (smooth-talker), and their daughter was Ingibiörg, who was married to Olaf Bitling (little bit), the King of the Sudreyar. Their second daughter was Margarét. Maddan's daughter, Frákork, was married to a man who was named Liót, Níding (miscreant), in Sutherland, and their daughter was Steinvör the Stout, who was married to Thorliót, at Rekavík.[1] Their sons were Olvir Rosta (strife), Magnus Orm, and Maddan Eindridi, and their daughter Audhild. A second daughter of Frákork was Gudrún, married to Thorstein Höld, Fiaransmunn (open-mouth). Their son was Thorbiörn Klerk (clerk).

Hákon, Paul's son, had a son named Paul, who was called Umálgi (speechless); he was a reserved man, but popular. When the brothers grew up they never agreed. Hákon, Paul's son, died on a sick-bed in the Islands, and his death was considered a great loss, for in the later days of his reign there was unbroken peace, and the Islanders suspected that the brothers would not agree well.

CHAPTER XLVI.

THE SLAYING OF THORKEL FOSTRI.

AFTER the death of Earl Hákon, his sons succeeded him; but they soon disagreed, and divided the dominions between

---

[1] Rekavík is either the modern Rackwick, on the northern point of the Island of Westray, in Orkney, or Rackwick, in the Island of Hoy; more probably the latter.

them. Then also dissensions arose between the great men, and the vassals of each were divided into factions. Earl Harald held Caithness from the King of the Scots, and he resided frequently there, but sometimes also in Scotland (Sutherland ?), for he had many friends and kinsmen there.

When Earl Harald was staying in Sutherland there came to him a man called Sigurd Slembir,[1] who was said to be the son of the priest Adalbrekt. He came from Scotland, having been staying with King David, who had held him in high esteem. Earl Harald received him extremely well. Sigurd went into the Islands with Earl Harald and Frákork, Maddan's daughter, for her husband, Liót Níding, was dead. She and her sister took a large share in the government with Earl Harald. Sigurd Slembir was a great favourite with all of them. At that time Audhild, the daughter of Thórleif, Maddan's daughter, was his concubine. Afterwards she was married to Hákon Kló (claw). Before that time she had been married to Eirík Stræta; their son was Eirík Slagbellir.

When Sigurd and Frákork came to the Islands great dissensions arose, and both of the Earls called together as many of their friends as they could get. The most attached to Earl Paul was Sigurd, at Westness,[2] who had married Ingibiörg the Noble, a kinswoman of the Earls', and Thorkel,

---

[1] Sigurd Slembir or Slembidiakn had a most romantic history. In his youth he was considered the son of a priest, Adalbrekt by name, and was brought up for the church. His tastes appear to have lain in quite another direction, however ; and he soon broke loose from the restraints of ecclesiastical life. He gave himself out as an illegitimate son of King Magnus Barelegs, and commenced a life of roving and adventure, visiting the Holy Land, and turning an honest penny occasionally by trading expeditions to Scotland, the Orkneys, Ireland, and Denmark. In the latter country he proved his paternity by the ordeal of hot iron, as King Harald Gilli had done. He then went to King Harald, and asked him to recognise him ; but instead of this he was placed on his trial for the slaying of Thorkel Fóstri, Sumarlidi's son. He managed to make his escape by jumping overboard with two of his guards in his arms, and soon after returned and killed King Harald Gilli in his bed in Bergen. Then he tried to place Magnus the Blind on the throne by assistance from Denmark ; but the expedition was met on the south coast of Norway by the sons of King Harald, and totally defeated. Magnus was slain, and Sigurd Slembir was taken, and put to death with almost incredible tortures. (See the account of him in the Sagas of Magnus the Blind and the sons of Harald in the Heimskringla.)

[2] Westness, in Rousey (Hrolfsey), see p. 73.

Sumarlidi's son, who was always with Earl Paul, and was called his foster-father. He was a kinsman of the holy Earl Magnus, and a most popular man. The friends of the Earl thought that no man would less deplore their dissensions than Thorkel, because of the injury done him by their father Hákon. At last Earl Harald and Sigurd Slembir went to Thorkel Fóstri,[1] and slew him. When Earl Paul heard this, he was very much displeased, and gathered men together; but when their mutual friends became aware of this, they went between them and tried to reconcile them; and all took part in making peace. Earl Paul was so wroth that he would not make peace, unless all those who were concerned in the manslaying were banished. But as the islanders thought their dissensions a great calamity, they all tried to pacify them; and the result was that Sigurd and all those who, in Earl Paul's opinion, were most concerned in this crime, were banished from the Orkneys. Earl Harald paid the manbote (compensation) for the slaughter of Thorkel. The terms of this peace were that their friendship should be confirmed, and that they should spend Christmas and all the chief festivals together.

Sigurd Slembir left the Orkneys, and went to Scotland, and stayed for a while with Malcolm, King of Scots, and was well entertained. He was thought a great man in all manly exercises. He remained for a time in Scotland, until he went to Jerusalem.

CHAPTER XLVII.

EARL HARALD SLAIN BY SORCERY.

ONCE the brothers were to be entertained at Orfjara (Orphir), one of Earl Harald's estates, and he was to bear the expense of the entertainment for both of them that Christmas. He was very busy, and made great preparations. The sisters Frákork and Helga were there with the Earl, and sat sewing

---

[1] Thorkel Fóstri Sumarlidi's son, foster-father to Earl Paul, not to be confounded with Thorkel Fóstri, Amundi's son, previously noticed as foster-father to Earl Thorfinn Sigurdson.

in a little room.[1]   Earl Harald went into the room where
the sisters were sitting on a cross-bench, and saw a linen
garment, newly made, and white as snow, lying between
them.   The Earl took it up, and saw that it was embroidered
with gold.   He asked, " To whom does this splendid thing
belong ? "

Frákork replied, " It is intended for your brother Paul."

" Why do you make such a fine garment for him ? You
do not take such pains in making my clothing."

He had just come out of bed, and was dressed in a
shirt and linen drawers, and had thrown a mantle over his
shoulders.   He threw off the mantle, and spread out the
dress.   His mother took hold of it, and asked him not to
envy his brother of his fine clothing.   The Earl pulled it
from her, and prepared to put it on.   Then Frákork snatched
off her head-gear, and tore her hair, and said that his life
was at stake if he put it on, and both of the women wept
grievously.   The Earl put on the garment nevertheless; but as
soon as it touched his sides a shiver went through his body,
which was soon followed by great pain, so that he had to
take to his bed; and he was not long in bed until he died.
His friends considered his death a great loss.

Immediately after his death his brother Paul took pos-
session of his dominions, with the consent of the Bœndr.
Earl Paul considered that the splendid underclothing which
Earl Harald had put on had been intended for him, and
therefore he did not like the sisters to stay in the Orkneys.
So they left the Islands with all their attendants, and went
first to Caithness, and then to Scotland to the estate which
Frákork had there.   Her son Erlend was brought up there
while he was young.   Olvir Rosta, the son of Thorliót, from
Rekavík (Rackwick), and Steinný (Steinvor ?), Frákork's
daughter, were also brought up there.   Olvir was a man of
great strength, a violent man and a great fighter.   Thorbiörn
Klerk, the son of Thorstein Höld, was brought up there,
and also Margarét, the daughter of Earl Hákon and Helga,

---

[1] Stofa.   In the twelfth century men began to live more comfortably, and
broke up their large halls into separate compartments.   Thus, a portion of
the Skáli at the upper end, where the pall or dais was, was shut off, and
called *stofa.* — (Dasent's preface to the Njals Saga.)

Moddan's daughter, and Eirík Slagbrellir. All these were men of great families, and accomplished, and thought they had claims to the Orkneys. The brothers of Frákork were Magnus Orfi (the liberal) and Earl Ottar, in Thórsey (Thurso), who was a noble man.

CHAPTER XLVIII.

OF EARL PAUL.

EARL PAUL then ruled the Orkneys, and was very popular. He was somewhat taciturn, spoke little at the Things, and gave others a large share in the government with himself. He was a modest man, and gentle to the people, liberal with his money, and spared nothing with his friends. He was not warlike, and kept himself very quiet. At that time there were many noble men descended from Earls in the Orkneys. Then there lived at Westness, in Hrólfsey (Rousey), a noble man, by name Sigurd, who had married Ingibiörg the Noble. Her mother Herborg was the daughter of Earl Paul, Thorfinn's son. Their sons were Brynjúlf and Hákon Pík (peak). All these were Earl Paul's vassals; so were also the sons of Hávard, Gunni's son—Hákon Kló, Thorstein, and Dúfniáll. Their mother was Berglíót, and her mother was Ragnhild, the daughter of Earl Paul. There was a man named Erling, who lived in Caithness. He had four sons, all of them accomplished men. A man named Olaf lived in Gáreksey (Gairsay), and had another estate at Dungalsbæ, in Caithness. Olaf was a great man, and highly honoured by Earl Paul. His wife was named Asleif, a wise woman, accomplished, and of a great family. Their sons—Valthióf, Swein, and Gunni—were all accomplished men. Their sister was named Ingigerd. Sigurd, the Earl's brother-in-law, had married Thóra, the mother of Earl Magnus, and their son was Hákon Karl (man). Both Sigurd and his son were great chiefs. In Rínarsey (North Ronaldsay) there lived a woman, by name Ragna, and her son was named Thorstein, a man of great strength. A farmer named Kugi, a wise and

wealthy man, lived at Gefsisness,[1] in Westrey. A farmer
named Helgi lived at a hamlet in Westrey. Thorkel Flétta
(a braid), a violent and powerful man, lived in Westrey.
Thorstein and Haflidi were unpopular men. At Swíney
(Swona), in the Pentland Firth, lived a poor man, and his
sons were Asbiörn and Margad, sturdy fellows. In Fridarey
(Fair Isle) lived a man by name Dagfinn. A man named
Thorstein lived at Fluguness,[2] in Hrossey (the Mainland of
Orkney), and his sons were Thorstein Krôkauga (crooked
eye) and Blán, both of them wild fellows. Játvör, the
daughter of Earl Erlend, and her son Borgar, lived at Knarrarstadir;[3] they were rather unpopular. Jón Vœng (wing)
lived at Uppland, in Háey (Hoy). Rikgard lived at Brekkur,[4] in Straumsey. They were poor men, and relatives of
Olaf Hrólfsson. A man named Grímkell lived at Glettuness.[5] All these men will be mentioned in the saga
afterwards.

[1] Gefsisness. No place answering to this name can now be traced in
Westray, but a various reading of the passage has Reppisness ; and there is a
place on the south-east side of the island still called Rapness, probably the
place here indicated.

[2] Fluguness does not again occur in the saga, and has not been identified.
It is the same as the Flydruness of p. 92.

[3] Knarrarstadir seems to signify the district at the head of Scapa Bay,
south of Kirkwall. Munch derives the name from *knörr*, a merchant-ship.
It is said at p. 110 that Játvör and her son Borgar lived at Geitaberg, which
seems to be the place now called Gatnip, on the east side of Scapa, anciently
Scalpeid.

[4] Brekkur in Straumsey may have been the name of a homestead in the
island of Stroma. There is some confusion as to the locality, however. It is
said in cap. lxvii. to have been in Stronsay. The name is not now recognisable in either of the islands.

[5] Glaitness, near Kirkwall, is probably the modern representative of the
ancient Glettuness. In the testament of Sir David Synclair of Swynbrocht
(Sumburgh, in Shetland), in the year 1506, there is a bequest "to Thorrald
of Brucht, and to his wife and his airis, ten merks land in Glaitness, and
fifteen merks land in Linggo, with all guids there contenit, and twenty-two
merks in Pappale, ten merks in Brucht."

CHAPTER XLIX.

OF KALI, WHO AFTERWARDS BECAME AN EARL.

KOL, who was a very wise man, resided on his estates at Agdir (in Norway), and did not go to the Orkneys. His son Kali grew up there, and was a most promising man. He was of middle size, well proportioned, and very handsomely shaped; his hair was of a light auburn colour. He was very affable and popular, and highly accomplished. He made the following verses :—

> At the game-board I am skilful;
> Knowing in no less than nine arts;
> Runic lore I well remember;
> Books I like; with tools I'm handy;
> Expert am I on the snow-shoes,
> With the bow, and pull an oar well;
> And, besides, I am an adept
> At the harp, and making verses.

Kali was frequently with his kinsman Sölmund, the son of Sigurd Sneis. He was treasurer at Túnsberg, and had estates at Austragdir. He was a great chief, and had a numerous retinue.

CHAPTER L.

OF KALI AND GILLICHRIST.

WHEN Kali was fifteen winters old, he went with some merchants to England, taking with him a good (cargo of) merchandise. They went to a trading place called Grímsbœ (Grimsby). There was a great number of people from Norway, as well as from the Orkneys, Scotland, and the Sudreyar. Kali met there a man who was called Gillichrist. The latter asked Kali about many things in Norway, and spoke chiefly with him, so that they became companions. Then he told Kali in confidence that his name was Harald,[1] that Magnus Barelegs was his father, and his mother was in the Sudreyar.

---

[1] Harald Gillichrist, who subsequently became King of Norway, under the name of King Harald Gilli. See p. 84, note.

He further asked him how he would be received in Norway if he came there. Kali said that he thought King Sigurd would be likely to receive him well, if others did not set him against him. Gillichrist and Kali exchanged presents, and at parting they promised each other mutual friendship wherever they might meet.

CHAPTER LI.

OF KALI AND JON.

AFTER that Kali went from the west in the same ship. They touched at Agdir, and from there they went to Björgvin (Bergen). Then he made a stanza :—

> Unpleasantly we have been wading
> In the mud a weary five weeks.
> Dirt we had indeed in plenty,
> While we lay in Grimsby harbour ;
> But now on the moor of sea-gulls
> Ride we o'er the crests of billows,
> Gaily as the elk of bowsprits
> Eastward ploughs its way to Bergen.

When they came to the town, there was a great number of people from the north and the south (of Norway), and from foreign lands, who had brought much merchandise. The crew of the ship went to some public places to amuse themselves. Kali was a great dandy, and made a great display, as he was newly arrived from England. He thought a great deal of himself, and many others thought a great deal of him too, because he was of a good family, and highly accomplished. In the inn where he sat drinking there was a man named Jón Pétrsson, the son of Serk, from Sogn. He was the king's vassal at the time. His mother was Helga, the daughter of Hárek, from Setr. Jón was a great dandy too. The dame who kept the inn where they were drinking was Unn by name, a woman of good repute. Jón and Kali soon became companions, and parted great friends. Whereupon Jón went home to his estates, and Kali went to his father, Kol, at Agdir. Kali stayed frequently with his kinsman

Sölmund.   Thus some years passed, in which Kali made trading trips during the summer, and spent the winters at home or with Sölmund.

CHAPTER LII.

KALI GOES INTO DOLLS CAVE.

ONE summer Kali went to Thrándheim; he was detained by weather in an island called Dolls, and there was a cave called Dollshellir.   It was said that money was hidden there. The merchants went into the cave, and found it very difficult to penetrate into it.   They came to a sheet of water stretching across the cave, and no one dared to cross it except Kali, and one of Sölmund's domestics called Hávard.   They swam across the lake, having a rope between them.   Kali also carried firewood and fire-making gear between his shoulders. They came to the opposite shore, which was rugged and stony; the smell also was there very bad, so that they could hardly make a light.   Kali said they should not go any farther, and piled up stones as a monument.   Then Kali sang a song:

> Here I raise a mighty stone-pile,
> In remembrance of our daring, ·
> In this Dolls cave, dark and gloomy,
> Where we sought the goblins' treasure.
> Yet I know not how the captain
> Of the ocean's gliding snow-skates
> May re-cross the dismal water:
> Long and dreary is the journey.

Then they returned, and came safe to their men, and it is not mentioned that anything else happened during their journey. When they came to Björgvin, Kali went to the same inn, to Dame Unn.   Jón Pétrsson was there, and one of his domestics, by name Brynjúlf.   Many other men were also there, although their names are not mentioned here.

CHAPTER LIII.

OF HAVARD AND BRYNJULF.

ONE evening, when Jón and Kali had gone to bed, many remained drinking, and talked a great deal. The guests were getting drunk, and at last they began comparing men,[1] and disputing about who were the greatest of the landed men of Norway. Brynjúlf said that Jón Pétrsson was the best man, and of the noblest family of all the young men south of Stad. Hávard, the companion of Kali, spoke of Sölmund, and said that he was in nothing inferior to Jón, adding that the men of Vík would esteem him more than Jón. Out of this a great quarrel arose, and as the ale spoke in them, they kept so little within bounds that Hávard jumped up, took a piece of wood, and struck Brynjúlf a blow on the head, so that he fainted. Those present took hold of Brynjúlf, and sent Hávard away to Kali, who again sent him to a priest called Rikgard, in Alvidra. "And tell him from me," said Kali, "to keep you till I come to the east." Kali sent a man with him, and they rowed to the south till they came to Grœningiasund. Then Hávard said to his fellow-traveller: "Now, as we are out of their reach, let us rest ourselves, and lie down to sleep."

When Brynjúlf recovered, he was conducted to Jón, and he told him all that had happened, and also that the man had been sent away. Jón guessed the truth about Hávard's destination, and ordered ten men, led by Brynjúlf, to take a rowing boat, in which they rowed till they came to Grœningiasund, and by that time it was daylight. They saw a boat on the beach. Brynjúlf said: "Perhaps these men may be able to tell us something of Hávard." Then they went up and found them when they had just woke up. Brynjúlf and his men attacked them immediately with arms, and Hávard and his companion were both slain. After this they returned

---

[1] Comparing men. This was a favourite occupation of their leisure hours among the Northmen. A curious instance of it occurs in the Saga of King Sigurd, the Jorsala-farer, in the Heimskringla, where the narrative states that as the ale was not good the guests were very quiet and still, until King Eystein said, "It is a common custom over the ale-table to compare one person with another, and now let us do so." As in this case, a quarrel was the usual result.

to the town and told the news to Jón, and then it was known to the whole town.

Kali considered these slaughters a great offence against himself; and when mediators went between him and Jón, the latter said that he would leave to him to say what amends he wished for the offence, without prejudice to the right of the King and the parties to the suit. Kali agreed to this, yet they were no friends from this time. Kali went home after this occurrence, and when he saw his father he told him the news and the result.

Then Kol said: "I think your judgment was rather strange, in that you should have agreed to any terms of reconciliation before Sölmund knew. I think your position is difficult, and that you can do little else than try to be reconciled. But Sölmund would not have acted like you if your man had been killed."

Kali replied: "I suppose it is true, father, that I have judged rather hastily in this matter, and you were too far away to advise me. It will often appear that I am not so deeply wise as you. But I thought that Sölmund had not a better chance of gaining honourable amends, though I refused what was offered to me. And I consider it no dishonour for you and Sölmund if he offers to allow you to determine your compensation, though I doubt whether such an offer will be made. But I consider myself under no obligation to Brynjúlf, while I have made no award and no money has been received."

Father and son had a long talk about this, and did not agree; then they sent men to tell Sölmund the news.

CHAPTER LIV.

OF JON AND SOLMUND.

AFTER that, Kol and Kali had an interview with Sölmund. Kol wished to send men to Jón to try to make peace between them; but Sölmund and Hallvard, Hávard's brother, refused everything but blood-revenge, and said it was not becoming to ask for settlement. Yet Kol's advice was taken, because he promised not to withdraw from the case until Sölmund had received honourable amends; and Kol was to lay all the plans. When the messengers returned, they said they had received a most unfavourable reply to their demands, and that Jón refused positively to make compensation for a man who by his own act had forfeited his personal security. Sölmund said that this had turned out just as he expected— namely, that little honour would be gained by asking Jón for settlement; and then he begged Kol to propose a plan that might be of some avail.

Kol replied: " Is Hallvard willing to run any risk in order to avenge his brother, even though it may come to little ? "

Hallvard said he would not spare himself in order to take revenge, even if there were danger connected with it.

" Then," said Kol, " you shall go secretly to Sogn, to a man called Uni, who lives not far from Jón. He is a wise man, but rather poor, for he has been a long time oppressed by Jón; he is a great friend of mine, and considerably advanced in years. You shall take to him from me six marks (of silver) weighed, in order that he may give you advice how to take revenge on Brynjúlf, or some other of Jón's men, whom he considers not less a loss to him. And if this can be brought about, Uni shall send you to my kins- man Kyrpinga Orm, at Studla, and his sons Ogmund and Erling, and there I consider you will be as if you were at home. Tell Uni to sell his farm and come to me."

Hallvard prepared to go, and we are not told of his journey or night quarters, until he came to Uni one evening. He did not tell his true name. They inquired of each other for current news; and in the evening, when they were sitting round the fire, the guest asked a great deal about noble men in Sogn and Hördaland. Uni said that none of the landed men were considered more powerful than Jón, on account of his family and his violence; and he further asked whether they had no experience of it in the south. When he had said this, the guest became silent. Then the people arose from the fire, and the two remained.

Then Uni said: " Did not you say just now that your name was Hallvard ? "

"No," said the guest; "I called myself Saxi this evening."

Uni said: "Then I am out of all difficulties; but if my name were Brynjúlf, I should think yours was Hallvard; and now let us go to sleep."

The guest took hold of him and said: "Let us not go yet." Whereupon he delivered the purse, and said: "Kol sends you his greeting and this silver, in order that you may be willing to advise me how to avenge my brother Havard on Brynjúlf." Then he told him Kol's plans.

Uni said: "Kol deserves well of me, but I cannot know what may be done about the revenge on Brynjúlf; but he is expected here to-morrow to fetch his concubine's clothes."

Thereafter he went with Hallvard to a stable which stood opposite the door of the house, and concealed him in the manger. This was before the people got up, but he had slept in the house during the night. When Hallvard had been a little while in the stable, he saw a brisk man coming to the house. He called into the house, and told the woman to make herself ready. She took her clothes and brought them out. Then Hallvard thought he knew who the man was, and walked out. Brynjúlf had put down his weapons while he was tying the clothes; and when Hallvard met him he dealt him a deadly blow, and returned to the stable and hid himself. While the slaughter was being committed the woman had gone into the house to take leave of the inmates, but when she came out she saw what had occurred, and ran in crying and frightened to such a degree that she was nearly fainting, and told the ·news. Farmer Uni ran out, and said that the man had probably been an assassin. He despatched a man to tell Jón the news, and urged his men with great eagerness to search for the murderer; therefore no one suspected him. Hallvard remained in the stable until the search had slackened. Then he went, with Uni's advice, to Orm and his sons at Studla, and they sent men with him to the east. Kol and Sölmund received him well, and were then well satisfied with their case. After a while the truth came out, and Jón was very much grieved. Thus that year passed.

Next winter, towards Yuletide, Jón left his home with

thirty men, saying that he was going to pay his uncle Olaf
a visit. This he did, and was very well received. Jón told
his uncle that he was going to Agdir to see Sölmund. Olaf
dissuaded him from it, and said that he had held his own
though they parted as matters stood then. But Jón said he
was not satisfied to let Brynjúlf remain unavenged. Olaf
said he thought he would gain very little by trying; yet he
had from there thirty men, and thus he went with half a
hundred men across the hills, intending to take Sölmund and
Kol by surprise. When Jón had just gone from the north,
Uni went in haste to Orm and his sons at Studla, and they
sent men with him to Kol. He arrived there at Yule,
and told them that Jón was going to attack them. Kol
despatched scouts immediately to all parts where Jón was
expected; and he himself went to see Sölmund, and they
and their kinsmen waited with a great number of men about
them. They had news of Jón's movements, and started
immediately to meet him. They met at a certain wood, and
the fight began immediately. Kol's men were much more
numerous, and came off victorious. Jón lost many men, and
fled into the wood. He was wounded in the leg, and this
wound healed so badly that he was lame ever after, and was
called Jón Fót (leg). He came to the north during Lent,
and his expedition was considered rather ignominious. The
winter thus passed, but the next summer Jón caused two of
Kol's kinsmen to be killed, Gunnar and Aslák.

CHAPTER LV.

THE RECONCILIATION OF THE ORKNEYMEN.

SHORTLY afterwards King Sigurd came to the town, and these
difficulties were laid before him. Then the King summoned
both to appear before him, and they came accompanied by
their kinsmen and friends. An attempt was made to reconcile them, and the result was, that the King should judge all
their differences, which both parties confirmed by shaking of
hands. King Sigurd, assisted by the advice of the wisest
men, then made peace between them. One part of the agree-

ment was, that Jón Pétrsson should marry Ingiríd, Kol's daughter, and their friendship should be confirmed by the connection. The killed were set off against each other. The attack on Kol, and Jón's wound, were set off against the loss of men in the east. Further wounds were matched, and the difference made up. Each should assist the other, both at home and abroad. As a result of this reconciliation, King Sigurd gave Kali, Kol's son, the half of the Orkneys, jointly with Paul, Hákon's son, and made him an Earl at the same time. He also gave him the name of Earl Rögnvald, Brúsi's son, because his mother, Gunnhild, said that Rögnvald was the most accomplished of all the Orkney Earls, and thought the name would bring good fortune. This part of the Orkneys had belonged to Earl Magnus, Kali's mother's brother. After this reconciliation, they who were enemies before parted good friends.

CHAPTER LVI.

KING SIGURD'S DEATH.

THIS winter King Sigurd resided in Osló.[1] During Lent he was taken ill, and died one night after Lady-day. His son Magnus was in the town, and held a Thing, and was accepted king throughout the land, agreeably to the oaths which the inhabitants had sworn to King Sigurd. He also took possession of all the royal treasures.

Harald Gilli was at Túnsberg when he heard of the death of King Sigurd. He had meetings with his friends, and sent for Rögnvald and his father, because they had always been friends since they met in England. Rögnvald and his father had also done most to help Harald to prove his paternity to Sigurd. In this they were assisted by many barons; among others Ingimar, Swein's son, and Thióstólf, Ali's son. Harald and his party resolved to hold the Hauga-Thing[2] at

[1] Osló, or Opslo, was the old capital of Norway. Its site is now included in that of Christiania.

[2] Hauga-Thing, so called apparently because the place of meeting was a *haug*, or barrow. Whether this was a local name at Túnsberg, or whether it refers to a special assembly held at the burial-place of the King, is not clear.

Túnsberg, and there Harald was accepted king of one-half of the land. The oaths with which he had given up his patrimony in order to be permitted to prove his paternity by an ordeal [1] were said to have been given under compulsion. Then people flocked to him, and gave in their allegiance, and soon he had many men about him.

Messages went between him and King Magnus, but it was not until four winters had passed that they were reconciled, on the terms that each of them should have one-half of the kingdom; but King Magnus had the long ships, and the table-service, and all the treasures (of his father), yet he was dissatisfied with his portion, and showed enmity to all the friends of King Harald. King Magnus would not hold valid King Sigurd's gift of the Orkneys and the earldom to Rögnvald, because he was the firmest partisan of King Harald, until all their dealings were concluded. Magnus and Harald were three winters Kings of Norway, and nominally at peace, but the fourth summer they fought at Fyrileif, [2] where King Magnus had nearly 6000, but Harald only 1500 men. These chiefs were with King Harald: his brother Kriströd, Earl Rögnvald, Ingimar from Ask, Thióstólf Ali's son, and Sölmund. King Magnus gained the victory, and Harald fled.

---

[1] Harald Gillichrist, illegitimate son of King Magnus Barelegs, was of Celtic extraction, his mother being a native of the Hebrides. He and his mother were brought over to Norway from the Southern Hebrides in a ship belonging to a Norwegian merchant named Halkel Húk. When the story of Harald's parentage was told to King Sigurd, he consented to allow Harald to prove his paternity by the ordeal of hot iron, but on condition, that if he succeeded in proving his descent according to his claim, he should not desire the kingdom in the lifetime either of King Sigurd or of his son, King Magnus, and to this Harald bound himself by oath. This seems to be the oath referred to as given under compulsion. "The ordeal," it is added in the Saga of King Sigurd, "was the greatest ever made in Norway, for nine glowing ploughshares were laid down, and Harald walked over them with bare feet, attended by two bishops, and invoking the holy St. Columba"—another testimony to his Celtic birth. His feet were then bound up, and he was laid in bed. After the customary three days had elapsed, his feet were examined, or, as the Saga has it, "the ordeal was taken to proof, and his feet were found unburnt." His claims were therefore held to have been proven, and made good. It is curious to find that among the privileges granted by the Scottish King David to the monks of Holyrood, they were specially empowered to make trials by the ordeal of hot iron.

[2] In Vík, in the south of Norway.

Kriströd and Ingimar were killed. Ingimar made the following stanza :—

> Fiends me drove to Fyrileif;[1]
> Not with my will did I fight there.
> Bit by arrows from the elmbow,
> Ne'er to Ask shall I return.

King Harald fled to his ships in Vík,[2] and went to Denmark to King Eirik Eymuni,[3] who gave him Halland for his maintenance, and eight long ships without rigging. Thióstólf, Ali's son, sold his lands, bought ships and arms, and went in autumn to King Harald, in Denmark. At Yuletide King Harald came to Biörgvin, and lay in Flóruvagár till after Yule. Then they attacked the town, and met with little resistance. King Magnus was seized on board his own ship, and maimed. King Harald then took possession of the whole kingdom, and the next spring he renewed the gift of the Islands and the title of Earl to Rögnvald.

CHAPTER LVII.

KOL'S SCHEMES.

KOL resolved to send men to the Orkneys to ask Earl Paul to give up half the Islands which King Harald had given to Rögnvald, and they should be friends and good kinsmen. But if Earl Paul refused, the same men should go to Frákork and Olvir Rosta, and offer them one-half of the land, jointly with Earl Rögnvald, if they were willing to take it from Earl Paul by force of arms. When they came to Earl Paul in the Orkneys, and delivered the message, he replied: " I understand this claim; it has been planned advisedly, and with long forethought; they sought the help of the Kings of Norway to obtain my possessions. Now, I will not repay this perfidy by giving away my possessions to a man who is

---

[1] Now Ferlof, in Sogn, Norway.

[2] Vík meant properly the bay of Oslo, the upper part of which is now called the Christiania Fiord, but it was also applied to the district bordering on the bay.

[3] Harald and Eric, Kings of Denmark, had sworn mutual brotherhood.

not nearer to me than Rögnvald is, and refusing them to my brother's son or sister's son. There is no need to talk any more of this, for with the assistance of my friends and kinsmen I shall defend the Orkneys as long as God grants me life."

Then the messengers saw what would be the result of their message to Earl Paul, and went away across the Pentland Firth to Caithness, and south into the country to Frákork, and delivered their message, to the effect that Kol and Rögnvald offered her and Olvir half the Islands if they were willing to conquer them from Earl Paul.

Frákork replied : " It is true that Kol is a very clever man, and it was wisely planned to seek assistance here, as we have a great many relatives and connections. I have now married Margaret, Hákon's daughter, to Moddan, Earl of Atjöklar (Athole), who is of the noblest family of all the Scottish chiefs. His father, Malcolm, is the brother (uncle?) of King Malcolm, the father of David, who is now King of Scots. We have many and just claims on the Orkneys. We ourselves have also some power. We are said also to be rather far-seeing, and during hostilities all things do not come on us unawares ; yet we will be glad to enter into alliance with Kol and his son for many reasons. Tell them from me that I and Olvir shall bring an army to the Orkneys against Earl Paul about the middle of the next summer. Let Earl Rögnvald meet us then, and come to a decisive battle with Earl Paul; and I will collect forces together during the winter from my kinsmen, friends, and connections in Scotland and the Sudreyar (Hebrides).

The messengers returned to Norway, and related how matters stood. Next winter Earl Rögnvald prepared to go west, and the chiefs Sölmund and Jón with him. They went the next summer, and had a fine body of troops, though not numerous, and five or six ships. They arrived at Hjaltland (Shetland) about the middle of the summer, but heard nothing of Frákork. Strong and contrary winds sprung up, and they brought their ships to Alasund,[1] and

---

[1] Alasund is now Yell Sound, the ancient name for the island of Yell being Jala. In the latest known Hjaltland document, written in Norse, and dated in 1586, the name of the island appears as " Yella."

went a-feasting over the country, for the Bœndr received them well.

But of Frákork it is to be told that in the spring she went to the Sudreyar, where she and Olvir gathered troops and ships together.   They got twelve ships, all of them small and somewhat badly manned; and about the middle of the summer they directed their course to the Orkneys, intending to meet Earl Rögnvald, according to their agreement.   The wind was rather unfavourable.   Olvir Rosta was the commander of these troops, and he was to obtain an earldom in the Orkneys if they gained the victory.   Frákork was there also with many of her retainers.

CHAPTER LVIII.

THE FIGHT BETWEEN EARL PAUL AND OLVIR ROSTA.

EARL PAUL was then at a feast with Sigurd at Westness, in Hrólfsey (Rousey), and when he heard that Earl Rögnvald had arrived in Hjaltland, and at the same time that an army which was going to attack him was gathering in the Sudreyar, he sent word to Kugi, in Westrey, and Thorkel Flettir, who were wise men, and many others of his chief men he called together.   At this meeting Earl Paul sought advice from his friends, but they differed in their opinions.   Some wished him to share his possessions with one of the two parties, so as not to have both as enemies.   Others advised him to go over to his friends in Ness (Caithness), and see what assistance he could get there.

Earl Paul replied, " I will not offer them my possessions now, since I refused peremptorily when they asked civilly. Besides, I think it would be unworthy of a chief to flee from my lands without a trial of strength.   My counsel is to send men to-night to collect troops throughout all the Islands.   Let us then go to meet Earl Rögnvald, and have matters decided between us before the Sudreymen come." Earl Paul's plan was adopted.

With Earl Paul there was a man by name Swein, called Brióstreip (breast-rope), who was his henchman, and highly esteemed by him. In the summer he was always on viking-raids, but in the winter [he stayed] with the Earl. Swein was a man of large stature and great strength, swarthy and ill-favoured. He was greatly skilled in ancient lore, and had frequently been engaged in outsittings.[1] His place was in the forecastle of the Earl's ship.

During the night the following chiefs came to Earl Paul: —Eyvind, Melbrigdi's son, in a ship fully manned; Olaf, Rólf's son, from Gáreksey (Gairsey), had another; Thorkel Flettir the third; Sigurd the fourth; and the Earl himself the fifth. With these five vessels they went to Hrólfsey (Rousey), and arrived there in the evening about sunset. Troops gathered to him during the night, but more ships were not to be had. The next day they were going to sail to Hjalt-land to meet Earl Rögnvald; but in the morning, shortly after sunrise, some men came to Earl Paul, who said they had seen longships coming from the Pentland Firth; whether ten or twelve they did not know. The Earl and his men were convinced that this was Frákork's party, and the Earl ordered his men to row against them as fast as possible. Olaf and Sigurd advised them to go leisurely, saying that their troops might arrive at any moment.

When they were east of Tannskáruness (Tankerness), the longships, twelve together, sailed to the west from Múli.[2] The Earl and his men fastened their ships together; then the Bondi, Erling from Tannskáruness, and his sons, came to the Earl and offered him their assistance; and then their ships were so crowded that they thought they could not use more men. The Earl asked Erling and his men to bring stones to them, until they were prevented by the fighting. When they had prepared themselves, Olvir came up and made the attack with a superior force, but his ships were smaller. Olvir (himself) had a large ship, which he placed beside the Earl's ship, and there was the severest fighting.

---

[1] Outsittings, a peculiar kind of sorcery resorted to in order to obtain foreknowledge of the future, in which the person sat out at night under the open sky, and by certain magical rites or incantations summoned the dead from their graves to consult them. A curious instance is given in the 40th chapter of the Færeyinga Saga, in which Sigmund Brestisson is brought from the dead, with his head in his hand, to show who was his murderer.

[2] The Moul Head of Deerness.

Olaf, Rólf's son, attacked the smallest ships of Olvir, and cleared three of them in a short time.   Olvir attacked the Earl's ships so fiercely that all the forecastle men were driven abaft the mast.   Then Olvir urged his men strongly to board, and jumped himself from the quarterdeck to the forepart of the ship, and was the first to board.

Swein Brióstreip was the foremost of all the Earl's men, and fought bravely.   When the Earl saw that Olvir had boarded his ship, he urged his men forward, and jumped himself from the quarterdeck to the forepart of the ship.   When Olvir perceived this, he grasped a spear, and hurled it at the Earl, who received it with his shield, but fell down on the deck.   Then there was a great shout; but in the same moment Swein Brióstreip seized a huge stone,[1] and threw it at Olvir.   It hit him in the chest with such force that he was thrown overboard, and sank; but his men were able to drag him up into one of their ships, and it was not known whether he was dead or alive.   Then some cut the cables, and wanted to flee.   All Olvir's men were also driven down off the Earl's ship, and began to withdraw.   At that moment Olvir recovered, and asked them not to flee; but all pretended not to hear what he said.   The Earl pursued the fugitives along the east of Hrossey and Rögnvaldsey, and into the Pentland Firth, where they parted.   Then he returned, and five of Olvir's ships remained where they had fought.   The Earl took them, and manned them with his troops.   The battle took place on Friday, but in the night the Earl had the ships made ready, and many troops and two longships came to him, so that in the morning he had twelve ships all well manned.

On Saturday he sailed to Hjaltland, and took by surprise those that had charge of Earl Rögnvald's ships.   He killed the men, and seized the ships with all their contents.   In

---

[1] The Norsemen were in the habit of carrying stones on board their warships to be used as missiles.   It is told in the Færeyinga Saga of Sigmund Brestisson that when about to attack the ships of another Viking lying on the opposite side of an island on the coast of Sweden, he spent the whole night in landing the goods and plunder from his vessels, and breaking up stones, and loading his vessel with them to serve as missiles in the attack. The same thing had been done by the Earl's men in this case before the commencement of the fight.

the morning Earl Rögnvald had news of this, and his men gathered together, and a great many of the Bœndr. Then they went down to the beach, and challenged Earl Paul and his men to come on shore and fight. Earl Paul did not put much faith in the Hjaltlanders, and would not go on shore; but he told them to take ships, and then they might fight. Earl Rögnvald saw, however, that they could get no ships in Hjaltland, such as would give them any chance, and they parted thus as matters stood. Earl Paul and his men went back to the Orkneys, but Earl Rögnvald and his men remained in Hjaltland during the summer. In the autumn they went back to Norway with some merchants, and it was thought their expedition had come to a most ridiculous end.

When Earl Rögnvald came to the east, he saw his father Kol, who asked him whether he was dissatisfied with his expedition. He replied that the result had brought little honour to himself.

Kol replied: " I do not think so ; I think a great deal has been done, since the Hjaltlanders are your friends, and the journey was better than staying at home."

Rögnvald replied : " If you praise this journey, then you are either more indifferent about my case than I thought, or you see something in it which I do not perceive. I should wish very much to have your counsels, and that you would go with us yourself."

Kol replied : " I shall not do both — call everything easy for you, and come nowhere near myself; but I think I shall hold fast to my own plans, so that there is no prejudice to your honour."

Rögnvald replied : " I will gladly follow your counsels."

Kol replied : " First, I advise you to send word to King Harald and other friends of yours, and ask them to give you men and ships to go to the west in the spring ; but during the winter we ourselves will collect all the forces we can, and then try a second time whether we can gain possession of the Islands, or find our graves there."

" I have made up my mind," said Earl Rögnvald, " not to make another journey like that we made just now, and I think that most of us who went are of the same mind."

CHAPTER LIX.

EARL RÖGNVALD'S PLANS.

EARL PAUL went back to the Orkneys, after having taken the ships of Earl Rögnvald. He had gained a great victory, and feasted all his friends and vassals.

It was now resolved to make a beacon in Fridarey (Fair Isle), which should be lighted if enemies were seen coming from Hjaltland. Another beacon was made in Rínarsey (North Ronaldsay), and others in some other islands also, so that they 'might be seen all over the Islands. Thorstein, the son of Hávard, Gunni's son, was to have charge of that on Rínarsey; his brother Magnus of the one in Sandey; Kugi of that in Westrey; and Sigurd, at Westness, of the one in Rólfsey. Olaf, Rólf's son, went to Dungalsbæ, in Caithness, and was to have the emoluments of that place. His son Valthióf lived at that time in Straumsey (Stroma).

Earl Paul gave presents to his men, and all promised him their unfailing friendship. He had many men about him in the autumn, until he heard that Rögnvald and his men had left Hjaltland. Nothing happened in the Islands until Yule. Earl Paul had a grand Yule feast, which he prepared at his estate in Jórfiara (Orphir), and invited many guests. Valthióf, Olaf's son, from Straumsey (Stroma), was invited. He went with his men in a ten-oared boat, and they perished all of them in the West Firth on Yule Eve. That was thought sad news, as Valthióf was a most accomplished man. His father, Olaf, had a large party in Caithness. There were his sons Swein and Gunni, and the sons of Grím of Swíney,[1] Asbiörn and Margad, brave-looking fellows, who always followed Swein. Three nights before Yule, Swein, Olaf's son, Asbiörn, and Margad, had put out to sea-fishing, and Asleif and her son, and Gunni, Olaf's

---

[1] Probably at the place now called Swiney, in Caithness, near Lybster. Though the context here seems to imply that Swiney, in Caithness, is meant, it seems that Grim was in the island of Swona (the small island between Hoy and South Ronaldsay), when Swein, Asleif's son, visited him (see p. 92). Perhaps Swiney, in Caithness, was so named from its being the property of Grim of Swona.

son, had gone a short distance to visit their friends. The
night after that Olvir Rosta arrived at Dungalsbæ with the
party that had been out with him on a viking-raid during
the summer. He surprised Olaf in the house, and set it on
fire immediately. There he was burnt with five others, but
the rest were permitted to escape. Olvir and his men took
all the movable property, and then went away.

After this Swein was called Asleif's son. He came
home on Yule Eve, and went immediately out north, on
the Pentland Firth. At midnight they came to Grím, the
father of Asbiörn and Margad, in Swefney (Swona); he went
into the boat to them, and they brought Swein to Knarrarstadir (Knarstane), in Skálpeid (Scapa). A man, by name
Arnkel, lived there. His sons were Hánef and Sigurd.
Grím and his sons returned, and Swein gave him a finger-
ring of gold. Hánef and Sigurd accompanied Swein to
Jórfiara (Orphir), where he was well received; and he was
conducted to his kinsman Eyvind Melbrigdi's son. Eyvind
conducted him to Earl Paul, who received him well, and asked
his news. He told him of his father's death, at which the
Earl was much grieved, and said it had in a great measure
happened through him. He invited Swein to stay witl
him, and he accepted the invitation with thanks.

CHAPTER LX.

SWEIN SLAYS SWEIN.

THEN they went to evensong. There was a large homestead there (at Orphir); it stood on the hill-side, and there
was a height behind the houses. From the top of the hill
Aurridafiörd[1] may be seen on the other side; in it lies
Damisey. In this island there was a castle; the keeper of
it was a man by name Blán, the son of Thorstein, at
Flydruness.[2] In Jórfiara there was a large drinking-hall;[3]

---

[1] Aurrida Firth, or Salmon-trout Firth, now the Bay of Firth.

[2] Flydruness seems to be the same as Fluguness, in Hrossey (Mainland),
mentioned as the residence of Blan and his father Thorstein, at p. 74.

[3] The Earl's seat at Orphir appears to have consisted of a cluster of buildings, of which the main hall or skáli answered to the public room of the re-

the door was near the east gable on the southern wall, and
a magnificent church was in front of the door; and one had
to go down to the church from the hall. On entering the
hall one saw a large flat stone[1] on the left hand; farther in
there were many large ale vessels; but opposite the outer
door was the stofa.

When the guests came from evensong, they were placed
in their seats. The Earl had Swein, Asleif's son, next to
him. On the other side, next to the Earl, was Swein
Brióstreip, and then Jón his kinsman. When the tables
were removed, there came in men with the tidings of
Valthióf's drowning. This the Earl considered sad news.
He said that no one should tell it to Swein while the
Yule feast lasted, adding that he had cares enow already.
In the evening, when they had finished drinking, the
Earl went to bed, and so did most of his guests. Swein
Brióstreip went out and sat out all night, as was his
wont. In the night (at midnight?) the guests arose
and heard mass, and after high mass they sat down to the
table. Eyvind Melbrigdi's son, shared the management of
the feast with the Earl, and did not sit down to the table.
Table-boys and candle-boys were standing before the Earl's
table,[2] but Eyvind handed drinking-cups to each of the

sidence. The descriptions given of the Orkney skális are wanting in that
minuteness which is necessary to enable us to understand the details of their
construction. No doubt they were similar to those of Iceland, the larger of
which were constructed partly of stone and partly of timber, the middle division
of the hall being higher in the roof than the "aisles" on either side of it, and
separated from them by a row of pillars running parallel to each of the side
walls. The walls of the aisles and the spaces between the pillars were covered
with wainscoting, sometimes with carved work, and on high days hung with
tapestry. Shields and weapons were hung along the sides of the hall, above
the benches, and the fires were lit on hearths in the middle of the floor. The
benches were ranged along both sides of the hall; the "high seat" of the
Earl, or owner of the skáli, was in the centre of the south side, and the seats
of highest honour were those next to him on either side.

[1] Probably a large flagstone set on end to serve as a partition-wall. This
is a common feature of the ancient structures in Caithness and Orkney. It
was in the shadow of this flagstone that Swein, Asleif's son, stood when he
killed Swein Briostreip (see p. 95).

[2] Serving the table, and holding lights. The light-bearers or candle-
holders were a distinct class of servants at the King's court. This custom is
said to have been first introduced by King Olaf Kyrre in the latter half of the
eleventh century.

Sweins. Swein Brióstreip thought Eyvind poured more into his cup than Swein, Asleif's son's, and that he took the cup away from the latter before he had emptied it, so he called Swein, Asleif's son, a sluggard at his drink. There had long been a coldness between Swein Brióstreip and Olaf, Hrólf's son, and also between him and Swein, Asleif's son, since he grew up. When they had been drinking for a while, the guests went to nones' service. When they came in again, memorial toasts[1] were proposed, and they drank out of horns. Then Swein Brióstreip wished to exchange horns with his namesake, saying his was a small one. Eyvind, however, put a big horn into Swein Asleif's son's hand, and this he offered to his namesake. Then Swein Brióstreip became angry, and was overheard by the Earl and some of the men muttering to himself, "Swein will be the death of Swein, and Swein shall be the death of Swein." But nothing was said about it. The drinking went on until evensong; and when the Earl went out, Swein, Asleif's son, walked before him; but Swein Brióstreip remained behind drinking. When they came out to the ale-room, Eyvind followed them, and craved a word alone with Swein, Asleif's son.

He said, " Did you not hear what your namesake said when you offered him the horn ? "

" No," he replied.

Then Eyvind repeated his words, and said that it was surely the devil that had spoken through his mouth in the night. " He intends to kill you," he added, " but you should forestall him, and slay him."

Eyvind put an axe into his hand, and told him to stand in the shadow beside the flat stone; he should strike him in front if Jón preceded him; but from behind if Jón followed him.

The Earl went to the church, and no one took heed of Eyvind and Swein; but when Swein Brióstreip and Jón walked out shortly after, the latter had a sword in his hand, as was his habit, though the others were unarmed. Jón

---

[1] The emptying of horns of ale to the memory of departed heroes and comrades, with the accompaniment of speeches setting forth their famous deeds, was a recognised custom at the festivals of the Northmen.

walked in front. Some light came through the outer door, but outside the sky was cloudy. When Swein Brióstreip came into the doorway, Swein, Asleif's son, struck him on the forehead, so that he stumbled, but did not fall; and when he regained his footing, he saw a man in the door, and thought it was he who had wounded him. Then he drew his sword, and struck at his head, splitting it down to the shoulders. This, however, was Jón, his kinsman, and they fell there both. Eyvind came up at the same moment, and led Swein, Asleif's son, into the stofa, opposite the door, and he was dragged out through a window. There Magnus, Eyvind's son, had a horse ready for him, and accompanied him away behind the house, and into Aurrida Firth. There he took a boat, and brought Swein to the castle in Damisey; and the next morning Blán accompanied him to Bishop William, in Egilsey. When they arrived there the Bishop was at mass, and after the mass Swein was conducted to him secretly. Swein told the Bishop the news—the death of his father and brother Valthióf, and the slaughter of Swein and Jón; then he besought the Bishop's assistance. The Bishop thanked him for the slaughter of Swein Brióstreip, and said it was a good riddance.[1] He kept Swein, Asleif's son, during the Yule-tide, and after that he sent him to a man called Höldbodi, Hundi's son, in Tyrvist (Tiree), in the Sudreyar (Hebrides). Höldbodi was a great chief, and received Swein very well, and there he spent the winter highly esteemed of all the people.

CHAPTER LXI.

OF EARL PAUL.

A SHORT time after the slaughters had been committed in Jórfiara, the men ran from the church, and carried Swein into the house, for he was not yet dead, but insensible, and he died during the night. The Earl commanded every one to take his seat, as he wished to know for certain who had

---

[1] Besides his evil repute as a turbulent fellow, Swein was suspected of sorcery, and thus obnoxious to the church (see p. 88).

committed the manslaughters.   Then Swein, Asleif's son, was
missed, and it was thought clear that he had done the deed.

Then Eyvind came and said that it was plainly seen that
Swein Brióstreip must have killed Jón.

The Earl said that no one should touch a hair of Swein,
Asleif's son's head, as this had not been done without provo-
cation.   "But if he avoids meeting with me," he said, "he
will harm himself by so doing."

It was thought most probable that Swein had gone to
Hákon Karl in Papuli,[1] the brother of Earl Magnus the holy.
He was a great chief, a quiet man and moderate.   The Earl
did not hear of Swein that winter, and then he outlawed
him.   In the spring the Earl visited many of the northern
islands, to collect his land-dues.   He made great friends of
the chiefs, and bestowed presents with both hands.   The
Earl visited Straumsey (Stroma), and gave Thorkel Flettir
the farm which Valthióf had, till such time as he should know
where Swein was.

Thorkel said: "Here the saying does not prove true,
that 'the King has many ears.'   Although you are an Earl,
I think it strange that you have not heard of Swein, for I
knew immediately that Bishop William had sent him to
Höldbodi, Hundi's son, in the Sudreyar, and there he has
been all winter."

The Earl replied: "What shall I do with a Bishop who
has acted thus?"

Thorkel replied: "The Bishop should not be blamed for
this in critical times like these; and you will need all your
friends if Rögnvald and his men come from the east."

The Earl said that was true.

From Straumsey he went to Rínarsey, and received an entertainment from Ragna and her son Thorstein.   Ragna was
a wise woman.   They (she and her son) had another farm in
Papey.   The Earl spent three nights there, as he was prevented by weather from going to Kugi, in Westrey.   The
Earl and Ragna spoke of many things.

---

[1] This must either be Paplay in South Ronaldsay, or Paplay on the Mainland.   Munch says that the circumstance that the name of the island is always
carefully added in the Saga when a Mainland district is not the one alluded
to favours the supposition that it is the latter which is here meant.

She said to him: "There was no great loss in Swein Brióstreip, although he was a brave warrior, for he brought on you the hatred of many. I should therefore advise you, in presence of the difficulties that face you, to make as many friends as possible, and be slow to resent offences. I could wish that you would not attach blame to Bishop William and other kinsmen of Swein, Asleif's son, but rather take the Bishop into favour, and send word to the Sudreyar after Swein to pardon him and restore him his possessions, in order that he may be to you such as his father was. It has long been the custom of the noblest men to do a great deal for their friends, and thus to secure support and popularity."

The Earl replied: "You are a wise woman, Ragna, but you have not yet been made Earl of the Orkneys, and you shall not rule the land here. Is it come to this, that I must give Swein money in order to be reconciled to him, thinking that it would be to my advantage?" Then he became wroth, and continued: "Let God decide between me and my kinsman Rögnvald, and may He let it happen to each of us according to his deeds. If I have offended against Rögnvald, I now make offer of reparation; but if he will invade my dominions, I will think him my greatest friend who assists me to defend them. I have never seen Rögnvald; and, so far from having ever offended him with my knowledge, it is known that I had no part in what my kinsmen did."

Many replied that to try to deprive him of his possessions by force of arms would be a most unprovoked assault; and no one spoke against this.

When the spring advanced, Earl Paul had beacons kept up in Fridarey (Fair Isle) and Rínarsey (North Ronaldsay), and almost all the Islands, so that each could be seen from the other. A man named Dagfinn, Hlödver's son, an active fellow who had a farm in Fridarey, was to keep that beacon, and light it if an army were seen coming from Hjaltland.

Earl Rögnvald spent the winter at home at Agdir (in Norway), where he and his father had farms, and sent messages to his kinsmen and friends. Some of them he visited himself, and asked them to assist him with troops and ships to go to the west, and most of them were willing to help him in his need.

H

During the month of Gói,[1] Kol sent away two transport vessels; one west to England to buy provisions and arms. Sölmund took the other south to Denmark, to buy such things as Kol told him, because he had all the management of their equipment. It was intended that these vessels should return about Easter, and they had arranged to start in the week after Easter. Kol and Rögnvald had one warship each, and Sölmund a third; they had also a transport ship with provisions. When they came to Björgvin, King Harald was there, and he gave Rögnvald a war-ship fully manned. Jón Fót (leg) had a war-ship also. Aslák, the son of Erlend, from Hernur, and the daughter's son of Steigar Thórir, had the sixth; he had also a barge with provisions. Thus they had six large ships, five boats, and three transports. When they were waiting for fair wind at Hernur, a ship came from the west, and they asked for news from the Orkneys, and also what preparations Earl Paul would have if Earl Rögnvald came to the west.

CHAPTER LXII.

KOL'S COUNSELS.

WHILE they were lying at Hernur, Earl Rögnvald called together a meeting of his men, and spoke of Earl Paul's preparations, and also of the great enmity the Orkneymen showed against himself, since they were going to prevent him taking possession of his patrimonial inheritance, which had been justly given him by the Kings of Norway. He made a long and eloquent speech, the conclusion of which was that he intended to go to the Orkneys and gain them or die there. His speech was approved of by all, and every one promised him faithful support.

Then Kol arose and said: "We have heard from the

---

[1] Gói, the fourth month of the year, corresponding to our February and part of March. The ancient mode of reckoning among the Northmen was by "winters," the year commencing on the 23d November. Gói was sometimes called "horning-month"—the month in which the deer shed their horns; and it was also the month in which, in heathen times, the great annual sacrifice took place at Upsala, as mentioned in the Saga of King Olaf the Holy.

Orkneys that all the islanders will rise with Earl Paul against you to keep you out of your inheritance. They are slow to lay aside the enmity which they have conceived against you, kinsman. Now it is my counsel to seek for help where it is likely to be had effectually, and to pray that he may permit you to enjoy these possessions, to whom they rightly belong—namely, the Holy Saint Magnus, your mother's brother. It is my wish that you should make a vow to him, that he may grant you your patrimony and his inheritance. You should promise one thing—that if you obtain those dominions you will build a stóne minster at Kirkiuvág (Kirkwall) in the Orkneys, more magnificent than any other in these lands, dedicating it to your kinsman, Earl Magnus the Holy, endowing it with money, so that it may be fitly established, and that his relics and the Bishop's see may be brought there."

Every one thought this good advice, and the vow was made and confirmed. Then they stood out to sea, and had a fair wind. They landed in Hjaltland, and the inhabitants there, as well as the Norwegians, were glad to see each other. The Hjaltlanders were able to tell them much from the Orkneys, and there they stayed for some time.

CHAPTER LXIII.

OF KOL AND UNI.

UNI, who has been mentioned before, and who was an accomplice in the slaughter of Brynjúlf, was now advanced in years.

Once Kol said to him : "What plan would you propose, Uni, in order to get the beacon in Fridarey discontinued, or how would you manage to prevent it from being lighted a second time? I put this question to you, because I know you are more ready-witted than most others here present, although here are men of more distinction."

Uni replied : "I am not a man of invention, and I do not wish the expedition to be made according to my plans; I would rather choose to come afterwards, for then I should follow my own devices."

Shortly after, Kol had many small boats made ready, and directed their course to the Orkneys. No chiefs took part in this expedition except Kol. When they had gone so far that they thought they could be seen from Fridarey, Kol had the sails spread on all the boats, but ordered his men to row backwards, in order that their speed might be as slow as possible, although the wind was right astern. The sails were at first hauled to the middle of the masts only, but afterwards higher, as if they were coming nearer to the island.

Kol said: " These manœuvres will be seen from Fridarey as if the boats were approaching nearer. They will then perhaps light the beacon, but they will go themselves to Earl Paul to tell him the news.

So when the beacon in Fridarey was seen, Thorstein, Ragna's son, lighted the beacon in Rínarsey; then the beacons were lighted one after another in all the Islands, and all the Bœndr went to the Earl, and there was a great gathering of men.

When Kol saw the beacon burning, he ordered his men to turn back, saying that this would now cause dissensions among their enemies. This done, Kol went back to Hjaltland, and said to Uni that he should now carry out his scheme.

Uni took with him three Hjaltlanders, and they took a six-oared boat, some provisions, and fishing tackle. They went to Fridarey. Uni said he was a Norwegian, but had been married in Hjaltland, and had sons there. He further said that he had been robbed by Earl Rögnvald's men, and spoke very ill of them. He took a house there, but his sons went out fishing, and he stayed at home himself and took care of the fish they caught. He entered into conversation with the men of the island, and became familiar with them, and was well liked.

CHAPTER LXIV.

OF THE ORKNEYMEN.

WHEN Dagfinn had lighted the beacon, he went to Earl Paul, as has been mentioned before. All the Earl's leading men came to him also. A watch was kept for Rögnvald's movements, and it was thought strange that he nowhere appeared. Still the troops were kept together for three days. Then the Islanders began to murmur, saying that it was great foolishness to light beacons when fishermen were seen in their boats.

Thorstein, Ragna's son, was blamed for having lighted the beacon in Rínarsey. He replied that he could do nothing but light his beacon when he saw the blaze in Fridarey, and said that this had all happened through Dagfinn.

Dagfinn replied: " People come more frequently to harm through you when you cannot blame me for it."

Thorstein told him to be silent, and leapt up with an axe and dealt him a heavy blow. Then each man seized his weapons, and there was a fray. This was in Hrossey, not far from Kirkiuvág. Sigurd from Westness, and his son Hákon Kló, and Brynjúlf, took part with Hlödver, Dagfinn's father, but Thorstein was aided by his kinsmen. Then the Earl was informed of what was going on, and it was a long time until he could part them.

Kugi of Westrey made a long speech, and said : " Do not disgrace the Earl by fighting among yourselves. Ere long you will need all your men ; let us take care then not to be disabled or at enmity among ourselves. This has probably happened according to the designs of our enemies, and has been a device of theirs to destroy the beacons in this way. Now they may be expected every day, and let us make our plans accordingly."

Dagfinn said : " No one has had any evil intention in this, but we have acted with more thoughtlessness than we ought to have done."

Kugi guessed the whole truth, and spoke many wise words about it. At last they both agreed that the Earl should judge between them ; and it was resolved to disperse the gathering, and the people went home.

A man by name Eirik was now appointed to take charge of the beacon in Fridarey. When Uni had stopped there a short time, he came to Eirik, and said : " Would you like me to take care of the beacon ; I have nothing else to do, and can give it my undivided attention." Eirik accepted his offer, and when no one was near Uni poured water over it, and made it so wet that it could not be lighted.

CHAPTER LXV.

THE BEACONS OF THE ORKNEYS DESTROYED.

EARL ROGNVALD and his men said they would wait until the tidal currents were met by an east wind, for then it is hardly possible to go from Westrey to Hrossey, but with east wind one can sail from Hjaltland to Westrey. For this Rögnvald and his men waited, and came one Friday evening to Höfn,[1] in Westrey, to Helgi, who dwelt there.

No beacons could be lighted, for when the sails were seen from Fridarey, Eirik prepared to go to Earl Paul, and sent a man to Uni to light the beacon, but when he came there Uni was away. When the man tried to light the beacon himself, it was so wet that it would not burn. When Eirik heard this, he knew what was the matter, and went to Earl Paul and told him.

When Earl Rögnvald had arrived in Westrey, the islanders ran together. Helgi and Kugi put themselves at their head, and their first plan was to try to make peace with the Earl ; and their dealings ended in such a way that the Westreymen submitted to Earl Rögnvald, and swore him oaths of fealty.

CHAPTER LXVI.

ROGNVALD RULES THE ORKNEYS.

ON Sunday Earl Rögnvald had mass celebrated there in the village.[2] As they were standing outside the church, they

---

[1] *Höfn*, the haven, in Westray, is probably the modern Pierowall, the only safe natural harbour in the island, and the only place entitled to the name of " the haven."

[2] The *thorp* or village of Höfn here mentioned most likely stood on the shore by the landing-place at Pierowall. The fact that there are a number of graves on the links here, in which have been found the swords peculiar to the Norse viking period, shield-bosses, bronze tortoise brooches (a distinctively

saw sixteen men approaching unarmed, and with their hair close cut. The Earl's men thought their dress singular, and spoke among themselves of who they might be. Then the Earl made a ditty:

> Sixteen have I seen together,
> With a small tuft on their foreheads;
> Surely these are women coming,
> All without their golden trinkets.
> Now may we of this bear witness.
> In the west here all the maidens
> Wear their hair short—that isle Elon [1]
> Lies out in the stormy ocean.

After Sunday, Earl Rögnvald's men visited the neighbouring districts, and all the people gave in their submission to the Earl. One night in Westrey the Earl's men became aware that the islanders were holding a secret meeting to devise some treachery against Earl Rögnvald. When the Earl heard of it, he rose and went to the place of meeting. When he came there, his men had beaten many of the islanders, and had taken Farmer Kugi and put him in fetters, saying that he was the author of all these proceedings. Kugi pled his cause eloquently, and many put in a word for him, and protested his innocence with him. Then the Earl sang:

Scandinavian form), and other relics unquestionably of Norse origin, shows that the neighbourhood must have been largely frequented by the Northmen, and perhaps made a permanent settlement long before this time. The Church of Westray is mentioned among those vacant in 1327-28 by the Papal Nuncio, who collected the tithes for these years.

[1] Although there is a curious similarity between this incident and that related in chap. lxxi. on the occasion of the visit of Bishop John to the Orkneys, yet the fact of Earl Rögnvald turning the procession into ridicule, whereas Bishop John's party appear to have been received with all due respect, suggests that the two narratives can scarcely refer to the same incident. The reference here to the "isle Elon," taken in connection with the statement in chap. xcix. that there were monks on Eller Holm (named "Helene-holm" by Fordun), may mean that there was a colony of clerics on the little island, whose dress and tonsure may thus have tickled the fancy of the rhyming Earl. In the rental of Schapinsay (1642), Elgin-holme is set in feu to Sir John Buchanan for payment of 12s. annually. In 1529 Jo. Ben mentions that there were foundations of houses and even of a chapel on Eloerholme, though it was then waste and uninhabited (see chap. xcix). Neale notices "the ruins of a very small chapel" on Ellerholm (Ecclesiological Notes, p. 111).

> I can see the crooked irons
> Fastened round the legs of Kugi ;
> Stray thou canst not in thy fetters,
> Old man ! fond of making night trips ;
> Now you must not hold night meetings,
> And must keep the peace established ;
> Kugi ! all your tricks are hinder'd,
> And your oaths you must keep sacred.

The Earl pardoned them all, and they renewed their compact.

CHAPTER LXVII.

OF EARL ROGNVALD AND PAUL.

AFTER Earl Rögnvald's arrival in the Orkneys, and when many had submitted to him, Earl Paul held a meeting in Hrossey with his men for consultation. The Earl asked their opinion of what was to be done in these difficulties. There were considerable differences of opinion. Some advised Earl Paul to share his dominions with Earl Rögnvald. But most of the more powerful men and Bœndr wished to buy Rögnvald away with money, and offered their means for that purpose. Others were for fighting, as they said that this had been the successful way before.

Earl Rögnvald had spies at the meeting, and when they came to him, the Earl asked a certain skald, who had been there, for news. He sang :—

> Of our foes I gain'd this knowledge
> That o'er secrets they are brooding.
> From the meeting of the Bœndr
> Has the great chief heard the tidings
> That among the powerful feeders
> Of the wolves, the wish prevails that
> All your ships should leave the islands
> And that Paul should rule the land here.

Then Earl Rögnvald sent men to see the Bishop, and asked for his intervention. He also sent for Thorstein, Ragna's son, and Thorstein, Hávard's son, in Sandey, and requested them to try to make peace between him and his

kinsman.   The Bishop procured a fortnight's truce, in order
that they might endeavour to establish a more lasting peace.
Then the islands were allocated that should maintain each
of them in the meantime.[1]   Earl Rögnvald went to Hrossey
(Mainland), and Earl Paul to Hrólfsey (Rousay).

At this time it happened that the kinsmen Swein,
Asleif's son, Jón Væng of Uppland in Háey, and Rikgard
of Brekkur in Stiórnsey (Stronsay), attacked Thorkel Flettir
on the estate which had belonged to Valthióf, and burnt
him in the house, with nine others.   After that they went
to Earl Rögnvald, and told him that they would go to Earl
Paul with the whole body of their kinsmen, if he would not
receive them ; but he did not turn them away.

As soon as Haflidi, Thorkel's son, heard of his father's
burning, he went to Earl Paul, who received him well.

After this Jón and his men bound themselves to serve
Earl Rögnvald, who had now many followers in the Islands,
and had become popular.   Earl Rögnvald gave leave to
Jón, Sölmund, and Aslák, and many others of his partizans,
to go home, but they said they preferred to wait until matters should be definitely settled.   Earl Rögnvald replied :
" If it is the will of God that I should gain possession of
the Orkneys, I think He and the Holy Earl Magnus, my
kinsman, will give me strength to hold them, even if you
go home to your estates."

Then they went home to Norway.

CHAPTER LXVIII.

SWEIN TAKES EARL PAUL CAPTIVE.

EARLY in the spring, Swein, Asleif's son, left the Sudreyar
(Hebrides), and went to Scotland to see his friends.   He
stayed a long time at Atjöklar (Athole) with Earl Maddad
and Margaret, Hákon's daughter, and had many secret con-
sultations with them.   Swein heard that there were disturbances in the Orkneys, and became desirous of going there

---

[1] The Iceland Annals place Earl Rögnvald's winning the Orkneys in the
year 1136.

to see his kinsmen.　He went first to Thórsey (Thurso), in
Caithness, accompanied by a nobleman by name Liótólf.
Swein had stayed with him a long time in the spring.　They
came to Earl Ottar, at Thórsey, the brother of Frákork.
Liótólf tried to make them compose the matters that had
been done by Frákork's orders, and Earl Ottar made compensation for his part.　He promised his friendship to
Swein, and he promised to Ottar, in return, to help Erlend,
the son of Harald Sléttmáli (smooth-talker), to obtain his
patrimony in the Orkneys when he should wish to claim it.

Swein changed ships there, and took a barge manned
by thirty men.　He crossed the Pentland Firth with a north-
westerly wind, and so along the west side of Hrossey, on to
Efjusund,[1] and along the sound to Hrólfsey (Rousay).　At
one end of the island there is a large headland and a vast
heap of stones beneath it.　Otters often resorted to this
stone-heap.　As they were rowing along the sound, Swein
said, "There are men on the headland, let us land and ask
them for news; let us change our dress, untie our ham-
mocks,[2] and twenty of us lie down there, and ten keep on
rowing: let us go leisurely."　When they came near the
headland the men in the island called to them to row to
Westness, and bring Earl Paul what was in their vessel,
thinking they were speaking to merchants.　Earl Paul had
spent the night at a feast with Sigurd, at Westness.　He had
been early up in the morning, and twenty men had gone
south on the island to catch otters, which were in the
stone-heap beneath the headland.　They were going home
to get a morning draught.　The men in the barge rowed
near the land; they asked the men on shore about all the
news, and were asked what news they brought, and whence
they came.　Swein's men also asked where the Earl was, and
the others said he was on the stone-heap there.　This was
heard by Swein and those that lay hid with him in the skin-
bags.　Swein told them to row to land, where they could not
be seen from the headland.　Then he told his men to get
their weapons, and slay the Earl's men wherever they found

[1] Evie Sound; from *Efja*, now Evie.
[2] *Húdfat*—skin-bags, or sleeping haps, made of hides sewed together, so
as to envelope the sleeper as in a sack.

them, and so they did. Swein's party killed nineteen men, and lost six. They seized Earl Paul with violence, and brought him on board their ship, and stood out to sea, returning by the same way, by the west side of Hrólfsey, and through the channel between Háey and Grímsey, and then by the east of Svelgr,[1] thence to Breidafiörd (the Moray Firth), until they came to Ekkialsbakki.[2] There he left his

---

[1] Still known as the Swelkie, a dangerous whirlpool in certain states of the tide, off the island of Stroma, fabled to be caused by the waters being sucked down through the eye of the quern " Grotti," which once belonged to King Fródi. Grotti was found in Denmark, and was the largest quern that had ever been known. It would grind for King Fródi gold or peace, which he pleased. But the sea-king Mýsing took Grotti, and caused white salt to be ground in his ships till they sank in Pentland's Firth. This is why the Swelkie has been there ever since. As the waters fall through the eye of the quern, the sea roars as the quern grinds ; and, moreover, this is how the sea first became salt.—(Elder Edda, Grottasöng.) Traces of this legend still linger in the locality.

[2] Ekkialsbakki is three times mentioned in the Flateyarbók, and Ekkial once by Arnór Jarlaskáld (see p. 22). Earl Sigurd, Eystein's son, who killed Malbrigd (Maormor of Mar according to Skene), was "hoy-laid" (buried in a how or barrow, *haugr*), on Ekkialsbakki. "There cannot be the least doubt," says Worsaae, in his ' Danes and Northmen,' "that Ekkial is the river Oykill (Oykel), which still forms the southern boundary of Sutherland. But nobody is able to point out the barrow of Sigurd Jarl. The tradition relating to it has vanished with the Norwegian population." But, fortunately, there are records more permanent and reliable than popular tradition, by which the truth of the Saga narrative may be verified, and the locality of Sigurd's grave-mound indisputably fixed. There is a place near the Ferry on the north bank of the Dornoch Firth (into which the Oykel runs) which is now somewhat inappropriately called Cyder Hall. In Blaeu's Atlas (1640) it appears as Siddera. In older charters it is conjoined with Skebo, and called Sythera. In a deed of the year 1275 the Bishop of Caithness claims right to " six davochs of Schythebolle and Sytheraw, with the ferry." In the deed of constitution of the Cathedral Chapter of Caithness, executed between 1223 and 1245, there are assigned to the treasurer the rectorial tithes of Scytheboll and *Siwardhoch*, its conjunction with Scytheboll showing it to be the same place which is called at subsequent periods Sytheraw, Siddera, and Cyder Hall. This place, named Siward's Hoch (*Sigurd's haug*) at that early date, could be no other than the traditional site of Earl Sigurd's grave-mound, and the Ekkialsbakki on which he was buried must ,thus have been the north bank of the Oykel's estuary. But the Ekkialsbakki twice mentioned in connection with Swein Asleifson's journey to Athole can scarcely be the same with that of the earlier narrative. It seems probable that in Swein Asleifson's narrative the word may have been originally Atjoklsbakki—the coast on the side of the Breidafiord (Moray Firth) next to Atjoklar (Athole). The word *bakki* is sometimes used for a " coast." The Saga writer may have been misled by the similarity of sound to substitute Ekkialsbakki for Atjoklsbakki. (See p. 115.)

ship with twenty men, and continued his journey until he came to Earl Maddad[1] and Margaret, Earl Paul's sister, at Atjöklar (Athole). There they were well received. Earl Maddad placed Earl Paul in his high seat, and when they were seated, Margaret entered with a long train of ladies, and advanced to her brother. Then men were procured to amuse them; but Earl Paul was moody, and it was no wonder, for he had many cares.

It is not recorded what passed between Earl Paul and Swein while they were on the journey together. Earl Maddad, Margaret, and Swein, had a consultation together; but in the evening, when the drinking was finished, Swein's followers were conducted to a sleeping-room by themselves, and the key turned upon them. This was done every evening while they were there.

CHAPTER LXIX.

OF SWEIN, ASLEIF'S SON'S, RETURN TO THE ORKNEYS.

ONE day Margaret announced that Swein, Asleif's son, should go to the Orkneys to see Earl Rögnvald, and ask him whom he preferred to share in the dominion of the Orkneys with him—Earl Paul, or Harald, the son of (her husband) Maddad, who was then three winters old.

When Earl Paul heard this, he said: "So far as my mind is concerned, I will say that I have left my dominions in such a way as has never been heard of before, I think; and I shall never return to the Orkneys any more. I see that this must be God's vengeance for the theft which I and my kinsmen committed. But if God thinks the dominion mine, then will I give it to Harald, if he may enjoy it; but I wish some money given to me, so that I may estab-

---

[1] The name of Maddad, Earl of Athole, appears in contemporary documents as Maddoc, Madach, and Madeth. In the foundation-charter of Scone by King Alexander I. and his queen Sibilla, "Madach Comes" is a witness. "Maddoc" and "Madeth Comes" also witness charters of King David I. From a charter by King Malcolm the Maiden, granting aid for the restoration of the Abbey of Scone, we learn that the style of the Earls of Athole was "Comes de Ethocl," the Atjokl of the Saga.—(Regist. de Dunferm. Regist. de Scone.)

lish myself in some monastery, and you can take care that I do not escape. And you, Swein, shall go out to the Orkneys, and say that I have been blinded, or still more mutilated, because my friends will fetch me if I am an unmaimed man. In that case I may not be able to refuse to return to my dominions with them, for I suspect that they will consider our parting a greater loss than it is."

What more the Earl said has not been placed on record.

Then Swein, Asleif's son, went to the Orkneys, and Earl Paul remained behind in Scotland.

This is how Swein related these matters. But some men tell the story in a way by no means so creditable (to those concerned)—namely, that Margaret induced Swein, Asleif's son, to blind her brother Earl Paul, then threw him into a dungeon, and subsequently induced another man to put him to death. We do not know which of these two statements is the more correct; but it is well known that Earl Paul came never again to the Orkneys, and that he had no dominions in Scotland.

CHAPTER LXX.

OF EARL ROGNVALD AND SWEIN, ASLEIF'S SON.

IT happened at Westness, when the Earl did not come home, that Sigurd sent men to search for him. When they came to the stone-heap they saw the slain, and then they thought the Earl had been killed. They went home and told the news. Sigurd went immediately to examine the bodies, and they recognised nineteen as the Earl's men; but six they did not know. Then Sigurd sent men to Egilsey, to the Bishop, to tell him the news. He went immediately to Sigurd. When they were talking about what had happened, Sigurd hinted that it had been done at the instigation of Earl Rögnvald; but the Bishop replied that it would be proved that Earl Rögnvald had not acted treacherously towards his kinsman Earl Paul. "It is my opinion," he said, "that some others have committed this crime."

Borgar, the son of Játvör, Erlend's daughter, who lived at Geitaberg,[1] had seen the barge coming from the south, and returning. When this was heard, it was believed to have been done at the instigation of Frákork and Olvir.

When the news spread in the Islands that Earl Paul had disappeared, and no one knew what had become of him, the Islanders had a consultation, and most of them went to Earl Rögnvald, and swore fealty to him; but Sigurd, of Westness, and his sons, Brynjólf and Hákon Kló, said they would not swear oaths of fealty to any man while they did not know anything of Earl Paul, or whether he might be expected to return or not. There were others also who refused to swear oaths to Earl Rögnvald. Others again fixed an hour or a day when they would become Earl Rögnvald's men, if Earl Paul had not then been heard of. But when Earl Rögnvald saw that he had to do with many powerful men, he did nöt refuse peremptorily anything which the people asked; and, as the time passed, he had frequent meetings with the inhabitants, and at each of them some submitted to him.

One day it happened in Kirkiuvág (Kirkwall) when Earl Rögnvald was holding a Thing meeting with the Bœndr, that nine armed men were seen walking from Skálpeid (Scapa) to the meeting. When they came near, Swein, Asleif's son, was recognised, and all were curious to know what news he had to tell. He had come in a ship to Scálpeid, and left it there, while he and his men walked to Kirkiuvág. When Swein came to the meeting, his kinsmen and friends turned to him, and asked him for news, but he did not say much. Swein sent for the Bishop, who welcomed him heartily, because they had long been friends. They went aside to talk, and Swein told the Bishop the whole truth about what he had done, and asked for his advice in these difficult circumstances.

The Bishop said : " Those are weighty tidings you have

[1] Geitaberg is probably the place now known as Gatnip, on the east side of Scapa Bay, near Kirkwall. It is formerly stated that Játvor and her son Borgar lived at Knarrarstad, which is evidently the name for the district, while Geitaberg was the name of Borgar's homestead. Gatnip is the highest point on that side of the bay, and thus Borgar was able to notice the barge rowed by Swein's men as it passed up and down the Firth.

brought, Swein, and we shall probably not be by ourselves sufficient in this matter. I wish you to wait here for me; but I shall plead your cause before the people and Earl Rögnvald."

Then the Bishop went to the meeting, and asked for silence. When silence was obtained, the Bishop pleaded Swein's cause, explaining for what reason he had left the Orkneys, and what penalties Earl Paul had inflicted on him for the slaying of Swein Brióstreip, a most wicked man. The Bishop concluded by asking Earl Rögnvald and all the people to grant security to Swein.

Earl Rögnvald replied : " For my part, I promise Swein three nights' security; but I think I can see from your countenance, Sir Bishop, that you and Swein know some great news which you have not yet made known. I wish you to take Swein into your keeping, and to be responsible for him, and I will speak to him to-morrow."

" I will," said the Bishop; " and he will be very glad to speak to you as soon as possible; for he wishes to become your man, if you are willing to receive him."

The Earl replied : " I do not think my friends are too many in these lands, yet I shall have some farther talk before I consent to this."

Then these four—Earl Rögnvald, his father Kol, the Bishop, and Swein, Asleif's son—had a private interview. Swein repeated everything, good and bad, that had happened between him and Earl Paul, and they came to the conclusion to send away the bulk of the people at the meeting. The Earl arose next morning and gave the people permission to go home; but when the multitude had gone away, he called together all those that remained, and made them all renew their promise of security to Swein, while he told the news.

In the morning, Magnus[1] Karl, the brother of the Holy Earl Magnus, was persuaded to tell Sigurd of Westness and his sons of Earl Paul's abduction, that he was not to be expected back to his dominions, and that he had been maimed.

Sigurd said : " Great news do I think this, about the

[1] Magnus, in the text here, is clearly a mistake for Hákon.

carrying away of the Earl; yet to me the saddest of all is
that he should have been maimed, for he would not be anywhere where I would not go to him." Afterwards he told
his friends that Hákon would not have left him unharmed,
if he had had a sufficient force with him when he told him
these tidings, so greatly was he moved by them.

When the news became generally known, all the Orkneymen submitted to Earl Rögnvald, and he became the sole
ruler of Earl Paul's dominions.

Not long after this the foundations of St. Magnus' Church[1]
were marked out, and craftsmen procured, so that more was
done during that year than in the ensuing four or five.
Kol took great interest in the erection of the building, and
had the principal oversight of the whole; but as it proceeded, it became very expensive to the Earl, and his means
were nearly exhausted. Then he consulted his father, and
he advised him to pass a law declaring that the Earls should
be considered to have inherited all the odal possessions
from the owners, but that they were to be redeemable by the
heirs.[2] This was considered a great hardship. Then Earl
Rögnvald called a Thing meeting, and proposed to the Bœndr
that they should purchase the odal possessions, so that it
would not be necessary to redeem them afterwards, and an
agreement was made with which all parties were satisfied.
It was to this effect, that they should pay the Earl one
mark (eight oz. of silver) for each plough's land all over the
Islands. From that time there was no want of money to
build the church; and it was made a magnificent structure.

[1] The erection of St. Magnus' Church was commenced apparently between
the years 1136 and 1138. The remains of St. Magnus appear to have been
transferred to it from Christ's Church, in Birsay, previous to the departure of
Earl Rögnvald to the Holy Land in 1152. After Earl Rögnvald's death, in
1158, the building of the cathedral was carried on by Bishop William, until
his death in 1168, after which we have no record of its progress.

[2] The odal tenure of the lands in the islands was first modified by Harald
Harfagri in the time of the Earl Torf Einar. Earl Sigurd Hlodverson restored the odal rights in return for the assistance of the Bœndr at the battle
of Skida Myre (see Appendix). This arrangement subsisted till the imposi-
tion of the succession-dues by Earl Rögnvald, which were subsequently bought
up, as here narrated.

CHAPTER LXXI.

BISHOP JÓN ARRIVES FROM SCOTLAND.

WHEN Earl Rögnvald had ruled the Orkneys two winters he had a Yule-feast at his estate called Knarrarstadir.[1]   The sixth day of Yule a ship was seen crossing the Pentland Firth from the south.   It was a fine day, and the Earl was outside the house, with many men, looking at the ship. There was also a man named Hrólf, the Earl's court priest. When the strangers landed, they left the ship, and the Earl's men calculated their number to be fifteen or sixteen.[2]   In front of them walked a man in a blue cloak, with his hair tucked up under the cap; the lower part of the chin was shaved,[3] but the lips unshaved, and the long beard was hanging down (from them).   They thought this man somewhat strange, but Hrólf said it was Bishop Jón from Atjöklar (Athole), in Scotland.   Then the Earl went to meet them, and gave the Bishop a gracious welcome.   He placed him in his high seat, but served at the table himself like a waiter.

Early next morning the Bishop held a service, and went to Egilsey to see Bishop William.   This was the tenth day of Yule.   Then both the Bishops went with a noble suite to visit Earl Rögnvald, and told him their business,

---

[1] Knarrarstad, as has been formerly explained, was applied to the district at the head of the Bay of Scapa.   It was so called because it was the place where the merchant-ships lay—from *Knarrar*, genitive of *knörr*, a merchant-ship ; and *stadr*, a stance or stead.   The name is preserved in old estate-lists as *Knarstane*.   In the near neighbourhood there is an ancient "broch" or "Pictish tower," recently excavated by Mr. George Petrie.   Remains of very extensive buildings have been found within and around it, evidently belonging to a secondary occupation of the tower, of later date than that of its original construction.   Among the relics found in these secondary buildings there are some which correspond with relics of the later Viking period found in Scandinavia.   This gives a certain amount of probability to the supposition that the ruins of this "Pictish tower" may have been occupied and utilised by Earl Rögnvald's men, as we know that the similar tower of Mousa, in Shetland, was on different occasions, one of which is narrated in chap. xcii. of this same Saga.

[2] This incident bears a remarkable similarity to that related in chap. lxvi.

[3] It is curious that Cæsar has described the ancient Britons as observing in his time the same custom of shaving the lower part of the chin, and wearing the hair long on the upper lip.

I

explaining the agreement between Swein, Asleif's son, and
Earl Maddad—namely, that their son Harald should bear the
title of Earl, and have half the Orkneys jointly with Earl
Rögnvald, but Earl Rögnvald should have the government in
his hands, even when Harald grew up; and if a difference
arose between them, Earl Rögnvald should have his own way.

Swein was present, and confirmed the Bishop's statement. It was resolved to hold a meeting during Lent in
Caithness, and there they agreed upon the terms above
mentioned, and their agreement was confirmed by the oaths
of the best men of the Orkneys and Scotland. Then Harald,
Maddad's son, went to the Orkneys with Earl Rögnvald, and
was invested with the title of Earl.

Harald was accompanied to the islands by Thorbiörn
Klerk, the son of Thorstein Höld, and Gudrún, the daughter
of Frákork. He was a wise and a great man. He was
foster-father to Harald at that time, and had great influence
with him. Thorbiörn married in the Orkneys Ingiríd,
Olaf's daughter, sister to Swein, Asleif's son. He was
sometimes in the Orkneys, and sometimes in Scotland. He
was a most valiant man, but overbearing in most things.

Swein, Asleif's son, took possession of all the estates
that belonged to his father Olaf and his brother Valthióf;
he became a great chief, and had always many men with
him. He was a wise man, and far-seeing in many things;
but overbearing and rash. No two men in the west were
considered at that time greater than the brothers-in-law
Swein and Thorbiörn, and there was a warm friendship
between them.

CHAPTER LXXII.

THE BURNING OF FRAKORK.

ON one occasion Swein, Asleif's son, asked Earl Rögnvald to
give him troops and ships to take vengeance on Olvir and
Frákork for the burning of his father Olaf.

The Earl said: "Do you not think, Swein, that Olvir
and that old hag Frákork, who is good for nothing, will
scarcely be able to do us any harm now?"

Swein replied: "They will always be mischievous while they live; and I expected something else when I did great things for you, than that you would refuse me this."

The Earl replied: "What will you be satisfied with?"

Swein said: "Two ships well equipped."

The Earl said he should have what he wished.

Then he made preparations for going. When he was ready he sailed south to Borgarfiörd,[1] and had a north-west wind to Dúfeyrar,[2] which is a trading-place in Scotland. From there he passed Moray to Ekkialsbakki,[3] and from there he went to Earl Maddad at Atjöklar (Athole). He gave Swein guides who knew the way across mountains and forests wherever Swein wished to go; and he went through the interior of the country, over mountains and through woods, away from all habitations, and came down in Hjálmundal,[4] near the middle of Sutherland. Olvir and Frákork had had spies wherever they thought they might expect enemies from the Orkneys, but this way they did not expect any. They did not, therefore, perceive the enemy till Swein and his men were in a certain slope behind the house. Olvir Rosta met them there with sixty men, and the fight began immediately. There was little resistance on the part of Olvir's men, and they retreated towards the houses, because they could not reach the wood. A great many were killed, and Olvir ran to Hjálmundal's river, and then up on the mountains. After that he went to Scotland's Firth (on

[1] Borgarfiord seems here to be a misreading for Breidafiord (the Moray Firth), unless we suppose that there was another Borgarfiord besides the one in Shetland. Jonæus has *nordr* instead of *sudr*, thus making Swein sail north to Borgarfiord, which in this case would be in Shetland. But it is hardly probable that he would have taken Shetland in his route from Orkney to the coast of Moray.

[2] Dúfeyrar must have been situated on the sandy shore of the parish of Duffus, on the Moray coast, *eyri* signifying a spit of sand. It has been supposed, with some degree of probability, that Burghead is the place here meant.

[3] Ekkialsbakki, probably for Atjoklsbakki. (See note on p. 107.)

[4] Hjalmundal, Strath Helmsdale, or Strath Ulli, which runs up along the south side of the Ord, the mountain chain separating Caithness from Sutherland. The expression "near the middle of Sutherland" must mean that Swein came up through the central or inland region of the country, and thus came down into Strath Helmsdale, a long way from the coast, or "near the middle of the land."

the west coast), and from there to the Sudreyar (Hebrides),
and he is not mentioned further in this Saga.

When Olvir escaped, Swein and his men approached the
houses, and plundered everything. Then they burnt the
houses, with all the inmates, and there Frákork perished.
Swein and his men committed many ravages in Sutherland
before they went to their ships. After that they were out
on raids during the summer, and ravaged in Scotland.

In the autumn Swein came to Earl Rögnvald in the
Orkneys, and was well received. Then he crossed over to
Ness (Caithness), and spent the winter in Dungalsbæ. At
this time Swein received a message from Höldbodi, in the
Sudreyar, that he should come and help him, because Höld
from Bretland had been there, driven him from his estates,
and taken much booty. The messenger was named Hród-
bjart (Robert), of English descent. When Swein received
the message, he quickly left for the Orkneys, and called on
Earl Rögnvald, and requested him to give him troops and
ships. The Earl asked Swein what he was going to do then.
He said that he had received a message from a man whom he
ought least of all to refuse, and who had proved his best friend
in his greatest need, and when most others were his enemies.

The Earl said : " It is well if you part good friends, but
most of those Sudreyarmen are treacherous. You must,
however, act a manly part, and I will give you two ships
fully manned."

Swein was well pleased with this, and went to the Sudreyar, but did not find Höldbodi till he came to the Isle of
Man, because the latter had fled thither. When Swein
came to the Isle of Man, Höldbodi was very glad to see him.
The British Höld had plundered and killed men, to a large
extent in the Isle of Man as well as in the Sudreyar. He
had killed a nobleman named Andrew, who left a widow by
name Ingiríd, and a son by name Sigurd. Ingiríd was
wealthy, and had large estates. Höldbodi advised Swein to
woo her ; and when he proposed marriage, she made it a
condition of her acceptance that he should avenge her late
husband Andrew.

Swein replied : " I may inflict some loss on the British,
but we cannot know how we may succeed in manslaying."

Then Swein and Höldbodi went out on an expedition with five ships. They plundered in Bretland, landing at a place called Jarlsness,[1] and committing great ravages. One morning they went into a certain village, and met with a little resistance. The inhabitants fled from the village, and Swein and his men plundered everything, and burnt six homesteads before dinner. An Icelander, named Eirík was with Swein, and sang the following:

> Half-a-dozen homesteads burning,
> Half-a-dozen households plundered:
> This was Swein's work of a morning—
> This his vengeance; coals he lent them.

After this they went to their ships. They were out reiving all the summer, and obtained much booty, but Höld fled into an island called Lund,[2] where there was a strong place. Swein besieged it for some time, to no purpose. In the autumn they went back to the Isle of Man.

CHAPTER LXXIII.

OF SWEIN AND HOLDBODI'S RAIDS.

THIS winter Swein married Ingiríd, and remained there, greatly honoured. In the spring he gathered men together, and went to see Höldbodi, and asked for his assistance, but he excused himself, saying that many of his men were occupied, and some on trading trips; so Swein got none there. But the truth was, that he had secretly made peace with Höld, and confirmed their alliance by exchanging presents. Swein went out, nevertheless, with three ships, but made little booty in the earlier part of the summer. Later they went south, under Ireland, and seized a barge belonging to some monks in Syllingar,[3] and plundered it. He made

---

[1] *Ines* in Jonæus; it has not been identified.
[2] Probably Lundy Island, in the Bristol Channel.
[3] Syllingar, the Scilly Islands. There was an ecclesiastical settlement there in Olaf Tryggvason's time. It was in the Scilly Islands that he was baptized, and embraced the faith which he afterwards propagated with the strong hand both in his own kingdom and in Orkney.

inroads in Ireland in many places, obtained a large booty, and returned to the Isle of Man in autumn.

When Swein had been a short time at home, he heard a report to the effect that Höldbodi was not faithful to him, but Swein shrank from believing it. One night in the spring Swein's watchmen came to him and said that enemies were approaching them. Swein and his men seized their arms, and ran out, and saw a great number of men carrying fire to the homestead. Then Swein and his men ran to a hill, and defended themselves from it. They had a horn[1] which they sounded. The neighbourhood was thickly inhabited, and men came flocking to help Swein, so that the assailants at last gave way. Swein and his men pursued them, and killed many in the flight, but many of both sides were wounded before they parted. The chief of the attacking band was Höldbodi. He escaped in the flight, and did not stop till he came to Lundey (Lundy Isle). Höld received him well, and they remained together. Swein went home, and kept a large number of his men about him, maintaining a strict watch, because he distrusted the Sudreyarmen. Late in the winter he sold his lands, and went early in the spring to Liódhús (Lewis). During this expedition he had committed many ravages.

CHAPTER LXXIV.

OF EARL ROGNVALD AND SWEIN.

WHILE Swein was in the Sudreyar, Earl Rögnvald went over to Caithness, and was entertained at Vík (Wick) by a man named Harald. His son was named Swein, an active fellow. While the Earl was there, Thorbiörn Klerk came up from Scotland, and said that his father, Thorstein Höld, had been killed by a certain Earl. People talked of how frequently Earl Rögnvald and Thorbiörn spoke together, because the Earl scarcely took leisure to discharge his duties for that

---

[1] *Lúdr.*—This same signal was used by the army of the Bœndr at the battle of Stiklestad (Flateyarbók, ii. 352). The signal-horn used at the present day by the Shetland fishermen still retains the ancient name, "the ludr-horn."

reason. Thorbiörn went with the Earl out to the Islands
(Orkneys), and Swein, Harald's son, became the Earl's table-
boy. Thorbiörn had been in Scotland for some time. He
had slain two men who had been with Swein, Asleif's son,
at the burning of Frákork.

When Swein came from the Sudreyar, he went home to
his farm in Gáreksey (Gairsay), and not to Earl Rögnvald,
as he used to do when he came from his expeditions. So
when the Earl heard that Swein had come home from the
Sudreyar in the summer, he asked Thorbiörn for what reason
he thought Swein did not come to him.

Thorbiörn replied: "I suppose Swein is offended with
me because I had those men slain who were with him at the
burning of Frákork."

The Earl said: "I do not like you to be enemies."

Then Earl Rögnvald went to Gáreksey, and tried to
reconcile them, which was easy, because they both wished
the Earl to judge between them. Then he made peace
between them, and it lasted for a long time after.

CHAPTER LXXV.

EARL ROGNVALD'S PLEASANTRIES.

At this time there came a certain Icelandic ship to the
Orkneys, in which was a man by name Hall, the son of
Thórarinn Breidmagi (broad waist). He went to Rínarsey
(North Ronaldsay), to stay with Thorstein and Ragna. He
became tired of staying there, and asked Thorstein to bring
him to Earl Rögnvald. They went to see him, but the Earl
would not receive Hall. When they came home, Ragna
asked how they had succeeded, and Hall replied by a ditty:

> It was to thy own son, Ragna,
> (Let truth be known among the people)
> I gave the noble task of asking
> My reception 'mong the courtiers;
> But the generous ring-giver,
> Who enjoys the highest honour,
> Has declined my clownish service,
> Having plenty of the bravest.

Shortly afterwards Ragna went to see Earl Rögnvald on
this errand herself.   She was so dressed that she had a
red head-gear of horse's hair; and when the Earl saw her he
sang :

> Never did I know before this
> How the ladies of the cross-bench
> Deck their heads with finest kerchiefs.
> If I use the proper language,
> Seems to me that this gold-wearer
> Hides the tresses of her hind-head
> With a chestnut filly's tail-locks,
> And her head-dress shows her temper.

Ragna said : "Now the saying comes true, 'that few are
so wise that they see everything as it is,' for this [hair] is of
a horse, and not of a mare."

Then she took a silken kerchief and wrapped it round
her head, continuing, nevertheless, her business with the
Earl.   He gave her a rather cold answer at first, but became
more pleasant as they spoke longer, and she obtained what
she wanted—namely, to procure for Hall a place at the
(Earl's) court.   He remained a long time with Earl Rögnvald.   They made jointly the "Old Metrekey," [1] with five
verses for each different metre.   Afterwards that was thought
too much, and now two verses only are made for each different metre.

CHAPTER LXXVI.

OF EARL ROGNVALD AND SWEIN, ASLEIF'S SON.

SWEIN, Asleif's son, is said to have heard that Höldbodi had
arrived in the Sudreyar.   Then he asked Earl Rögnvald to
give him troops to avenge himself.   The Earl gave him five
ships, and Thorbiörn Klerk was the commander of one of
them ; Haflidi, the son of Thorkel Flettir, of another; Dúfniál, the son of Hávard, Gunni's son, the third ; Ríkgard
(Richard), Thorleif's son, the fourth ; and Swein, Asleif's son,

---

[1] *Clavis Rhythmica,* apparently a kind of rhyming dictionary or repertory
of versification.   Torfæus states that this joint production of Earl Rögnvald
and Hall, Ragna's son, is still extant in the library at Upsala.

the fifth. When Höldbodi heard of Swein, he fled from the Sudreyar. Swein and his men killed many people in the Sudreyar, and ravaged and burnt far and wide. They obtained great booty, but could not catch Höldbodi, and he never came to the Sudreyar after that. Swein wished to remain in the Sudreyar during the winter, but Thorbiörn and the others wished to go home, and went in the autumn to Caithness, and arrived at Dungalsbæ. When they were going to divide their booty, Swein said they should all share equally, but that he himself should have a chief's share besides, saying that he had been the chief, and that the Earl had sent the others to his assistance. Besides, he added further that he alone had the quarrel with the Sudrey-armen, while the others had none. Thorbiörn, however, said he did not deserve less than Swein, and had not been less a leader than he. They also wished that all the ships' commanders should have equal shares; but they had to submit to Swein, because his men were by far the most numerous there on the Ness (in Caithness).

Thorbiörn went out to the Orkneys and told Earl Rögnvald how matters had gone between him and Swein, and that they were very much displeased to have been deprived by him of their just proportion of the spoil.

The Earl said it would not be only once that Swein had turned out not to be an equitable man, yet he would in the end receive retribution for his injustice; but, he added : " You shall not quarrel about this. I shall give you as much money of my own as you have lost through him, and it is my will that you do not claim it of him. It will be a good thing if this does not lead to greater difficulties with him."

Thorbiörn replied : " May God reward you, my lord, for the honour you do us, and we shall not quarrel with Swein about this; but I shall never be his friend any more, and I shall do him some despite in return." And after that Thorbiörn divorced himself from Ingiríd, Swein's sister, and sent her to him over to Ness (Caithness). Swein received her well, but considered Thorbiörn's conduct a great insult to himself. There was then fierce enmity between them. Then the saying proved true that monsters are best matched together.

When Swein was in the Sudreyar, he had placed Margad, Grím's son, over his affairs at Dungalsbæ, and transferred to him the office (of deputy or factor) which he held from Earl Rögnvald, but Margad was resentful and overbearing, and became unpopular on account of his violence. Those who were the first objects of his oppression ran to Hróald (at Wick), and remained there. From this enmity arose between the two. Shortly after Margad went south to Vík (Wick) on business with nineteen men, and before he left he attacked Hróald, and killed him and several others. Then he went to Dungalsbæ to see Swein. The latter gathered men together, and went to Lambaborg,[1] where he fortified himself. It was a strong place, and there he remained, with sixty men, and brought thither provisions and other necessaries. The borg (castle) was situated on a sea-girt rock, and on the landward side there was a well-built stone wall. The crags ran a long way along the sea on either side. Swein and his men committed many violent robberies in Caithness, and brought everything into the stronghold, and became greatly hated.

CHAPTER LXXVII.

OF SWEIN, ASLEIF'S SON'S MOVEMENTS.

THIS news came to the ears of Earl Rögnvald, and Swein, Hróald's son, and he asked the Earl to help him to obtain redress in this cause; and many supported Swein's request. At last Earl Rögnvald crossed over to Ness (Caithness), and the following chiefs with him :—Thorbiörn ; Haflidi, Thorkel's son ; and Dúfniál, Hávard's son. These counselled the most severe measures against Swein. They went to Dungalsbæ, but Swein was not there. They heard that he was in Lambaborg, and then the Earl went thither. When they came to the borg, Swein asked who their leader was, and he was told that it was Earl Rögnvald. Swein asked him what

---

[1] From the description of Lambaborg, and its situation with regard to the coast and the river at Freswick, it seems to have been the fortalice now called Bucholly Castle, from a Mowat of Bucholly who possessed it in the 17th century, and by whom it was partially rebuilt.

he wanted.   The Earl said he wished him to deliver Margad
up to them.   Swein asked whether he was to receive quarter.
The Earl said he would not promise.   Then Swein said : " I
have not the heart to deliver Margad into the power of Swein,
Hróald's son, or of my other enemies who are with you, but
I should wish very much to be at peace with you, my lord."

Then Thorbiörn Klerk said : " Hear what the traitor
says, that he would willingly be at peace with his lord after
he has plundered his land, and betaken himself to the high-
ways like a thief.   You make a bad return to the Earl for all
the honour he has done you, and so you will do to all you can."

Swein replied : " You need not say much in this case,
Thorbiörn, for no respect will be paid to your words.   But
it is my foreboding that you will repay him worse for all the
honour he has done to you, before you part, for nobody will
gain good fortune from any dealings with you."

Then Earl Rögnvald said that men should not rail at each
other.

Then they besieged the borg, and cut off all communication, and a long time passed, as they could not make an
assault.   And when the provisions were exhausted, Swein
called his men together, and consulted with them.   But they
all said, as with one mouth, that they wished to follow his
guidance as long as they were able.

Then Swein said : " I think it most disgraceful to starve
here, and afterwards to surrender to our enemies.   It has
turned out, as was likely, that our skill and good fortune
should fail against Earl Rögnvald.   We have tried to obtain
peace and security for life, but neither was to be had for my
companion Margad.   Though I know that the others will be
able to obtain quarter, yet I have not the heart to deliver
him under the axe.   Still, it is not right that so many here
should suffer for his difficulties, although I am unwilling to
part from him for a time."

Then he tied together ropes which they had, and during
the night they let Swein and Margad down from the borg
into the sea.   They swam along the cliffs till they came to
the end of them, then they got on shore and went to Sutherland, thence to Moray, and then to Dúfeyrar.[1]   There they

---

[1] Probably now represented by Duffus in Moray.

met with some Orkneymen in a trading vessel. Hallvard
and Thorkel were the commanders, and they were ten altogether. Swein and Margad went on board with them, when
they were twelve together, and then they sailed south off
Scotland, until they came to Máeyar (the Isle of May).
There was a monastery, the head of which was an abbot, by
name Baldwin.[1] Swein and his men were detained there
seven nights by stress of weather. They said they had been
sent by Earl Rögnvald to the King of Scots. The monks
suspected their tale, and thinking they were pirates, sent to
the mainland for men. When Swein and his comrades
became aware of this, they went hastily on board their ship,
after having plundered much treasure from the monastery.
They went in along Myrkvifiörd (the Firth of Forth), and
found David, the King of Scots, in Edinburgh. He received
Swein well, and requested him to stay with him. He told
the King explicitly the reason of his visit, how matters had
gone between him and Earl Rögnvald before they parted, and
also that they had plundered in Máeyar. Swein and Margad stayed for a while with the King of Scots, and were well
treated. King David sent men to those who had been robbed
by Swein, and told them to estimate their loss themselves, and
then of his own money he made good to every one his loss.

King David proposed to Swein to bring his wife from
the Orkneys, and to bestow upon him such honours in
Scotland as he might be well satisfied with. Swein declared all his wishes to the King. He said it was his wish
that Margad should remain with him, and that the King
should send word to Earl Rögnvald to be reconciled to him;
but he said he would himself leave his case entirely to the
decision of Rögnvald, adding that he was always well pleased
when there was friendship between them, but ill at ease
when they were at enmity.

King David replied: " I suppose this Earl is a good
man, and you value nothing except what comes from him,
since you prefer the risk of surrendering yourself to his
good faith, and refuse my offers."

---

[1] This passage supplies the name of a prior of the monastery of May, not
otherwise on record. (See records of the Priory of the Isle of May, issued by
the Soc. Antiq. Scot. 1868).

Swein said he would never give up his friendship, yet he asked the King to grant him this, and the King said it should be as he wished.

King David sent men to the Orkneys with presents, and a message requesting that the Earl would make peace with Swein. Then Swein went north to the Islands, and Margad remained behind with the King. King David's messengers went to Earl Rögnvald, who received them well, and also the presents, promising peace to Swein. Then he was fully reconciled to Swein, who now returned to his estates.

CHAPTER LXXVIII.

EARL VALTHIOF'S DEATH.

WHEN Swein and Margad had left Lambaborg,[1] those that were in the fort resolved to surrender it to Earl Rögnvald. He asked them what they knew last of Swein and Margad, and they told the truth.

When the Earl heard it, he said : " To tell the truth, Swein has no equal among those that are now with us, and such feats are both brave and hardy ; but I will not abuse my power over you, although you were involved in these troubles with Swein. Every one of you shall go home in peace as far as I am concerned."

The Earl went home to the Orkneys, and sent Thorbiörn Klerk in a ship with forty men south to Breidafiörd (the Moray Firth), to search for Swein; but he heard nothing of him.

Thorbiörn then said to his men : " Our journey is a strange one ; we are all this time wandering after Swein, but I have heard that Earl Valthióf, who slew my father,[2] is not far off, with but a few men ; and if you will attack him with me, I will promise you that I shall not act as Swein did—namely, to deprive you of your share if we get any booty, for you shall have all we get, except what you wish to give me, because I think glory is better than booty."

Then they went to the place where Earl Valthióf was at a banquet, and surprised them in the house, and set it on

[1] See p. 123.   [2] See chap. lxxiv.

fire immediately. Valthióf and his men ran to the door, and asked who was the raiser of the fire. Thorbiörn told his name. Valthióf offered compensation for Thorstein's slaying, but Thorbiörn said it was useless to ask for peace. They defended themselves bravely for a time; but when the fire pressed them they ran out; after that their defence was short, because the fire had overcome them. Earl Valthióf fell, and thirty men with him. Thorbiörn and his men got a great deal of booty, and he kept all his promises to them faithfully. Then they went to the Orkneys to Earl Rögnvald, who was well satisfied with what they had done. Then there was peace and quiet in the Islands.

At that time a young man lived in the Islands,[1] by name Kolbein Hrúga (heap), a very overbearing man; he built a fine stone castle,[2] which was a strong defence. Kolbein's wife was Herbiörg, the sister of Hákon Barn (child), but their mother was the daughter of Herborg, Paul's daughter. Their children were Kolbein Karl, Bjarni Skáld, Sumarlidi, Aslák, and Frída; they were all well mannered.

CHAPTER LXXIX.

OF EINDRIDI UNGI (THE YOUNG).

AT that time the sons of Harald Gilli[3] ruled over Norway. Eystein was the oldest of them, but Ingi was a legitimate son, and he was most honoured by the Lendermen, because he let them have their way in all things as they liked. At this time the following Lendermen (Barons) assisted him in

[1] The Stockholm translation of the Saga has "in Vigr," instead of "in the Islands."

[2] In the Saga of Hakon Hakonson it is stated that Kolbein Hrúga's castle was on the island of Vigr, now Weir. It was to this stronghold that Snækoll Gunnason fled when he had slain Earl John (son of Harald Maddadson), the last of the Norse Earls of Orkney, in A.D. 1232; and the Saga states that the castle was so strong that it resisted all the efforts of the Earl's friends to take it. In 1529 we learn from Jo. Ben that the ruins were still visible. Barry describes it as a small square tower, 15 feet square inside, and the walls 7 feet thick, strongly built with large stones, well cemented with lime. It is now a green mound, like the older Pictish towers; but to this day among the peasantry of the locality the mound bears the name of *Cobbie Row's* (Kolbein Hruga's) Castle.　　　　[3] See note on p. 84.

the government :—Ogmund and Erling, the son of Kyrpinga Orm. They advised King Ingi to send word to Earl Rögnvald, and give him an honourable invitation, saying truly that he had been a great friend of his father, and desired him to become as intimate with the Earl as he could, so that he might be a dearer friend of his than of his brother, whatever might happen between them. The Earl was related to the brothers, and a great friend of theirs; and when he received this message, he quickly prepared to go, because he felt a desire to go to Norway to see his friends and kinsmen. Earl Harald asked to be permitted to go with him, out of curiosity and to amuse himself; he was then nineteen winters old.

When the Earls were ready, they started from the west with some merchants, having a noble retinue, and arrived in Norway early in the spring. They found King Ingi in Biörgvin (Bergen), and he received them very well. Earl Rögnvald saw many of his friends and kinsmen, and spent a great deal of the summer there. Eindridi Ungi (the young) arrived from Mikligard (Constantinople) that summer; he had been long in service [1] there, and was able to tell many things from there; and it was thought good entertainment to inquire from him about things in that part of the world. The Earl conversed frequently with him.

[1] Probably in the body-guard of the Greek Emperor, which, the Byzantine historians of the period inform us, was composed of natives of the remote north, whom they call Varangians. The name Varangi first appears with them in the year 935, but they are said to have served of old in the body-guard, and to have come partly from Thule and partly from England. In the Saga of Harald Hardradi his exploits during his sojourn in the East are minutely detailed, and it is recorded that he became chief of the Værings, who were at that time in the Imperial service. For several centuries these mercenaries in the pay of the Emperors were renowned for their bravery, discipline, and fidelity. After the Norman conquest of England, a body of Anglo-Saxon youth, under Siward of Gloucester, choosing exile rather than the ignominy of submission to the conquerors, went to Constantinople, and enrolled themselves among the Værings. So many followed them that a mixture of Danish and Saxon became the official language of the guards of the Imperial Palace. Hoards of Eastern coins and ornaments are almost annually discovered in Norway and Sweden, and occasionally in Orkney and the North of Scotland. The museum of Stockholm possesses a collection of more than 20,000 Cufic coins found in Sweden, dating from the close of the 8th to the end of the 10th century, and vast quantities of those silver ornaments of peculiar forms and style of workmanship, which are also believed to have been brought from the East, partly by trade and partly by the returning Værings.

Once when they were talking, Eindridi said : " It seems strange to me that you do not think of going out to Jór-salaheim (Jerusalem), and that you should be satisfied with being told of the things that are there; it would best suit such men as you are to be there on account of your great accomplishments, and you will be honoured above all others wherever you come among noble men."

When Eindridi had said this, many spoke in favour of it, and exhorted the Earl to become the leader of such an expedition. Erling made a long speech in support of the proposal, and said he would join the party himself, if the Earl would consent to be their chief. And as many men of note seemed eager for the journey, he promised to go. And when he and Erling were settling matters between them, many noble men joined the party. These Lendermen (Barons) were among them : Eindridi Ungi, who was to be their guide, Jón Pétrsson, Aslák Erlendsson, Guttorm Möl, and Kol from Halland. It was resolved that none of them should have a larger ship than with thirty benches, except the Earl, and no one should have an ornamented vessel but he. This was done in order that no one should envy an-other because he had finer men or a better ship than he. Jón Fót (leg) was to build a ship for the Earl, and to have it as finely fitted out as possible. Earl Rögnvald went home in the autumn, and intended to stay at home two winters. King Ingi gave the Earl two long ships—small, but very beautiful, and specially built for rowing ; they were, therefore, of all the ships the swiftest. Earl Rögnvald gave Harald one of them, called Fífa ; the other was called Hjálp. In these ships the Earls went to sea, holding west-ward. Earl Rögnvald had received large presents from his friends. It was Tuesday evening when the Earls put out to sea, and they had a fair wind during the night. On Wednesday there was a great storm, and in the evening they saw land. It was very dark, and they saw signs of breakers surrounding them on all sides. Up to this time they had kept together. There was nothing to be done except to run the vessels on shore, and this they did.[1] The beach before them was stony and narrow, enclosed behind

---

[1] The scene of the shipwreck seems to have been near Gulberwick.

by crags. All the men were saved, but they lost a large quantity of their stores. Some of the things were thrown up by the sea during the night. As usual, Earl Rögnvald bore himself as the bravest of all the men there. He was so merry that he played with his fingers, and spoke nearly all his sayings in rhyme. He took a golden ring from his hand, and sang this ditty:

> Thus I hang the hammer-beaten
> Hand-ring from my rounded fingers ;
> Thus I put my fingers through it :
> So the nymph of crashing waters
> Threw me, joyful, in a rock-rift
> There to play me with my fingers.

When they had carried their things up from the sea, they went farther inland to search for habitations, because they thought they knew they had landed in Hjaltland. They soon found farms, and distributed themselves among them. The people were glad to see the Earl, and when he was asked about his voyage, he sang:

> Both my ships on beach went crashing ;
> When the surges swept my men off,
> Sore afflicted by the billows
> Were the friends of Hjalp and Fifa.
> Certainly this misadventure
> Of the danger-seeking rovers
> Will not soon be quite forgotten
> By those who got such a wetting.

The mistress of the house brought a fur cloak to the Earl, who, stretching his hands forward to receive it, and laughing, sang this ditty:

> Here I shake a shrunken fur coat ;
> Surely 'tis not ornamental.
> All our clothes are in the ship-field,
> And it is too wide to seek them.
> Lately, all the young sea-horses
> Left we dressed in splendid garments,
> As we drove the steeds of mast-heads
> To the crags, across the surges.

Large fires were made, and there they warmed them-

K

selves. A female servant entered shivering all over, and her words were unintelligible on account of her shiver. The Earl said he understood her:

> Asa! you seem quite exhausted.
> Atatata! 'tis the water.
> Hutututu! where shall I sit?
> By the fire—'tis rather chilly.

The Earl sent twelve of his men to Einar in Gullberu-vík, but he said he would not receive them unless the Earl came himself. When Earl Rögnvald heard this, he sang:

> Einar said he would give food to
> None of all the lads of Rögnvald,
> He himself alone excepted—
> (Empty words I now am talking),
> For I know that he, the friendly,
> Never failed to keep his promise.
> Go we in then where the fires are
> Burning brightly all the evening.

The Earl stayed a long time in Hjaltland, and in the autumn he went south to the Orkneys, and resided in his dominions. That autumn two Hjaltlanders [1] came to him. One was named Armód, a poet; the other was Oddi the little, the son of Glúm: he made verses well. The Earl received them both as his men. The Earl had a grand Yule feast, to which he invited guests, and gave his men presents. He handed a spear, inlaid with gold, to the poet Armód, shook it at him, and told him to make a song on the spur of the moment:

> Princely gifts the battle-fanner
> With no niggard hand distributes:
> Scaldic honours are not measured
> By the gifts bestowed on others.
> The defender of his country,
> And the best of all commanders,
> With his own hand brings to Armód
> This blood-candle, golden pointed.

One day during Yule the guests were looking at the tapestry. The Earl said to Oddi the little: " Make a song

---

[1] The MS. translation at Stockholm reads "two Icelanders."

about the workman's handicraft on the tapestry, and have it
made by the time that I have finished my stanza, and use
none of the same words that are in mine.   The Earl sang:

> The old one on the hangings standing,
> Has a sheath-rod on his shoulder,
> But, in spite of all his anger,
> He will not get one step farther.

Oddi sang:

> For a stroke himself prepares the
> Warrior in stooping posture,
> Where the tapestry is parted ;
> Yet his danger will be greatest.
> Time it is for ships' commanders
> Peace to make ere harm does happen.

During Yule-tide, the Earl entertained Bishop William
and many of his chiefs.   Then he made known his intention
to go to Jórsalaheim (Jerusalem), and requested the Bishop
to go with him, because he was a good Parisian scholar,[1] and
the Earl wished him to be their interpreter.   The Bishop
agreed to the Earl's request, and promised to go.   The following chiefs went with Earl Rögnvald :—Magnus, the son
of Hávard, Gunni's son ; Swein, Hróald's son ; and the following men of lesser note :—Thorgeir Skotakoll, Oddi the
little, Thorberg Svarti, Armód the scald, Thorkel Krókauga,
Grímkell of Flettuness, and Bjarni his son.   When the two
winters appointed for their preparations were passed, Earl
Rögnvald went early in the spring from the Orkneys east to
Norway, to see how far the Lendermen (Barons) had pro-
gressed with their preparations ; and when he came to
Biörgvin, he found there Erling, Jón, his brother-in-law, and
Aslák, but Guttorm arrived shortly after.   To Biörgvin came
also the ship which Jón Fót had caused to be built for the
Earl.   It was a most exquisite piece of workmanship, and
all ornamented.   The whole of the carved work on the prow,
the vanes, and many other parts of the ship, were gilt.
Altogether, it was a most splendid ship.   Eindridi came

---

[1] Having studied probably at the University of Paris.   Schröder gives the
names of several Swedish students at the University of Paris as early as
1275.   (De Universitate Parisiensi : Joh. Hen. Schröder.)

frequently to town during the summer, and said he should
be ready in a week. The Earl's men murmured greatly at
having to wait so long, and some proposed not to wait for
him, saying that such voyages as this had been made without
Eindridi.   A short time after Eindridi came to town and said
he was ready.   Then the Earl commanded his men to set sail
when they thought there was favourable wind ; and when the
day came when they thought they might expect a favourable
wind, they left the town, and set sail.   The breeze was faint,
and the Earl's ship moved slowly, because it required strong
wind.   The other chiefs lowered their sails, and would not
leave the Earl.   When they were outside the Islands, the
breeze increased to such a degree that in the smaller vessels
they had to take in sail, but the Earl's ship now went at a
great speed.   They saw two large ships coming after them,
and soon they passed them.   One of these two ships was
highly finished.   It was a dragon ; both its head and stem
were richly gilded ; it was white on the bows, and painted
everywhere above the sea where it was thought it would look
well.   The Earl's men said that was very likely Eindridi's,
adding : " He has not kept well the agreement that no one
should have an ornamented ship except you, sire."

The Earl replied : " Eindridi's pride is great, and he may
be excused for not liking to be on the same level with us,
as we are so much his inferiors ; but it is difficult to see
whether his good fortune runs before him or goes along with
him.   But let us not direct our movements according to his
hotheadedness."

Eindridi soon passed them in the larger vessel, but the
Earl kept all his ships together, and had a successful voyage.
They arrived all safe in the Orkneys in the autumn.

CHAPTER LXXX.

OF EARL ROGNVALD AND THE ORKNEYMEN.

IT was resolved that they should spend the winter there.
Some lived at their own expense, others were quartered with
the Bœndr, and many were with the Earl.   There was a great

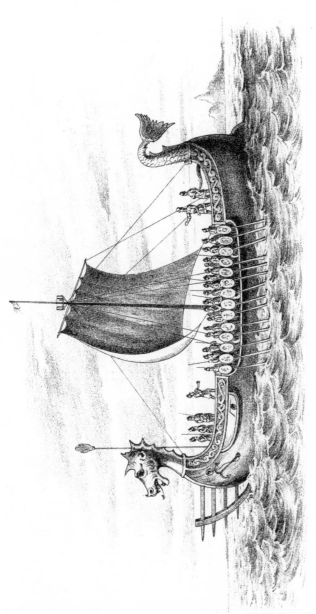

DRAGON SHIP OF THE VIKING PERIOD
(from Holmberg's Nordbon i Hednatiden)

Waterstone & Son Edinr. Lith.

turmoil in the Islands; the Orkneymen and the Eastmen quarrelled frequently about bargains, and women, and other things. The Earl had a very difficult task to keep peace among them, for both parties considered that he deserved well of them and they of him.

Of Eindridi it is to be told that when they came to Hjaltland (Shetland) his fine ship was totally wrecked, and he lost a great quantity of goods, but the smaller ship was saved. He spent the winter in Hjaltland, and sent men to Norway to have another ship built for the voyage to the East.

One of Eindridi's crew was called Arni Spítulegg (stickleg). He went to the Orkneys during the winter with nine men. Arni was a very violent man, daring and turbulent. He and his comrades lived at their own expense during the winter. He bought malt and meat of a tenant of Swein, Asleif's son, and when he demanded payment Arni delayed to pay. When he demanded it a second time, he was overwhelmed with abuse; and before they parted Arni struck him with the back of his axe, saying, "Go and tell your champion, Swein, whom you are always praising, to obtain redress for you; you will need no more." The man went and told Swein, requesting him to obtain redress. He gave him a cold answer, and said he would promise nothing. One day in the spring Swein went to collect his rents. They were four together in a ten-oared boat. They had to pass the island in which Arni was staying, and Swein said he would land there. It was ebbing tide. Swein went on shore alone, carrying an axe with a short handle, and no other weapon. He told his men to keep the boat from getting aground. Arni Spítulegg and his comrades were lying in an outhouse not far from the sea. Swein walked up, and found them indoors. They greeted him. He acknowledged their greeting, and spoke to Arni, saying that he should settle the farmer's account. Arni replied that there was plenty of time for that. Swein asked him to do it for his intercession, but still Arni refused. Then Swein said he would not ask any further, and at the same time he drove the axe into Arni's skull, so that the iron was buried in it, and he lost hold of the handle. Swein ran out, and Arni's companions

after him, to the beach. As they ran fast along the muddy
shore, one of them, who was the swiftest, came to close quarters with him. There were large roots of seaweed lying in
the mud. Swein seized one of them, and thrust it into the
face of the man who had come up with him, and he grasped
at his eyes to clear the mud away, but Swein escaped to his
boat, and went home to Gáreksey. Shortly after he went on
his own business over to Caithness, and sent word to Earl
Rögnvald to settle the matter about Arni Spítulegg's slaying.
And when the Earl received the message, he summoned
together those who were entitled to compensation for Arni,
and settled the matter to their satisfaction, he himself paying
the compensation money. Many other acts of violence per-
petrated by the Eastmen and the Orkneymen during the
winter the Earl made good out of his own [funds].

Early in the spring he called a Thing meeting in Hrossey
(Mainland), to which came all the chiefs residing in his
dominions. He then made it known to them that he intended
to leave the Orkneys and to go to Jórsalaheim (Jerusalem),
saying that he would leave the government in the hands of
his kinsman Harald, and praying all his friends to obey him,
and help him faithfully in whatever he required while he
was obliged to be away himself. Earl Harald was then
nearly twenty, tall and strong, but ugly; yet he was a wise
man, and the people thought he would be a good chief.

In the summer Earl Rögnvald prepared to leave the
Orkneys; but the summer was far advanced before he was
ready, because he had to wait a long time for Eindridi until
his ship came from Norway. When they were ready, they
left the Orkneys in fifteen large ships. The following were
commanders of ships:—Earl Rögnvald; Erling Skakki;
Bishop William; Aslák, Erlend's son; Guttorm; Magnus,
Hávard's son; Swein, Hróald's son; Eindridi Ungi; and the
others who were with him are not named. From the Orkneys
they sailed to Scotland, and then to England, and when they
sailed to Nordymbraland (Northumberland), off the mouth of
Hvera (the Wear), Armód sang:

> High the crests were of the billows
> As we passed the mouth of Hvera;
> Masts were bending, and the low land

> Met the waves in long sand reaches ;
> Blind our eyes were with the salt spray
> While the youths at home remaining,
> From the Thing-field fare on horseback.

Then they sailed till they were south off England, and so on to Valland.[1] There is no account of their voyage until they came to a seaport called Verbon.[2] There they learned that the Earl who had governed the city, and whose name was Geirbiörn, had lately died; but left a young and beautiful daughter, by name Ermingerd. She had charge of her patrimony, under the guardianship of her noblest kinsmen. They advised the Queen to invite Earl Rögnvald to a splendid banquet, saying that her fame would spread far if she gave a fitting reception to noblemen arrived from such a distance. The Queen left it to them; and when this had been resolved upon, men were sent to the Earl to tell him that the Queen invited him to a banquet, with as many men as he himself wished to accompany him. The Earl received her invitation gratefully, selecting the best of his men to go with him. And when they came to the banquet there was good cheer, and nothing was spared by which the Earl might consider himself specially honoured. One day, while the Earl sat at the feast, the Queen entered the hall, attended by many ladies. She had in her hand a golden cup, and was arrayed in the finest robes. She wore her hair loose, according to the custom of maidens, and a golden diadem round her forehead. She poured out for the Earl, and the maidens played for them. The Earl took her hand along with the cup, and placed her beside him. They conversed during the day. The Earl sang :

> Lady fair ! thy form surpasses
> All the loveliness of maidens,
> Though arrayed in costly garments,
> And adorned with precious jewels :
> Silken curls in radiant splendour
> Fall upon the beauteous shoulders
> Of the goddess of the gold-rings.
> The greedy eagle's claws I redden'd.

---

[1] Valland, probably for Gaul-land, the Norse name for the west coast of France. [2] Verbon has not been identified.

The Earl stayed there a long time, and was well entertained.
The inhabitants of the city solicited him to take up his residence there, saying that they were in favour of giving the
Queen to him in marriage.   The Earl said he wished to
complete his intended journey, but that he would come there
on his return, and then they might do what they thought fit.
Then the Earl left with his retinue, and sailed round Thrasness.   They had a fair wind, and sat and drank, and made
themselves merry.   The Earl sang this song:

>Long in the Prince's memory
>Ermingerd's soft words shall linger;
>It is her desire that we shall
>Ride the waters out to Jordan;
>But the riders of sea-horses,
>From the southern climes returning,
>Soon shall plough their way to Verbon
>O'er the whale-pond in the autumn.

Then Armód sang:

>Ne'er shall I see Ermingerda
>More, from this time, if it be not
>That my fate shall be propitious;
>Many now are grieving for her.
>Happy were I if I could but
>Be beside her just for one day;
>That, indeed, would be good fortune,
>Once again to see her fair face.

Then Oddi sang:

>Truth to tell, we two are scarcely
>Worthy of fair Ermingerda;
>For this wise and lovely Princess
>May be called the Queen of Maidens:
>This the title that beseemeth
>Best the splendour of her beauty.
>While she lives beneath the sun-ray,
>May her lot be ever happy.

They went on till they came west to Galicialand,[1] five
nights before Yule-tide, and intended to spend it there.   They
asked the inhabitants whether they were willing to sell them

---

[1] Galicialand, the modern Galicia, the north-west corner of Spain.

provisions; but food is scarce in that country, and they thought it a great hardship to have to feed such a numerous host.   It so happened that the country was under the rule of a foreigner, who resided in the castle, and oppressed the inhabitants greatly.   He made war on them if they did not do everything he wished, and menaced them with violence and oppression.   When the Earl asked the inhabitants to sell him victuals, they consented to do so until Lent, but made certain proposals on their part — to wit, that Earl Rögnvald should attack their enemies, and should have all the money which he might obtain from them.   The Earl communicated this to his men, and asked them what they would be inclined to do.   Most of them were willing to attack the castle, thinking that it was a very likely place to obtain booty.   Therefore Earl Rögnvald and his men agreed to the terms of the inhabitants.

When the Yule-tide was close at hand the Earl called his men together, and said: "We have been resting for a while, and have not disturbed the men of the castle, and the inhabitants are getting tired of supplying us.   I suppose they will think our promise will come to nothing; and it is not manly in us not to try to do what we promised.   Now, I wish to hear your advice as to how we are to take the castle, as I know you here are men of great discretion; therefore I ask every one here present to state what plan he thinks most likely to succeed."

Erling replied to the Earl, and said : " I will not be silent since you command us to speak, although I am not a man of sage counsels; and those ought rather to be asked who have seen more and are more experienced in such undertakings, as Eindridi Ungi.   But I suppose we must do here as the saying is, 'Shoot at the bird before we catch it.'   I may try to give some advice, whatever may be its value.   If you and the other ship-commanders do not think it a bad plan, we shall to-day go all of us to the wood, and carry three bundles of faggots each to the castle, because it appears to me that the lime would not stand well if much heat were applied to it. Let us do this for the next three days, and see what happens."

They did as Erling advised, and when they had finished their work Yule was close at hand.   The Bishop would not permit the inhabitants of the castle to be attacked during the Yule-tide.

The chief inhabiting the castle was named Gudifrey.   He was a wise man, and somewhat advanced in years.   He was a good scholar, had travelled much, and knew many languages.   He was a covetous man, and overbearing.

When he saw what the strangers were doing, he called his men together, and said : " The plan adopted by the Northmen seems to me a wise one, and likely to do us great harm. We shall see, when fire is applied to the stone wall round the castle, that it is not strong.   Moreover, the Northmen are valiant, and men of great strength, and we may expect a fierce attack from them if they get an opportunity.   Now, I wish to hear your advice about the difficult position in which we are placed."

But all his men asked him to do what he thought best.

Then he said : " My first plan is to tie ropes together, and you shall let me down over the castle wall.   I will dress myself in rags, and go to the camp of the Northmen, and see what I can ascertain."

They did as he told them, and he came to Earl Rögnvald pretending to be a beggar, and speaking Valska, as they understood a little of it.   He walked throughout the camp and begged food.   He perceived that there was much jealousy among the Northmen, and that they were divided into two factions.   Eindridi Ungi was the leader of one, and the Earl of the other.

Gudifrey went to Eindridi and spoke to him.   He said that the chief of the castle had sent him there, wishing to form an alliance with him.   " He expects that you will give him quarter if the castle is taken ; and he is more willing to let you have his treasure, if you will do this in return, than those who wish to have him a dead man."

Such things they spoke, and many others, but it was concealed from the Earl, as at first they observed profound secrecy.   When Gudifrey had been some time with the Earl's men, he returned to his castle.   But they did not remove their property from it, because they did not know whether the attack would be successful, and they could not put faith in the inhabitants.

CHAPTER LXXXI.

EARL ROGNVALD TAKES A CASTLE.

THE tenth day of Yule-tide was a fine day, and Earl Rögnvald arose and commanded his men to arm themselves, and
summoned them with trumpets to the attack of the castle.
They dragged the wood close to it, and heaped up large piles
round the walls. Then the Earl gave orders where each
should make the attack. He himself with the Orkneymen
had the attack from the south, Erling and Aslák from the
west, Jón and Guttorm from the east, and Eindridi Ungi
from the north. When they were ready for the attack, they
set fire to the wood, and the Earl sang:

> Maids in lace and snow-white linen
> Bring us here the white wine sparkling.
> Fair to see was Ermingerda,
> When we met her in our travels.
> Fare we now to try the castle
> With our flaming oaken firebrands;
> Quickly leaping from the scabbard
> Gleams the sharp-edged smiter.   Forward!

Now they began to attack the castle vigorously, both with
weapons and with fire. They shot missiles into it, for that
was the only way of attack. The besieged did not stand
firm on the walls, because they had to guard themselves
against the missiles. They poured down burning pitch and
brimstone, which, however, did very little harm to the Earl's
men. What Erling had foretold came to pass; the lime
could not stand the fire, and the wall fell down, leaving large
breaches open.

A man named Sigmund Ongul (fish-hook), the Earl's
stepson, was one of the keenest in the attack, and frequently
went in front of the Earl, although he was then hardly a
full-grown man. When the attack had lasted for a while,
all the besieged were driven from the wall. The wind blew
from the south, and drove all the smoke towards Eindridi,
and when the fire began to spread rapidly the Earl had water
poured on it to cool the burnt stones, and then there was a
short pause in the attack. The Earl sang a song:

> Now I mind me of the Yule-tide
> Which I spent with friends and brave men
> On the east of Agdir's mountains,
> With the valiant warrior Solmund;
> Now, again, another Yule-tide
> Am I in the same way busy
> At the south side of this castle,
> Adding to the din of weapons.

Further he sang:

> Glad I was when that fair lady
> Listened to my love-tale's telling;
> Hopelessly was I led captive
> By a Valland maid in autumn.
> Still I love the noble lady,
> And I spread the feast for eagles.
> Stone and lime, well bound together,
> Now before me fall asunder.

Then Sigmund Ongul sang:

> When, in spring-time, o'er the waters
> Ye go homeward to the Orkneys,
> Tell the lady whom I most love—
> Lady of the splendid garments—
> That, beneath the castle ramparts,
> There was none who stepped more boldly
> 'Mong the young men than her lover.

Then the Earl and Sigmund prepared to force their way into the castle, and meeting with little resistance, they entered it, and many were killed; but those that surrendered to the Earl received quarter. They obtained a great deal of property, but did not find the chief, and almost no treasure. There was a great discussion about the escape of Gudifrey, and how he had effected it; and they soon suspected Eindridi Ungi that he had given him the means of escaping, and that he had followed the smoke, and thus gained the forest.

After this Earl Rögnvald and his men stayed a short time in Galicialand, and directed their course along the west of Spain. They plundered far and wide in heathen Spainland,[1] and obtained great booty. They went into a certain

---

[1] Heathen Spainland must refer to the provinces then in possession of the Moors. The Saga of Sigurd the Jórsala-farer says that when he visited Lisbon,

village, but the villagers ran together and offered fight.
They made a stout resistance, but fled at last, when many of
them had been killed.   The Earl sang :

> When in Spainland I went fighting,
> Quickly we o'erthrew the foemen,
> For, when tired of our hard hewing,
> Home they ran to see their sweethearts :
> All the land was strewed with corpses.
> Our deeds in song shall now be famous ;
> And my hope is, to be worthy
> Of the lovely Ermingerda.

Then they sailed along the west of Spain, and were overtaken by a gale.   There they lay at anchor three days, and
great waves broke over them, so that the vessels nearly foun-
dered.   Then the Earl sang :

> Here I'm storm-tossed, but undaunted,
> While the cables hold together,
> And the tackle of the vessel
> Breaks not, as she breasts the billows ;
> I am promised to the fair one
> Whom we left out in the North-land ;
> Now again there comes a fair wind ;
> Speed we on into the channel.

Then they set sail, and ran into Njörfasund [1] with a fair
wind, and Oddi sang :

> When the faithful friend of heroes,
> In the guest-hall sweet mead quaffing,
> Sat beside the fair ring-giver,
> That was a week to be remembered.
> Now the splendid steeds of billows
> Bear the noble-minded Rögnvald
> And his warriors, wearing bucklers,
> Quickly through the Sound of Njörfi.

When they were tacking into the Sound, the Earl sang :

> By an east wind, breathing softly,
> As from lips of Valland lady,

---

four years after the fall of King Magnus Barelegs (circa A.D. 1107), " there lies
the division between Christian Spain and heathen Spain, and all the districts
that lie west of the city are occupied by heathens "—meaning Moslems.

[1] Njorfasund, the Straits of Gibraltar.

> Are our ships now wafted onward,
> As we push the yards out farther ;
> Though we had to tie the canvas
> Tighter than we had expected
> To the middle of the sailyard,
> South off Spain—we bear away now.

They sailed through Njörfasund, and then the gale began to
abate ; and when they had cleared the Sound, Eindridi Ungi
parted from the Earl with six ships, and sailed across the sea to
Marselia (Marseilles), but Earl Rögnvald and his men remained
at the Sound.   It was said that Eindridi now himself proved
that he had allowed Gudifrey to escape.   The Earl's men
sailed out to sea, and stood southwards to Serkland.[1]   Then
Earl Rögnvald sang :

> Now our good ship, land forsaking,
> Laves her breast in limpid waters.
> Long ere he who sings these verses,
> Sees again the northern islands ;
> With the sharp prow I the yielding
> Earth-surrounding sea am carving,
> Far off Spain-land, sweeping southward.

More is not said of the Earl's progress till they came south
off Serkland, and lay near Sardinia, not knowing where the
land was.   It was very calm, and a thick fog spread over
the water, so that they could hardly see anything from the
ships, and they sailed therefore slowly.   One morning the
mist disappeared, and the crew arose and looked around and
saw two islets.   When they looked for them the second time,
there was but one islet.   This they told to the Earl.   Then
he said : " This cannot have been islets which you have seen ;
it must be ships such as they have in this part of the world,
and which they call Drómundar.[2]   From a distance they look
as big as holms.   But where the other Drómund lay, a puff
of wind has probably swept over the water, and she has
sailed away ; but they are likely some rovers."

---

[1] Serkland, or Saracen land—the north coast of Africa.

[2] *Dromones*, originally used for long and swift ships, was in later times
applied to the larger ships of war (Du Cange *sub voce*).   In the early French
romances it appears as "Dromons," and "Dromont."   Matthew Paris, in his
account of the crusading expedition of Richard I. of England (A.D. 1191)
notices the capture of a Saracen ship—"navis permaxima quam Dromundam
appellant."—*Hist. Angl.* vol. ii. p. 23, Rolls Ed.

Then he summoned the Bishop and all the ship-commanders, and said: "I ask of you my Lord Bishop, and
Erling my kinsman, whether you see any chance or device
by which we may overcome those in the Drómund."

The Bishop replied: "I think you will find it difficult
to attack the Drómund in your long-ships, for you will hardly
be able to reach their bulwarks with a boarding-pike, and
they have probably brimstone and boiling pitch to pour under
your feet and over your heads. You may see, Earl Rögnvald, wise as you are, that it would be the greatest rashness
to place yourself and your men in such jeopardy."

Then Erling said: "My Lord Bishop, it may be that you
are right in thinking that we shall not obtain the victory by
rowing at them; yet I cannot help thinking that if we try
to push close to the Drómund, their missiles will fall beyond
our ships lying close alongside; but if this be not the case,
we can push away quickly, for they will not be able to chase
us in the Drómund."

The Earl said: "That is bravely spoken, and very much
to my own mind. I will now make it known to the ships'
commanders and all the men, that every one may arm and
prepare himself, each in his own place, as well as he can.
Then let us attack them, and if they are Christian merchants,
we can make peace with them; but if they are heathens,
which I think they are, by the favour of Almighty God we
shall be able to overcome them, but of the booty we obtain
we shall give every fiftieth penny to the poor."

Then they unfastened their arms, prepared the bulwarks
of their ships for battle, and made themselves ready in other
ways as their circumstances permitted. The Earl assigned
to each vessel its place in the attack; then they pulled
vigorously onwards.

CHAPTER LXXXII.

RÖGNVALD CONQUERS THE DRÓMUND.

WHEN the men in the Drómund saw the ships pulling
towards them, to attack them, they spread fine clothing

and costly stuffs out on the bulwarks, and made a great
shouting, which the Earl's men took as a challenge. Earl
Rögnvald brought his ship close under the stem of the
Drómund, on the starboard side. Erling did the same on
the larboard side. Jón and Aslák brought theirs under
her bows, and the others amidships on either side, all stick-
ing as close to her as possible. But when they came close
under the Dromund, she was so high in the side that the
Northmen were unable to use their weapons, and the others
poured blazing brimstone and burning pitch over them; but
most of it fell outside the ships, as Erling had foreseen, and
they had no need to shield themselves from it. However,
when the attack did not succeed, the Bishop moved away
his ship and two others, and they told off their bowmen to
go in them. After having got to a convenient distance for
shooting, they shot their arrows into the Drómund, and this
was the most effective mode of attack. The men in the
Drómund protected themselves with their shields, and paid
little heed to what those were doing who were in the ships
close under the Drómund.

Earl Rögnvald then ordered his men to take their axes,
and cut the planks of the Drómund, where the iron fastenings were fewest; and when the men in the other ships saw
what the Earl's men were doing, they did the same. Now,
where Erling had stationed himself, there was a large anchor
hanging from the Drómund, which had its fluke hooked over
the gunwale, but the shank hung down towards Erling's
ship. One of his forecastle men was named Audun Raudi
(red); he was lifted up on the anchor-stock, and then he
pulled up others. Standing there as close as they could,
they hacked away at the planks with all their might; and
this was far higher than the others could reach. When
they had made an opehing large enough to admit them, they
prepared to board the Drómund. The Earl and his men
entered on the lower deck, and Erling and his men on the
upper; and when they both got in, there began to be severe
fighting. Those in the Drómund were Saracens, whom we
call Mahometan infidels. There were also many black men,
who withstood them most fiercely. Erling received a severe
wound in the neck, near the shoulder, when he jumped on

board; it healed so badly that he carried his head to a side
ever after, and therefore he was called crick-neck (Skakki).

When Earl Rögnvald and Erling joined each other, the
Saracens were driven to the forepart of the ship; and the
Earl's men boarded one after another until they were more
numerous, and then they pressed the enemy hard. In the
Drómund they saw one man far superior to the others in
appearance and stature, and they were persuaded that he
must be their chief. Earl Rögnvald ordered his men not
to wound him, if they could seize him in any other way.
Then they surrounded him, and pressed him with their
shields, and thus caught him. He and a few others with
him were sent to the Bishop's ship. All the rest they
killed, and obtained great booty and many precious things.
When they had finished the hardest part of their work,
they sat down and rested, and the Earl sang:

> At the spreading of the banner,
> Erling, mighty tree of battle,
> Went to victory and honour
> Foremost when we fought the Drómund;
> Then we felled the black-skinned fighters;
> Everywhere the blood ran streaming,
> And the keen-edged swords were reddened
> As we hewed among the heathen.
>
> We have had our fill of slaughter,
> Round us lie the heaps of corpses;
> Gory swords have been red-painting
> At the Drómund all this morning;
> Soon the news will spread to northward
> Of this furious sword-tempest;
> It will soon be known at Verbon,
> How we dealt death-blows this morning.

There was much talk about what had been done; every one
told what he had seen. Then they talked of who had been
the first to board, but were not all of one opinion. Some
said it would not be creditable to them if they did not all
relate this great exploit in the same way. At last they
all agreed to let Earl Rögnvald decide, and every one should

afterwards tell the story in the same way as he did. Then the Earl sang:

> Audun Raudi was the man who
> First, with energy and valour,
> Scaled the black sides of the Dromund;
> Soon the brave one seized his booty.
> By the help of God's good favour
> Have we overcome the heathen;
> Steeped our swords are all in red blood;
> Round us lie the sable corpses.

When they had cleared the Drómund, they set it on fire. When the big man whom they had taken prisoner saw this, he changed colour and became pale, and could not keep himself still. But though they tried to make him speak, he did not say a word, neither did he make any kind of sign; he was immovable to fair promises and menaces alike. But when the Drómund began to blaze up, they saw a glowing stream, as it were, run into the sea. At this the captive man was greatly moved. They concluded that they had not made a careful search for the money, and now the metal, whether gold or silver, had melted in the fire.

Then Earl Rögnvald and his men sailed south, under Serkland, and lay off a certain town of Serkland, and had seven nights' truce with the men of the town, and sold them silver and other valuables. No one would buy the big man; and then the Earl gave him leave to go away with four men. He came back on the morning after, with his men, and told them that he was a nobleman of Serkland, and that he had been ransomed from there with the Drómund and all its contents. " It grieved me most," he said, " that you should burn it, and thus destroy so much treasure, without any one's having the benefit of it. Now you are in my power, but it counts for your benefit with me that you spared my life, and did me such honour as you could. But I would gladly never see you again, and now may you live hale and well." Then he rode away into the country.

Earl Rögnvald sailed to Crete, and anchored in a strong gale. When Armod kept watch during the night, he sang:

Lie we now, where stormy billows
Break above the sturdy bulwarks;
My lot is to keep the watch well,
On this wave-surmounting seahorse;
While the lads are snugly sleeping,
I, to Crete, look o'er my shoulder.

They lay off Crete until they had fair wind to Jórsalir (Jerusalem), and arrived early on a Friday morning at Akursborg (Acre). They went on shore with great pomp and splendour, such as seldom had been seen there. Thorbiörn Svarti sang:

Oft have I, with comrades hardy,
Been in battle, in the Orkneys,
When the feeder of the people
Led his forces to the combat.
Now our trusty Earl we follow,
As we carry up our bucklers
Gaily to the gates of Acre
On this joyful Friday morning.

They stayed in Akursborg for a while, and a disease broke out among their men, of which many died. Thorbiörn Svarti died there. Oddi Litli sang:

Bravely bore the Baron's vessels
Thorbiorn Svarti, scald and comrade,
As he trod the sea-king's highway,
Round by Thrasness, south to Acre.
There I saw them heap the grave-mould
Of the High Church o'er the King's friend.
Earth and stones now lies he under
In that southern land of sunshine.

Earl Rögnvald and his men left Akursborg, and visited all the holiest places of Jórsalaland. They went all to Jórdan and bathed. Earl Rögnvald and Sigmund Ongull swam across the river, and went to some shrubs and tied large knots.[1] The Earl sang:

[1] The tying of knots at the Jordan is also alluded to in the saga of Sigurd the Jórsala-farer. King Sigurd and his brother Eystein are "comparing each other's exploits," and Sigurd says:—"I went to Palestine, and I came to

> Long the way is I have travelled
> To this heath, enclosed by deserts,
> And the wise maid will remember,
> Too, my crossing over Jordan.
> Seems to me, that those who tarry
> At their homesteads, will not find it
> A short journey here to travel.
> Warm the blood falls on the wide plain

Then Sigmund sang:

> This day I have tied a strong knot
> For the churlish clown that's sitting
> By the home-hearth; 'tis no falsehood
> That we play him now a fine trick.

The Earl sang:

> On this feast-day of St. Lawrence,
> Tie we knots for this fine fellow.
> Tired I came to this nice corner,
> Where the shrubs grow close together.

And when they were going from Jórsalaland Earl Rögnvald sang:

> From the scald's neck hangs the cross now,
> In his hand a palm he carries.
> Now should cease unkindly feelings:
> From the heights my men rush downwards.

During the summer Earl Rögnvald and his men left
Jórsalaland, and were going to Mikligard. In the autumn
they came to a town called Imbolum,[1] and stayed there a
long time. When two persons met where the street was

Apulia, but I did not see you there, brother. I went all the way to Jordan,
where our Lord was baptized, and swam across the river; but I did not see
thee there. On the edge of the river-bank there was a bush of willows, and
there I twisted a knot of willows, which is waiting thee there; for I said this
knot thou shouldst untie, and fulfil the vow, brother, that is bound up in it."
The tying of knots seems also to have had another meaning covertly alluded
to in the stanzas.—(See the story of Gunnhild and Hrut in the Njáls Saga,
p. 18.)

[1] This seems to be no place-name, but a name formed, as the Turks formed
the name Istambol, from hearing the Greeks constantly talking of going
" εις την πολιν"—"to the city," meaning Constantinople.

crowded, and one of them thought it necessary to go to one
side, he cried out to the other, "Midway, midway!" One
evening the Earl's men, among whom was Erling Skakki,
walked from the town, and on the bridge leading to the
ship, some inhabitants of the town met them, and cried
out, "Midway, midway!" Erling was very drunk, and pretended not to hear it; and when they met, he jumped from
the bridge into the mud; his men ran to his assistance, and
dragged him out, and had to undress him completely. Next
morning, when the Earl saw him, and was told what had
happened, he smiled and sang:

> Bad the luck my friend has met with;
> In the mud he tumbled, splashing;
> As he would not cry out "Midway!"
> Loudly, like the foreign people.
> I suppose the prince's brother,
> When upset, looked rather rueful.
> Black the mud that on the ground is
> In Imbol, as Erling knoweth.

Some time after, it happened that they came from the
town very drunk, and Jón Fót was missed by his men,
and no one else was missing. They sent immediately to
the other ships to search for him, but he was not found.
They could not search for him on shore during the night;
but in the morning, when it was daylight, they found him
murdered under the wall of the town; but it was never
known who had slain him. They buried him honourably
at a holy church, and then they went away, and came north
to Ægisness,[1] and there they waited some nights for a fair
wind to sail to Mikligard. They made their ships look
splendidly, and sailed with great pomp, as they knew Sigurd

---

[1] Probably the promontory of Sigeum, at the mouth of the Dardanelles.
It might be called Ægisness, from its being at the entrance to the Ægean Sea.
It is called Engilsness in the saga of "King Sigurd the Jórsala-farer," and it
is stated that Sigurd's fleet also lay here for a fortnight waiting a side-wind,
that they might show off their sails (which they had stitched over with silks)
as they passed up to Constantinople. There was, however, a town called
Ægos, at the mouth of a stream of the same name, near the northern end of
the Dardanelles, a little below the modern Gallipoli.

Jórsalafari had done.   While they were crossing the sea
northward the Earl sang this song :

> Let us ride the sea-king's horses,
> Leave the plough in field untouched.
> As we drive the wet prows onward
> All the way to Mikligardr.
> There we'll take the royal bounty,
> Paid for wielding well our weapons,
> While we fill the wolf's red palate,
> And on battlefields win honour.

CHAPTER LXXXIII.

OF EARL RÖGNVALD.

RÖGNVALD and his men came to Mikligard, and were well
received by the Emperor and the Væringiar.[1]   At this time
Menelaus, whom we call Manuli,[2] was the Emperor of Mikligard.   He gave them a great deal of money, and offered
them pay if they would stay there permanently.   They
spent there a great part of the winter.   Eindridi Ungi was
there when they came, and was highly honoured by the
Emperor.   He had little to do with the Earl and his
men, but rather spoke slightingly of them to others.   Rögnvald commenced his journey from Mikligard during the
winter, and went first to Dýraksborg[3] in Bólgaraland.
From there they sailed west to Púll.[4]   Earl Rögnvald,
Erling, Bishop William, and most others of their noblest
men left their ships there, procured horses, and rode first
to Rómaborg (Rome), and then from Róm until they came
to Denmark.   From there they went to Norway, where the

---

[1] See note at p. 127.

[2] Manuel I., successor of John Comnenus, who reigned from 1143 to
1180.

[3] Dýraksborg must be Durazzo, the ancient Dyrachium, a seaport in
Albania, on the Adriatic, opposite to Brundusium in Italy.

[4] Pull, the ancient Apulia or Puglia, in Italy, on the opposite shore of the
Adriatic from Dyrachium.   Apulia had been under the dominion of its Norman dukes from the middle of the eleventh century, and this may have been
the reason why the route homewards through Apulia was chosen both by
Sigurd the Jórsala-farer and Earl Rögnvald.

people were glad to see them. This journey became very famous, and all those who had made it were considered greater men afterwards than before.

Ogmund Dreng, Erling Skakki's brother, had died while they were away; while both were alive, he was considered the greater of the two. After the death of King Ingi, Magnus, the son of Erling and Kristín, the daughter of Sigurd Jórsalafari, was made King, but the government of Norway was in the hands of Erling alone. Valdimar, King of the Danes, gave him the title of Earl, and he became a great chief. Eindridi came from the south some winters after Earl Rögnvald, and went to King Eystein, because he would not have anything to do with Erling. But after King Eystein's death Eindridi and Sigurd, the son of Hávard Höld of Reyr, raised a party, and made Hákon Herdabreid,[1] the son of King Sigurd, son of Harald Gilli, their king. They slew Gregorius Dag's son and King Ingi. Eindridi and Hákon fought with Erling, under Sekkr,[2] where Hákon was killed; but Eindridi fled. Earl Erling had Eindridi Ungi killed some time after in Vik.[3]

Earl Rögnvald spent the summer in Hördaland, in Norway, and heard many tidings from the Orkneys. There were great disturbances there, and most of the chiefs were divided into two factions, few remaining neutral. Earl Harald was at the head of one of these factions, and Earl Erlend and Swein, Asleif's son, of the other. When the Earl heard this, he sang:

> Though the most part of my nobles
> Have forgot the oaths they sware me
> (Such the wickedness of men is),
> Yet will their designs be thwarted.
> Traitors plotting in my absence,
> Will not by it grow more loyal;
> Slow but sure shall be my motto
> While a beard on chin I carry.

---

[1] Hákon Herdabreid (the broad-shouldered) became King in 1161. (For an account of his death, and that of King Ingi and Gregorius Dagson, see the sagas of the sons of Harald Gilli and Hákon Herdabreid, in the Heimskringla.)

[2] Near Bergen.   [3] Viken, in the south of Norway.

The Earl had no ships, but he asked his kinsmen and friends to build some long-ships for him during the winter. They gave a favourable answer, and consented to everything he proposed, and built the ships.

CHAPTER LXXXIV.

EARL RÖGNVALD GOES TO THE ORKNEYS.

In the summer the Earl made himself ready to go west to his dominions in the Orkneys, but it was late before he was ready, because many things kept him back. He went to the west in a merchant-vessel belonging to Thórhall, Asgrím's son, an Icelander of a noble family, who had a farm south in Biskupstungur.[1] The Earl had a numerous train of noblemen on board the vessel. When they came to Scotland the winter was far advanced, and they lay at Torfnes.[2] The Earl arrived in his dominions shortly before Yule.

CHAPTER LXXXV.

KING EYSTEIN TAKES EARL HARALD PRISONER.

Now we have to tell what happened in the Orkneys while Earl Rögnvald was away. The same summer that the Earl went on his journey, King Eystein, son of Harald Gilli, arrived from Norway with a numerous army, which he had landed at Rínansey.[3] He heard that Earl Harald had gone over to Caithness in a ship of twenty benches, with eighty men, and lay then at Thórsá. When King Eystein heard of him, he manned three boats, and crossed the Pentland Firth, going westward, and on to Thórsá. When he arrived there the Earl and his men did not know anything of them until the King's men boarded the ship, and took the Earl pri-

---

[1] Bishop's-tongues, a district lying between three rivers in the south of Iceland, also mentioned in the Njáls Saga.

[2] See note on p. 21.

[3] One of the MS. copies of the saga has "Rognvaldzeyiar."

soner. He was brought before the King, and the result was that the Earl ransomed himself with three marks of gold, and surrendered his dominions to King Eystein, so that he should hold them from him in the future. Then he became King Eystein's man, and confirmed their compact with oaths. From there King Eystein went to Scotland, and ravaged there during the summer. During this expedition he plundered in many parts of England, considering that he was taking revenge for King Harald, Sigurd's son.[1]

CHAPTER LXXXVI.

OF KING EYSTEIN.

THEN King Eystein returned to his kingdom, and his expedition was variously thought of. Earl Harald remained in his dominions in the Orkneys, and most of the inhabitants were satisfied with his rule. At this time his father, Earl Maddad, was dead; but his mother, Margarét, had gone to the Orkneys. She was a handsome woman,[2] but a virago. At this time David, the King of Scots, died, and his son Malcolm[3] was made king. He was quite a child when he succeeded his father.

CHAPTER LXXXVII.

OF EARL HARALD.

ERLEND, the son of Harald Sléttmáli, spent most of his time in Thórsá. Sometimes he was in the Sudreyar, or on war expeditions, after the death of Earl Ottar. He was a very promising man, and accomplished in most things, liberal in

---

[1] Harald Hardradi, son of Sigurd Syr, who was slain in the battle of Stamford Bridge. See p. 47.

[2] See the account of her elopement with Earl Erlend Ungi in chap. xcii., and of her relations with Gunni, Olaf's son, chap. lxxxvii.

[3] This was Malcolm the Maiden, the grandson, and not the son, of King David I.

money, gentle, open to advice, and greatly loved by his men. He had a large following.

There was a man named Anakol, who had fostered Erlend, and to his counsels he chiefly listened. He was of a noble family, and hardy. He was Earl Erlend's right-hand man.

When Earl Rögnvald had left his dominions to go to Jórsalaheim, Erlend went to Malcolm,[1] the King of Scots, and requested him to give him an Earl's title, and Caithness for his support, as his father Earl Erlend had. And because Erlend had many friends, and Malcolm was a child in years, it was brought about that he bestowed the title of Earl on Erlend, and gave him the half of Caithness jointly with his kinsman Harald. Then Erlend went to Caithness to see his friends.

After that he gathered troops together, went out to the Orkneys, and sought to be accepted by the inhabitants. When Earl Harald, Maddad's son, heard this, he gathered troops together, and had many men. Some parties went between the kinsmen and tried to make peace between them. Erlend asked for half of the Islands jointly with Earl Harald, but Earl Harald refused to give them up. Truce was, however, made between them for that year; and it was resolved that Erlend should go to the east and see the King of Norway, and ask for that half which belonged to Earl Rögnvald, which Earl Harald said he would surrender. Then Erlend went east to Norway, but Anakol and some of his party remained behind.

Gunni, Olaf's son, the brother of Swein, Asleif's son, had children by Margarét, Earl Harald's mother, but Earl Harald had banished him, and therefore enmity arose between him and Swein. The latter sent his brother Gunni south to Liódhús (Lewis) to his friend Liótólf, with whom he had been staying himself. Fugl, the son of Liótólf, was with Earl Harald, and there was therefore coldness between him and Swein. When Earl Erlend went east to Norway, Earl Harald went over to Caithness, and resided at Vík (Wick) during the winter. Swein, Asleif's son, was then at Thrasvík (Freswick), in Caithness, and took care of the estate which his stepsons had there, for his former wife was Ragnhild,

---

[1] Malcolm the Maiden.

Ingimund's daughter, though they lived but a short time together. Their son was Olaf. After that he married Ingirid, Thorkel's daughter. Their son was Andreas.

On Wednesday in Passion week Swein went with some others to Lambaborg. They saw a transport vessel coming from the north across the Pentland Firth, and Swein concluded that they were Earl Harald's men whom he had sent to collect his revenues (scat) in Hjaltland. Swein ordered his men to take a boat and attack the barge, which they did. They seized all its cargo, and put Earl Harald's men on shore, and they went to Vík (Wick) and told him. Earl Harald did not say much to this, yet he said: "Swein and I shall have our turns." He distributed his men to be entertained during Easter. The Caithnessmen called this —that the Earl was in guest-quarters.

CHAPTER LXXXVIII.

OF SWEIN, ASLEIF'S SON.

IMMEDIATELY after Easter week, Swein, Asleif's son, went with a barge and a boat rowed by oars to the Orkneys; and when they came to Skálpeid (Scapa), they took there a ship from Fugl, Liótólf's son. He was coming from his father at Liódhús (Lewis), and was going to Earl Harald. During the same trip they took twelve ounces of gold from Sigurd Klaufi, a housecarl of Earl Harald's. This money had been left at the homestead, but the owners were in Kirkiuvag (Kirkwall). Then Swein went over to Ness (Caithness), and up through Scotland. He found Malcolm,[1] King of Scots, who was then nine winters old, in Apardion (Aberdeen). Swein spent a month there, and was well entertained. The King of Scots insisted upon his enjoying all those emoluments of Caithness which he had before he became Earl Harald's enemy.

[1] Malcolm the Maiden was twelve years old when he came to the throne. Perhaps the Saga-writer meant that he had then been nine winters king.

CHAPTER LXXXIX.

OF SWEIN AND ANAKOL.

AFTER this Swein prepared to go away, and the King of Scots and he parted very good friends. Then Swein went to his ships, and sailed from the south to the Orkneys. Anakol was at Dýrness when Swein sailed from the south, and they saw them sailing east off Múli.[1] They sent Gauti, a bondi of Skeggbjarnarstadir,[2] to Swein, and Anakol requested him to come to terms with Fugl about the seizure of the ship, because Anakol and Fugl were related to each other. When Gauti found Swein, and told him Anakol's message, he sent a messenger back to Anakol, asking him to go to Sandey, that they might meet there, because he (Swein) had to be there himself. They had a peaceful meeting there, and came to terms; and the result was that Swein should make the award as he liked himself. After that Anakol formed an alliance with Swein, and bound himself to make peace between Swein and Earl Erlend, when he came from the east—for they were bitter enemies on account of the burning of Frákork. Swein and Anakol went to Striónsey, and lay off Hofsness[3] some nights. At this time Thorfinn Bessason lived at Striónsey. His wife was Ingigerd, Swein's sister, who had been deserted by Thorbiörn Klerk.

CHAPTER XC.

THE RECONCILIATION OF EARL ERLEND AND SWEIN.

WHEN Swein and Anakol were lying off Hofsness, Earl Erlend arrived there from Norway. Anakol and Thorfinn endeavoured to reconcile him to Swein, but he gave an unfavourable answer, saying that Swein had always been

---

[1] The Mull of Deerness, or Moulhead of Deerness, as it is called in the maps, in the north-east of the Mainland, Orkney.

[2] Skeggbjarnarstad was probably a homestead on Skebro Head, in Rousay. The old form of Skebro Head might be Skeggbjarnarhöfdi.

[3] Hofsness, probably Huipness, the most northerly point of Stronsay.

opposed to his kinsmen, and had not kept the agreement between him and Earl Ottar, that he should help him to the dominion. Then Swein offered the Earl his support, and they were negotiating the whole day; yet the Earl would not be reconciled until Anakol and Thorfinn declared that they would follow Swein from Orkney if the Earl would not make peace with him. Earl Erlend then told the message from King Eystein, that he should have that part of the Orkneys which had formerly been held by Earl Harald.

When they had made peace, Swein gave the advice that they should go to Earl Harald before he heard this from others, and ask him to surrender the dominion. Swein's advice was acted upon. They found Earl Harald on board his ship, off Kjárekstadir.[1]

It was in the evening of Michaelsmas that Harald and his men saw long-ships approaching, and suspecting them to be enemies, they ran from the ships into the castle. There was a man named Arni, Rafn's son, who ran from Earl Harald's ship to Kirkiuvag. He was so frightened that he forgot that he had his shield at his shoulder until it stuck fast in the door. Earl Erlend and Swein ran from their ships, and pursued Earl Harald to the castle, and attacked them both with arms and fire. The assailed defended themselves bravely, until night parted them. Many were wounded on both sides, and Harald and his men would soon have been exhausted if the attack had lasted longer. The next morning the Bœndr and their mutual friends arrived, and tried to make peace between them. Earl Erlend and Swein were very reluctant to make peace. In the end, however, they agreed, on condition that Harald should swear to let Earl Erlend have his part of the Islands, and never demand it from him. These oaths were made in the presence of the best men in the Islands.

[1] Kjarekstad.—Munch identifies this place with the modern Karston or Careston, which lies on the inlet leading to the Loch of Stennis, a little to the north-east of Stromness. But this would make Arni, Rafn's son, run a good ten miles without once remembering that he had his shield on his shoulder until it stuck in the door at Kirkwall. If this Kjarekstad be not the same with Knarrarstad at Scapa, which was Earl Rögnvald's homestead (see p. 113), and might be the castle here spoken of, there is a Corness near Kirkwall (in old maps Carisness) which may be more readily supposed to be the Kjarekstad from which Arni ran than Careston near Stromness.

After that Earl Harald went over to Ness (Caithness), and to his friends in Scotland, accompanied by only a few men from the Orkneys.

Earl Erlend and Swein called together a Thing-meeting with the Bœndr in Kirkiuvag, and they arrived from all the Islands. Earl Erlend pleaded his cause, saying that King Eystein had given him that part of the Orkneys of which Earl Harald had charge, and he requested the Bœndr to receive him, showing them King Eystein's letters, which proved his words. Swein, and many others of his friends and kinsmen, spoke in favour of the Earl; and at last the Bœndr promised obedience to Earl Erlend. Then he took possession of all the islands, and became ruler over them. It was an agreement between Earl Erlend and the Bœndr that he should not hinder Earl Rögnvald from taking possession of that part of the islands which belonged to him, if it should be granted him to come back; but if Earl Rögnvald should demand more than one-half of the islands, they should help Earl Erlend to resist his claims. Swein, Asleif's son, was frequently with Earl Erlend, and asked him to be on his guard, and not to trust Earl Harald or the Scots. The most part of the winter they were on board their ships, and had scouts on the look-out. Towards Yule-tide the weather began to grow boisterous, and Swein went home to his estate in Gáreksey, and asked the Earl not to relax his vigilance though they parted, and the Earl did so. He remained on board his ships, and had nowhere a Yule feast prepared for him in the Islands.

CHAPTER XCI.

EARL HARALD COMES UNPERCEIVED TO THE ORKNEYS.

THE eleventh day of Yule-tide, it happened in Gáreksey that Swein was sitting at his drink with his men. Rubbing his nose, he said: "I think Earl Harald is now on his way to the Islands."

His men replied that this was unlikely, on account of the strong gales prevailing at that time.

He replied : " I know such is your opinion, and I shall not therefore send intelligence to the Earl now, merely on the strength of my presentiment; yet I suspect it is necessary." Then the subject was dropped, and they went on drinking as before.

Earl Harald commenced his voyage to the Orkneys during Yule-tide. He had four ships, and a hundred men. Two nights he lay under Gáreksey (Grimsey ?). They landed in Hafnarvag,[1] in Hrossey, and the thirteenth day of Yule-tide they walked to Fiörd (Firth). They spent the Yule-holiday at Orkahaug.[2] There two of their men were seized with madness, which retarded their journey. It was near day when they came to Fiörd (Firth). There they learned that Earl Erlend was on board his ship, but that he had been drinking during that day at a house on shore. There Harald and his men killed two men—one was named Ketill, the name of the other is not mentioned—and made four prisoners : Arnfinn, Anakol's brother, another man called Liótólf, and two others. Harald and Thorbiörn Klerk returned to Thórsá ; the brothers Benedict and Eirík went to Lambaborg, taking Arnfinn with them.

[1] Munch says of this passage that the text reads, very improperly, "Gareksey" for "Grimsey." Hafnarvag he identifies with the Medalland's hofn of Hakon Hakonson's saga, which is the "Midland Harbour" lying between the Holm of Houston and the Mainland on the south side of Orphir. The name Hafnarvag, however, simply signifies a landing-place in a voe or inlet, and might more appropriately be applied to some place near the head of the inlet immediately opposite Grimsey, which goes up to the Loch of Stennis. If Harald and his men landed at "Midland Harbour," they took the longest land route to walk to Firth ; if they landed near the head of the inlet above mentioned, they chose the shortest land route.

[2] The word Orkahaug is only known to occur twice—once here, and once in one of the Runic inscriptions on the walls of the chamber of Maeshow. Here it is given merely as the name of the place where Earl Harald and his men had a Yule-tide carouse, which disabled two of them from proceeding on their journey, so that they failed in surprising Earl Erlend at his Yule feast. In the inscription in the chamber of Maeshow it appears as the name of the burial-mound which was broken into by the Jórsala-farers in search of treasure. There seems to be little doubt that this name "Orkahaug" was the name by which the Maeshow was then known. The Orkahaug of the text must either mean the actual "how" itself, or a homestead near it which was named from it. There is an Orkhill (Orquill) not very far from Maeshow, and there was another Orkhill near Knarstane, Scapa, which is called Orquile in "the coppie of my Lord Sinclairis Rentale that deit at Flowdin." No other Orkahaug, however, is known. (See under Maeshow in the Introduction.)

As soon as Earl Erlend became aware of the enemy, he sent men during the night to Gáreksey to tell Swein. He pushed out his boats immediately, and went to see Earl Erlend, according to the message, and they stayed on board the ships a great part of the winter. Benedict and his brother sent word that Arnfinn would not be liberated unless Earl Erlend sent them back their ship which had been seized off Kjárekstadir. The Earl was willing to give up the ship, but Anakol dissuaded him from it, saying that Arnfinn would get away without this sacrifice.

On the Wednesday before Lent, Anakol and Thorstein, Ragna's son, went over by night to Ness (Caithness) in a boat with twenty men. They hauled the boat ashore under a cliff in a hidden creek. Then they went up and hid themselves in some copsewood a short distance from Thrasvík (Freswick). They had fitted up the boat in such a way that the men seemed to be each in his place. Some men had come past the boat in the morning, and had not suspected anything.

Anakol and his men saw some men rowing from the borg[1] and landing at the river-mouth.[2] Then they saw a man riding from the borg, and another walking, whom they recognised to be Eirík. Then they divided themselves into two parties. Ten went along the river down to the sea, to prevent them from getting to the boat; other ten went to the hamlet. Eirík came a short time before them to the hamlet, and walked towards the drinking-hall. Then he heard armed men moving about, and ran into the hall, and out through another door, and down to his boat; but there he came upon men who seized him, and brought him out to the Islands to Earl Erlend. Then messengers were sent to Earl Harald to tell him that Eirík would not be liberated until Arnfinn and his companions came safe to Erlend. And the wishes of both were complied with.

---

[1] The castle at Freswick, elsewhere called Lambaborg (see p. 122).
[2] The mouth of the burn of Freswick.

CHAPTER XCII.

THE RECONCILIATION OF THE EARLS HARALD AND ERLEND.

IN the spring Earl Harald prepared to go from Caithness north to Hjaltland. His intention was to take the life of Erlend Ungi, who had wooed his mother Margarét, although the Earl (Harald) had refused him. Then Erlend gathered men together, and carried her off from the Orkneys, and took her north to Hjaltland, took up his residence in Moseyjarborg,[1] and made great preparations (for defence). When the Earl (Harald) came to Hjaltland, he besieged the borg, and cut off all communication; but it was difficult to take it by assault, and men went between them and tried to reconcile them. Erlend asked the Earl to give him the woman in marriage, and in return he offered to assist the Earl, saying it was of greater consequence for him to recover his dominions than this, and it would be advisable for him to make as many friends as he could. Many spoke in favour of Erlend's proposal; and the result was that they made peace, and Erlend married Margarét. Then he became an ally of Earl Harald, and during the summer they both went east to Norway.

When these tidings came to Orkney, Earl Erlend and his men laid their plans. Swein counselled to go on a harrying raid to obtain booty. This they did, and went south to Breidafiörd,[2] and made inroads on the east of Scotland. They went south to Beruvík (Berwick-on-Tweed). There was a man named Knút the wealthy, who was a merchant, and always resided in Beruvík. Swein and Erlend seized a large and fine vessel belonging to Knút. On board was a valuable cargo, and Knút's wife. Then they sailed south to

---

[1] Moseyjar-borg, the burg or castle on the little island of Mousa, in Shetland. This curious structure is the best preserved example of the old Celtic strongholds, or "Pictish towers," which were so thickly planted over the northern and western districts of Scotland, and specially in those districts exposed to the ravages of the Northmen. We learn from the Saga of Egill Skallagrimson that fully two centuries before the event here narrated Mousa had been occupied in a precisely similar manner by a couple who fled from Norway, and after celebrating their marriage in the deserted burg, lived in it for a whole winter. (See under Mousa in the Introduction.)

[2] The Moray Firth.

M

Blýhólmar.[1]   Knút was at Beruvík when he heard of the
plunder.   He induced the Beruvík men for a hundred marks
of silver to try to recover the goods.   Of those who went in
pursuit most were merchants.   They went in fourteen ships
to search for them.   When Earl Erlend and Swein were
lying under Blýhólmar, Swein said in the night that they
should sleep without awnings, saying that he expected that
the Beruvík men might come upon them during the night in
great numbers.   A gale was blowing, and no heed was paid
to Swein's words, and they slept under the awnings, except
in Swein's ship, where there was no awning abaft the mast.
Swein was sitting on a chest in a fur coat, saying that he
wished to be ready during the night.

One of Swein's crew was called Einar Skeif.   He said
that Swein's bravery was much talked of, that he was called
a bolder man than others, but now he dared not have awnings on board his ship.   Watchmen were on shore in the
island.   Swein, hearing that they did not agree about what
they saw, went up to them and asked what they were disputing about?   They said they were not sure what it was
that they saw.   Swein had keener sight than any of his
men, and when he looked he saw fourteen ships approaching
them from the north.   Then he went on board his ship
again, and told his men to wake up and take down the awnings, and then a great outcry arose, every one asking Swein
what they should do.   He told them to be silent, and said
that his advice was to moor the ships between the island
and the mainland, adding : "We shall see whether they do
not pass by us, and if they do we shall part ; but if they
attack us, we shall row against them as vigorously as possible, and let us make a stout resistance if we meet."

Others spoke against this plan, saying the only way was
to sail from them, and so they did.

Swein said : "If you wish to sail away, then stand out
to sea."   Swein was not so soon ready as the others, but
Anakol waited for him.   Swein's ship was, however, a
swifter sailer, and he took in sail and waited for Anakol,
not wishing him to be left behind in a single ship.   When

---

[1] Bly-holmar (lead islands) must refer to a group of islands not far to the
south of Berwick, probably the Fern Islands.

they stood off, with all sail set, Einar Skeif said : "Swein, does our ship stand still ? "

Swein replied : "I do not think so; but I advise you not to question my courage any more, since through your fright you cannot tell whether the ship moves or stands still, yet it is one of the swiftest sailers."

They put in under Mosey,[1] and Swein sent men to Eidinaborg to tell the King of Scots of his plunder; but before they came to the town they met twelve men on horse-back who had saddle-bags filled with silver, and when they met they inquired after Swein, Asleif's son. The others told where he was, and asked what they wanted with him. The Scots said they had been told that Swein was taken prisoner, and the King of Scots had sent them to ransom him. Thus they told their errand.

The King did not make much of Knút's loss, but sent a costly shield to Swein, and other presents besides.

Earl Erlend and Swein arrived rather late in the Orkneys in the autumn. This summer Earl Harald went east to Norway. At the same time, Earl Rögnvald and Erling Skakki came to Norway from Mikligard, and he arrived at his dominions in the Orkneys shortly before Yule.

CHAPTER XCIII.

PEACE BETWEEN EARL RÖGNVALD AND EARL ERLEND.

THEN there went men immediately between Earl Erlend and Earl Rögnvald, and tried to make peace between them, the Bœndr pleading the agreement they had come to with Earl Erlend, that he should not prevent Earl Rögnvald from taking possession of his part of the Islands. A conference took place between the Earls at Kirkiuvag (Kirkwall), and at that conference they confirmed their peace with oaths. It was two nights before Yule when they made peace, and the terms were, that they should each have one-half of the Islands, and both should defend them against Earl Harald or any other if he claimed them. Earl Rögnvald had no

---

[1] Mosey, the Isle of May.

ships till his own came from the east in the summer. This
winter all was quiet, but in the spring the Earls prepared
their plans in case Earl Harald should come from the east.
Earl Erlend went to Hjaltland to intercept him if he should
come there. Earl Rögnvald went over to Thórsá, because
Earl Harald was expected to go there if he came from the
east, as he had there many friends and kinsmen. Earl
Erlend and Swein were in Hjaltland during the summer,
and kept back all ships, so that none went to Norway.

In summer Earl Harald left Norway with seven ships,
and landed in the Orkneys. Three of the ships, however,
were driven by stress of weather to Hjaltland, and these
were seized by Swein and Earl Erlend. When Earl Harald
came to the Orkneys he heard of the agreement of Earl Rögnvald and Earl Erlend, that each of them should have one-
half of the Islands; and then he saw that no territory was
intended for him. He resolved to go over to Ness (Caithness) to Earl Rögnvald before Earl Erlend and Swein came
from the east. They were in Hjaltland, when they heard
that Earl Harald had arrived in the Orkneys with five
long-ships, and prepared to go thither immediately. In
Dynröst[1] they had strong currents and severe gales, and
there they parted. Swein was driven back to Fridarey
(Fair Isle), with twelve ships, and they thought the Earl
had perished. From Fridarey they went to Sandey, where
they found Earl Erlend with three ships. It was a joyful
meeting for them. Then they went to Hrossey (Mainland),
and inquired about Earl Harald's movements.

CHAPTER XCIV.

PEACE IS TALKED OF.

Now it is to be told that Earl Harald came to Thórsá with
six ships. Earl Rögnvald was in Sutherland, at the wedding of his daughter Ingiríd, whom he married to Eirík Slagbrellir. He heard immediately that Earl Harald had arrived

---

[1] Off Sumburgh Head, now called Sumburgh Roost.

at Thórsá, and rode from Beruvík[1] to Thórsá, attended by many men. Eirík was related to Earl Harald; and with many others he tried to make peace between them, saying that it was absurd for them to be at enmity, because of their relationship, their up-bringing, and their long alliance. At last matters came so far that a meeting was appointed, and truce made. They should meet in a certain castle at Thórsá,[2] and talk together alone; but an equal number of their men should be outside the castle. They talked a long time, and agreed very well. They had not seen each other since Rögnvald returned. Late in the day information was given to Earl Rögnvald that Earl Harald's men were coming there armed. Earl Harald said that no harm would be done. Then they heard heavy blows outside, and ran out. Thorbiörn Klerk had arrived there with a large party, and attacked Rögnvald's men immediately. The Earls called to them that they should not fight. Then the inhabitants of the town came running to the spot to separate them. Thirteen of Earl Rögnvald's men were killed, and he himself was wounded in the face.

CHAPTER XCV.

SWEIN'S PLANS.

AFTER this their friends made an effort to establish peace between them, and the result was that they made peace, which they confirmed by oaths. They renewed their alliance, pledging their faith and shaking hands; and it was resolved that they should go that very night out to the Orkneys to attack Earl Erlend. They went out on the Pentland Firth with ten ships, taking the course to Rínarsey.[3]

---

[1] Beruvík, probably the inlet at the mouth of the Berriedale water, on the north side of the Ord of Caithness, where there is an old tower called Berriedale Castle. (See note at p. 18.)

[2] This was probably the castle which was destroyed by King William the Lion in the end of the twelfth century, when he sent his troops against Earl Harald "to Turseha," and destroyed the Earl's residence there.

[3] This is evidently a mistake in the text for Rognvaldsey, or South Ronaldsay. In the MS. the contraction R.ey is used both for Rinarsey and Rognvaldsey.

They landed in Vidivag,[1] and went on shore. Erlend and his men lay on board their ships in Bardvik,[2] and from there they saw a crowd on Rognvaldsey, and sent out spies. When they heard of the reconciliation of the Earls, it was also said that Earl Erlend would not be permitted to plunder on shore, or to obtain provisions in any other way; and their intention was to prevent them from getting any food in the island. Earl Erlend held a meeting and consulted his men, and they agreed to leave it to Swein to say what should be done. Swein replied that they should sail that very night over to Caithness, saying that they had no strength to contend with both the Earls there in the Islands. He gave out that they intended to go to the Sudreyar (Hebrides), and winter there.

It was Michaelmas-eve when they sailed out on the Firth, but when they came over to Ness (Caithness), they ran up into the country, and drove down a great number of cattle, which they brought on board their ships. There were strong currents and bad weather, so that the Firth was frequently impassable; but when favourable weather came, Swein sent a man in a boat from Ness, to give information that Earl Erlend had made a great strand-hewing[3] in Caithness, and was ready to sail to the Sudreyar when there was a favourable wind. When this came to the ears of Earl Rögnvald, he called his men together and made a speech to them, telling them to be on their guard, to be wary, and sleep every night on board their ships; "For now," he said, "Swein may be expected every hour in the Islands; the more certainly the more he talks of going away."

Early in the winter Earl Erlend and Swein left Thórsá, and took their course by the west of Scotland. They had six large long-ships, all well manned. They had to row, and when they had gone some distance from Caithness, Earl Rögnvald's spies went out to the Islands, and told him the

---

[1] Vidivag, the voe or creek of the beacon; now Widewall, in South Ronaldsay.

[2] Bardvik, the bay beside Barth Head; now Burswick, in South Ronaldsay.

[3] Strandhögg, strand-hewing, or victualling the ships of a viking squadron, by driving cattle to the shore, and killing them there.

news.   Then the Earls moved their ships to Skálpeid (Scapa), and Earl Rögnvald wished them to stay a while on board.

When Swein and Erlend came west off Staur,[1] the former said that they should not distress themselves by rowing any farther, and asked his men to put the ships about and set the sails.   This action on the part of Swein was thought foolish, yet his men did as he desired them. When they had been sailing for a while the ships began to speed, because there was a fine breeze, and nothing is said of their voyage until they came to Vagaland,[2] in Orkney. There they heard that the Earls were lying at Skálpeid, off Knarrarstadir,[3] with thirteen ships.   There were Erlend Ungi, Eirík Slagbrellir, and many other men of note.   Thorbiörn Klerk had gone out to Papuley,[4] to Hákon Karl, his brother-in-law.   It was four nights before Simon's-mas when Swein, Asleif's son, decided to attack the Earls during the night, but it was thought rather hazardous, as their followers were so much more numerous.   Yet Swein insisted on having his own way; and so he did, because the Earl wished to follow his advice.

CHAPTER XCVI.

BATTLE BETWEEN THE THREE EARLS.

DURING the night there fell a shower of sleet, and Earl Rögnvald left his ship with six men, intending to go to his residence at Jórfiara (Orphir), because he expected no danger. During the shower they came to Knarrarstadir.   An Icelander, by name Bótólf Begla, an excellent skald, lived there. He pressed Earl Rögnvald with many invitations to stay there during the night.   Earl Rögnvald and his men entered the house; their clothes were pulled off them, and they

---

[1] Ru Stoer in Assynt, on the west coast of Sutherlandshire.

[2] Walls, in the Island of Hoy, Orkney.

[3] Knarston, at Scapa, in the Mainland of Orkney.   (See note at p. 113.)

[4] Paplay, in Mainland, where Hákon Karl, the brother of Earl Magnus the Holy, had his residence.   (See p. 96.)

went to sleep; but Bótólf was to keep watch. This same night Earl Erlend and Swein attacked Earl Harald and his men, and took them by surprise, and they knew of nothing till they heard the battle-cry. They flew to arms, and defended themselves bravely. Many were killed, and the attack ended in this way—that Earl Harald leaped on shore when there were only five men left in his ship. Bjarni, brother of Erlend Ungi, a noble man, fell there, and a hundred men with him; and a great number were wounded. All the Earl's men jumped from the ships to reach the shore, and fled. Few of Earl Erlend's men were killed, and they took fourteen ships belonging to the Earls, with all the valuables they contained. When the most part of their work was done, they heard that Earl Rögnvald had left his ship the evening before, and walked first to Knarrarstadir, and thither they went. Bondi Bótólf was outside the door when they came, and greeted them well. They asked whether Earl Rögnvald was there. Bótólf said he had been there during the night. They became very violent, and demanded where the Earl was then, saying that he no doubt knew where he was. He pointed with his hand behind the farm-yard, and sang:

> This way went the Prince a-fowling;
> Skilful are his men with arrows.
> Now is many a heathcock meeting
> Death beside the verdant hillocks,
> Where the elmbow of the hunter,
> Keenly bent, as if by magic,
> Makes the moorfowl quickly perish.
> The Prince's sword the land defendeth.

The Earl's men ran away from the homestead, and he who could run fastest considered himself luckiest, as he would be the first to catch Earl Rögnvald. Bótólf went into the house, awoke the Earl, and told him what had happened during the night, and also what the Earl's men were doing. Rögnvald and his men started up instantly, and put on their clothes; then they went away to the Earl's residence at Jórfiara; and when they came there they found Earl Harald in hiding. The Earls [Harald and Rögnvald] went immediately over to Ness each in a separate boat; one had two men, the other three. All their men went over to Ness, wherever they could get a boat.

Earl Erlend and Swein took the ships belonging to the Earl, and a great quantity of other property. Swein took for his share all Earl Rögnvald's treasures that were in his ship, and sent them to him over to Ness. Swein advised Earl Erlend to move his ships out to Vagaland (Walls), and to lie in the Firth, where they could see ships coming from Ness, as he thought it would be convenient to run out upon them if there was opportunity. But Earl Erlend yielded to the persuasions of his men that they should go north to Daminsey (Damsey), and in a large castle there they drank all day, but fastened the ships together every night, and slept on board. Thus time passed on till the Yule-feast.

CHAPTER XCVII.

EARL ERLEND'S DEATH.

FIVE nights before Christmas, Swein, Asleif's son, went east to Sandvík,[1] to his kinswoman Sigríd, because he had to make peace between her and her neighbour by name Björn. Before he went away he told Earl Erlend to sleep on board by night, and not to be less on his guard that he himself was absent. Swein spent one night with his kinswoman Sigríd. A tenant and dear friend of Sigríd's, by name Gisl, asked Swein to stay with him, as he had been brewing ale, and wished to entertain him. When they came to Gisl they were told that Earl Erlend had not gone on board that night; and as soon as Swein heard it, he sent Margad, Grim's son, and two other men to the Earl, and asked him to pay heed to his advice, although he had not done so the preceding night, and then he added: " I suspect that I shall not have long to provide for this Earl."

Margad and his companions found Earl Erlend, and told him Swein's words. The Earl's men said: " He is a strange man; sometimes he is afraid of nothing, at other

---

[1] Sandwick, in Deerness.

times he is so frightened that he does not know where to look for shelter to himself or others." They said they would sleep quietly on shore, and not go on board. The Earl said they should do as Swein advised them, and he went on board with four-and-twenty men; the others slept at a house. Margad went to another creek, not far away. This very night the Earls Rögnvald and Harald surprised Earl Erlend, and neither the watchmen who kept guard on the island nor those on board the ship perceived them until they were climbing on board. A man named Orm and another Ufi were in the forepart of the Earl's ship. Ufi jumped up and tried to rouse the Earl, but could not, for he was dead-drunk. Then he took him in his arms, and jumped overboard with him into a boat alongside the ship, and Orm jumped overboard on the other side, and escaped on shore. There Earl Erlend was slain, and most of those on board. Margad and his men were awakened during the night by the battle-cry, and took to their oars, and rowed round the headland. It was clear moonlight, and they saw when the Earls went away; and they felt sure that fate had decided between them. They rowed away first to Rennadal (Rendale), and sent men to Swein, Asleif's son, to tell him what they had seen. Earl Harald wished to give Earl Erlend's men peace, but Earl Rögnvald wished to wait, in order to know whether the Earl's body would be found or not. The body was found two nights before Yule. A spear was seen standing in a heap of seaweed; and that spear was fast in Earl Erlend's body.[1] Then it was brought to church, and peace was given to the Earl's men, as well as to four of Swein's men who had been taken.

A man named Jón Vœng was a sister's son of that Jón Vœng who was mentioned before.[2] He had been with Hákon Karl, and had a child by his sister; then he ran away, and was with Anakol on piratical expeditions; but now he was with Erlend, yet he was not in the battle. All Erlend's men went to Kirkiuvag, and took refuge in St. Magnus's church. The Earls went there, and a meeting for peace-making was held in the church. The Earls would not pardon Jón until he promised to marry the woman. All

---

[1] The Iceland Annals place the fall of Earl Erlend in A.D. 1154.   [2] See p. 74.

the men swore oaths of fealty to the Earls, and Jón Vœng became Earl Harald's steward.

CHAPTER XCVIII.

SWEIN SLAYS ERLEND.

AFTER Earl Erlend's death Swein, Asleif's son, went to Rennadal (Rendale), and there he saw Margad, who was able to give him all the tidings of what happened in Daminsey. Then Swein went to Hrólfsey (Rousay), and arrived there at high-water. He and his men brought all the tackle of the ships on shore, and placed it in safety. They divided themselves among the farms, and kept watch on the movements of the Earls and other chiefs. Swein, Asleif's son, mounted the hill with five men, and went down to the sea on the other side; they hid themselves at the homestead in the darkness, and heard a great talking. There were Thorfinn, his son Ogmund, and their brother-in-law Erlénd.[1] He boasted of having given Earl Erlend the death-blow, and all of them were declaring they had done right well. When Swein heard this, he and his companions went in upon them. Swein was quickest, and immediately dealt Erlend a death-blow. They took Thorfinn prisoner, and brought him away; but Ogmund was wounded. Swein went to Thingavöll,[2] to his father's brother Helgi; and there they spent the first days of Yule in hiding. Earl Rögnvald went to Daminsey, but Earl Harald was at Kirkiuvag during Yule-tide. Earl Rögnvald sent men to Thingavöll, to Helgi, and asked him to tell his kinsman Swein, if he knew anything of his whereabouts, that Earl Rögnvald invited him to spend the Yule with him, and he would try to make peace between him and Earl Harald. When Swein received this message, he went to Earl Rögnvald, and remained with him during the rest of the Yule-tide, and was well treated.

[1] None of these men are again mentioned in the Saga.
[2] In the "Coppie of my Lord Sinclaire's Rentale, that deit at Flowdin," dating between 1497 and 1503, there is a Tyngwale in Rendale, set to John Sclatter. The name still remains, but there is no other trace of an Orkney thing-stead in the Islands. (See p. 61.)

CHAPTER XCIX.

OF EARL HARALD AND SWEIN, ASLEIF'S SON.

AFTER Christmas a meeting was appointed to make peace between the Earls and Swein, when they should finally settle all matters about which reconciliation had been made.   When they met, Earl Rögnvald took great pains to make peace between them.   Others, however, who were not Swein's friends or kinsmen, spoke against him, saying that he would always be causing disturbances if he were not expelled from the Islands.   At last, however, they agreed upon this—that Swein should pay a mark of gold to each of the Earls, and should keep one-half of his estates and a good long-ship.

When Swein heard the award, he replied : " Our agreement will be good only in case I am not oppressed."

Earl Rögnvald would not accept the payment from Swein, saying that he would in no way oppress him, as he considered his faithfulness and friendship worth more than money.

After the peace-meeting, Earl Harald went to Gáreksey, and used Swein's corn and other property rather wastefully. When Swein heard this he complained of his loss to Earl Rögnvald, and said, that " this was a breach of their agreement, and that he would go home to look after his property."

Earl Rögnvald said : " Stay with me, Swein : I shall send a message to Earl Harald, for he will be more than a match for you to deal with, strong and brave as you are."

Swein was not to be dissuaded, and went with ten men in a boat to Gáreksey, and arrived there late in the evening. They went behind the houses, and Swein wished to set fire to the hall, and burn down the homestead, and the Earl within it.   A man named Swein, Blákári's son, the most notable of Swein's companions, dissuaded him from doing so, saying that the Earl was not perhaps in the homestead; and if he was there, he would neither permit Swein's wife nor his daughter to go out, and it was never to be thought of to burn them.   Then they went up to the door, and into the entry.   Those who were inside the hall jumped up and

closed the door, and then Swein and his men became aware
that the Earl was not in the house.   Those who were
within soon ceased resisting, surrendered their weapons to
Swein, and went out unarmed.   Swein gave quarter to all
Earl Harald's men.   He poured out all his beer, and took
away his wife and daughter.   He asked his wife Ingirid
where Earl Harald was, but she would not tell him.   He
then said : " Say nothing then, but point to where he is."
She would not do that either, because she was related to
the Earl.   Swein gave up some of the arms, when they
came on board the ships.   But the effect of this was that
their agreement of·peace was at an end.

Earl Harald had gone out to a certain island to hunt
hares.[1]   Swein went to Hellisey.[2]   It rises abruptly from
the sea, and there is a large cave in the cliffs, the mouth of
which is flooded at high-water.   When the Earl's men got
their weapons from Swein, they went to Earl Harald and
informed him of these doings of Swein's.   The Earl had his
ship set afloat, and ordered his men to row after him.   He
said : " This time our meeting with Swein shall be decisive."
Then they rowed in pursuit of him, and soon they saw and
recognised each other.

When Swein saw that they gained on him, he said :
" We must devise some scheme, because I do not care to
meet the Earl with so great odds against me as I suspect
there are.   Let us go to the cave and see how we fare."

When Swein came to the cave it was ebb tide.   They
hauled up the boat into the cave, which ran into the cliff,
and the water rose before the mouth of the cave.   During
the day Earl Harald and his men searched for Swein
throughout the island, and did not find him, neither did they
see any boat leave the island.   They wondered very much
at this, as they thought it unlikely that Swein's boat had
gone down.   They rowed round the island in search of the
boat, but did not find it.   Then they concluded that he must

---

[1] Mackaile and Sir Robert Sibbald both notice the existence of white hares
in the hill of Hoy. Low, in his "Fauna Orcadensis," states that they did
not exist in his day ; and he adds, "nor is there a hare of any kind to be
found in the Orkneys."

[2] Cave Isle—now Eller Holm, a small island between Shapinsay and the
Mainland of Orkney.

have gone to some of the other islands, and they went where
they thought it most likely. It so happened that, when the
Earl rowed away, the tide was back from the mouth of the
cave. Swein had overheard the talk between the Earl and
his men. He left his own boat in the cave, and took a small
boat which the monks[1] had, and went to Sandey. There they
landed, and pushed off the small boat, which drifted about
till it was wrecked. They came to a homestead called
Völuness,[2] where a man lived by name Bárd, who was Swein's
kinsman. They made themselves known to him secretly,
and Swein said he wished to stay there. Bárd said he
might do as he liked, but that he dared not keep him here
unless in hiding. They went in, and sat by themselves in
a part of the house separated from the other inmates by a
partition-wall. There was a secret door to it, filled up with
loose stones. That evening Jón Vœng, Earl Harald's
steward, arrived there with six men, and Bárd received them
well. Large fires were made, at which they warmed themselves. Jón was excited, and spoke of the dealings of Swein
and the Earls. He blamed Swein very much, said he was a
truce-breaker, and faithful to no one. He had lately made
peace with Earl Harald, and yet he went to attack him and
burn him in the house, adding that there would never be
peace in the land till Swein was banished from it. Bárd
and Jón's companions put in some words in Swein's defence.
Then Jón began to blame Earl Erlend, saying there was no
loss in his death, as he was a violent man, and nobody could
live in safety for him. When Swein heard this, he could
not restrain himself, but seized his weapons, and ran to the
secret door. He pushed the stones down, thus making a
great noise. Swein's design was to leap before the hall-door.
Jón was sitting in his shirt and linen breeches, and when he
heard Swein coming he tied on his shoes and sprang out
from the fire and away from the house. The night was pitch

---

[1] This seems to indicate that there was an ecclesiastical settlement on Eller
Holm. Possibly it may have been the "isle Elon" referred to in the stanza
made by Earl Rögnvald on the occasion of the singular apparition of the sixteen shaven crowns described in cap. lxvi. It is suggestive of this that Fordun
gives the name of this island as Helene-holm instead of Eller Holm. (See
note, chap. lxvi.)

[2] Völuness has not been identified.

dark, and it was hard frost. During the night he came to another farm. His feet were very much frost-bitten, and some of his toes fell off. Through the intercession of Bárd, Swein gave peace to Jón's companions. He remained there during the night, but in the morning he and his men went away in a boat belonging to Bárd, which he gave to him. They went south to Bardsvík,[1] and stayed in a certain cave. Sometimes Swein took his meals at a house during the day, but slept during the night down by his boat, and thus he guarded himself against his enemies.

CHAPTER C.

OF ROGNVALD AND SWEIN.

ONE morning early Swein and his men saw a large long-ship coming from Hrolfsey (Hrossey?) to Rognvaldsey,[2] and Swein recognised it immediately as Earl Rögnvald's ship, which he used to command himself. They put in at Rognvaldsey, where Swein's boat was lying, and five of them went on shore. Swein and his men were on a certain headland, and threw stones at the Earl's men. When those on board saw this, they drew forth their arms; and when that was seen by Swein, they ran down to the beach, and pushed their boat afloat, and jumped into it. The long-ship stuck fast on the beach. When they rowed past it, Swein was standing up with a spear in his hand. When Earl Rögnvald perceived it, he took a shield and held it before him, but Swein did not throw the spear. When the Earl saw that they would get away from them, he ordered a truce-shield to be held aloft, and asked Swein to go on shore. When Swein saw this, he told his men to put to land, saying that it was his greatest satisfaction to be at peace with Earl Rögnvald.

---

[1] This must be Barswick, near Barthhead, in South Ronaldsay, as it is afterwards stated that from this headland Rögnvald and Swein saw Earl Harald's ship coming across the Firth from Caithness to Walls.

[2] In the text it is "Hrolfsey to R(inans)ey"—Rousay to North Ronaldsay, but Munch's reading of the passage seems to be the true one. (See the next chapter.)

CHAPTER CI.

OF EARL HARALD AND SWEIN.

THEN Earl Rögnvald and Swein went on shore, and had a long conversation by themselves, and agreed very well. While they were talking, they saw Earl Harald sailing from Caithness to Vagaland (Walls), and when the ship approached the island, Swein asked what was to be done. The Earl said Swein should go over to Ness immediately. This was during Lent. They left Rognvaldsey at the same time. The Earl went to Hrossey,[1] but Swein went west to Straumsey (Stroma). Earl Harald saw the boat, and thought he recognised it as Swein's, and went immediately into the Firth in pursuit. When Swein saw the pursuit, they left the boat, and hid themselves. When Earl Harald came to Straumsey (Stroma) he saw the boat, and suspected that the men were somewhere near, and would not therefore go on shore. A man named Amundi, the son of Hnefi, who was Earl Harald's friend, and father's brother to Swein, Asleif's son's stepchildren, went between them, and succeeded so far that they agreed to keep the agreement of peace which they had made the previous winter. A gale arose, and they were both obliged to remain there during the night, and Amundi put Earl Harald and Swein in the same bed, and many of their men slept in the same house.

After this Swein went over to Ness (Caithness), and Earl Harald to the Orkneys. Swein heard that the Earl had said that their agreement to be at peace had been rather loose. He paid little heed to this, however, and went south to Dalir, and spent the Easter there with his friend Sumarlidi; but Earl Harald went north to Hjaltland, and was there a long time during the spring.

After Easter Swein went from the south, and met on his way two of Jón Vœng's brothers—one was called Bunu-Pétr, the other Blán. Swein and his men seized them, and took from them all their goods, and brought them to land. A

---

[1] The Mainland of Orkney. This shows that in all likelihood it is Hrossey that is meant where the text has Hrolfsey at the beginning of the previous chapter.

gallows was erected for them, and when everything was ready Swein said they should be allowed to run up the country, adding that they were greater shame to their brother Jón alive than dead. They were a long time out on the hills, and when they came to some habitations they were very much frost-bitten.

From thence Swein went to Liódhús, in the Sudreyar, and stayed there some time. When Jón Vœng heard that Swein had taken his brothers prisoners, and not knowing what he had done with them, he went to Eyin Helga (Enhallow), and took Olaf, the son of Swein, Asleif's son, and Kolbein Hrúga's foster-son, and brought him to Westrey. They met Earl Rögnvald at Hreppisnes,[1] and when he saw Olaf, he said : " Why are you here, Olaf ? "

He said : " It is the work of Jón Vœng."

The Earl looked to Jón, and said : " Why did you bring Olaf here ? "

He replied : " Swein took my brothers, and I don't know but he may have killed them."

The Earl said : " Take him back again as quickly as you can, and do not dare to do him any harm, whatever may have become of your brothers, for if you do, you will not be safe in the Islands from either Swein or Kolbein.

CHAPTER CII.

OF EARL RÖGNVALD.

AFTER Easter Swein commenced a journey to the Sudreyar, taking with him sixty men. He went to the Orkneys, and landed first in Hrólfsey (Rousay). There they took a man, by name Hákon Karl,[2] who had been with Earl Harald when Earl Erlend was slain. Hákon ransomed himself with three marks of gold, and thus saved himself from Swein. In Hrólfsey Swein found the ship which the Earls had taken from him, and two of the planks were cut, which had been

---

[1] Probably Rapness, in the south-east of the island of Westray.
[2] It does not appear whether this is the Hákon Karl who lived at Papuli or not.

done by Earl Rögnvald's order, because Swein had refused
to buy it or to accept it as a gift from the Earls. Swein
went from there to Hrossey, and met Earl Rögnvald at Birgishérad (Birsay). The Earl received him well, and Swein
spent the spring with him. Earl Rögnvald said that he had
ordered the planks of the ship to be cut, because he did not
wish him to row about rashly among the Islands when he
came from the Sudreyar. Earl Harald came from Hjaltland
in the spring during the Whitsuntide, and when he came to
the Orkneys Earl Rögnvald sent men to him to say that he
wished the compact of peace between him and Swein to be
renewed, and a peace meeting was appointed in St. Magnus's
church on Friday during the holy week. Earl Rögnvald
carried a broad axe to the meeting, and Swein went with
him. Then the peace compact which had been made in the
winter was confirmed.

CHAPTER CIII.

OF SWEIN, ASLEIF'S SON.

THEN Earl Rögnvald gave Earl Harald the ship which had
belonged to Swein, but all other things which had been
awarded him from Swein he returned to him. Earl Rögnvald and Swein were standing at the church-door while the
sail, which had been lying in St. Magnus's church, was carried out, and Swein looked rather gloomy. The following
Saturday, after noontide service, Earl Harald's men came to
Swein, Asleif's son, and said the Earl wished him to come
to speak with him. Swein consulted Earl Rögnvald, but he
did not say much in favour of his going, and added that one
did not know whom to trust. Swein went, nevertheless,
with five men. The Earl was sitting on a cross bench in a
small room, and Thorbiörn Klerk beside him. A few other
men were with the Earl, and they sat for a while and drank.
Then Thorbiörn left the room, and Swein's companions said
to him that they distrusted the Earl's conduct very much.
Thorbiörn returned shortly after, and presented Swein with a
scarlet tunic and a cloak, saying that he did not know

whether he would call it a gift, because these things had been taken from Swein in the winter. Swein accepted the gifts. Earl Harald restored to him the long-ship which had belonged to him, and the half of his property and estates. He asked him to stay with him, and said their friendship should never be dissolved. Swein accepted all this gladly, and went immediately the same night and told Earl Rögnvald how matters had turned out between him and Earl Harald. Earl Rögnvald said he was much pleased with this, and told Swein to take care that they did not become enemies again.

CHAPTER CIV.

OF THE EARLS.

A SHORT time after, the three chiefs—Swein, Thorbiörn, and Eirik—went out on a plundering expedition. They went first to the Sudreyar, and all along the west to the Syllingar, where they gained a great victory in Maríuhöfn[1] on Columba's-mas (9th June), and took much booty. Then they returned to the Orkneys.

When the Earls Harald and Rögnvald had made peace with Swein, Asleif's son, they were always together, and Earl Rögnvald governed, but they agreed very well. When they came home from the Syllingar, Thorbiörn Klerk went to Earl Harald, and became his counsellor. Swein went home to Gáreksey, and resided there during the winter with many men, living upon his booty, and other stores which he possessed there in the Islands. He was most attached to Earl Rögnvald. Every summer he was out on marauding expeditions. It was said that Thorbiörn did not improve the harmony between Earl Harald and Earl Rögnvald.

Thórarinn Killinef was one of Earl Rögnvald's men, a great friend of his, and was always with the Earl. A man named Thorkell was one of Thorbiörn Klerk's followers, and a friend of his. Thórarinn and Thorkell quarrelled over their drink at Kirkiuvag, and Thorkell wounded Thórarinn, and then escaped to Thorbiörn. Thórarinn's companions

---

[1] St. Mary's, the largest of the Scilly Isles, called Syllingar in the Sagas.

pursued Thorkell, but Thorbiörn and his men defended
themselves in a loft. The Earls were informed of this, and
they went to part them. Thorbiörn refused to leave the
decision of this case to Earl Rögnvald, as it was his men
that were concerned in the pursuit. When Thórarinn had
recovered from his wounds, he slew Thorkell as he was going
to church. He ran into the church, but Thorbiörn and his
men pursued him. Earl Rögnvald was told what was
happening, and he went there with his men, and asked
Thôrbiörn whether he was going to break the church open.
Thorbiörn said the church ought not to shelter him who was
within. Earl Rögnvald said there should be no violation of
the church at this time, and Thorbiörn was pushed away
from it. No agreement was come to about this case.

Thorbiörn went over to Caithness, and was there for a
while. Then many things happened to estrange them, for
Thorbiörn was often guilty of violence to women, and of
manslaying. He went secretly out to the Orkneys in a
boat with thirty men, and landed at Skálpeid, and walked to
Kirkiuvag with three men. In the evening he went alone
into an inn where Thórarinn was drinking, and struck him a
death-blow immediately. Then he ran out into the darkness
and far away. For this the Earl made him an outlaw in
every part of his dominions. Thorbiörn went over to Ness,
and remained in hiding with his brother-in-law, Hösvir, who
was called the strong. He had married Thorbiörn's sister,
Ragnhild, and their son was Stefán Rádgiafi (counsellor),
Thorbiörn's follower. Shortly afterwards Thorbiörn went to
Malcolm, King of Scots, and remained there a while, in high
favour with the King. There was a man called Gillaodran
with the King of Scots. He was of a great family, but a
violent man. He had incurred the displeasure of the King
of Scots for violent acts and manslaughters which he had
committed in his kingdom. He fled to the Orkneys, and
the Earls received him. Then he went to Caithness, and
acted as a steward for the Earls. There was a noble Bondi
in Caithness, by name Helgi, a friend of Earl Rögnvald's.
Gillaodran quarrelled with him about the stewardship, and
Gillaodran attacked and killed him. After the slaughter he
went west to Scotland's Fiord, and was received by a chief

named Sumarlidi Höld,[1] who had possessions in Dalir, on Scotland's Fiord. His wife was Ragnhild, the daughter of Olaf Bitling (little bit), King of the Sudreyar. Their sons were King Dufgall, Rögnvald, and Engull.[2] They were called the Dalverja family.

Earl Rögnvald sent for Swein, Asleif's son, before he went out on his expedition. When they met, Earl Rögnvald asked him to have an eye on Gillaodran if he had an opportunity. Swein said he did not know how far he might succeed.

CHAPTER CV.

SWEIN SLAYS SUMARLIDI.

THEN Swein went on a marauding expedition, having five long-ships. When he came west to Scotland's Fiord, he heard that Sumarlidi Höld had gone on board a ship, and was about to set out on an expedition. He had seven ships, and Gillaodran commanded one. He had gone into the firths to bring up some troops that had not arrived. When Swein heard of Sumarlidi, he gave him battle, and it was a fierce fight. Sumarlidi Höld was killed in that fight, and many men with him. When Swein became aware that Gillaodran was not there, he went in search of him, and slew him in Myrkvifiörd,[3] and fifty men with him. Then he went

---

[1] This was the famous Somerled, styled by the Chronicle of Man "Regulus Herergaidel"—ruler of Argyle. This chronicle also adds the information that his marriage with Ragnhild was the cause of the ruin of the monarchy of the Isles. Although the Saga here makes Swein, Asleif's son, kill Somerled about the year A.D. 1159, we learn from the more trustworthy sources of Fordun and the Chron. de Mailros that Somerled was killed at Renfrew on the 1st January 1164, having landed there with a fleet of 160 galleys in the attempt to make a conquest of Scotland. He had given his sister in marriage to Wimund, ex-bishop, *alias* Malcolm M'Heth, whom the Saga calls Earl of Moray. After the unsuccessful termination of Malcolm M'Heth's attempt to gain possession of the crown of Scotland, his brother-in-law, Somerled, seems to have continued the hostilities against King David, and to have joined the party against Malcolm IV. when the attempt was made to place the "Boy of Egremont" on the throne. (See Fordun Skene's ed.) II. 250, and Munch, *Chron. Man.* p. 80.

[2] Dugald, Reginald, and Angus ; from Reginald sprang the Macrories, Macdougalls, and Macdonalds of the Isles.

[3] This is the Firth of Forth in chapter lxxvii. Here it evidently refers to

on his expedition, and returned home in the autumn, as his custom was. He went to see Earl Rögnvald soon after his return, and he was much pleased with these deeds.

CHAPTER CVI.

OF EARL RÖGNVALD AND EARL HARALD.

Every summer the Earls were wont to go over to Caithness, and up into the forests to hunt the red-deer or the reindeer.[1] Thorbiörn Klerk was with the King of Scots, and sometimes he went to Caithness and stayed in hiding with his friends. He had three friends in Caithness whom he trusted most. One was his brother-in-law, Hösvir; the second, Liótúlf, who lived in Thórsdal; and the third was Hallvard, Dúfa's son, in Kálfadal (Calder), at a certain promontory off Thórsdal. All these were his intimate friends.

one of the sea-lochs on the west coast, and may probably be Loch Gleann Dubh, the inner portion of Kyle Scow. At least the Norse name "Dark Fiord," and the Gaelic "Loch of the Dark Glen," are suggestively similar, and both equally descriptive of the upper part of the Kyle.

[1] In reference to this passage, Jonæus, in his edition of the Saga (Hafniæ, 1780), says, that what is of the greatest moment is the fact which it points out, that at this date (circa 1158) there were reindeer in Scotland. In his Latin version of the original he translates the phrase "*at veida rauddyri edr hreina*" as "*feras rubras et rangiferos venari*," and has no doubt or hesitancy about the matter. It is established by geological evidence that the reindeer was widely distributed in Great Britain in post-glacial times, although the instances of its occurrence within the human period, and in association with the remains of man, have been comparatively rare. Recently, however, evidence has been supplied by excavations in the ruins of the brochs, or "Pictish towers," of the north of Scotland, which fully corroborates the statement of the Saga that the reindeer was actually hunted and eaten by the later occupants of these structures, their latest occupation on record being an occasional one by the Norsemen. In the refuse-heaps of several of these towers, the horns of the reindeer have been found, in some instances cut and sawn as if to be utilised for artificial purposes; while in other cases it is evident that the animals must have been killed when the horns were in the velvet. It is also significant that the reindeer moss (*Cladonia rangiferina*) still grows abundantly in Caithness. The question is very fully and ably discussed in a paper on "The Reindeer in Scotland," by Dr. J. A. Smith, in the eighth volume of the Proceedings of the Society of Antiquaries of Scotland.

CHAPTER CVII.

THE SLAYING OF EARL RÖGNVALD.

WHEN Earl Rögnvald had been an Earl two-and-twenty winters from the time that Earl Paul was taken prisoner, the Earls went over to Caithness during the latter part of the summer as usual, and when they came to Thórsá they heard a rumour to the effect that Thorbiörn was there in hiding with not a few men, and that he intended to attack them if he had an opportunity. Then the Earls called men together, and went with a hundred men, twenty of whom were on horseback and the rest on foot. In the evening they went up into the valley,[1] and took up their quarters for the night. When they were sitting by the fire in the evening, Earl Rögnvald sneezed very much. Earl Harald said: " That was a loud sneeze, kinsman." In the morning they went along the valley.

During the day Earl Rögnvald rode always ahead of his men, and a man with him called Asólf, and another by name Jómar, his kinsman. They rode five together along Kálfadal; and when they came to the farm, farmer Höskuld was on the top of a corn-stack piling up the corn, which his servants brought to him. Earl Harald was some distance behind. When Höskuld recognised Earl Rögnvald, he saluted him by name, and asked for news, speaking very loud, so that he could be heard far away. This was a short distance from the sitting-room of the house. The home-

---

[1] It is plain from the original that some words are here omitted from the text. One of the MS. copies of the Saga has had the additional words, which are thus rendered in the Danish translation preserved at Stockholm, "*Der som vaar noget* erg, *det kalde vi setter*," etc. " There were there some shielings (erg), which we call setter; and there they took up their quarters for the night." What is remarkable about this passage is that the Gaelic word for a shieling, *Airidh*, given phonetically by the old Norse saga-writer as "erg," is glossed in the Danish translation by the word "setter"—summer pasturing-place, where rude huts were erected for temporary occupation. The word setter, which is common in the place-names of Caithness and the Northern Isles, is to this day understood by the inhabitants in the same sense, although the custom of sending the cattle to the hill-pastures in summer, and living in "shielings," has now ceased, on the mainland at least. (See also the note on "Asgrim's ærgin," p. 187.)

stead stood on an eminence, and one had to go through
narrow and very steep passages up to it.   Thorbiörn was at
this farm, and was sitting indoors drinking.   The passages
led to the end of the house close to the gable, which had a
door filled loosely with stones.   Thorbiörn and his men,
hearing the words of Höskuld when he saluted Earl Rögnvald, seized their weapons, pushed the stones from the concealed door, and ran out.   Thorbiörn ran round the gable,
and on to the wall of the passage.   The Earl was then
close to the door.   Thorbiörn struck at him, and Asólf
warded off the blow with his hand, and it was cut off; and
then the sword touched the Earl's chin, inflicting a great
wound.

On receiving the blow Asólf said : " Let them serve the
Earl better who have to thank him for greater gifts."   He
was then eighteen winters old, and had lately entered the
Earl's service.

Earl Rögnvald was going to jump off his horse, and his
foot stuck fast in the stirrup.   At that moment Stefán
arrived and stabbed him with a spear ; and Thorbiörn
wounded him again ; but Jómar stabbed Thorbiörn in the
thigh, the spear entering the bowels.   Then Thorbiörn and
his men ran behind the homestead, and down a steep bank,
into a wet morass.   Then Earl Harald and his men arrived
and met Thorbiörn.   They recognised each other, and the
Earl's men, when they knew his intentions, advised to pursue
him ; but Earl Harald dissuaded them from it, saying that
he wished to wait for Earl Rögnvald's opinion, " Because,"
said he, " I am very intimately connected with Thorbiörn,
as you know, both through relationship and other ties."

Those who were with Earl Rögnvald stood sorrowing
over his dead body, and some time passed before Earl
Harald heard the news.   Thorbiörn and his men had got
out on the bog, and across the moss-hag running along it.
But through the urgency of the Earl's followers, he and his
men ran down to the bog, and they met at the moss-hag
—the two parties standing one on either side.   Thorbiörn's
party defended themselves from the bank, and his followers
ran to his assistance from the neighbouring homesteads,
until they were fifty in number.   They defended themselves

bravely, for they had a strong position.   The moss-hag
was both deep and broad, and the bog was soft; so they
could only hurl spears at each other.   Thorbiörn told his
men to throw none back; and when the Earl's party had
exhausted their missiles they spoke to each other, and
Thorbiörn called to Earl Harald, saying, "Kinsman! I
wish to ask you to give me quarter, and I am willing
to leave the decision of this case entirely in your hands.
I will reserve nothing which may contribute to your honour.
I also think, kinsman, you must remember that there have
been quarrels in which you would not have made such a
difference between Earl Rögnvald and me that you would
have killed me for having done this deed, when he had you
under his thumb, and left you no more power than if you
had been his page; but I gave you the best gifts, and
endeavoured to further your honour in every way I could.
The deed which I have committed is indeed a great crime,
and weighs heavily upon me, but the whole of his dominions
revert to you.   You may also know that Earl Rögnvald
intended for me the same fate which he met at my hands.
And I suspect, kinsman, that if it had so happened that I
were dead, and Earl Rögnvald alive, you would not have
quarrelled with him; and yet you wish to take away my
life."

Thorbiörn urged his case with many fair words, and
many pleaded for him, and begged that quarter might be
given him.   And at last, when so many pleaded, the Earl
began to listen to them.

Then Magnus, the son of Gunni, Hávard's son, a chief
and a kinsman of the Earl's, and the noblest born of Earl
Harald's followers, took speech as follows:—"We are not
able to counsel you, Earl, after these great deeds, but I shall
tell you what will be said if quarter is given to Thorbiörn
when he has done such a deed, and even dared to say to
your face, almost in so many words, that he has done this
wickedness in your interest, or for your honour; and it
will be an everlasting shame and dishonour to you and to
all the Earl's kinsmen if he is not avenged.   I think Earl
Rögnvald's friends will believe it to be the truth that for
a long time you have been planning his death, and that it

is your plan which has now been accomplished. Do you think he will acquit you from complicity in his guilt when he has to defend himself; since no one says a word for you when he tells you to your face that he has committed this crime in your interest? And how can you better confirm this suspicion than by now granting him peace? I have resolved, for my part, never to give him quarter, if any doughty men are willing to follow me, whether you like it or not."

His brother Thorstein, and Hákon, and Swein, Hróald's son, spoke to the same effect. Then they left the Earl and went along by the moss-hag, trying to find a place where they might cross.

When Thorbiörn saw Magnus and his followers walking along the moss-hag, he said: "Now, I suppose, they must have disagreed in their counsels; the Earl has wished to give me peace, and Magnus has spoken against it."

While they were thus talking, Thorbiörn and his men went farther away from the moss-hag.

Harald's party stood on the brink, and when he saw that no quarter would be given, he leapt across in full armour, though it was nine ells[1] broad. His followers leapt after him, but none of them were able to leap so far; and most of them caught the bank and crawled up out of the mud.

Thorbiörn's men urged him to advance against Magnus and his men, and decide the matter with them; but he said: "I think the best plan is, that each of you do what he thinks likely to be best, but I shall go to Earl Harald."

Most of his men dissuaded him from this, and begged him rather to flee to the woods and save himself. He did not, however, accept that advice. Then his followers left him, and tried to save themselves in various ways, and at last there were eight men only with Thorbiörn. When he saw that Earl Harald had crossed the ditch, he went to him and fell on his knees, saying that he brought his head to him. Many of the Earl's men asked that peace might

---

[1] A Norwegian ell is half a yard. The leap was thus four yards and a half.

be given him ; and the Earl said : " Save yourself, Thorbiörn ; I have not the heart to kill you."

While they were talking, they moved down the valley
along Kálfadalsá,[2] and Magnus's party pursued them. When
the Earl saw it, he said : " Save yourself, Thorbiörn, I will
not fight for you against my men." Then Thorbiörn and
his men left the Earl's party, and went to some deserted
shielings called Asgrím's ærgin.[1] Magnus's party pursued
them, and set the buildings on fire immediately. Thorbiörn
and his men defended themselves bravely ; and when the
buildings began to fall down with the burning, they went
out and were attacked by the other party with their weapons,
as soon as they could reach them. They were already very
much exhausted by the fire, and fell there all nine. When
Thorbiörn's wounds were examined, it was found that the
intestines protruded through the wound inflicted by Jómar.
Earl Harald led his men down the valley, but those who
were with Magnus went to Fors (Forss), wrapped up Earl
Rögnvald's body, and brought it down to Thórsá.

[1] Kalfadalsá, the Kalfadal's stream, is the Burn of Calder, which, issuing
from the Loch of Calder, falls into the Thurso water. The situation of Kalfadal, a valley running up from the valley of the Thurso water towards Forss,
is exactly that of the valley of Calder.

[2] The word ærgin is not Norse. It is, however, a Norse corruption of the
Gaelic word for a shieling—airidh, plur. aridhean, which enters into the
composition of many of the place-names in Caithness—e.g. Halsary, Dorrery,
Shurrery, Blingery, etc. Asgrim's ærgin is still recognisable in the modern
Askary or Assary, near the north end of the Loch of Calder. It is curious to
find thus incidentally in the Saga an indication of the blending of the folk-
speech of the time, and to find also in the modern names of Norn Calder and
Scotscalder a record (preserved on the spot) of the time when one portion of
the dale was possessed by the Norsemen and another by the natives. Passing
from Calder towards the coast the place-names are mostly Norse ; and passing
from Calder in the opposite direction towards the uplands, the place-names
are almost entirely Gaelic.

CHAPTER CVIII.

THE REMOVAL OF EARL RÖGNVALD'S BODY.

EARL RÖGNVALD KALI died five nights after the summer Marymas.[1] Earl Harald brought the body with a splendid following to the Orkneys, and it was buried at the Magnus Kirk; and there it rested until God manifested Rögnvald's merits by many and great miracles. Then Bishop Bjarni had his holy remains exhumed with the permission of the Pope.[2] Where the blood of the Earl fell on the stones when he died, it may be seen to this day as fresh as if it had just come from the wounds.

Earl Rögnvald's death was much lamented, because he was very popular in the Islands and in many other parts. He had been helpful to many, was liberal with his money, gentle, and a true friend, highly accomplished, and a good scald. He left a daughter, Ingigerd, an only child, who was married to Eirík Slagbrellir. Their children were Harald Ungi, Magnus Mangi. Rögnvald, Ingibiörg, Elín, and Ragnhild.

CHAPTER CIX.

OF HARALD AND SWEIN.

AFTER Earl Rögnvald's death, Earl Harald took possession of the whole of the Islands, and became their sole ruler. He was a mighty chief, and a man of large stature and great strength. His wife was Afreka, and their children were — Heinrek, Hákon, Helena, and Margarét. When Hákon was only a few winters old, Swein, Asleif's son, offered to foster him, and when he was able to take his part with other men, Swein took him out on marauding expeditions every summer, and honoured him in everything. Swein used to reside at home in Gáreksey, in winter, keeping there eighty men at his own expense. He

---

[1] The feast of the Assumption of St. Mary, or the 15th August. The Iceland Annals give 1158 as the year of Rögnvald's death.

[2] Earl Rögnvald was canonised A.D. 1192.

had such a large drinking-hall that there was none equal to it anywhere else in the Orkneys. In the spring he was very busy sowing a large breadth of seed, and he usually did a great part of the work himself. When this work was finished, he went every spring on marauding expeditions. He plundered in the Sudreyar and Ireland, and returned home after midsummer. This he called spring-viking. Then he stayed at home till the fields were reaped and the corn brought in. Then he went out again, and did not return until one month of winter had passed. This he called autumn-viking.

CHAPTER CX.

SWEIN GOES TO IRELAND.

ONCE it happened that Swein went out on a spring expedition, taking with him Hákon, the son of Earl Harald. They had five rowing ships, all large. They plundered in the Sudreyar. All the inhabitants were so afraid of him that they hid all their movable property in the ground or in heaps of loose stones. Swein went all the way south to Man, and obtained very little booty. Then they went to Ireland and plundered there, but when they were approaching Dýflin (Dublin) two merchant-ships came from England, laden with English cloth and other merchandise; they were going to Dýflin. Swein made for the vessels, and offered them battle. There was little resistance by the English, and Swein's party took every penny in the vessels, leaving to the Englishmen only what they stood in, and a small quantity of provisions. They sailed away in the vessels, but Swein's party went to the Sudreyar, and divided their booty. They sailed from the west with great pomp. When they were lying in harbours, they covered their ships with the English cloth, to make a show; and when they sailed to the Orkneys, they sewed the cloth upon their sails, and then it looked as if the sails were made entirely of the fine stuffs. This they named the Skrud-viking.[1]

---

[1] Skrud, a general term for fine cloth and costly stuffs.

Swein went home to his estate in Gáreksey. He had taken a large quantity of wine and English mead from the vessels. When he had been at home a short time he invited Earl Harald, and prepared a splendid feast for him. When Earl Harald was at the feast a great deal was said of Swein's magnificence. The Earl said : " I wish, Swein, you would now leave off your marauding expeditions ; it is good now to drive home a whole waggon. You know that your plundering has fed you and your men a long time, but to most men of violence it happens that they perish in their raiding, if they do not leave it off in time."

Swein looked to the Earl and said, smiling : " This is well said, my Lord ; you have spoken like a friend, and it is good to take sound advice from you ; but some complain that you are not an over just man yourself."

The Earl replied : " I must be responsible for my own acts, but I spoke as it occurred to me."

Swein replied : " Your intention is no doubt good, my Lord ; and it shall be so, that I will discontinue my marauding expeditions, for I am getting old, and my strength is wasting away in the wet work and the fighting. I am now going to make an autumn expedition, and I wish it to be not less glorious than the spring one. Then I shall leave off war-going."

The Earl replied : " It is difficult to know, comrade, which comes first—death or lasting fame."

Then their conversation ceased. When Earl Harald left the feast honourable gifts were presented to him, and he and Swein parted very good friends.

CHAPTER CXI.

SWEIN, ASLEIF'S SON'S (LAST) EXPEDITION.

SHORTLY after this Swein prepared to go on a marauding expedition with seven long-ships, all of them large. Hákon, the son of Earl Harald, went with him. They went first to the Sudreyar, and found there little booty. Then they went to Ireland, and plundered there in many places. They went all the way south to Dýflin (Dublin), and took the inhabitants by surprise, so that they did not know till they were in the town. They took a great deal of plunder, and took captive the rulers of the city, and their negotiations ended in the surrender of the town to Swein, and they promised to pay as much money as he might levy on them. He was to quarter his men on the town, and have the command of it, and the Dýflin men confirmed this arrangement with oaths. Swein and his men went down to their ships in the evening, but in the morning they were to come into the town and receive hostages from the inhabitants.

Now it is to be told what was going on in the town during the night. The rulers of the town had a meeting, and considered the difficulties in which they were placed. They thought it a grievous hardship that they should have to surrender their town to the Orkneymen, especially to him whom they knew to be the most exacting man in the whole West; and they came to the determination to play him false if they could. They resolved to dig large pits inside of the city gates, and in many other places between .the houses, where it was intended that Swein's men should come in, and armed men were hidden in the houses close by. They placed such coverings over the pits as were sure to fall in when the weight of the men came upon them. Then they covered all over with straw, so that the pits could not be seen, and waited till morning.

CHAPTER CXII.

SWEIN, ASLEIF'S SON'S FALL.

NEXT morning Swein and his men arose and armed themselves, and went to the town; and when they came near the gates the Dýflin men ranged themselves on both sides from the gates along by the pits. Swein and his men, not being on their guard, fell into them. Some of the townsmen ran immediately to the gates, and others to the pits, and attacked Swein's men with weapons. It was difficult for them to defend themselves, and Swein perished there in the pit,

with all those who had entered the town.   It was said that
Swein was the last man who died there, and that he spake
these words before his fall : " Know all men, whether I die
to-day or not, that I am the holy Earl Rögnvald's henchman,
and my confidence is where he is with God."   Swein's surviving followers went then to their ships, and put out to sea;
and nothing is said of their voyage until they came to the
Orkneys.   Here is the end of Swein's history ; and it has
been said that he was the greatest man in the Western
lands, either in old times or at the present day, of those who
had not a higher title than he had.   After his death his sons
Olaf and Andrés divided their patrimony.   The next summer
after his death they raised the end walls of the large drinking-
hall which he had in Gáreksey.   Andrés, the son of Swein,
married Frída, the daughter of Kolbein Hrúga, and sister to
Bishop Bjarni.

CHAPTER CXIII.

OF EARL HARALD AND HIS SONS.

Now Earl Harald ruled the Orkneys, and was a great chief.
Afterwards[1] he married Hvarflöd,[2] the daughter of Earl
Malcolm,[3] of Mærhæfi (Moray).   Their children were
Thorfinn,[4] David, Jón, Gunnhild, Herborga, and Langlíf.

---

[1] After the death of his first wife Afreka. (See chap. cix.)

[2] The Celtic form of her name is Gormlath.

[3] This "Malcolm, Earl of Moray," has a curious history.   He appears
first as Wimund, a monk of Savigny, and priest in the Isle of Skye.   Afterwards he became Bishop of Man, and subsequently appeared in the character
of a pretender to the Scottish crown, giving himself out to be Malcolm Mac-
Heth, son of that Angus MacHeth who was defeated by King David, and
slain at Strickathro A.D. 1130.   Assisted by Somerled of Argyle and by this
alliance with the Earl of Orkney, he ravaged the western coasts of Scotland,
until he was captured by King David, and confined in the Castle of Roxburgh
in 1134.   He was released by Malcolm the Maiden after the death of King
David, and received from the young king the sovereignty of a portion of the
ancient kingdom of Cumbria.   His tyranny was such that his subjects re-
volted, took him prisoner, put out his eyes, and confined him in the monastery of Bellaland (Byland), in Yorkshire. (Munch, *Chron. Man.* p. 80.)

[4] Thorfinn, the son of Earl Harald, appears on record about the year A.D.
1165.   In the Chartulary of Scone there is a document by "Harald, Earl of

When Bishop William the Second was dead, Bjarni, the son of Kolbein Hrúga, was made bishop after him. He was a very great man, and a dear friend of Earl Harald. Bishop Bjarni had a large party of kinsmen in the Islands. The sons of Eirík Slagbrellir were Harald Ungi, Magnus Mangi, and Rögnvald. The brothers went east to Norway to see King Magnus, Erling's son, and he gave Harald the title of Earl, and one half of the Islands, which had belonged to the holy Earl Rögnvald, his mother's father. Earl Harald Ungi went to the west, and with him Sigurd Murt, the son of Ivar Galli. The mother of Ivar, who fell at Akr with Erling Skakki, was the daughter of Hávard, Gunni's son. Sigurd Murt was young, handsome, and a great dandy. Magnus Mangi remained with the King, and fell with him in Sogn.

Harald (Ungi) and his followers came first to Hjaltland. Then they went over to Caithness, and then into Scotland, to William, King of Scots.[1] Earl Harald requested King William to give him the half of Caithness which Earl Rögnvald had held. The King granted him this; and Earl Harald went then down to Caithness, and gathered troops. Then Lífólf Skalli, his brother-in-law, came to him. He had many noble kinsmen there. Lífólf had married Ragnhild, the sister of Earl Harald. He was called Earl Harald Ungi (the younger); but Harald, Maddad's son, the elder. Lífólf had the command of the Earl's troops. They sent men to the Orkneys, to Earl Harald the elder, requesting him to give up one half of the Islands, since the King had given them to Earl Harald Ungi. When the Earl received this message, he refused absolutely to divide his dominions on any condition. Lífólf Skalli was the messenger, and the Earl upbraided him greatly before he left. After this, Earl Harald the elder collected troops, and obtained a great many. Earl Harald Ungi's party were in Caithness, and had some gathering too. When they heard that Harald the elder was collecting troops,

Orkney, Hetland, and Cataness," granting to the monks of Scone a mark of silver to be paid annually by himself, his son Turphin, and their heirs.—*Lib. Eccles. de Scone*, p. 37. Thorfinn died in prison in Roxburgh Castle, after being mutilated by King William the Lion, to whom he had been given as a hostage for his father.

[1] William the Lion.

they sent Lífólf a second time across the Pentland Firth
to gather information about the enemy's forces. He landed
east in Rognvaldsey, and ascended a hill, where he found
three of Harald's watchmen. Two of them he killed, and
one of them he took with him for information. Then Lífólf
saw the Earl's fleet, which consisted of many ships, most
of them large. Then he went down from the hill to his
boat, and told his companions what he had ascertained. He
said Earl Harald had so large an army that it was quite
hopeless for them to fight with him. " I would advise," said
Lífólf, " that we should go to-day to Thórsá, and there many
troops will come to us at once. If you wish to offer battle
to Earl Harald now, it is most imprudent, whatever the result
may be."

Then said Sigurd Murt : " Ill has the Earl's brother-in-
law fared across the Pentland Firth if he has left his heart
behind him ;" adding, further, that their prospects were not
bright if all should lose heart when they saw Earl Harald's
army.

Lífólf replied : " It is difficult to see, Sigurd, where each
one carries his heart when courage is required ; and I believe
you men of mark will think it a serious matter to remain
behind when I run from Harald Ungi."

They did not go to Thórsá ; but shortly after they saw
Earl Harald's fleet coming from Rognvaldsey, and then they
prepared for battle. Earl Harald went on shore, and placed
his men in battle array. They far exceeded the others
in number. Sigurd Murt and Lífólf arranged the troops
of Earl Ungi. The former was dressed in a scarlet tunic,
and tucked the skirt under his belt. Some said that the
same should be done behind, but he told them not to do
it, " for," said he, " I shall not go backwards to-day." Lífólf
and Sigurd led one wing each, and when they had arrayed
their men the battle began with great fury. Among the
troops of Earl Harald the elder there were many hardy,
fierce, and well-armed men, the Bishop's kinsmen, and
many others of the Earl's champions. When the battle had
lasted for a while, Sigurd Murt fell, having borne himself
well and bravely. Lífólf behaved the most valiantly of them
all. The Caithnessmen say he broke three times through

the ranks of Earl Harald's men, yet he fell in this fight, after having earned great fame. When both were dead—Lífólf and Sigurd Murt—Earl Ungi's men fled. Earl Harald Ungi fell at some turf-pits,[1] and that very night a great light was seen where his blood fell on the ground. People said he was truly a saint, and there is now a church where he fell. He is buried in Ness (Caithness). Innumerable miracles are by God granted through his merits, which testify that he wished to go to Orkney to his kinsmen Earl Magnus and Earl Rögnvald. After the battle Earl Harald subdued the whole of Caithness, and went back triumphant to the Orkneys.

CHAPTER CXIV.

OF THE ORKNEYMEN.

WILLIAM, King of Scots, heard that Earl Harald (Ungi) had been killed, and also that Earl Harald, Maddad's son, had subdued the whole of Caithness without asking his leave. He became enraged at this, and sent men to the Sudreyar to Rögnvald, Gudröd's son, the King of the Sudreyar. Gudröd's mother was Ingibiörg, daughter of Earl Hákon, Paul's son. King Rögnvald was the greatest warrior then in the western lands. Three winters he had been out in war-ships without coming under a sooty rafter. When this message came to Rögnvald, he collected an army from all the kingdom of the Sudreyar and from Satiri (Kintyre). He had also a large army from Ireland. Then he went north to

---

[1] The "Fagrskinna" has (p. 148) "er fell i Vik"—he fell at Wick ; but there is nothing to fix the locality of this battle more definitely. The tradition of the district points to Clairdon Hill, between Murkle and Thurso, as the scene of the encounter. The church which is here said to have been erected on the spot where Harald fell, and which is spoken of as standing there when the Saga was written, is not now in existence. The ruins of a chapel, which was traditionally believed to mark the spot, were removed when the ground was brought under cultivation by the late Sir John Sinclair. A remonstrance by the late Rev. Mr. Pope, of Reay, seems to have had the effect of causing the erection of an edifice (now used as the tomb of the Sinclair family) over the place where an old chapel stood. It is now known locally as "Harold's Tower." Large quantities of human bones, and several of the peculiarly-shaped Norse swords which Mr. Pope describes as "odd machines resembling ploughshares, all iron," have been dug up in the neighbourhood.

Caithness, took possession of the whole of the territory, and remained there some time. Earl Harald kept in the Orkneys, and took no heed of the King's movements. Towards winter King Rögnvald prepared to go home to his dominions in the Sudreyar. He left three stewards (sýslumenn) over Caithness. One was Máni, Olaf's son; the second Rafn, the lawman; and the third, Hlífólf Alli. Some time after, King Rögnvald returned to the Sudreyar. Earl Harald sent a man over to Ness (Caithness), saying that he would consider his journey a lucky one if he could kill any of the stewards or all of them. This man was brought across the Pentland Firth, and he went on till he came to Lawman Rafn. Rafn asked him where he was going, and he had little to say in reply. Rafn said: "I can see in you that Earl Harald has sent you over here for some evil purpose, but I have not the heart to slay you, because you are my kinsman." Thus they parted, and he went away to Hlífólf, and their intercourse ended in Hlífólf's murder. Then he fled to the Orkneys to Earl Harald, and told him what he had done.

CHAPTER CXV.

HARALD TORTURES THE BISHOP.

Now Earl Harald prepared to leave the Orkneys, and when he was quite ready he went first to Thórsá, and landed from his ships there. The Bishop was in the borg at Skárabólstad (Scrabster). When the Caithnessmen saw Earl Harald's army, they perceived it was so numerous that they had no chance to withstand them. They were told also that the Earl was in such an evil temper that there was no knowing what he might do. Then the Bishop took speech, and said: "If our dealings turn out well, he will give you peace."[1] They did as the Bishop told them. The Earl's men rushed from the ships up to the borg. The Bishop went to meet the Earl, and saluted him with bland words, but their dealing turned out in this way, that Earl Harald

---

[1] The Bishop advised the people to allow him first to speak with the Earl, in the hope that he would be able to mollify him.

had the Bishop seized, his tongue cut out, and then he caused a knife to be thrust into his eyes, and blinded him. Bishop Jón prayed to the holy virgin Tröllhæna during his torture, and then he went on a certain bank, when they let him go. There was a woman on the bank, and the Bishop asked her to help him. She saw that blood was flowing from his face, and said: "Be silent, my lord, and I shall willingly help you." The Bishop was brought to the resting-place of the holy Tröllhæna,[1] and there he recovered both his speech and sight.

Earl Harald went up to the borg, and it was immediately surrendered to him.[2] He proceeded at once to punish the inhabitants severely, and imposed heavy fines on those whom he considered most guilty of treachery to him; and he made all the Caithnessmen acknowledge him by oath as their lord, whether they liked it or not. Then he took possession of all the property belonging to the stewards, who had fled to the King of Scots. Then Earl Harald resided in Caithness with many men.

[1] This seems to imply that it was at the grave of the holy Tröllhæna that the Bishop received his sight. Tröllhæna seems to be the Celtic St. Triduana or St. Tredwell, who, according to her legendary history, came from Achaia with St. Regulus in the fourth century. Being of extraordinary beauty, she was solicited by a Gallic prince, and to put an end to his solicitations she cut out both her eyes, and sent them to him skewered on a twig. Sir David Lindsay alludes to this :—

> "Sanct Tredwall, als, there may be sene,
> Quhilk on ane prick hes baith her ene."

She died at Restalrig, near Edinburgh, and her tomb there continued, so late as Lindsay's time, to be a resort of pilgrims who came to "mend their ene." There is a chapel dedicated to St. Tredwell in the island of Papa Westray, which Munch considers likely to have been erected by Celtic ecclesiastics previous to the Norse invasion. There was another chapel dedicated to her at Kintradwell, in Sutherlandshire, where she is known as St. Trullen ; but there is now no trace of a St. Tredwell's chapel in Caithness.

[2] The letter of Pope Innocent to the Bishop of Orkney, prescribing the penance to be performed by the man Lomberd, who cut out the Bishop's tongue, gives the additional information that when the Earl's men took the "borg" they killed almost all that were in it. (See the Introduction.) The "borg," or castle, at Scrabster, may have been an earlier building on the site of the "Bishop's Castle," an old fortalice on the cliff near the present hamlet of Scrabster, or it may have been the ruins of one of the still older Pictish towers, not far off, which the Caithnessmen may have occupied for the occasion as a defensible position.

CHAPTER CXVI.

OF THE STEWARDS.

Now it is to be told of the stewards (sýslumenn) that they went six together to Scotland, and saw the King during Advent. They were able to give particular intelligence of everything that had happened in Caithness during Earl Harald's stay there. The King was highly enraged at hearing the news, but he said he would pay back double to those who had lost their own. The first day they stayed with the King twenty-five ells of cloth and an English mark in ready money was given to each of them. They spent the Yule-tide with the King, and were well treated.

After Yule-tide the King sent word to all the chiefs in his kingdom, and collected a large army throughout the country, and with all these troops he went down to Caithness against Earl Harald. With this great army he pursued his journey till he came to Eysteinsdal,[1] where Caithness and Sutherland meet. The camp of the King of Scots stretched far along the valleys.

Earl Harald was in Caithness when he heard the news, and he drew troops together immediately. It is said he obtained six thousand men, and yet he had no chance to withstand the King of Scots. Then he sent men to him to sue for peace. When this request was brought before the King, he said it was no use asking for peace unless he had every fourth penny that was to be found in all the land of Caithness.

When the Earl received this message, he called together the inhabitants and chiefs, and consulted with them. As, however, they had no means of resisting, it was agreed that the Caithnessmen should pay one-fourth of all their property to the King of Scots, except those men who had gone to see the King in winter. Earl Harald went out to the Orkneys, and was to have Caithness as he had it before it was given to Earl Harald Ungi by the King of Scots. Thorfinn, the son of Earl Harald, who was a hostage with the King of Scots, was blinded during these hostilities.

When peace had been made, the King returned to Scot-

---

[1] Eysteinsdal is not now represented in the topography of the district.

land. Earl Harald was now the sole ruler of the Orkneys. In the later part of the days of Earl Harald, his brother-in-law, Olaf, and Jón, Hallkell's son, raised a party in the Orkneys, and went east to Norway against King Sverrir. They made Sigurd, the son of King Magnus, Erling's son, their King. Many men of noble birth in the Orkneys joined this party, and it was very strong. They were for a while called Eyjarskeggjar (Islanders) or Gullbeinir (golden-legs). They fought with King Sverrir in Flóruvogar, and were beaten.[1] Both Jón and Olaf were killed, as also their King, and most of their men. After this King Sverrir became a great enemy of Earl Harald, laying it to his charge that he was the cause of the party being raised. At last Earl Harald went from the west, and Bishop Bjarni went along with him. The Earl left his case without reservation to the decision of King Sverrir. Then King Sverrir took all Hjaltland from Earl Harald, with its taxes (scat) and dues, as a fine; and the Earls of Orkney have never had it since.[2]

Earl Harald was five winters old when he was made Earl, and for twenty winters he and Earl Rögnvald were together Earls of Orkney. After Earl Rögnvald's death, he was forty-eight winters Earl of Orkney, and he died in the second year of the reign of King Ingi, Bard's son.[3] Earl Harald's sons, Jón and David, succeeded him; and Heinrek, his son, had Ross in Scotland.

The following have been the most powerful of the Earls of Orkney, according to the relation of those who have made histories of them :—Sigurd, Eystein's son ; Earl Thorfinn, Sigurd's son ; and Earl Harald, Maddad's son.

The brothers Jón and David ruled the land after their father, until David died from disease, the same year as Hákon Galinn died in Norway.[4] After that Jón took the title of Earl of all the Orkneys.

---

[1] The battle of Floruvogar took place in 1194, according to the Iceland Annals appended to the Flateyjarbók.

Shetland then passed into the immediate possession of the Crown of Norway. Its revenues were granted by King Hakon Magnusson, in 1312-19, to the Mary-kirk in Osloe (Christiania) for the completion of the fabric, with the proviso that then they should revert to the crown.

[3] According to the Iceland Annals of the Flateyjarbók, King Ingi Bardson "took the kingdom" in 1204, and Harald Maddadson died in 1206.

[4] The death of Hakon Galinn took place in the year 1214, according to the Annals appended to the Flateyjarbók.

CHAPTER CXVII.

THE BURNING OF BISHOP ADAM.

WHEN Bishop Jón, he who was maimed by the order of Earl
Harald, died in Caithness, a man who was called Adam was
made Bishop in his stead. None knew his family, because
when a child he was found at the door of a certain church.
The Caithnessmen found him rather exacting in his office, and
blamed a certain monk who was with him chiefly for that.
It was an ancient custom that the Bishop should receive a
spann[1] of butter of every twenty cows. Every Bondi in
Caithness had to pay this—he more who had more cows, and
he who had fewer less, and so in proportion. Bishop Adam
wished to increase the impost, and demanded a spann of every
fifteen cows; and when that was obtained, he demanded it
of twelve; and when this too was conceded, he demanded it
of ten. But this was thought by all men most unreasonable.

Then the Caithnessmen went to see Earl Jón, who was
then in Caithness, and they complained of this before the
Earl. He said he would have nothing to do with it, adding
that the case was not a difficult one. There were two alternatives: this was not to be endured, yet he would not say
what the other might be.

Bishop Adam was at Há Kirkia,[2] in Thorsdal, and Earl
Jón was a short distance off. The Caithnessmen held a
meeting on a hill above the village where the Bishop was.
Lawman Rafn was with the Bishop, and begged him to spare
the inhabitants, saying that otherwise he feared the consequences. The Bishop asked him to be of good cheer, saying
that the Bœndr (farmers) would become quiet of their own
accord. Then a man was sent to Earl Jón, requesting him
to make peace between them and the Bishop. But the
Earl would not meddle with the matter at all. Then the
Bœndr ran down from the hill in great excitement, and
when Lawman Rafn saw it he warned the Bishop to take
care of himself. The Bishop and his friends were drinking
in a loft there, and when the Bœndr arrived the monk went

---

[1] A spann = 24 marks, or 12 lbs. Scottish.—*Balfour's Odal Rights*, p. 99.
[2] Halkirk, in the Thurso valley.

to the door, and he was immediately hewn across the face, and fell back into the room dead.   When the Bishop heard it, he said : " This did not happen sooner than might have been expected, for his interference in our transactions has generally been unfortunate."   Then Rafn asked the Bishop to tell the Bœndr that he was willing to come to an agreement with them; and when they heard it, all the wiser men among them were very glad.   Then the Bishop went out to make an arrangement with them; but when he was seen by the more wicked ones, who were most furious, they seized the Bishop, brought him into a small house, and set fire to it, and the house burnt so quickly that those who wished to save the Bishop could not do anything.   Bishop Adam perished there.[1]   His body was not much burnt when it was found.   Then the body was buried suitably and honourably; but those who had been the best friends of the Bishop sent men to the King of Scots.   Alexander, son of the holy King William, was then King of Scotland.   When he heard the tidings, he became so enraged that the punishments inflicted by him for the burning of the Bishop, by mutilation and death, confiscation and outlawry from the land, are still in fresh memory.

And now we cannot relate more distinctly than we have here done the events concerning the Earls of Orkney.

---

[1] The Icelandic Annals place the burning of Bishop Adam in the year 1222, and add that the King of Scots caused the hands and feet to be hewn off eighty men who had been concerned in the Bishop's burning.   Among the documents found in the King's treasury at Edinburgh in 1282 (and subsequently lost) was one entitled : " A quit-claiming of the lands of the Bondi of Caithness for the slaughter of the Bishop."   A bull of Pope Honorius, dated 23d January 1223, and addressed to the Bishops of St. Andrews, Glasgow, Dunkeld, and Dunblane, speaks in terms of high commendation of King Alexander's zealous desire to avenge such an unheard-of crime as the burning of a bishop, and thoroughly corroborates the Saga account of the manner of Adam's death, stating that these "wolves" and "demons," having stripped their Bishop of his garments, stoned him, mortally wounded him with an axe, and finally burned him in his own kitchen. (Theiner's *Vetera Monumenta*, p. 21.)

APPENDIX.

———◆———

SAGA OF OLAF, TRYGGVI'S SON.

(From the Flateyjarbók.)

THE DOMINIONS OF KING HARALD AND EARL ROGNVALD.

179. Earl Rögnvald assisted Harald Harfagri (fair-haired) to conquer the country (Norway), and he gave him the revenues of both Mæri and Raumsdal. Rögnvald had married Ragnhild, the daughter of Hrólf Nefia (nose). They had a son named Hrólf, who conquered Normandy. Hrólf was so big that no horse could carry him, and he was therefore called Gönguhrólf (Hrólf the walker). From him the Earls of Rúda (Rouen) and the Kings of England are descended. They had two other sons, Ivar and Earl Thórir Thegiandi (the silent). Rögnvald had also sons by his concubines. They were Hallad, Hrollaug, and Einar, who was the youngest. One summer Harald Harfagri went to the west across the sea to punish the Vikings, as he was weary of their devastations. They plundered in Norway during the summer, and spent the winters in Hjaltland or the Orkneys. Harald subdued Hjaltland, the Orkneys, and the Sudreyar (Hebrides). He went west as far as the Isle of Man, and destroyed all the dwellings in Man. He fought many battles there, and extended his dominion so far to the west that none of the Kings of Norway since his time has had wider dominions. In one of these battles, Ivar, the son of Earl Rögnvald, fell. So when King Harald sailed from the west he gave Hjaltland and the Orkneys to Earl Rögnvald as a compensation for [the loss of] his son; but Earl Rögnvald gave the Islands to his brother Sigurd, who was King Harald's forecastleman; and the King gave him the title of Earl before he left the west. Sigurd remained out in the west.

EARL MELBRIGD SLAIN BY SIGURD.

180. Earl Sigurd became a great chief. He formed an alliance with Thorstein the Red, son of Olaf the White, and Aud Djúpaudga

(the very wealthy), and together they conquered all Caithness and much more of Scotland—Mærhæfui (Moray) and Ross. He built a borg on the southern border of Mærhæfui. Melbrigd Tönn (tooth), an Earl of the Scots, and Earl Sigurd, made an arrangement to meet in a certain place, with forty men each, in order to come to an agreement concerning their differences. When the appointed day arrived Earl Sigurd was suspicious of treachery on the part of the Scots. He therefore caused eighty men to be mounted on forty horses. When Earl Melbrigd saw this, he said to his men :—"Now we have been treacherously dealt with by Earl Sigurd, for I see two men's legs on one side of each horse, and the men, I believe, are thus twice as many as the beasts. But let us be brave, and kill each his man before we die." Then they made themselves ready. When Sigurd saw it, he also decided on his plan, and said to his men :—"Now, let one-half of our number dismount and attack them from behind, when the troops meet, while we shall ride at them with all our speed to break their battle array. There was hard fighting immediately, and it was not long till Earl Melbrigd fell, and all his men with him. Earl Sigurd and his men fastened the heads [of the slain] to their saddle-straps, in bravado, and so they rode home triumphing in their victory. As they were proceeding, Earl Sigurd, intending to kick at his horse with his foot, struck the calf of his leg against a tooth protruding from Earl Melbrigd's head, which scratched him slightly ; but it soon became swollen and painful, and he died of it. Sigurd the powerful was buried in a mound at Ekkialsbakki.[1]

Sigurd's son was named Guthorm. He reigned one winter, and died childless.

When Earl Rögnvald heard of the death of Earl Sigurd and his son, he sent his son Hallad out to the west, and King Harald gave him the title of Earl. Hallad came out to the west, and took up his residence in Hrossey,[2] but Vikings went prowling about the islands and outlying headlands, slaying men and seizing booty. The Bœndr complained of their losses to Earl Hallad, but they thought he did not get them much redress for their wrongs. Then Hallad grew tired of the dignity, and resigned the earldom, took up his odal rights, and returned to Norway, and his journey was regarded as a very ignominious one.

EINAR COMES TO THE ISLANDS.

181. Two Danish Vikings took up their quarters in the Islands ; one of them was called Thórir Tréskegg (wooden beard), the other Kálf Skurfa (scurf). When Earl Rögnvald heard this he became

---

[1] See note at p. 107.　　　　　　　　[2] The Mainland of Orkney.

very angry, and called his sons Thórir and Hrollaug. Hrólf was at that time on a war expedition. Rögnvald asked which of them would go to the Islands. Thórir said he would follow his advice.

The Earl replied : " I foresee that your power will be greatest here ; and your ways do not lead from home."

Hrollaug said : " Father, would you like me to go ? "

The Earl replied : " It will never be your fortune to become an Earl. Your way lies towards Iceland. There you will increase your family, and it will be a noble one."

Then Einar, his youngest son, came forward and said : " Would you like me to go to the Islands ? One thing I will promise, which will be very acceptable to you—viz. that I shall never more come into your presence ; little honour do I enjoy at home, and it is hardly likely that my success will be less elsewhere than it is here."

The Earl said : " You are not likely to become a chief, on account of your birth, for all your kin on the mother's side are thrall-born ; but it is true that the sooner you go and the longer you stay the more agreeable it will be to me." Earl Rögnvald gave him a fully-equipped vessel, with twenty benches, and King Harald gave him the title of Earl.

The Vikings slain.

182. Einar sailed to Hjaltland, and there many men gathered round him. Then he went to the Orkneys to meet Kálf Skurfa and Thórir Tréskegg. There was a great battle, and both the Vikings were killed. This was said about it :

> Tré-skegg gave he to the Trows :
> Skurfa fell before Torf-Einar.

Then Einar took possession of the lands, and soon became a great chief. He was the man who first cut turf (peat) from the ground for fuel at Torfnes in Scotland, for fuel was scarce in the Islands. Einar was a tall man, ugly, and with one eye, yet he was very keen-sighted.

Battle between Earl Einar and Prince Halfdan.

183. When the sons of Harald Harfagri grew up they became men of great violence and turbulence, as has been told before. The sons of Snæfríd, Hálfdán Hálegg (high legs) and Gudröd Liomi (splendour) killed Rögnvald, Earl of Mæri. King Harald became very angry at this, and Hálfdán had to flee over seas to the west, but Gudröd became reconciled to his father. When Hálfdán Hálegg came to the Orkneys, Earl Einar fled from the Islands to Scotland, and Hálfdán became King over the Islands. Earl Einar came back

during the same year, and when they met there was a great battle,
in which Einar had the victory, and Hálfdán fled away.   Einar sang
this song :

> Why are not the spear-shafts flying,
> From the hands of Hrólf and Hrollaug,
> Thickly 'gainst the press of warriors ?
> Now, my father ! I avenge thee.
> While we here are closed in battle,
> Sits Earl Thorir all the evening,
> Silent o'er his cheerless drink.

Next morning they found Hálfdán Hálegg on Rinar's Hill.   The
Earl made a blood eagle be cut on his back with the sword, and had
his ribs severed from the back-bone, and his lungs pulled out.   Thus
he gave him to Odinn as an offering for victory, and sang this song :

> Oft it is that bearded men
> Are guilty deemed for taking sheep ;
> But my offence is that I slew
> The young son of the Islands' king.
> Men may say that danger waits me
> From the great king's speedy vengeance ;
> But his wrath shall never daunt me,
> In whose shield I've made a dint.

Then he had a cairn raised over him, and sang this song :

> Vengeance for my father's death
> I have ta'en for my fourth share.
> In him the people's champion fell ;
> But it was the Norns' decree.
> Heap we now a cairn o'er High-leg,
> Thus the hard skatt we shall pay him
> Which as victors we are due him.
> Let the wise to me now listen.

When this was heard in Norway his brothers became greatly enraged, and threatened an expedition to the Islands to avenge him, but
Harald delayed their journey.   When Earl Einar heard of their threats,
he sang :

> Men of no ignoble birth
> Are they who, from my native land,
> Seek my life for vengeance' sake ;
> But the truth is, that they know not,
> Till their swords have surely slain me,
> Whom the eagles' claws shall rend.

Some time afterwards King Harald set out for the western seas,
and came to the Islands.   Einar fled from the Islands to Caithness.

Then men went between them, and they made peace. King Harald imposed a fine upon the Islands, adjudging them to pay sixty marks of gold. Earl Einar offered [to the Bœndr] to pay the money himself, on condition that he should become proprietor of all their freeholds. The Bœndr accepted this, because the wealthy men thought they might redeem their freeholds, and the poorer men had no money. Einar paid the whole sum, and for a long time afterwards the Earls held all the odal lands, until Earl Sigurd gave back their odal possessions to the Orkneymen. King Harald went back to Norway, but Earl Einar ruled over the Orkneys a long time, and died on a sickbed. He had three sons : one was named Arnkell, the second Erlend, and the third Thorfinn Hausakliúf (skull-splitter).

When Harald Harfagri died, Eirík Blódöx (bloody-axe) was King for two winters. Then Hakon, Athelstan's foster son, came to the land, and Eirík fled. Arnkell and Erlend, the sons of Torf Einar, fell with Eirík Blódöx in England. Gunnhild and her sons then went to the Orkneys, and took possession of them, and stayed there for a time. From thence they went to Denmark, but before they went away they married Ragnhild, the daughter of Gunnhild and Eirík, to Arnfinn, the son of Earl Thorfinn [Hausakliúf], and Earl Thorfinn took up his residence in the Islands : he was a great and warlike chief. He died on a sick-bed, and was buried in a mound on Hauga Heath,[1] in Rognvaldsey, and was considered to have been a great man.

The Murder of Havard.

184. Thorfinn had five sons. One was named Hávard Arsæli (blessed with good seasons), the second Hlödver, the third Liót, the fourth Skúli, and the fifth Arnfinn. Ragnhild, the daughter of Eirík, killed her husband Arnfinn at Myrkhol (Murkle), in Caithness, and then she married Hávard Arsæli, his brother. He became Earl, and was a good chief, and blessed with good seasons. There was a man named Einar Klíning (buttered bread), the son of Hávard's sister. He was a great chief, and had many men, and went usually on war expeditions during the summer. He accepted an invitation from Hávard, and at that feast he and Ragnhild talked much together. She said that it was more suitable that such a man as he should be

[1] Haugaheith, now Hoxa, a peninsula on the north-west side of South Ronaldsay, on which there are still several ancient grave-mounds, and one mound larger than the rest, which has been ascertained to cover the ruins of a Pictish tower. The grave-mound of Earl Thorfinn has not been identified, but Low mentions that in his time there was a tradition that the son of a King of Norway had been buried in the How (*haug*) of Hoxa (*Haugs-heith*).

chief and Earl than Hávard his kinsman, adding that the woman was
well married who had him for a husband. Einar told her not to
speak of such things, saying that Hávard was the noblest man in the
Islands, and that she was well matched. Ragnhild replied : "Hávard
and I shall not be long together after this. But it is true that men
will be found in the Islands who will not stick at trifles if you grudge
me the dignity." By her persuasion Einar was moved to covetousness
and treachery against his kinsman. They agreed that he should kill
the Earl, and that she should marry him. Some time after Einar prepared to take out his men, but a certain spaeman who was with him
said : "Do not engage in this business to-day ; wait till to-morrow, or
else family murders will be frequent in your family." Einar pretended
not to hear this. At this time Hávard was at Steinsness,[1] in Hrossey.
There they met, and there was hard fighting, and it was not long till
the Earl fell. The place is now called Hávard's teigar.[2] When this
became known, Einar was considered a great nithing[3] for the deed.
Ragnhild would have nothing to do with him, saying it was a mere lie
that she had given him any promises. Then she sent for Einar Hardkiöpt (hard mouth), who was the son of another sister of Hávard.
And when they met, she said it was a great shame to Hávard's kinsmen that they did not avenge him, adding that she would do anything
that the Earl might be avenged. "It is evident," she said, "that he
who avenges the Earl will be most esteemed by good people, and will
most deserve his dominions." Einar replied : "It is said that you
sometimes speak differently from what you think. But he who does
this deed will expect in return that you will help him to the dominions,
as well as to other things which he will consider not less important."
This was the end of their talk. After this Einar Hardkiöpt went to
Einar Klíning and killed him. But Ragnhild sent for their brother
Liót, and married him. Liót became Earl, and was a great chief.
Now Einar Hardkiöpt had killed his kinsman, and was not any nearer
the earldom than before. He was highly dissatisfied, and wished to
collect men together and subdue the Islands by force. He had great
difficulty in getting men, for the Orkneymen wished to serve the sons
of Thorfinn Hausakliúf. Some time afterwards the Earl had Einar
Hardkiöpt slain.

[1] Steinsness, in Hrossey, is the "ness" or promontory at the Loch of
Stennis on the Mainland of Orkney, now so well known as the site of the
"standing stones of Stennis." The Norsemen evidently named it Steinsness
from the stone circles and monoliths which stood on it when they first knew
it. (See the Introduction, under "Stennis.")

[2] There is a place at Stennis called Havard's-teigr by the country people
to the present day ; teigr meaning an individual's share of the tún-land.

[3] Nithing—cowardly miscreant.

BATTLE BETWEEN LIOT AND SKULI.

185. Skúli, the brother of Liót, went to Scotland, and had an Earl's title given him by the King of Scots. Then he went down to Caithness, and collected forces together; from thence he went to the Islands, and fought with his brother for the dominion of them. Liót collected a numerous army, and went against Skúli. When they met, Skúli would nothing but fight. There was a severely contested battle. Liót gained the victory, and Skúli fled over to Ness (Caithness). Liót pursued him, stayed there for a while, and got many men together. Then Skúli came down from Scotland with a large army, and met Liót at Dalir (Dale), in Caithness, and a great battle ensued. Skúli had a large army given him by the King of Scots and Earl Magbiód.[1] In the beginning of the battle the Scots fought hotly. Earl Liót told his men to act on the defensive, and to stand firm; and when the Scots could not make any impression on them, Liót incited his men, and fought very fiercely himself. When this had been going on for some time, the array of the Scots was broken, and then they fled; but Skúli continued the battle, and was ultimately killed. Liót took possession of Caithness, and he and the Scots were at war, because they were vexed at their defeat. When Earl Liót was in Caithness, Earl Magbiód came down from Scotland with a large army, and they met at Skida-mire (Skitten), in Caithness. Although Earl Liót's forces were not equal to those of the Scots, he fought so bravely that the Scots gave way, and the battle had not continued long when those of the Scots who were left alive fled, and many of them were wounded. Liót returned from the pursuit victorious, but with many men wounded, and he himself had received wounds, of which he died.

BATTLE.

186. Hlödver was Earl after Liót, and became a great chief. He married Audna, the daughter of Kiarval, the King of the Ivar.[2] Their son was Sigurd the stout. Hlödver died on a sick-bed, and was buried at Hofn (Huna), in Caithness. His son Sigurd succeeded him, and became a great chief, with extensive possessions. He kept Caithness

---

[1] The name Magbiód is suggestive of Macbeth, but the date is too early for Macbeth Mac-Finlay.

[2] Audna is probably the Irish name *Eithne*. Kiarval, her father, is the Cearbhal or Carrol of the Irish Annals, who was King of Dublin 872-887. He is mentioned in the opening chapter of the Landnamabók as King of Dublin when Harald Harfagri ruled in Norway and Sigurd was Earl of the Orkneys. The two branches of the Hy Ivar, Kings of Dublin and Limerick, were the descendants of Ivar the Boneless, son of Ragnar Lodbrok. (See War of the Gaedhil with the Gaill, App. pp. 271, 299.)

by main force from the Scots, and went every summer on war expeditions to the Sudreyar (Hebrides), Scotland, and Ireland. One summer
Finnleik, an Earl of the Scots, challenged Sigurd to meet him at Skida-
mire on a certain day; but Sigurd went to consult his mother, who
was a wise woman. The Earl told her that the difference in numbers
would not be less than seven to one. She replied: "I should have
reared thee up long in my wool-bag if I had known that thou wouldst
wish to live for ever. It is fate that rules life, and not the place
where a man may go. It is better to die with honour than live with
shame. Take thou here this banner which I have made with all my
skill, and I ween that it will bring victory to him before whom it is
borne, but death to its bearer." The banner was wrought with cunningly executed handiwork and elaborate art. It was made in the
shape of a raven, and when floating in the wind it resembled the
raven flying. Earl Sigurd was very wroth at his mother's words. He
restored their odal rights to the Orkneymen to induce them to assist
him, and went to meet Earl Finnleik at Skida-mire, where they both
placed their men in battle array. When the forces met, Earl Sigurd's
standard-bearer was killed by an arrow. The Earl ordered another to
bear the banner, and when they had fought for a while he also fell.
Three standard-bearers were killed, but the Earl gained the victory,
and the Orkneymen regained their freeholds.

MEETING BETWEEN OLAF (TRYGGVI'S SON) AND THE EARL.

187. Olaf, Tryggvi's son, sailed west to the Orkneys, as has been
mentioned before. But as the Pentland Firth was not to be passed
at the time, he moored his ships in Asmundarvag (Osmondwall) opposite Rognvaldsey. Earl Sigurd, Hlödver's son, was there before him
with three ships, for he was going on a war expedition. When King
Olaf became aware that the Earl was there, he called him into his
presence. But when the Earl came to the King's ship, the King
spoke as follows:—

"You know, Earl Sigurd, that Harald Harfagri came here to the
west with an army when he had obtained possession of all Norway.
King Harald conquered the Orkneys and Hjaltland, and many other
lands here in the west. The King gave the Islands to Rognvald the
Powerful as a compensation for his son, but Rognvald gave them to
his brother Sigurd, and he became the Earl of King Harald. King
Harald went a second time against Earl Einar with a large army; but
well-disposed men mediated between them, and they agreed to the
following terms:—The King claimed all the Orkneys and Hjaltland
as his own; and the result of their negotiations was that the Earl paid

the King sixty marks of gold for the murder of his son, Halfdan Halegg, and Earl Einar then held the lands from King Harald. Shortly afterwards, King Eirík, Harald's son, came from Norway. Then also the Earls, the sons of Torfeinar, were his vassals. This appears from the fact that they gave him many men for his war expeditions. When King Eirík came to the Islands a second time, he took away with him the two Earls, Arnkell and Erlend, and appointed their brother Thorfinn to rule over the land. They were both killed in England with King Eirík. Then the sons of Eirík came from England and ruled over the Islands, and when they departed they appointed Arnfinn, their brother-in-law, ruler of the Islands. Havard first succeeded his brother (Arnfinn), then Liót, and lastly your father, Hlödver. Now you, Sigurd, are Earl over these lands which I claim as my possessions, with all other lands possessed by Harald Harfagri and his kinsmen, and descending from them to me by inheritance from generation to generation. You know that most of the sons of Eirík and Gunnhild have now been killed. And although their sister Ragnhild is still alive, it seems to me that she has been guilty of such wickedness in the Orkneys that she ought not to have dignity or power anywhere; indeed, my view is that she has completely forfeited both property and life if it be true that she has done all the shameful deeds that are reported of her, and generally believed. Now, since it has so happened, Earl Sigurd, that you have come into my power, you have to choose between two very unequal alternatives. One is, that you embrace the true faith, become my man, and be baptized with all your subjects. In that case you may have certain hope of honour from me. You shall hold in full liberty as my subject, and with the dignity of an Earl, all the dominions which you have had before. And besides, you will gain what is much more important—namely, to reign in eternal joy in the kingdom of Heaven with the Almighty God. Of this you may be sure if you keep his commandments. The other alternative is a very hard one, and quite unlike the former—viz. that you shall be slain on the spot, and after your death I will send fire and sword throughout the Orkneys, burning homesteads and men, unless this people is willing to accept immunity by believing in the true God. And if you and your subjects choose the latter alternative, you and they, who put your trust in idols, shall speedily die, and shall thereafter be tormented in hell-fire, with wicked devils, without end."

When Earl Sigurd had listened to King Olaf's long and eloquent harangue, he hardened his mind against him, and said : " I will tell you, King Olaf, that I have absolutely resolved that I will not, and I dare not, renounce the faith which my kinsmen and forefathers had before me, because I do not know better counsels than they, and I do

not know that the faith which you preach is better than that which
we have had and have held all our lives."

When the King saw that the Earl persisted obstinately in his
error, he caught hold of his young son, who was with him, and who
had been brought up in the Islands.   The King carried this son of
the Earl to the forepart of the ship.   There he drew his sword, and
made ready to hew the boy down, saying at the same time : " Now I
will show you, Earl Sigurd, that I shall spare no man who will not
serve Almighty God, or listen to my preaching of the blessed message.
Therefore I shall kill your son before your eyes this instant, with the
sword now in my hand, unless you and your men will serve my God.
For I shall not leave these Islands until I have completely fulfilled his
blessed commission, and you have been baptized along with this son
of yours whom I now hold."

And because the Earl was situated as he was, he chose the better
alternative of doing as the King desired, and so he embraced the true
faith.   Then the Earl was baptized, and so were all the people of the
Orkneys.   Then Earl Sigurd became the Earl of King Olaf according
to this world's dignity, and held from him lands and dominions, and
gave him as a hostage his son who has already been mentioned.   His
name was Hvelp or Hundi (whelp or hound).   King Olaf had him
baptized by the name of Hlödver, and took him with him to Norway.
Earl Sigurd confirmed all their agreement with oaths.   After this
King Olaf sailed from the Orkneys, leaving priests to instruct the
people in the holy faith.   King Olaf and Earl Sigurd parted friends.
Hlödver lived but a short time, and after his death Earl Sigurd paid
no homage to King Olaf.   Then he married the daughter of Melkólf,
the King of Scots, and their son was Thorfinn.

INDEX.

ERRATA.

Page lxxix.—*For* " Há Kirkiu," *read* " Há Kirkia."

Page 44.—*For* " She was married to Kolbein Hruga," *read* " She was the mother of Hakon Barn and of Herborg, who was married to Kolbein Hruga."

Page 135.—*After* " Verbon," *read* " (Nerbon)."

Page 157.—*For* " Corness," *read* " Carness."

Page 192.—*For* " death," in Note 1, *read* " divorce."

THE END.

CPSIA information can be obtained
at www.ICGtesting.com
Printed in the USA
LVHW011818020719
623009LV00001B/92/P